Medieval Self-Coronations

Based on narrative, iconographical and liturgical sources, this is the first systematic study to trace the story of the ritual of royal self-coronations from ancient Persia to the present. Exposing as myth the idea that Napoleon's act of self-coronation in 1804 was the first extraordinary event to break the secular tradition of kings being crowned by bishops, Jaume Aurell vividly demonstrates that self-coronations were not as transgressive or unconventional as has been imagined. Drawing on numerous examples of royal self-coronations, with a particular focus on European kings of the Middle Ages, including Frederic II of Germany (1229), Alphonse XI of Castile (1328), Peter IV of Aragon (1332) and Charles III of Navarra (1390), Aurell draws on history, anthropology, ritual studies, liturgy and art history to explore royal self-coronations as privileged sites at which the frontiers and limits between the temporal and spiritual, politics and religion and tradition and innovation are encountered.

Jaume Aurell is Professor of Medieval History at the University of Navarra, Spain. His previous publications include *Authoring the Past: History, Autobiography, and Politics in Medieval Catalonia* (2012), *Theoretical Perspectives on Historians' Autobiographies* (2015) and, as editor, *Rethinking Historical Genres in the Twenty-First Century* (2017).

Medieval Self-Coronations
The History and Symbolism of a Ritual

Jaume Aurell
University of Navarra

CAMBRIDGE
UNIVERSITY PRESS

Shaftesbury Road, Cambridge CB2 8EA, United Kingdom

One Liberty Plaza, 20th Floor, New York, NY 10006, USA

477 Williamstown Road, Port Melbourne, VIC 3207, Australia

314–321, 3rd Floor, Plot 3, Splendor Forum, Jasola District Centre, New Delhi – 110025, India

103 Penang Road, #05–06/07, Visioncrest Commercial, Singapore 238467

Cambridge University Press is part of Cambridge University Press & Assessment, a department of the University of Cambridge.

We share the University's mission to contribute to society through the pursuit of education, learning and research at the highest international levels of excellence.

www.cambridge.org
Information on this title: www.cambridge.org/9781108794176

DOI: 10.1017/9781108879279

© Jaume Aurell 2020

This publication is in copyright. Subject to statutory exception and to the provisions of relevant collective licensing agreements, no reproduction of any part may take place without the written permission of Cambridge University Press & Assessment.

First published 2020
First paperback edition 2024

A catalogue record for this publication is available from the British Library

| ISBN | 978-1-108-84024-8 | Hardback |
| ISBN | 978-1-108-79417-6 | Paperback |

Cambridge University Press & Assessment has no responsibility for the persistence or accuracy of URLs for external or third-party internet websites referred to in this publication and does not guarantee that any content on such websites is, or will remain, accurate or appropriate.

Contents

List of Figures	*page* vii
Acknowledgements	xi
Introduction	1
1 Self-Coronation As Ritual	36
Part I Heritage	**59**
2 Consecration without Mediation in Antiquity	61
3 The Hand of God	85
4 Symbolic Self-Coronations in Byzantium	96
5 The Sacralisation of Carolingian Accessions	127
6 Anglo-Saxon and Ottonian Christocentrism	147
Part II Infamy	**173**
7 Roger II of Sicily: Imagining Self-Coronation	175
8 Frederick II of Germany: Desacralising Rituals	196
Part III Convention	**219**
9 Alfonso XI of Castile: From Self-Knighting to Self-Crowning	221

10 Peter IV of Aragon's Self-Coronation: A Conventionalisation Programme	242
11 Charles III of Navarra: Juridical Implications of Self-Coronations	274
12 Early Modern Dramatisation: The Road to Napoleon	296
Conclusion	302
Index	318

Figures

1 *The Victorious Youth*, a statue of an athlete crowning himself with an olive wreath, 300–100 BC. Bronze with inlaid copper. The J. Paul Getty Museum, Villa Collection, Malibu, California. © Getty Images. The J. Paul Getty Museum (Los Angeles). *page* 2
2 Coronation of Empress Josephine in the Cathedral of Notre-Dame de Paris on 2 December 1804, by Jacques-Louis David, 1807. Louvre Museum in Paris, France. © Musée du Louvre, Dist. RMN-Grand Palais / Angèle Dequier. 3
3 *The Coronation of Edward III*. Miniature by Loyset Liédet, Chroniques de Jean Froissart, *c.*1470–5. BNF, Ms. Fr. 2643, fol. 12. © Bibliothèque nationale de France. 6
4 One of the pages of the *Ceremonial de consagración y coronación de los reyes de Aragón*. Annex to the *Ordinacions de Cort*, second half of the fourteenth century. Biblioteca de la Fundación Lázaro Galdiano, reg. 14425, fol. 19 r. © Museo Lázaro Galdiano. Madrid. 20
5 Relief depicting King Darius facing a group of men, roped together, representing rebels defeated by the king. The figure at the top is the god Ahuramazda in a winged disc. The relief is carved into a rock face at Behistun, Bisotun, Iran. © www.BibleLandPictures.com / Alamy Stock Photo. 72
6 Relief depicting Ares, the god of war, crowning the honouree after a military victory, third quarter of the fourth century BC. Acropolis Museum, Athens, Greece, piece EAM 2947. © Acropolis Museum, 2011. Photo: Socratis Mavrommatis. 75
7 Relief depicting King Ardashir I receiving the ring of power from the divinity Ahura Mazda, third century. Relief in Naqsh-e Rostam, Iran. © Interfoto / Alamy Stock Photo. 79
8 Self-coronation of Shah Mohammad Reza Pahlavi, Palace of Golestan, Teheran, 26 October 1967. © Bettmann / Contributor, Getty Images. 83

9 Constantine being crowned by the hand of God. Constantius II Medallon, revers, Kunsthistorisches Museum, Vienna, Münzcabinett, circa 330, KHM 1754/19. © Kunsthistorisches Museum, Vienna. 88
10 *Master of Tahüll*, the hand of God as an isolated motif. Fresco from the Church of Sant Climent de Taüll, Catalonia, Spain. © Museu Nacional d'Art de Catalunya (Barcelona, 2019). 92
11 Constantine VII being crowned by the patriarch of Constantinople. Codex Graecus Matritensis Ioannis Skylitzes, Skylitzes Chronicle, Byzantine Italy, eleventh and twelfth centuries, *Synopsis of Histories* by John Skylitzes. Biblioteca Nacional de España manuscript Graecus Vitr. 26–2, folio 114 verso – Codex Graecus, Madrid. © Biblioteca Nacional de España. 105
12 Leo VI being crowned by the Virgin Mary. Berlin, Bode Museum, Inventory 2006. © Skulpturensammlung und Museum für Byzantinische Kunst, Staatliche Museen zu Berlin – Stiftung Preußischer Kulturbesitz. Photo: Antje Voigt, 2019. 113
13 Solidus issued by Alexander I (912–13), showing him being crowned by Christ. Dumbarton Oaks Byzantine Collection (BZC.1948.17.3002). © Dumbarton Oaks Byzantine Collection. 117
14 Ivory table depicting Constantine VII being crowned by Christ. State Pushkin Museum of Fine Arts, II 2b 329, Moscow. © Pushkin Museum of Fine Arts, Moscow. 118
15 Romanus II of Byzantium and his wife, Eudocia, being crowned by Christ. Constantinople, ivory, c.945–9. Bibliothèque Nationale, Cabinet des Médailles. Paris. © Bibliothèque Nationale de France. 120
16 Illustration from the psalter of Basil II, showing the armed emperor being crowned by the archangel Gabriel. Biblioteca Nazionale Marciana, Venice. cod. gr. 17, f. 3 r. © Biblioteca Nazionale Marciana, Venice, Italia. 122
17 *The Judgement of Solomon*. Bible of San Paolo Fuori le Mura, fol. 188 v. Frontispiece to Proverbs. © Abbazia of San Paolo Fuori le Mura, Roma. 137
18 Maiestas Domini. London, British Library, MS Add. 49598, fol. 70 r. © The British Library Board. 152
19 Angels crowning King Cnut as he and his wife, Aelfgifu of Northampton, present the Winchester Cross to the church. The *New Minster Liber Vitae*, Winchester, New Minster, 1031.

List of Figures ix

London, British Library MS. Stowe 944, fol. 6 r. © The British Library Board. 156
20 Holy Roman Emperor Otto II and his wife, Theophanu, being crowned by Christ, engraving after ivory carving, tenth century (C10 Byzantine ivory). © Paris, Musée de Cluny and Musée national du Moyen Âge. 159
21 *Otto II in Majesty*, fol. 16 v, Ottonisches Evangeliar, Domschatzkammer Aachen. © Domkapitel Aachen. Photo: Pit Siebigs. 160
22 Charles the Bald being crowned by a hand of God from above. *Sacramentary of Metz*, 1141, Bibliothèque Nationale de France, f. 2 v. © Bibliothèque Nationale de France. 165
23 Crowning of Henry II by Christ. *Sacramentary of Henry II*. Regensburg, 1002–14. Munich, Bayerische Staatsbibl, Clm. 4456, f. 11. © Bayerische Staatsbibliothek München. 167
24 Mosaic depicting Roger II receiving the crown from Christ. Church of Martorana, Santa Maria dell' Ammiraglio in Palermo, Italy, around 1143. © Image BROKER / Alamy Stock Photo. 186
25 The automated statue of Saint James. Monasterio de las Huelgas, Burgos, Spain. Second half of the thirteenth century. © Album / Oronoz. 235
26 Miniature showing King Peter IV of Aragon crowning himself. *Ceremonial de consagración y coronación de los reyes de Aragón*, fol. 19 r. Annex to the *Ordinacions de Cort*, second half of the fourteenth century. Biblioteca de la Fundación Lázaro Galdiano, Reg. 14425. © Museo Lázaro Galdiano. Madrid. 243
27 King Peter IV of Aragon crowning the queen. *Ceremonial de consagración y coronación de los reyes de Aragón*, fol. 35 v. Annex to the *Ordinacions de Cort*, second half of the fourteenth century. Biblioteca de la Fundación Lázaro Galdiano, reg. 14425. © Museo Lázaro Galdiano. Madrid. 263
28 A king being crowned and anointed by a bishop. Bibliothèque Nationale de France, MS., LAT. 1246, f. 37 v. *Ordre de la consécration et du couronnement des rois de France*. Circa 1250. © Bibliothèque Nationale de France. 264
29 Self-coronation of Peter the Ceremonious. *Ordinacions de Cort*, c.1370–80. Bibliothèque Nationale de France, ms. Esp. 99, fol. 129 r. © Bibliothèque Nationale de France. 266
30 Peter the Ceremonious crowning the queen. *Ordinacions de Cort*, c.1370–80. Bibliothèque Nationale de France, ms. Esp. 99, fol. 147 r. © Bibliothèque Nationale de France. 266

31 Ivory seal of Charles III of Navarra, annexed to the document of the act of investiture of Charles III. Archivo Real y General de Navarra, Camara de Comptos, Documentos, Registro 225, Caja 59, número 10, f. 1, dated 13 February 1390. © Archivo Real y General de Navarra. 290

32 Coronation of Jean-Bédel Bokassa as emperor of the Central African Empire. Bangui, 4 December 1977. © Keystone Press / Alamy Stock Photo. 300

Acknowledgements

This research began in 2010, while I was finishing my monograph *Authoring the Past: History, Politics and Autobiography in Medieval Catalonia* (University of Chicago Press, 2012). Rereading Peter IV of Aragon's autobiography, I was struck, once more, by the passage in which the king narrates his self-coronation, performed in 1336 when he was sixteen years old, and the liturgical ordo he later commissioned to fix the ritual as an established ceremony for his successors. When I discovered that story, I could not understand how such a meaningful historiographical passage, and Peter's impressive liturgical ordo, complete with miniatures, had been virtually unknown by scholars beyond the few Catalan specialists on that king. Figure 26 of this book, coming from one of the manuscripts of that liturgical ordo, shows King Peter holding the crown just before crowning himself under the passive gaze of the bishop.

In the long time it took me to write this volume, I have benefited from the generous help of many colleagues and friends. My analysis and understanding of the ritual of self-coronations necessarily developed from an interdisciplinary approach from history, symbolic anthropology, political philosophy, art history, theology and liturgy. Thus, this book falls within the framework of the Religion and Civil Society project of the Institute for Culture and Society (ICS) of the University of Navarra (Spain). It owes a great deal to the comprehensive dynamic of this project, to the intense debates of the almost biweekly seminars and to frequent conversations with my colleagues. I particularly appreciate the advice I received from the head of the project, the political philosopher Montserrat Herrero.

My research has greatly benefited from visits to various campuses of the University of California. At UCLA I learned much from the advice of the historians Patrick J. Geary, Lynn Hunt and Teófilo F. Ruiz, and from the anthropologists Andrew Apter and Sherry B. Ortner. During my stays at UC Berkeley I spoke with the historians Anthony Adamthwaite and Martin Jay and the anthropologist Geoffrey Koziol. Finally, I *crowned* this book in a fruitful stay at Stanford University, thanks to the invitation of Marisa Galvez, who was generous with advice as well as hospitality.

In the middle of my research, I developed some of my theories in the seminars held at Johns Hopkins University, where I found always-inspiring advice from Gabrielle M. Spiegel and her colleagues of the department of history, and at Wesleyan University, where I largely benefited from the comments of Gary Shaw, Ethan Kleinberg and their colleagues in history and anthropology.

In the course of this project, I learned from many colleagues from numerous disciplines. I thank Michael Axworthy and Rolf Strootman for their suggestions for the chapter on antiquity (Chapter 2); José Marín Riveros and Patricia Varona for information on Byzantium (Chapter 4); Jinty Nelson, my brother Martin Aurell, János Bak, Björn Weiler, Mirko Vagnoni, Stefano Manganaro and Nikolas Jaspert for their comments on the chapters on the Carolingians (Chapter 5), Sicily (Chapter 7) and Germany (Chapter 8); Adam M. Kosto, Paul Freedman, Alfons Puigarnau, José Enrique Ruiz-Domènec, Flocel Sabaté and Marta Serrano-Coll for their feedback on the chapter on Aragon (Chapter 10); Julia Pavón, Eloísa Ramírez, Juan Carrasco, Ángel Sesma and María Narbona for their input in the chapter on Navarra (Chapter 11); Laura Delbrugge and Álvaro Fernández de Córdova for their contributions to the chapter on Castile (Chapter 9); Peter Burke and Pablo Vázquez Gestal for their help with the chapter on early modern coronations (Chapter 12); Robert A. Rosenstone and Kalle Pihlainen for necessary theoretical perspectives; and Philippe Buc and Lynn Hunt for the shifting but always stimulating relationship between history and anthropology. I particularly thank the anonymous readers of the previous drafts for their comments and suggestions: my initial daze in receiving their advice turned into a genuine appreciation when I began working hard on their (literally) hundreds of suggestions.

To work with Cambridge University Press has been an enjoyable example of professionalism. My deepest thanks go to Elisabeth Friend-Smith and Atifa Jiwa. I also thank Gabriela Alba for her efficient job on the index.

Finally, I greatly appreciate the enthusiastic support of my parents during the long process of the writing of this book. Their love for culture, books, history and tradition has always been a genuine impulse for my dedication to history.

Earlier versions of some chapters of this book have already appeared as: 'The Self-Coronation of Peter the Ceremonious (1336): Historical, Liturgical, and Iconographical Representations', *Speculum* 89 (2014): 66–95 (with Marta Serrano-Coll); 'The Self-Coronations of Iberian Kings: A Crooked Line', *Imago Temporis* 8 (2014): 151–75; 'Strategies of Royal Self-Fashioning: Iberian Kings' Self-Coronations', in *Self-Fashioning and Assumptions of Identity in Medieval and Early Modern Iberia*, ed. Laura Delbrugge (Leiden: Brill, 2015), 18–45; 'The Self-Coronation of Frederick II: A Non-sacred Consecration', in *Political Theology in Medieval and Early Modern Europe: Discourses, Rites, and Representations*, ed. Montserrat Herrero, Jaume Aurell and Angela Miceli (Turnhout: Brepols, 2017), 245–66; and 'Charles III of Navarra's Oath and Coronation: The Juridical Implications of Self-Coronations', in *Le sacré et la parole: le serment au Moyen Age*, ed. Martin Aurell, Jaume Aurell and Montserrat Herrero (Paris: Garnier, 2018), 227–49.

Introduction

> *Non aspettar mio dir più ne mio cenno:*
> *libero, dritto e sano è tuo arbitrio*
> *e fallo fora non fare a suo senno:*
> *per ch'io te sovra te corono e mitrio*
> Dante, *Divina Commedia, Purgatorio*, Chant 27[1]

In a small room in a corner of the Getty Villa in Los Angeles, a gorgeous full-body bronze sculpture of a young athlete crowning himself with an olive wreath, dating back to Greece from between 300 and 100 BC, is on display. The museum's catalogue calls the figure *The Victorious Youth* (see Figure 1), and describes it in these terms:

> In the traditional pose of a victorious athlete, a relaxed and confident youth crowns himself with a wreath, probably olive. The olive wreath was the prize for a victor in the Olympic Games and identifies this youth as a victorious athlete. He may have carried palm branches, another attribute of victory, in his left hand. The figure's eyes were once inset with stones of glass paste to create a naturalistic impression. This statue probably commemorated an athletic triumph at Olympia, where the olive wreath was given as a prize. It may have stood in the sanctuary there or in the athlete's hometown.[2]

Although this is a self-coronation in an athletic rather than a political context, the statue's iconographic motif proves that the ancient world was familiar with the custom of placing a crown on one's own head.[3] From the start of the Christian era, this gesture of

---

[1] 'I do not give you sign or word; // free, upright and whole is thy will; // 'twere a fault not to act according to its prompting; // wherefore I do crown and mitre thee over thyself' (Virgil's declaration to Dante at the Paradiso's thresholds, in Dante, *Divina Commedia, Purgatorio*, Chant 27, verses 139–42). See Ernst H. Kantorowicz, *The King's Two Bodies* (Princeton, NJ: Princeton University Press, 1957), 483–95.
[2] Catalogue, Getty Villa museum in Los Angeles, available at www.getty.edu/art/collection/objects/7792/unknown-maker-statue-of-a-victorious-youth-greek-300-100-bc/ (accessed 29 March 2017).
[3] I do not intend to engage with the intensive historiographical debate on the meaning of the gesture of this statue, which I noticed on my first visit to the Getty Villa museum. Rather,

Figure 1 *The Victorious Youth*, a statue of an athlete crowning himself with an olive wreath, 300–100 BC. Bronze with inlaid copper. The J. Paul Getty Museum, Villa Collection, Malibu, California. © Getty Images. The J. Paul Getty Museum (Los Angeles).

I just take it as iconographic data for this book, taking into account its most probable sense. The text describing the statue has actually changed several times in the past few years, and the latest inscription states that the victorious athlete 'is about to remove his wreath' rather than 'crowning himself'. The most extensive work on the sculpture is Carol C. Mattusch, *The Victorious Youth* (Los Angeles: Getty Museum, 1997). She adds another example of the apparent self-crowning in a figure of the goddess Eros (Mattusch, *The Victorious Youth*, 9, figure 9).

Figure 2 Coronation of Empress Josephine in the Cathedral of Notre-Dame de Paris on 2 December 1804, by Jacques-Louis David, 1807. Louvre Museum in Paris, France. © Musée du Louvre, Dist. RMN-Grand Palais / Angèle Dequier.[4]

royal self-coronation has conventionally been considered a transgression of tradition on the part of the sovereign who practises it. The sovereign who puts a crown on his own head clearly defies the priest, to whom it naturally falls to act as mediator between the divinity that confers temporal power from above and the person receiving this authority on earth. The popularity and spread of the rite of self-coronation reached its zenith with Napoleon's imperial self-coronation in Paris on 2 December 1804, an event that achieved world notoriety in large part because of the monumental painting by the court artist Louis David, currently on display at the Louvre (see Figure 2).

The scene actually represents the coronation of Empress Josephine by the emperor, but activates an inevitable reference to the transgressive gesture of Napoleon's self-coronation that preceded it.

---

[4] Complete information on this painting may be found in Antoine Schnapper and Arlette Sérullaz, 'Le Couronnement de l'Empereur et de l'Impératrice, 169 à 181', in *Jacques-Louis David, 1748–1825*, ed. Antione Schnapper and Arlette Sérullaz (Paris: Ministère de la Culture, 1989), 399–432.

Notably, Pope Pius VII appears in the painting as a passive spectator, an attitude reflected in the apparently melancholy smile on his face. Received through heredity, election, military victory or usurpation, royal dignity is usually established through a solemn ceremony of investiture that tends to take multiple ritual forms. In the post-Constantinian Christian world, the recognition of self-coronation as a transgressive gesture presupposes the belief that the king should receive sacred authority, with the necessary mediation of a priest, solemnised in the ceremony of the investiture of the sovereign.

It is obvious that between the relaxed and confident figure of the Greek athlete and Napoleon's authoritative gesture lies a complex evolution of historical context, ritual forms and iconographic motifs through which self-coronations have been enacted and represented – a multilayered development this book examines and interprets. Though Napoleon's self-coronation in 1804 is generally taken to have been an extraordinary event that broke the long tradition of kings being crowned by bishops, research shows that the ritual of self-coronation was already known and practised by Christian European kings. Thus, considering both the imaginary representations and the ceremonial experience of self-coronation, and in order to reflect on its symbolic meaning and its ritual dimension, this book focuses on the self-coronations imagined and/or performed by sovereigns. It traces the origins of these specific rituals and their continuity and discontinuity, as well as their evolution from exceptionality to normativity, from ancient civilisations to the present, particularly focusing on the Middle Ages. It narrates the long history of self-coronations, highlighted by placing the chronological accounts of self-coronations in their own particular context. It challenges previous assumptions, since it shows that self-coronations began in the very distant past, that they were not extraordinary events at all, and they were not as transgressive or non-conventional as we might perhaps want to imagine. It poses two essential questions: one historical – 'What is the long-term story of royal self-coronations?' – and the other anthropological – 'What does self-crowning reveal about the operation of ritual, and what is its symbolic meaning?'

* * *

One may naturally question the ability of coronations to generate social transformations, especially if one considers the ostensibly passive role of the king during the ceremony, as traditional scholarship on the subject has argued. Richard A. Jackson notes that 'the king seems to play a role definitely minor' during the ceremony of

Introduction 5

his own investiture.⁵ Meyer Fortes states that 'the part played by ecclesiastical dignitaries in these ceremonies is significant' and that 'the occupant of [the] office cannot legitimately install himself.'⁶ That priests make kings in Europe, Africa and Asia has been posited by scholars who have published comprehensive approaches to the topic, such as Arthur M. Hocart and, more recently, David Graber and Marshall Sahlins.⁷

Royal investment in the different kingdoms of medieval Europe was usually composed by an addition of ceremonies. The most common were the unction and the crowning by the bishop.⁸ The normative structure of the ceremony requires that, at the climax of the event, the bishop places the crown on the king's head, as most medieval Western European iconography shows (see Figure 3).

This practice was certainly normative in England, France and Germany, and was quickly adopted in Sicily and Jerusalem. In those

---

⁵ Richard A. Jackson, 'Le pouvoir monarchique dans la cérémonie du sacre et couronnement des rois de France', in *Représentation, pouvoir et royauté à la fin du moyen âge*, ed. Joël Blanchard (Paris: Picard, 1995), 237–51, here 237.

⁶ Meyer Fortes, 'Of Installation Ceremonies', *Proceedings of the Royal Anthropological Institute of Great Britain and Ireland* (1967): 5–20, here 6 and 11.

⁷ Arthur M. Hocart, *Kingship* (Oxford: Clarendon, 1927) and David Graeber and Marshall Sahlins, *On Kings* (Chicago: Hau, 2017). For a general vision of medieval kingship see, among others, Henry A. Myers, *Medieval Kingship* (Chicago: Nelson-Hall, 1982) and Bernhard Jussen, ed., *Die Macht des Königs* (Munich: C. H. Beck, 2005).

⁸ Classical works on medieval coronations include: Cornelius A. Bouman, *Sacring and Crowning* (Groningen: J. B. Wolters, 1957); János M. Bak, ed., *Coronations: Medieval and Early Modern Monarchic Ritual* (Berkeley: University of California Press, 1990); Richard A. Jackson, *Ordines coronationis Franciae. 2 vols.* (Philadelphia: University of Pennsylvania Press, 1995); Joachim Ott, *Krone und Krönung* (Mainz: Philipp von Zabern, 1998); Janet L. Nelson, *Politics and Ritual in Early Modern Europe* (London: Hambledon Press, 1986). For coronation's connection with political and legal theory see Fritz Kern, *Kingship and Law in the Middle Ages* (Oxford: Basil Blackwell, 1956); Frederic W. Maitland, *Roman Canon Law* (New York: Burt Franklin, 1968); Walter Ullmann, *The Carolingian Renaissance and the Idea of Kingship* (London: Methuen, 1969). For a more specific analysis of medieval European coronations see Percy E. Schramm, *A History of the English Coronation* (Oxford: Clarendon, 1937); Roy Strong, *Coronation: A History of Kingship and the British Monarchy* (London: Harper Collins, 2005); H. G. Richardson, 'The Coronation in Medieval England: The Evolution of the Office and the Oath', *Traditio* 16 (1960): 111–202; Ernst H. Kantorowicz, 'Inalienability: A Note on the Canonical Practice and the English Coronation Oath in the Thirteenth Century', *Speculum*, 29 (1954): 488–502; Paul L. Ward, 'The Coronation Ceremony in Medieval England', *Speculum* 24 (1939): 160–78; Eloísa Ramírez, ed., *Ceremonial de la Coronación, unción y exequias de los reyes de Inglaterra* (Pamplona: Gobierno de Navarra, 2008); Richard A. Jackson, *Vive le Roi!* (Chapel Hill: University of North Carolina Press, 1984). For analyses of the long-term continuity of the political symbols see Ernst H. Kantorowicz, 'Oriens Augusti – Lever du roi', *Dumbarton Oaks Papers* 17 (1963): 117–77; Percy E. Schramm, *Der König Von Frankreich. 2. Das Wesen Der Monarchie Vom 9. Zum 16. Jahrhundert* (Darmstadt: Wissenschaftliche Buchgesellschaft, 1960); Jacques Le Goff, Eric Palazzo, Jean-Claude Bonne and Marie-Noël Collette, eds., *Le Sacre Royal a L'epoque De Saint-Louis* (Paris: Gallimard, 2001).

6   Introduction

Figure 3 *The Coronation of Edward III*. Miniature by Loyset Liédet, Chroniques de Jean Froissart, c.1470–5. BNF, Ms. Fr. 2643, fol. 12. © Bibliothèque nationale de France.

European kingdoms other forms of coronations were not practised at all, with the possible exceptions of the intriguing story of the auto-investiture of King Cnut (1016–35)[9] and the self-coronation of

---

[9] Henry of Huntingdon documents that Cnut enthroned himself at the seashore. Since he was at the peak of his power, he ordered the incoming tide not to presume to wet the ruler of England. The tide, however, rose and soaked the king. Cnut then regretted his arrogance and humbly recognised that the power of earthly kings was worthless and that the only one

Richard I of England in 1189,[10] both clearly seen as opprobrium. From the thirteenth century onwards, departure from established tradition was not really an option for the French and English, since they could not truly become kings in the medieval and early modern eras until they had been anointed and crowned by the bishops. But the variety of rituals of coronations and, crucially, the diversity of the places in which they were performed, show that the French, English and German models should not be taken as conventional elsewhere. Thus, this book aims to demonstrate that at some points in the Middle Ages, and particularly in some areas, such as Iberia and other Central and Northern European kingdoms, the coronation by the bishop was not the more common or even orthodox or conventional ritual of investiture. In these kingdoms, coronations by bishops were replaced by coronations by the kings themselves, or other forms of

worthy of the name was He who ruled the universe. Consequently, Cnut never again wore the gold crown that he had given himself and put it on the head of Christ crucified instead (Robert Deshman, 'Christus Rex et Magi Reges: Kingship and Christology in Ottonian and Anglo-Saxon Art', *Frühmittelalterliche Studien* 10 (1976): 367–405, here 404–5). Matthew of Paris relates the same story in his *Chronica Majora* when telling of Cnut's death. He confirms that 'rex quoque deinceps nunquam coronam portavit; sed coronam suam super caput imaginis Crucifixi componens, magnum regibus futuris praebuit humilitatis exemplum' – 'the king never wore the crown again; it was put on the head of a Crucifix image, offering a great example of humility for future kings' (Matthew of Paris, *Mattaei Parisiensis, monachi Sancti Albani, Chronica majora*, ed. Henry Richards Luard [London: Rerum Britannicarum Medii Aevi Scriptores, Rolls Series, Kraus Reprint, 1964], vol. 57: 1, p. 510). The tale seems to have some basis in reality, since in 1023 Cnut recorded in a charter to Christchurch, Canterbury, that he laid 'the royal crown from my head with my own hands upon the altar of Christ in Canterbury' (Agnes J. Robertson, *Anglo-Saxon Charters* [Cambridge: Cambridge University Press, 1956], 159, n. 82, 407). A posterior list of Canterbury donors states that Christ's crown was kept on the head of Christ in Canterbury (William A. Chaney, *The Cult of Kingship in Anglo-Saxon England: The Transition from Paganism to Christianity* [Manchester: Manchester University Press, 1970], 139). Cnut's regret for having put the crown on his own head sends the message that self-coronation was not approved of in England at the time Henry of Huntingdon and Matthew of Paris wrote their chronicles – the mid-twelfth to mid-thirteenth centuries.

[10] The chronicler Roger of Howden records that Richard I's ceremony of investiture, performed on 13 September 1189, consisted of the usual anointing by Baldwin, Archbishop of Canterbury. Yet, at the moment of coronation, Richard himself picked up the crown and handed it to the archbishop, instead of the bishop taking it from the altar. However, the bishop actually placed the crown on the king's head, with the assistance of two nobles: 'Deinde ipse [the king] cepit coronam de altari, et tradidit eam archiepiscopo, et erchiepiscopus posuit eam super caput illius, quam duo comites sustinebant propter ponderositatem ipsius' (Roger of Howden, *Chronica. Magistri Rogeri de Houedene*, ed. William Stubbs. 4 vols. [Oxford: Macmillan, 1870], 3:11). In later coronations, the archbishop would take the crown from the altar in order to place it on the king's head. Yet it is not clear if Richard I finally crowned himself or if he just took the crown from the altar (as the chronicler says) before the bishop put the crown on his head. In any case, whether or not this was an innovation, it was a real gesture of self-affirmation: John Gillingham, *Richard I* (New Haven, CT: Yale University Press, 1999), 107.

investiture, more than we tend to think. Perhaps the time has come to revise a paradigm so deeply established, not only in the popular imagination that sees Napoleon's self-coronation as the paradigm of originality, unconventionality and transgression, but also in scholarship.

More specifically, these supposed conventional forms of coronation were not practised in Denmark and Norway until the second half of the twelfth century, in Bohemia until the thirteenth century or in Poland and Scotland until the fourteenth century, and they were only occasionally practised in other European kingdoms, especially in Wales and Ireland. Iberian rulers temporarily adopted unction and coronation or occasionally abandoned them. Unction and coronation were introduced, sought out and petitioned for by kings across the Latin West without a particular chronological or special regularity and uniformity.[11] The general perspective provides one of the key data for this project.

Consequently, we should clarify the difference between the notions of 'coronation' and 'self-coronation', and examine the historical and symbolic implications of the latter term. While the French, English and imperial coronations by the bishops and the Pope have been largely examined, expanding this particular model to all the Western kingdoms, the *allegedly* unconventional strategy of self-coronations deserves more attention. Some primary sources speak clearly of the essential difference between coronations and self-coronations, beginning with Charlemagne's initial reluctance to be crowned by the Pope. According to Einhard, if the emperor 'had known beforehand the [P]ope's plan, he would never have entered the church [to be crowned by the Pope]'.[12] The Franks believed Charlemagne owed his title of emperor not to papal coronation but to an acknowledgement of his power by the people he ruled.[13]

---

[11] For detailed evidence on the European kingdoms' different rhythms of the adoption of the installation ceremonies see Matthias Becher, ed., *Die mittelalterliche Thronfolge im europäischen Vergleich* (Ostfildern: Jan Thorbecke, 2017). For Scandinavian kingdoms see Philip Line, *Kingship and State Formation in Sweden, 1130–1290* (Leiden: Brill, 2007), 388–400; Elisabeth Vestergaard, 'A Note on Viking Age Inaugurations', in *Coronations: Medieval and Early Modern Monarchic Ritual*, ed. János M. Bak (Berkeley: University of California Press, 1990), 119–24; Erich Hoffmann, 'Coronations and Coronation Ordines in Medieval Scandinavia', in *Coronations: Medieval and Early Modern Monarchic Ritual*, ed. János M. Bak (Berkeley: University of California Press, 1990), 125–51. For East-Central European kingdoms see Aleksander Gieysztor, 'Gesture in the Coronation Ceremonies of Medieval Poland', in *Coronations: Medieval and Early Modern Monarchic Ritual*, ed. János M. Bak (Berkeley: University of California Press, 1990), 152–64; Paul W. Knoll, *The Rise of the Polish Monarchy* (Chicago: Chicago University Press, 1972), 27, 38–40, 65–6.

[12] Einhard, *Vita Caroli Magni*, ed. Oswald Holder-Egger (Hannoverae: Impensis Bibliopolii Hahniani, 1965), 32 (chapter 28).

[13] Percy E. Schramm, *Kaiser, Könige und Päpste. 4 vols.* (Stuttgart: Hiersemann, 1968), 1:215–63, and Janet L. Nelson, 'Kingship and Empire', in *The Cambridge History of*

Further evidence of the difference between coronations and self-coronations, and their respective symbolic implications, comes from the chronicler William of Malmesbury, who documents that on 29 January 1121 Henry of England married Adeliza of Louvain at Windsor. The next day, as Ralph d'Escures, Archbishop of Canterbury, was presiding over Adeliza's coronation, he

> noticed that the king was seated on his throne wearing the crown. Furious that another man had anticipated a duty he should have carried out himself, he went up to the king, just as he was, in his holy pallium. The king rose, out of respect for him. Ralph said: 'Who crowned you?' The king excused himself, saying he did not know. 'You have been crowned unlawfully,' Ralph said. 'Either you must take off your crown, or I will not celebrate [M]ass.' 'No, lord father,' answered the king, 'correct the error, and do what should be done.' Ralph therefore put out his hands to take off the crown ['*Illo ergo manus ad auferendum diadema compnente*'], and the king began to untie the fastening at his chin.[14]

Malmesbury views Ralph's angry action as a result of the archbishop's conviction that 'when something was done that affected the rights of his church, he would resent it and seek a sharp revenge.'[15] Kings were not expected to put on their crowns habitually or casually. This is what Archbishop Gervais wanted to emphasise when he crowned Philip I of France in 1059: 'Taking the staff of Saint-Remi, he explained quietly and peacefully how the election and consecration of the king pertained especially to him[self] as successor to the holy Remigius, who had baptized and consecrated Clovis.'[16]

A fourth testimony comes from the nineteenth century, when Henry de Saint-Simon argued for the hegemony of his own class of nobles, which he identified as possessing the same dignity as the old Peers of France. Thus, he stated, without their agreement, it was impossible for the king to be crowned:

Medieval Political Thought, c. 350–c. 1450, ed. James H. Burns (Cambridge: Cambridge University Press, 1988), 211–51, here 231.

[14] William de Malmesbury, *Gesta Pontificum Anglorum: The History of the English Bishops, 1: Text and Translation*, ed. Michael Winterbottom and Rodney M. Thomson. 2 vols. (Oxford: Clarendon, 2009), chapter 1, 71, 1–4 (here pp. 210–13). The story is also told by Eadmer of Canterbury; see *Historia novorum in Anglia*, ed. Martin Rule (London: Rolls Series, 1884), 292–4. See Robert Bartlett, *England under the Norman and Angevin Kings, 1075–1225* (Oxford: Clarendon, 2000), 127. The story is also told in Eadmer, *Historia novorum*, 4:292; Geoffrey Koziol, 'England, France and the Problem of Sacrality in Twelfth-Century Ritual', in *Cultures of Power: Lordship, Status and Power in Twelfth-Century Europe*, ed. Thomas N. Bisson (Philadelphia: University of Pennsylvania Press, 1995), 124–48, here 138.

[15] Malmesbury, *Gesta Pontificum*, 211.

[16] See Thomas N. Bisson, *The Crisis of the Twelfth Century: Power, Lordship, and the Origins of European Government* (Princeton, NJ: Princeton University Press, 2009), 158, who takes it from Jackson, *Ordines coronationis Franciae*, 1:217–32.

The king cannot bear the great weight of the crown except with the aid of those who have placed it upon his head and who support it there. That is to say that the great affairs of the kingdom ought to be equally shared with them in writing, in counsel, in power because they equally support the Crown; that without them there is no important sanction, no law, no new structure; that *they are those who come closest to approaching and supporting the Crown and are even the only who may place their hand upon it*, that is to say, who may join together with the king, establish laws with the king, coexecute the most important things with him, constitute, colegislate, and validate, authorize by the power, by virtue of the whole nation residing in them, all that it pleases the king to do with their concurrence.[17]

From these accounts, it would appear that the practice of self-coronation was viewed as a transgression of the norm, leading to a generalised idea that might have actually artificially projected Napoleon's legendary self-coronation in 1804 back to those performed during the Middle Ages. Yet, as I try to show in this book, the assumption of self-coronations as a transgressive ritual is valid only for French, English and German kingdoms, where the ceremonial norm of the king being crowned by the bishop was firmly established, particularly in France, where it became a symbol 'for the principle that political authority was sacrosanct'.[18] But this was not the case for other kingdoms of medieval Europe, which witnessed very different ritual formulas of accession, self-coronations among them. Here also appears the anachronism of projecting our modern ideas about 'secularisation' back to the Middle Ages which, once again, leads to multiple misunderstandings.

Historians do not use the word 'coronation' to describe accession rituals in medieval Europe because they consider it misleading. Apart from the fact that more occurs in this ceremony than the specific gesture of the coronation by the bishop, the reduction of the royal accession to the 'coronation' would exclude *other* ceremonial forms such as self-coronations – which have not necessarily been conceived as 'transgressive rituals'.[19] I think the modern word 'coronation' can be obstructive because it stresses one particular act. This complicates our approach to coronations in non-inaugural circumstances. For instance, the Germans felt the need to invent the term *Festkrönung* to designate events medieval

---

[17] Saint-Simon, 'Mémoire succincte sur les formalités desquelles nécessairement la renonciation du Roy d'Espagne', in *Escrits inédits de Saint Simon*, ed. Prosper Faugère. 6 vols. (Paris: Hachette, 1880), 2:1, 179–408, here 212–13 (emphasis added).
[18] Koziol, 'England, France and the Problem of Sacrality', 148.
[19] Johanna Dale has examined medieval chronicles to see how inaugurations were described and, although chroniclers occasionally do use the word 'coronation' or linked words (i.e. 'crowning'), they more often prefer other terms, particularly those linked to anointing or consecration: see Johanna Dale, *Inauguration and Liturgical Kingship in the Long Twentieth Century: Male and Female Accession Rituals in France, England and the Empire* (Suffolk: Boydell & Brewer, 2019), chapter 3.

people simply called 'coronations'. Other historians have highlighted the double meaning of the concept of 'accession': 'The Latin word "accessio" can be translated into English both as "accession" (i.e. enthronement or the adoption of royal status) and as "access" (i.e. the right of non-royal persons to approach or petition the person seated on the royal throne).'[20]

In any case, no one can deny that the specific gesture of 'putting the crown on the king's head' has a special relevance relating to the other ceremonies of the investiture, because of its intrinsic symbolic meaning and ritual dramatisation. Then, the decision of *who* places the crown on the king's head in the ceremony of investiture is not a trivial choice, since the formula of royal investiture as declared in the first imperial ceremonials clearly states that 'the Pontiff [or bishop] must stay at the altar and put the diadem on the emperor's [or king's] head.'[21] In opposition to what is usually believed, there are multiple forms of transferring the office of the kingdom to an individual apart from ecclesiastical mediation.[22] Björn Weiler has analysed the theme of the *rex renitens*, in which 'reluctant kingship was not merely confined to being hesitant before assuming office; it could also, and just as frequently, include an unwillingness to accept the trappings of office, that is the title, insignia, or ceremonial of kingship', as happened with Saint Ladislaus of Hungary, Henry I of France and Godfrey I of Jerusalem.[23] Jacek Banaszkiewicz gives details of Conrad II of Germany's peculiar investiture – or its propagandistic narrative – in which four petitioners with a separate claim and an individual complainant approach the king. Conrad had to attend to these four claimants – a peasant, an orphan, a widow and a vagabond – before being anointed.[24] Philip Lane details some of the 'rituals of ruling' in medieval Scandinavia, in which 'the

---

[20] Nicholas Vincent, 'Royal Sacrality in England, 1154–1272', in *El acceso al trono. Concepción y ritualización* (Pamplona: Gobierno de Navarra, 2017), 167–90, here 168.

[21] Reinhard Elze, *Ordines coronationis imperialis* (Hannover: Hahnsche Buchhandlung, 1960), 18 (Pontifical of Mainz, in which is included the *Ordo Coronationis* of Ottonian kings).

[22] A good number of them are gathered in Björn Weiler, 'Crown-Giving and King-Making in the West ca. 1000–ca. 1250', *Viator* 41(1) (2010): 57–88.

[23] Björn Weiler, 'The *Rex Renitens* and the Medieval Idea of Kingship, ca. 900–ca. 1250', *Viator* 31 (2000): 1–42, here 7. On a related approach for ecclesiastical offices see Timothy Reuter, '*Pastorale Pedum ante Pedes Apostolici Posuit*: Dis- and Reinvestiture in the Era of the Investiture Context', in *Belief and Culture in the Middle Ages: Studies Presented to Henry Mayr-Harting* (Oxford: Oxford University Press, 2001), 197–210.

[24] Jacek Banaszkiewicz, 'Conrad II's "Theatrumrituale": Wipo on the Earliest Deeds of the Salian Ruler', in *Central and Eastern Europe in the Middle Ages: A Cultural History. Essays in Honour of Paul W. Knoll*, ed. Nancy van Deusen and Piotr Górecki (London: Tauris Academic Studies, 2009), 50–63, and Ludger Körntgen, *Königsherrschaft und Gottes Gnade. Zu Kontext und Funktion sakraler Vorstellungen in Historiographie und Bildzeugnissen der ottonisch-frühsalischen Zeit* (Berlin: Akademie Verlag, 2001), 136–47.

crown was normally placed by nobles' under the archbishop's supervision; in others, 'German emperors conferred the crowns on Danish princes or kings in return for an act of submission.'[25] Dusan Zupka offers a variety of rituals of accession enacted by Central European rulers in Germany, Bohemia and Hungary. He describes several forms of these ceremonies, whose variation depended on specific occasions and circumstances. The sources do not always allow us to identify clearly demarcated boundaries among them: *Erstkrönung*, *Festkrönung*, *Mitkrönung*, *Beikrönung*, *Unter-Krone-gehen* and *Kronentragen*, among others.[26]

Another variation of the alleged conventional ritual (the bishop crowning the king) is the practice of self-coronations. When a king decides to crown himself, this gesture not only has symbolic implications which affect the content of the ceremony, but it also reshapes the entire ritual and subverts participants' expectations. So the self-crowned kings analysed in this book, such as Alfonso IV of Aragon (1328), Alfonso XI of Castile (1332), Peter IV of Aragon (1336), Charles III of Navarra (1390), Martin I of Aragon (1399) and Ferdinand I of Aragon (1414), were using their agency to emphasise their authority as well as their autonomy in temporal matters over the sacred hierarchy.[27] Certainly, there can be many types of self-coronation, as many as there can be self-investitures. In the first place, the self-coronation could occur in the context of the royal consecration Mass, which would therefore be a properly sacred context. That was the case with the fourteenth-century Iberian kings, whose self-coronations preserved all the ceremonies established by the rituals, except at the solemn moment of the actual crowning, when the kings placed the crown on their heads themselves. In the second instance,

---

[25] Line, *Kingship and State Formation in Sweden*, 389, with other examples in 388–400.

[26] Dusan Zupka, *Ritual and Symbolic Communication in Medieval Hungary under the Árpád Dynasty* (Leiden: Brill, 2016), 38.

[27] Perhaps Henry I the Fowler, king of East Francia (919–36) and founder of the Ottonian Dynasty should be added to this list. It seems that Archbishop Heriger of Mains offered to anoint him according to the usual ceremony, but he refused because he wished to be king not by the church's authority but by the people's acclaim. Nevertheless, scholars agree that the evidence is insufficient to assert this: Weiler, '*Rex Renitens* and the Medieval Idea of Kingship', 5–6; Johannes Fried, 'Die Königserhebung Heinrichs I. Erinnerung. Mündlichkeit und Traditionsbildung im 10. Jahrhundert', in *Mittelalterforschung nach der Wende 1989*, ed. Michael Borgolte (Munich: Oldenbourg, 1995), 267–318; Ernst Karpf, 'Königserhebung ohne Salbung. Zur politischen Bedeutung von Heinrichs. I. Ungewöhnlichern Verzicht in Fritzlar (919)', *Hessisches Jahrbuch für Landesgeschichte* 34 (1984): 1–24; Walter Schlesinger, 'Die Königserhebung Heinrichs I. zu Fritzlar im Jahre 919', in *Fritzlar im Mittelalter. Festschrift zur 1250-Jahrfeier* (Fritzlar: Magistrat der Stadt Fritzlar, 1974), 121–43, here 137–8; Schramm, 'Vom Tode Karls des Grossen (814) bis zum Anfang des 10. Jahrhunderts', in *Kaiser, Könige und Päpste*, 2:303–4. See the previous notes on the *rex renitens*.

self-coronation may be orchestrated directly by the king crowning his heir without resorting to the ecclesiastical hierarchy, as happened in some Byzantine and Carolingian investitures. Finally, there may be a self-coronation (or, more properly, a ceremony of wearing the crown) without the presence of a sacred minister or any ceremony and therefore, strictly speaking, without consecration, as appears to have been the case with Frederick II in Jerusalem.

Previous scholarship has rarely analysed self-coronations. Carlrichard Brühl uses the concept of self-coronation in 1984, in an article which referred to the practice of self-coronation by kings and emperors from the thirteenth to nineteenth centuries.[28] Hans E. Mayer documents the (supposed) self-coronation of Frederick II of Hohenstaufen in Jerusalem in 1229.[29] Teófilo F. Ruiz discusses this in his article on the self-coronation of Alfonso XI of Castile in 1332, connecting it with the concept of (de)sacralisation.[30] Marta Serrano-Coll and I use the concept in our historical and iconographic analysis of Peter IV of Aragon's self-coronation in 1336.[31] Finally, Christopher Clark and Philippe Buc have published valuable articles on the self-coronation of Frederick I of Prussia (1701).[32]

In addition to the analysis of these *ceremonies* of self-coronation, this book also focuses on what the Byzantinist André Grabar calls 'celestial coronation' or 'symbolic coronation' (*couronnement symbolique*) to refer to the imaginative iconographic dimension of the ritual of self-coronation developed in the East by ancient and medieval empires such as Persia and Byzantium.[33] Rather than the emperor being crowned by the priest, those

---

[28] Carlrichard Brühl, 'Les auto-couronnements d'empereurs et de rois (XII–XIXe siècles)', *Comptes rendus des séances de l'Académie des Inscriptions et Belles-Lettres* 128(1) (1984): 102–18, and Carlrichard Brühl, 'Kronen- und Krönungsbrauch im frühen und höhen Mittelalter', *Historische Zeitschrift* 234 (1982): 1–31. See also the section 'Selbstkrönung', in Ott, *Krone und Krönung*, 127–8.

[29] Hans E. Mayer, 'Das Pontifikale von Tyrus und die Krönung der lateinischen Könige von Jerusalem', *Dumbarton Oaks Papers* 21 (1967): 141–232.

[30] Teófilo F. Ruiz, 'Une royauté sans sacre: la monarchie castillane du Bas Moyen Age', *Annales. Économies, Sociétés, Civilizations* 39 (1984): 429–53.

[31] Jaume Aurell and Marta Serrano-Coll, 'The Self-Coronation of Peter the Ceremonious (1336)', *Speculum* 89 (2014): 66–95.

[32] Christopher Clark, 'When Culture Meets Power: The Prussian Coronation of 1701', in *Cultures of Power in Europe during the Long Eighteenth Century*, ed. Hamish M. Scott and Brendan Simms (Cambridge: Cambridge University Press, 2007), 15–35; Philippe Buc, '1701 in Medieval Perspective: Monarchical Rituals between the Middle Ages and Modernity', *Majestas* 10 (2002): 91–124.

[33] André Grabar, *L'Empereur dans l'Art Byzantin* (Paris: Les Belles lettres, 1936), 112–22. See also Andrea Torno Ginnasi, *L'incoronazione celeste nel mondo bizantino* (Oxford: Archaeopress, 2014). A rich and interdisciplinary approach on the relationship between images and ritual is presented in *Bild und Ritual*, ed. Claus Ambos, Petra Rösch and Stefan Weinfurter (Darmstadt: WBG, 2010).

societies developed the iconography of the divinity Ahura Mazda (in Persia) or Christ himself (in Byzantium) crowning the ruler. This peculiar iconography conveys the idea of the divinity of the sovereign, who need not be crowned by the priest-mediator because he already has direct access to God. Yet paradoxically, and contrasting with these symbolic self-coronations, we have historical evidence that the ritual of coronation was performed by the priest or the patriarch in most cases, in both Persia and Byzantium.

* * *

I have used three different primary sources for analysing the ritual of self-coronation: historiographical, liturgical and iconographic imprints.

First, and guided by my own work on medieval historiography in the book *Authoring the Past*, I have employed the descriptions written by witnesses of those coronations as well as the historical narratives produced by chroniclers at the time or shortly after the event. The use of narrative texts in the analysis of the ritual connects with debates around the correct understanding of these sources to enter the substance of the rituals. Here the core of the issue is divided into two main problems: first, on the veracity of the sources and, second, on the danger of projecting modern interpretive categories back to the medieval spirit of these sources. In his study on the *rex renitens*, Weiler gives one of the keys for approaching the first of these dilemmas:

> Many of our sources contain anecdotes, legends, and episodes which bear little or no resemblance to what we know to have happened. At the same time, their veracity is of only marginal concern here. Although an awareness of the wider background will be useful, it is not our primary aim to establish whether a king had really been reluctant, but rather why a particular author may have described him as such.[34]

To deal with medieval self-coronations is thus not only to try to establish what really happened, especially when we can base our historical knowledge of the event on a variety of sources – as in the case of Peter the Ceremonious' self-coronation, for which we have the narrative account, the liturgical ordo and some iconographic representations. It is also, and crucially, to learn how a particular ritual of self-coronation was represented and interpreted by people at the time or by the next generations of chroniclers.

As for the second issue, the projection of modern interpretive categories, Buc has alerted historians to the danger of constructing their interpretations of medieval rituals on modern social scientific models rather than on medieval hermeneutics and theological models. This was especially

---

[34] Weiler, '*Rex Renitens* and Medieval Ideas of Kingship', 3.

Introduction 15

notable in interwar Germany, where Percy E. Schramm developed his work. In his influential *Dangers of Ritual*, Buc opens a lively debate between history and anthropology of the rituals to medieval studies, which I analyse in Chapter 1.[35] Buc's perspectives are particularly useful for my own theories on the practice of self-coronations since this book is in part an inductive demonstration that 'the ceremonies that the early modernist takes for granted were not central to medieval kingship at all times and in all places.'[36] As I argue, it is wrong to take the coronation enacted by the bishop as a model for ceremonies of royal accession in the Middle Ages, as a plurality of ceremonies, self-coronations among them, existed.

One of Buc's main conclusions is that 'medieval sources seldom present a ceremony as it actually happened.'[37] Yet Buc does not promote scepticism towards these sources because, though subjective, they constitute our only access to medieval rituals. The same heuristic scepticism could be actually applied to all narratives and historiographical texts used as sources of all aspects of the past.[38] Yet the very existence of narratives implies the explicit recognition of the ritual, as well as its relevance beyond its actual enactment. More properly, these narrations of the rites by the medieval chroniclers 'meant not so much to report a ritual as to influence how a ritual would come to be interpreted. ... It was not some magical power of ritual but rather a ritual's reception that shaped society and politics'.[39]

Buc concludes that the process of interpreting ritual began at the time of performance and continued thereafter.[40] To be sure, the record of a ritual constitutes an event in itself: although of a narrative nature, it

---

[35] Philippe Buc, *The Dangers of Ritual* (Princeton, NJ: Princeton University Press, 2001), 1–28. See also David A. Warner, 'Ritual and Memory in the Ottonian Reich: The Ceremony of Adventus', *Speculum* 76 (2001): 255–83; Timothy Reuter, 'Pre-Gregorian Mentalities', *Journal of Ecclesiastical History* 45 (1994): 465–74; Mayke de Jong, 'Power and Humility in Carolingian Society: The Public Penance of Louis the Pious', *Early Medieval Europe* 1 (1992): 29–52; Mayke de Jong, *The Penitential State: Authority and Atonement in the Age of Louis the Pious, 814–840* (Cambridge: Cambridge University Press, 2009). A good example of how medievalists have applied these ideas is presented in the detailed analysis of one 'case study'; see Simon MacLean, 'Ritual, Misunderstanding, and the Contest for Meaning: Representations of the Disrupted Royal Assembly at Frankfurt (873)', in *Representations of Power in Medieval Germany, 800–1500*, ed. Simon MacLean and Björn Weiler (Turnhout: Brepols, 2006), 97–120.

[36] Buc, '1701 in Medieval Perspective', 94.

[37] Buc, '1701 in Medieval Perspective', 110.

[38] Jaume Aurell, *Authoring the Past: History, Autobiography, and Politics in Medieval Catalonia* (Chicago: University of Chicago Press, 2012), 155–76.

[39] Buc, '1701 in Medieval Perspective', 110.

[40] Philippe Buc, 'Ritual and Interpretation: The Early Medieval Case', *Early Medieval Europe* 9 (2000): 1–28, here 4.

generates a new historical reality, as we consider its effects on its audience. The act of remembering 'changed the very nature of what would be preserved'.[41] As David A. Warner argues:

In any case, whether the ritual in question actually occurred or not, the ability to impose a particular reading on it implied a kind of power or authority, which, in the case of literary account, had the potential to increase as the event itself receded into the past and competing, nonliterary accounts faded.[42]

Compared to legal briefs, notarial documentation and chancellery records, narrative sources are probably less reliable from a strict heuristic point of view. But they convey more accurately the richness of cultural manifestations, and the historian should not discard them because of their heuristic ambiguity or epistemic complexity. Actually, in some of the self-coronations analysed in this book, particularly those of Frederick II of Germany and Peter IV of Aragon, we explore how the informant has manipulated the historical account to articulate an approach to reality in order to achieve certain political aims. Thus, the story narrated by the chronicler should be contrasted with other documents. This comparative analysis of sources, though useful, nonetheless cannot provide a detailed and definitive reconstruction of the facts. Since the question of whether the ritual narrated 'really happened' and 'in what form' is certainly relevant but unanswerable in the end, it is perhaps more useful to analyse what criteria might have led a chronicler to include an account of a ritual in his historical narrative, how these criteria affected the content of his work and how the narration was shaped and the event remembered.[43]

In addition to narrative accounts, I have also used sources of a liturgical nature: missals, pontificals and *ordines* and, for the fourteenth century onwards, the books of ceremonies or liturgical collections.[44] Since verbal and gestural ritual are too easily corrupted by the passage of time, lapses of memory and deliberate falsifications, ecclesiastics firstly and rulers later commissioned liturgical ceremonials, before or after the events, in order to establish and validate the ritual performed in the ceremonies of

---

[41] Patrick Geary, *Phantoms of Remembrance: Memory and Oblivion at the End of the First Millennium* (Princeton, NJ: Princeton University Press, 1994), 177. On the literary implications of the remembering see Brian Stock, *The Implications of Literacy* (Princeton, NJ: Princeton University Press, 1983), 15–25.

[42] Warner, 'Ritual and Memory in the Ottonian Reich', 256.

[43] David A. Warner, 'Thietmar of Merseburg on Rituals of Kingship', *Viator* 26 (1995): 53–76, here 75.

[44] For an interesting comment on the nature of liturgical text as sources see Johanna Dale, 'Inauguration and Political Liturgy in the Hohenstaufen Empire, 1138–1215', *German History* 2 (2016): 191–213. See also Johanna Dale, 'Royal Inauguration and the Liturgical Calendar in England, France and the Empire, c.1050–c.1250', *Anglo-Norman Studies* 37 (2015): 83–98.

investiture. Some historians have turned to royal consecration *ordines* for insights about medieval kingship.[45] These *ordines* were subsequent to royal consecrations since they first emerged in Carolingian Europe. Liturgical texts prescribe the actions and words during a rite. The theological discipline of the liturgy, mostly applied to medieval and early modern religious ceremonies, has been of great value for the interpretation of this kind of resource: any ceremony connected with the sacred represents the liturgification of a ritual.[46] Coronation orders, liturgical plays and the ceremonial scripts fill the signs of rulership with life through the codification of the most auspicious and politically important ceremonies and spectacles of the Middle Ages.[47] Though they are not always accurate descriptions of what really happened in a ritual, *ordines* provide us with primary evidence for the motives, perceptions and beliefs of their promoters and compilers. The ceremonial commissioned by Peter the Ceremonious to consolidate the specific gesture of self-coronations (see Chapter 10) has been particularly useful in my research on this ritual. Johanna Dale is right when she states that 'the narrative and liturgical testimonies are rarely complementary',[48] so that Peter's propagandistic programme – gathering narrative, liturgical and iconographic evidence – has provided us with an extraordinary ensemble of sources and inspired historical interpretations.

In my analysis of the ceremonies of the investiture through liturgical sources I have also used as a model some works published by medievalists interested in the ritual dimension of the coronations.[49] Ritual studies has

---

[45] Elze, *Ordines coronationis*, chapter xii (with an exhaustive bibliographical annotation); Michel Andrieu, *Les Ordines Romani du haut moyen âge* (Louvain: Spicilegium Sacrum Lovaniense, 1931–61) and Andrieu, 'Die Ordines der mittelalterlichen Kaiserkrönung. Ein Beitrag zur Geschichte des Kaisertums', *Archiv für Urkundenforschung* 11 (1930): 285–390; Ernst H. Kantorowicz, *Laudes Regiae: A Study in Liturgical Acclamations and Mediaeval Ruler Worship* (Berkeley: University of California Press, 1946); Walter Ullmann, *Liber Regie Capelle* (London: Henry Bradshaw, 1961) and 'Der Souveränitätsgedanke in den mittelalterlichen Krönungsordines', in *Festschrift Percy Ernst Schramm*, ed. Peter Classen and Peter Scheibert. 2 vols. (Wiesbaden: F. Steiner, 1964), 1:72–89; Otto Treitinger, *Die oströmische Kaiser- und Reichsidee nach ihrer Gestaltung im höfischen Zeremoniell* (Darmstadt: Herman Gentner, 1956); Richardson, 'The Coronation in Medieval England', 111–82.

[46] Eric Palazzo, *Liturgie et société au Moyen Âge* (Paris: Aubier, 2000); Matthew Cheung Salisbury, 'Establishing a Liturgical Text: Text for Performance, Performance As Text', in *Late Medieval Liturgies Enacted*, ed. Sally Harper, P. S. Barnwell and Magnus Williamson (London: Routledge, 2016), chapter 6.

[47] János M. Bak, 'Medieval Symbology of the State: Percy E. Schramm's Contribution', *Viator* 4 (1973): 33–63, here 41.

[48] Dale, 'Inauguration and Political Liturgy', 193.

[49] Some excellent surveys on the different scholarship approaches to medieval rituals appear in Giovanni Isabella, 'Rituali altomedievali: le ragioni di un dibattito', *Storica* 41–2 (2008): 165–91; Christina Pössel, 'The Magic of Early Medieval Ritual', *Early Medieval Europe* 17 (2009): 111–25; Geoffrey Koziol, 'The Dangers of Polemic: Is

shifted between a comparative-*presentist* tendency, privileging the analysis of contemporary rituals in some traditional societies preserved in different places of Africa, America, Australia and Asia, and the very influential 'myth-ritual school' of Cambridge in the 1920s–1930s, entirely based on ancient studies. Therefore, medieval and early modern rituals did not fit well between these two poles, so the scholars of ritual studies have not usually paid attention to those intermediary periods. Nevertheless, three very qualified exceptions serve as forerunners of current medieval ritual studies: Marc Bloch's *Les rois thaumaturges* (1924), Ernst Kantorowicz's *Ladues Regiae* (1949) and Percy E. Schramm's *Kaiser, Könige und Päpste* (1968). In the 1980s, British medievalists, notably Janet L. Nelson, connected medieval studies on investitures with the best of the Cambridge ancient studies developed in the 1920s and 1930s. At that time, certain French medievalists of the *mentalités*, notably Jacques Le Goff and afterwards Jean-Claude Schmitt, Eric Palazzo and Philippe Buc, were inspired by classic historians of the first generation of the *Annales* like Marc Bloch, and they found their own path to medieval ritual and liturgy. In addition, Central European and American medievalists, including Gerd Althoff, Geoffrey Koziol, János Bak, Teófilo Ruiz and Patrick Geary, also found different ways to approach the rituals of accession, and engaged themselves in an interesting debate on the nature of medieval rituals and the limitations of the negotiation with anthropological ritual studies and social sciences-oriented approaches.[50] Finally, a new generation of scholars, such as Björn Weiler, Johanna Dale, Simon John, Nicholas Vincent, Christina Pössel and Simon MacLean, most of them trained in the British historiographical tradition pioneered by Timothy Reuter and Janet Nelson, have approached medieval rituals of accession blending narrative and liturgical sources, have provided a convincing analytical prospection, and have taken the best of the recent debate on medieval rituals just mentioned. Since self-coronations occurred mostly in medieval Iberia, I have also based my research on the work of scholars such as Bonifacio Palacios, José Manuel Nieto Soria and Peter Linehan, who have analysed Iberian royal coronations in depth.[51]

Ritual Still an Interesting Topic of Historical Study?', *Early Medieval Europe* 11 (2002): 367–88; Philippe Buc, 'The Monster and the Critics: A Ritual Replay', *Early Medieval Europe* 15 (2007): 441–52.

[50] Geoffrey Koziol, *Begging Pardon and Favor* (Ithaca, NY: Cornell University Press, 1992); Gerd Althoff, *Die Macht der Rituale* (Darmstadt: Wissenschaftliche Buchgesellschaft, 2003); Nelson, *Politics and Ritual in Early Modern Europe*; Frans Theuws and Janet L. Nelson, eds., *Rituals of Power* (Leiden: Brill, 2000); Bak, *Coronations*; Geary, *Phantoms of Remembrance*; Ruiz, 'Une royauté sans sacre'.

[51] Bonifacio Palacios Martin, *La coronación de los reyes de Aragón, 1204–1410* (Valencia: Anubar, 1975); Peter Linehan, *History and the Historians of Medieval Spain* (Oxford:

Introduction   19

In addition to narrative and liturgical sources and to this rich tradition of scholarship, I have collected numerous iconographic representations of self-coronations. These primarily include reliefs, sculptures, mural pictures and coins for the chapter on the forms of mediation in antiquity (Chapter 2), and miniatures, pictures and mosaics from the Middle Ages. Some of these images reveal coronations performed historically while most of them show coronations without historical referentiality, as an event imagined by artists or promoted by their patrons. Nevertheless, I deploy both forms of images, the referential and the non-referential, as examples of 'symbolic' or 'heavenly' coronations, and they provide us with keys to the meaning of self-coronations as well. Relevant literature has been published on the *historical* function of miniatures and other medieval images, especially those promoted by or connected with royal power. They teach us how to locate the images in their textual and historical context.[52] This operation of 'putting the events and the images in context' shapes my research on self-coronations since, as Robert Darnton argues, 'symbols work not merely because of their metaphorical power but also by virtue of their position within a cultural frame.'[53] Understanding the specific ritual of self-coronation involves comprehending both its metaphorical dimension (the general meaning encoded in this ceremony and its location in the entire system of the nature of the ritual to which it belongs) and the particular context in which this dimension is enacted. Thus, we comprehend both its common system of meaning and how this meaning is socially shared.

Nevertheless, the operation of taking the iconographic sources for historical inquiry should take into account the function of the audience of these images. Most of the images I have used as historical evidence – particularly those miniatures I discuss in the chapters devoted to Iberian monarchies – were limited to an aristocratic and clerical audience. They were usually placed in ceremonial books, which were read by a small audience (see Figure 4).

Clarendon, 1993); José Manuel Nieto Soria, 'Dialécticas monocráticas. El acceso al trono y la legitimidad de origen', in *El acceso al trono. Concepción y ritualización* (Pamplona: Gobierno de Navarra, 2017), 11–36.

[52] Solid literature on art history helps us understand the image in a particular context: Carra F. O'Meara, *Monarchy and Consent* (London: Harvey Miller, 2001); Anne D. Hedeman, *The Royal Image: Illustrations of the Grandes Chroniques de France, 1274–1422* (Berkeley: University of California Press, 1991); Robert A. Maxwell, ed., *Representing History, 900–1300* (University Park: Pennsylvania State University Press, 2010); Henry Mayr-Hasting, *Ottonian Book Illumination* (London: Harvey Miller, 1991).

[53] Robert Darnton, 'The Symbolic Element in History', *Journal of Modern History* 58 (1986): 218–34, here 227.

Figure 4 One of the pages of the *Ceremonial de consagración y coronación de los reyes de Aragón*. Annex to the *Ordinacions de Cort*, second half of the fourteenth century. Biblioteca de la Fundación Lázaro Galdiano, reg. 14425, fol. 19 r. © Museo Lázaro Galdiano. Madrid.

The subject and the composition of the image inserted in one of the pages of Peter the Ceremonious' ceremonial, in which the king crowns his wife (see Figures 27 and 30), is strikingly similar to David's drawing of Napoleon's self-coronation (see Figure 2). Yet the former was designed for contemplation by a small ecclesiastical and noble elite, and probably just for practical purposes, while the latter was intended to be seen by multiple visitors to the ruler's palace. Actually, the later story of both images validates their designers' original purpose. Peter's miniature was produced for a reduced contemporary audience and for a few scholars who have been fortunate enough to see the manuscript, which lies in a corner of the Lázaro Galdiano Library in Madrid. By contrast, Napoleon's imposing painting is visited by hundreds of thousands of people a year in the Louvre museum in Paris.

Paradoxically, images related to ceremonies of royal investiture usually develop a more elaborate symbolic language so as to reinforce the authority of the king. As John Elliott argues:

> It is as if a form of 'Avis principle' operates in the world of imagery and propaganda: those who are only second try harder. Where ... the supremacy of the king is taken for granted, political imagery can be studiously understated, and there is no need to deck out the ruler with elaborate allegorical trappings.[54]

This would also justify the distinction between the symbolic and ritual self-coronations that govern the structure of this book. Those powerful kings who were able to perform self-coronations such as Frederick II of Germany, Alfonso XI of Castile or Peter IV of Aragon did not need to return to the iconographic motif of Jesus Christ crowning the king, unlike the Byzantine emperors or Roger II of Sicily.

* * *

Apart from these historical sources, this project has also been framed by methodological choices and theoretical assumptions such as the emphasis on political theology, the use of long-term chronology and cultural comparative exercise, the concept of agency, and the use of the ritual studies and theories.

Political theology, as first developed by the political philosopher Carl Schmitt in the 1920s, is based on the analysis of the transferences between the spiritual and the temporal, the sacred and the profane, the political and the religious.[55] It is therefore a useful methodological tool that

---

[54] John H. Elliott, 'Power and Propaganda in Spain of Philip IV', in *Rites of Power*, ed. Sean Wilentz (Philadelphia: University of Pennsylvania Press, 1985), 145–73, here 151.
[55] Carl Schmitt, *Political Theology: Four Chapters on the Concept of Sovereignty* (Cambridge, MA: MIT Press, 1985) and *Political Theology II: The Myth of the Closure of Any Political*

recognises the affinity between the systematic structure of theological and juridical concepts and the political consequences that this resemblance or analogy entails. This analogy is relevant because all significant concepts of the theory of the modern state are secularised concepts. For instance, the state of exception in modern jurisprudence would be the secularised version of the miracle in theology just as the 'king's two bodies' would be the secularised version of the doctrine of the two natures of Jesus Christ in theology. The monarchical sovereignty would be the secular version of the monotheistic conviction in religion just as the idea of utopia would be the secularised version of paradise, and the communist ideal would be a secular version of chiliastic eschatology.[56] As Schmitt declared in his foundational definition of the term in 1922:

> All significant concepts of the modern theory of the state are secularised theological concepts not only because of their historical development – in which they were transferred from theology to the theory of the state, whereby, for example, the omnipotent God became the omnipotent law-giver – but also because of their systematic structure.[57]

Schmitt offers a methodological tool that has also been relevant for the examination of the development of political and religious ideas and cultural practices. To be sure, Schmitt conceived this methodology for the analysis of the early modern and modern eras rather than the medieval. Nevertheless, some medievalists have used it, more or less explicitly, in their studies, and scholars of law, theology and sociology have expanded it to their respective disciplines. Kantorowicz is probably the most relevant of them, in applying it to his monograph *The King's Two Bodies* (1957), which he subtitled *A Study on Medieval Political Theology*.[58]

Theology (New York: Polity Press, 2014). See also the epigraph on 'Theologie Politique', in Henri de Lubac, *Théologies d'occasion* (Paris: Desclée de Brouwer, 1984), 215–54, in which he applies this methodology to the historical evolution of the church. On the theoretical and practical assumptions of this concept for historiographical purposes see two recent collective works: Montserrat Herrero, Jaume Aurell and Angela C. Miceli Stout, eds., *Political Theology in Medieval and Early Modern Europe* (Turnhout: Brepols, 2017) and Karolina Mroziewicz and Aleksander Sroczynski, eds., *Premodern Rulership and Contemporary Political Power: The King's Body Never Dies* (Amsterdam: Amsterdam University Press, 2017).

[56] A survey of the definition and theoretical and practical implications of the concept of 'political theology' is presented in Montserrat Herrero, *The Political Discourse of Carl Schmitt* (London: Rowman & Littlefield, 2015), chapter 8, 'Political Theology', 157–77, here 157. See also Álvaro d'Ors, 'Teología Política: una revisión del problema', in *Sistema de las ciencias, IV*, ed. Álvaro d'Ors (Pamplona: Eunsa, 1977), 86–135.

[57] Schmitt, *Political Theology*, 36.

[58] Robert E. Lerner, *Ernst Kantorowicz: A Life* (Princeton, NJ: Princeton University Press, 2017), 344–57, and György Geréby, 'Carl Schmitt and Erik Peterson on the Problem of Political Theology: A Footnote to Kantorowicz', in *Monotheistic Kingship*, ed. Aziz Al-Azmeh and János M. Bak (Budapest: Central European University, 2004), 31–62.

Kantorowicz was aware of the dual nature of the concept, which embodies both historical-temporal development and systematic-normative structure. This normative structure allows the concept to be applied to the examination of any period, but particularly those after the Christianisation of the Roman Empire after the fourth century.

Approaching medieval self-coronations under the light of political theology allows us to discern parallels, contrasts, transferences, transpositions, filters and dualities between the temporal power exercised by kings and the spiritual authority proper to bishops. Political theology avoids misunderstandings in the necessary dual approach – from the temporal to the spiritual – in royal coronations since 'a world wholly demystified is a world wholly depoliticized.'[59] Philosophers of religion such as Mircea Eliade and historians of kingship such as Arthur M. Hocart have arrived to the same conclusion after their ambitious comparative approach: 'When it is prayed that he [the king] may defend the "fortresses of God", it is as ... to say whether these fortresses are material or spiritual. The fact is, they are both, for the material and the spiritual cannot be separated.'[60] The question of the universality of kingship and its eventual divinity has allowed historians and anthropologists to approach it through cross-cultural, multi-disciplinary and cross-temporal comparisons, as visible in the collective volumes edited by Nicole Brisch, Rolf Gundlach and Hermann Weber, Franz-Reiner Erkens and Declan Quigley.[61] This approach promotes general visions and theories, so that anthropologists such as Michael Puett have related the conviction of the divinity of kingship with the development of and reaction to imperial policies.[62]

Kantorowicz's article 'Mysteries of State: An Absolutist Concept and Its Late Medieval Origins', *Harvard Historical Review* 48 (1955): 65–91, is another example of the efficacy of political theology for interpreting medieval political theory and practice, as Kantorowicz opens the article by stating that the concept 'mysteries of State' is the result of the *infinite cross-relations* between church and state (p. 31, emphasis added).

[59] Clifford Geertz, 'Centers, Kings, and Charisma: Reflections on the Symbolics of Power', in *Culture and Its Creators*, ed. Joseph Ben-David and Terry Nichols Clark (Chicago: University of Chicago Press, 1977), 150–71, here 168.

[60] Arthur M. Hocart, *Kings and Councillors* (Chicago: University of Chicago Press, 1936), 160.

[61] Nicole Brisch, ed., *Religion and Power: Divine Kingship in the Ancient World and Beyond* (Chicago: Oriental Institute of the University of Chicago, 2008); Rolf Gundlach and Hermann Weber, eds., *Legitimation und Funktion des Herrschers: Von ägyptischen Pharao zum neuzeitlichen Diktator* (Stuttgart: Franz Steiner, 1992); Franz-Reiner Erkens, ed., *Die Sakralität von Herrschaft: Herrschaftslegitimierung im Wechsel der Zeiten und Räume* (Berlin: Akademie-Verlag, 2002); Declan Quigley, *The Character of Kingship* (Oxford: Berg, 2005).

[62] Michael Puett, 'Human and Divine Kingship in Early China: Comparative Reflections', in *Religion and Power: Divine Kingship in the Ancient World and Beyond*, ed. Nicole Brisch (Chicago: Oriental Institute of the University of Chicago, 2008), 207–20.

Thus, the practice of self-coronation, with all its symbolic implications, serves as an excellent field from which to discuss the tensions and transferences between these realms: spiritual and temporal, religious and political, supernatural and natural, ecclesiastical and civil and transcendent and mundane. In addition, the use of the political theology allows us to evade the presentism and anachronism that might arise from applying contemporary concepts, such as that of 'political religion', to medieval cultural phenomena.[63] In the public sphere, a nuanced approach to the relationships between the spiritual and temporal spheres avoids in its turn artificial fusions between the religious and the political which could potentially damage social stability.[64]

My second methodological strategy assumes the long-term approach that compares the sixth century BC with its establishment of the new Persian-Achaemenid dynasty to Napoleon's self-coronation in Notre-Dame of Paris in 1804, although certainly privileging my own speciality of medieval history, and its extensive geographical framework from Spain to Persia and from Sicily to Sweden. This broad approach carries the risk of falling into historical anachronism and diachronism, but it activates the aim of all historical narration, what Reinhardt Koselleck calls 'the synchrony of the anachronism': the historian uses synchronic and diachronic procedures simultaneously, 'favoring synchrony when he describes, and diachrony when he narrates'.[65] As Alexander Beihammer argues, 'approaching rituals and symbolic communication as historical phenomena of *longue durée* stretching from the early Middle Ages to the early modern period and as phenomena shared by different cultural and religious spheres is no doubt a forward-looking and future-oriented viewpoint.'[66]

This tactic is not new in the scholarly approach to ceremonies of investiture. Traditional anthropology began working on parallels among the royal investiture ceremonies of kings from Africa, Europe, America, Asia and Oceania from different periods and ages, namely

---

[63] Philippe Burrin, 'Political Religion: The Relevance of a Concept', *History and Memory* 9 (1997): 321–49, and Hans Maier, 'Political Religion: A Concept and Its Limitations', *Totalitarian Movements and Political Religions* 8 (2007): 5–16.

[64] Clifford Geertz, 'Ritual and Social Change: A Javanese Example of Funeral', *American Anthropologist* 59 (1957): 32–45, here 44–5.

[65] Reinhardt Koselleck, *Futures Past* (New York: Columbia University Press), 217. See also Hans-Georg Gadamer, *Truth and Method* (London: Sheed & Ward, 1989), 297, and Paul Ricoeur, *Time and Narrative*. 3 vols. (Chicago: University of Chicago Press, 1990), 3:220.

[66] Alexander Beihammer, 'Comparative Approaches to the Ritual World on the Medieval Mediterranean', in *Court Ceremonies and Rituals of Power in Byzantium*, ed. Alexander Beihammer, Stavroula Constantinou and Maria G. Parani (Leiden: Brill, 2013), 1–36, here 7.

Arthur M. Hocart,[67] Meyer Fortes[68] and Robert S. Ellwood.[69] More recent anthropologists such as Roy Rappaport and Catherine Bell still believe that there is something *universal* and *common* among, 'say, rites such as the Catholic Mass, the Sun Dance, the rites of passage in the deserts of Central Australia, Papua New Guinea curing rituals, and human sacrifice in Aztec Mexico'.[70] They have tried to explore 'what makes us identify some acts as ritual, what such a category does for the production and organization of knowledge about other cultures, and how we might assess the assumptions that create and constrain the notion of ritual'.[71] Francis Oakley has published a general review on the nature of kingship, arguing that kingship may be the most common form of government known to humankind, beyond the formal differences among the pharaohs of Egypt, the emperors of Japan, the Maya rulers of Mesoamerica and the medieval popes and emperors of the European monarchies.[72] All these general approaches demonstrate that rituals have been one of the privileged fields of anthropological studies, beyond theoretical assumptions or methodological concerns supporting their approach: 'functionalism with authority, Marxism with contradiction and change, structuralism with binary contrast and equivalence, phenomenology with the construction of experience', as Andrew Apter notes.[73]

Though I am aware of the limitations of the essentialist method, I argue that this comparative approach may be still revisited, not only from the geographical-synchronical terms within which it has been traditionally practised, but also in its chronological-anachronical dimension – which particularly interests me in my long-term approach to royal self-coronations. In this way I have tried to diminish the natural divergence between 'the theoretical and the observational language', as Wolfgang Stegmüller puts it in his analysis of the language of theory in the hard

---

[67] Hocart took as a case study ceremonies performed 'from the Aegean to the Ganges' (Hocart, *Kingship*, 98) and he enumerates twenty-five common features of these royal coronations. See also Reginald M. Woolley, *Coronation Rites* (Cambridge: Cambridge University Press, 1915), 165–76, section 'The Inter-relation of the Different Rites'.

[68] Meyer Fortes argues for the 'confirmation for the thesis in Hocart's study, namely, that installation ceremonies have much the same structure, use similar procedures, and serve broadly the same ends in all societies' (Fortes, 'Of Installation Ceremonies', 19).

[69] Robert S. Ellwood, *The Feast of Kingship* (Tokyo: Sophia University, 1973), 1–36. For African ceremonies of investitures see Hilda Kuper, *An African Aristocracy* (Oxford: Oxford University Press, 1947), 72–87 and 197–225.

[70] Roy A. Rappaport, *Ritual and Religion in the Making of Humanity* (Cambridge: Cambridge University Press, 1999), 29.

[71] Catherine Bell, *Ritual Theory, Ritual Practice* (Oxford: Oxford University Press, 1992), 4.

[72] Francis Oakley, *Kingship: The Politics of Enchantment* (Oxford: Blackwell, 2006).

[73] Andrew Apter, 'The Embodiment of Paradox: Yoruba Kingship and Female Power', *Cultural Anthropology* 6 (1991): 212–29, here 223.

sciences.[74] Approaches on self-coronations actually oscillate between the two opposing points of view: synchronicity and diachronicity. Anthropologists privilege the study of culture as a system of meanings which encapsulates the primordial values of a specific community. From this point of view, coronation rituals may be read synchronically and, as a consequence, analysed like a text, as a coherent script or a master narrative that actors follow and participants believe.[75] Historians, on their part, privilege the specificity of each ritual, given its particular context, circumstances and the agency of its promoters. They consequently proceed diachronically, acknowledging the manipulation, artificiality and historicity of the ritual rather than its essentialist, permanent and universal nature. This approach adopts a perspective through which each ritual performance constitutes one link in a chain of causes and consequences extending through time.[76]

The progressive specialisation of modern historiography, which has privileged micro- rather than macro-historical approaches, has alerted us not to fall into abstract and, ultimately, imaginative generalisations. But recent historiographical trends argue in favour of a more comprehensive chronological perspective, in order to establish reasonable comparisons among agents from different places and ages, and to provide society with historical models that may empathically connect with an audience beyond the academic world.[77] Since my story of the self-coronations is, in the end, the genealogy of a ritual, it requires a large-scale temporal and comparative approach rather than a microscopic historical analysis. This larger-time-scale approach also facilitates a more multilayered contextualisation of the ritual of self-coronation, within the general system of coronations. Thus, I have moved from the necessary detailed historical account of the singular events in each chapter to the comparative and comprehensive anthropological approach in the conclusions.

To take advantage of what each discipline has to offer, I have tried, in this book, to analyse like a historian and to interpret like an anthropologist.[78] I have followed Marshall Sahlins' attempt to blend the

---

[74] Wolfgang Stegmüller, *The Structure and Dynamic of Theories* (New York: Springer, 1976), 24.

[75] Sherry B. Ortner, 'Introduction', *Representations* 59 (1997): 1–13, here 8–9; Lisa Wedeen, 'Conceptualizing Culture: Possibilities for Political Science', *American Political Science Review* 96 (2002): 713–28, here 716; Clark, 'When Culture Meets Power', 15–16.

[76] William H. Sewell Jr, 'Geertz, Cultural Systems, and History: From Synchrony to Transformation', *Representations* 59 (1997): 35–55, here 40.

[77] Jo Guldi and David Armitage, *The History Manifesto* (Cambridge: Cambridge University Press, 2014).

[78] See an interesting example of this double approach in Clark, 'When Culture Meets Power'.

methods of history and anthropology rather than simply searching for more mutual collaboration between the disciplines: 'The problem now is to explode the concept of history by the anthropological experience of culture so that the historical experience will surely explode the anthropological concept of culture – structure included.'[79] Royal rituals share 'universal characteristics of the symbolic construction of authority and also gain specific meaning through their adoption and adaptation of symbolic forms which organized non-royal life'.[80] Structure and symbol, particularism and generalisation, system and individual, and analysis and interpretation naturally converge in my medieval self-coronation approach since, as Victor Turner argues, 'we see the meaning of a symbol as deriving from its relation to other symbols in a specific cluster or gestalt of symbols whose elements acquire much of their significance from their position in its structure.'[81] Thus, one self-coronation must be connected, in comparative terms, not only with its particular historical context and with the historical reality of other self-coronations performed in medieval Europe, but also with the whole system of that ritual perceived as a ceremony of investiture. In this direction, I question, in this book, up to what extent self-coronations are a simple 'variety' of the ritual of investiture, or rather are an 'anomaly' or 'failure' of the form, or even another kind of ritual.

Most of these questions require deep reflection on the historical context in which self-coronations were enacted. That is why I open each chapter with the temporal, geographical, political, social and cultural circumstances of each self-coronation analysed. The exercise of contextualising each ritual is necessary so as to understand that the degree of transgressivity of each event does not depend only on the nature of the ceremonies enacted within the ritual itself, but also, and more properly, on the particular circumstances during which they were performed. In the Crown of Aragon, for instance, the most transgressive self-coronation was probably that of Alfonso the Benign, while his successors Peter, John, Martin and Ferdinand used the same ritual, following an 'established' tradition. Thus, one understands Turner's insistence on the 'semantic bipolarity' of ritual symbols which involves the diverse meanings resulting from the different circumstances in each ceremony.[82] An accurate knowledge of the performance context is necessary to determine which particular

---

[79] Marshall D. Sahlins, *Islands of History* (Chicago: University of Chicago Press, 1985), xvii. See especially chapter 5, 'Structure and History', 136–56.
[80] Maurice Bloch, *Ritual, History and Power* (Oxford: Berg, 2004), 188.
[81] Victor Turner, 'The Syntax of Symbolism in an African Religion', *Transactions of the Royal Philosophical Society* 25 (1966): 295–303, here 295.
[82] Victor Turner, *The Ritual Process* (Chicago: University of Chicago Press, 1966), 69.

connotations are intended, because 'the same symbols have varying significance in different contexts.'[83] As Clyde Kluckhohn puts it, myths and rituals may convey symbolic realities, since they 'may express not only the latent content of ritual [depending on the ceremonial itself] but of other culturally organized behaviours [depending on the context in which the ritual is inserted]'.[84]

This leads to my scepticism regarding the alleged transgressivity of self-coronations. This label was probably established because of the great symbolic power of Napoleon's self-coronation in 1804 and the uncritical projection of Capetian – and successively English – coronation models onto other medieval and early modern realms. Weiler explains,

> As a kind of historiographical commonplace, high medieval European is often equated with Capetian kingship. As with historians of feudalism who experience an existential crisis on realizing that in their chosen region patron–client relationships did not resemble those of the Mâconnais, many historians of kingship also set their regional case against the image of kingship as developed by the learned denizens in and around St. Denis in the decades after the 1270s. ... That is, the prestige claimed by the descendants of St. Louis may have led modern historians to project backwards in time a cultural hegemony that only emerged, and only for a short period, in the closing decades of the thirteenth and the first quarter of the fourteenth century.[85]

Medieval rituals are rather inserted in a general context in which the ritual behaviour and symbolic gestures become relevant, but they may passively express or actively react against their own context. Rituals are conditioned by tradition, since they must reiterate an earlier performance, and they depend on the precise repetition of specific words or symbolic gestures. Of course, there were variations in the rites, but it is difficult to find sources which describe the attendants' reactions to them. But we have enough evidence to assert that the emphasis of the medieval rituals was placed on the ability to repeat certain formulas in the proper order and in the proper language. Nevertheless, it is also true that some royal rituals, such as the royal and triumphal entries in the cities, 'though with certain recognizable elements maintained over long periods of time, were quite malleable, and the symbols displayed in these performances quite fluid. Exact reiteration, such as that of the Mass, was not required: changes and slight variations could occur'.[86]

---

[83] Turner, *The Ritual Process*, 53.
[84] Clyde Kluckhohn, 'Myths and Rituals: A General Theory', *Harvard Theological Review* 35 (1942), 45–79, here 54.
[85] Weiler, 'Crown-Giving and King-Making', 85–6.
[86] Teófilo F. Ruiz, 'The Symbolic Meaning of Sword and Palio in Late Medieval and Early Modern Ritual Entries', *Memoria y Civilización* 12 (2009): 13–48, here 15–16.

Thus, based on this long-term approach, I analyse the (historical) action-field context in which the ritual enacted is simply a phase, and the (anthropological) cultural context in which symbols become clusters of abstract meanings. I also include a third approach, the historical-genealogical perspective, which blends both the event and interpretations of the whole system. I do not merely describe and interpret each coronation, but also read its place within the entire cultural system of 'self-coronation' – in the end, not a cultural event but a conceptual construction. Combining these three approaches (the action-field, the cultural context and the interpretation of the cultural system) allows me to clarify the meaning of the particular symbols that emerge from this complex ritual. They are full of cultural rather than material implications: what distinguishes self-coronations from other rituals is that their performance is not concerned, like most traditional rituals, with natural phenomena, technological processes, human life crises or the breach of crucial social relationships, but with the emergence, legitimation and representation of the complex reality of power. In addition, this comparative approach helps gather the three basic coordinates in which all rituals are encompassed: the spatial (the physical and architectonic context, usually sacral such as the cathedral, but also civil, such as the royal palace), the temporal (the development of the ritual following the rhythm of the liturgy) and the visual (the iconographic representations and the artistic programme conveyed in the ceremony itself).

The third key concept I use in my reading of self-coronation is an emphasis on agency. Self-coronations are dense crossroads of semiotically charged royal ceremonies that require both an anthropological and a historical approach. They arise from a tradition that obeys the symbolic logic of European kingship, anchored on the solid foundation of the culture of a given society, but at the same time they are highly purposive and manipulative, an opportunity to activate their actors' agency. This fits well with the formula proposed by Lisa Wedeen and Christopher Clark, who see the rituals as 'processes of meaning-making' in which 'the intentions and strategies of actors interact with language, ritual and other symbolic systems'.[87] As Gabrielle Spiegel argues, we are experiencing a partial restoration of the concept of agency, after the double determinism of social (Marxist) and subsequently cultural studies constructionism, via methodologies associated with the linguistic turn, postmodernism and post-structuralism:

---

[87] Wedeen, 'Conceptualizing Culture', 713 and 716, and Clark, 'When Culture Meets Power', 16.

Rather than being governed by impersonal semiotic codes, historical actors are now seen as engaged in inflecting the semiotic constituents (signs) that shape their understanding of reality so as to craft an experience of that world in terms of a situational sociology of meaning, or what might be called a social semantics. This shift in focus from semiotics to semantics, from given semiotic structures to the individual and social construal of signs – in short, from culture as discourse to culture as practice and performance – entails a recuperation of the historical actor as a rational and intentional agent.[88]

As Goethe wrote recalling the investiture of Joseph II at Frankfort:

A politico-religious ceremony possesses an infinite charm. We behold earthly majesty before our eyes, surrounded by all the symbols of its power; but while it bends before that of heaven, it brings to our minds the communion of both. For even the individual can only prove his relationship with the Deity by subjecting himself and adoring.[89]

Thus, part of the interest and, as Goethe would say, the *charm* of self-coronation is that it responds to the action of individual agency rather than to social structures. In the end, the interest for ritual studies among medievalist since the 1990s, in which they have applied the theories and practices that emanated from symbolic anthropology during the 1970s and 1980s, is the result of an attempt 'to move away from structure and to find new ways of talking about individuals' agency'.[90] Historians and anthropologists have argued, in one way or another, that 'in the institutions of a given society changes are slow and subtle; transformations are mostly the result of an adaptation to exigencies of the moment, rather than of conscious innovations.'[91] Yet some rituals show that sometimes new traditions – or, at least, variations of traditions – are shaped by conscious innovations by individuals.

My own interest in issues associated with the concept of agency has materialised in my projects on authorship in the Middle Ages and modern historians' autobiographies.[92] Now, I see in the practice of self-coronation not only a palpable manifestation of human agency

---

[88] Gabrielle M. Spiegel, 'Reflections on the New Philology', in *Rethinking the New Medievalism*, ed. R. Howard Bloch, Alison Calhoun, Jacqueline Cerquiglini-Toulet, Joachim Küpper and Jeanette Patterson (Baltimore, MD: Johns Hopkins University Press, 2014): 39–50, here 48–9. See also Amanda Anderson, *The Way We Argue Now: A Study in the Cultures of Theory* (Princeton, NJ: Princeton University Press, 2006).
[89] Johann W. Goethe, *The Autobiography of Goethe*, trans. John Oxenford. 2 vols. (London: Bell, 1864), 1:168.
[90] Pössel, 'The Magic of Early Medieval Ritual', 125.
[91] Marion F. Facinger, 'A Study on Medieval Queenship: Capetian France, 987–1237', *Studies in Medieval and Renaissance History* 5 (1968): 3–47, here 31.
[92] Jaume Aurell, *Theoretical Perspectives on Historians' Autobiographies* (London: Routledge, 2016) and Aurell, *Authoring the Past*.

Introduction 31

susceptible to systematic analysis, but also that move 'from culture as discourse to culture as practice and performance', as Gabrielle Spiegel puts it, which has inspired my approach to anthropological studies via studies of ritual. Medieval kings actively employed the language of ritual to one extent or another, since their opportunities to shape the form through which they governed were limited to certain solemn occasions.[93]

Emphasis on agency has also allowed me to reflect on the bipolar nature – active and passive – of the ritual of self-coronation. To be sure, agency is not the only force behind a self-coronation since, as Mary Douglas explains, 'rituals, as a form of social interaction, will be suspect when social interaction itself is troubled.'[94] The practice of self-coronation shows that when political authority and social stability are in danger the king searches for the symbols through which to recover normality, even if he may be accused of transgressing a tradition. Then, the king's aggressive agency in ritual reflects social transformation in context.[95]

Finally, the concept of self-fashioning complements that of agency and helps to discern how individuals or groups define or express identity and authority through a variety of performative practices.[96] In the creation and expression of identity, authors and historical agents employ inherited attributes, acquired skills and performed actions to persuade contemporaries in ways that exemplify – and, in the case of some self-coronations, challenge – the traditional values and expectations prevalent in their historical context. In fact, Stephen Greenblatt uses Clifford Geertz's definition of culture to argue that self-fashioning is 'the cultural system of meanings that creates specific individuals by governing the passage from abstract potential to concrete historical embodiment'.[97] Subjects and authors are connected by texts and contexts and their ability to highlight authorial agency and to self-create a new identity. From this perspective, self-coronations become an artfully manipulative process in which a new identity is purposefully created and then presented to the world – a process which fits very well in the cases of Alfonso XI, Peter IV, Charles III, Frederick II and Frederick of Prussia. This concept of self-fashioning has been applied extensively to literary and historical texts, yet

---

[93] Warner, 'Thietmar of Merseburg on Rituals of Kingship', 55.
[94] Mary Douglas, *Natural Symbols* (New York: Routledge, 2003), 144.
[95] Margaret Thompson Drewal, *Yoruba Ritual* (Bloomington: Indiana University Press, 1992).
[96] Stephen Greenblatt, *Renaissance Self-Fashioning: From More to Shakespeare* (Chicago: University of Chicago Press, 1980).
[97] Greenblatt, *Renaissance Self-Fashioning*, 4–5.

may be also a good instrument for the interpretations of rituals, ceremonies and performative practices – what we could call gestural or performative self-fashioning.

* * *

The analysis, description and interpretation of and the comparative approach to the rituals of accession without ecclesiastical mediation I propose in this book are governed by a double dimension. On one hand, I provide the particularised analysis of each of the ceremonies in its specific context, which immunises against an eventual static, essentialist and ahistorical vision of these rituals. On the other, I establish these rites' long-term development, which examines their continuities and discontinuities. If history allows us to fix the relationship between the particular characteristics of each of the self-coronations and to look for continuities in long-term historical processes, anthropology may serve to analyse the symbolic dimension and the meaning of these ceremonies.[98] Thus, the structure of this book reflects this long-term transformation of the ritual of self-coronation from ancient pagan societies to late antiquity and the early medieval Christianised world ('Tradition'), and from being considered as a transgressive ritual ('Opprobrium') to its Iberian normativity ('Convention') and early modern theatricality ('Dramatisation'). Another basic plot is the distinction between *imagining how the world can be* (symbolic self-coronations: Chapters 2–6) and *how things actually are* (performed self-coronations: Chapters 7–12).

The first chapter provides a theoretical exposition of the key theories around the ritual nature of self-coronation and its symbolic implications, focusing on historians and anthropologists' theoretical perspectives. The second chapter explores diverse forms of mediation in pre-Christian civilisations, from the Israelite to the Mesopotamian, Egyptian, Persian and Greek monarchies, and the symbolic meanings connected with the idea of 'consecration without mediation'. Based on textual, epigraphic and iconographic evidence, it privileges the analysis of the royal investiture ceremony in Achaemenid and Sassanid Persia, since the practice of self-coronation decisively influenced subsequent periods, reaching Islamic and even contemporary Persia (including the self-coronation by Shah Reza Pahlavi in 1926 and his son Mohammad Reza Pahlavi in 1967) and expanding beyond its borders, to Byzantium and

---

[98] I am thus particularly sympathetic to try to find that 'middle ground' between the historical and anthropological approaches and between facts and interpretation argued in Maclean, 'Ritual, Misunderstanding, and the Contest for Meaning', 99.

central Asia. We learn from these data that the practice of self-coronation was certainly not unprecedented.

The third chapter examines the iconography of the 'hand of God' spread during the late Roman Empire from the mid-third century onwards, and in the context of interactions between the pagan, Jewish and Christian cultures. This particular iconography leads directly to the idea of self-coronation – although still an iconographic rather than a performative reality – since it conveys the emperor being crowned by a celestial hand from above, without priestly intervention. Numismatic sources emerge here as crucial evidence, particularly in the case of third- and fourth-century Roman emperors. The iconography of the emperor being crowned by the hand of God did not extend to early Byzantium, but survived in medieval art through the iconography of the king or emperor being crowned by Jesus Christ.

With the expansion of Christianity throughout the Mediterranean, self-coronation and the mediation of priests became a point of divergence. Emperors in Christian Byzantium are thus to be crowned by the patriarchs in the ritual practice, but they are frequently crowned by the iconographic representation of the 'hand of God'. Thus, the fourth chapter analyses what scholars have called 'symbolic' or 'heavenly' coronation in Byzantium. It engages in a comparative analysis of the reality of the church's intervention in the real performative ceremony of the imperial coronation and the imaginative fiction of the crowning of the emperor directly by Christ and his angels and saints, as established in some iconographic representations. In Byzantium, imperial art was given the task of translating into a visual and symbolic – but not necessarily referential – language the values and ideology that prevailed in each dynasty concerning the source of its power.

The fifth and sixth chapters explore the sacralisation and liturgification of the royal investiture ceremony in eighth- to eleventh-century Western Europe, with the progressive fusion of the rites of unction and coronation in the same ceremony and the increasing prominence of the bishop as its ordinary minister. This sacralisation, particularly among Carolingian, Anglo-Saxons and Ottonian rulers, preludes the allegedly transgressive nature of the performance of self-coronation among some Western late medieval kings, in which the mediating function of the priest will be modified. The iconographic Christ substitutes (or, perhaps more accurately, is transferred from) the pagan and theocentric models of pre-Carolingian ceremonies and rites, and they symbolise that the office of king must be bestowed by the priest. These chapters show that the error of considering self-coronation a transgressive act arises from the projection of the French and, to a lesser extent, English models – clearly a heritage of Carolingian, Anglo-Saxon and Ottonian ritual and iconographic models of coronation – to other areas of medieval Europe.

The seventh chapter focuses on the image of Roger II of Sicily being crowned by Christ, as depicted in the mosaic in the Martorana Church in Palermo, one of the strongest indications of the Christocentric evolution outlined in the sixth chapter, and a formidable example of symbolic self-coronation. Roger II's respect for his Muslim Arab subjects, as well as his attempt to assimilate Arab and Byzantine cultural traditions, are at the root of his iconographic programme: the visual language could be understood by Arabs, Normans, Greeks and Latins. This supra-linguistic, multinational, multi-ethnic and multicultural form is a typical inheritance of the Norman kingdom of Sicily, and would without doubt have inspired the universalist and imperial politics of Roger II's grandson Frederick II, specifically at his majestic self-coronation in Jerusalem.

The eighth chapter explores the possible occurrence of Frederick II's self-coronation in the Church of the Holy Sepulchre in Jerusalem on Sunday, 17 March 1229, an event that remains shrouded in mystery. It is still difficult to discern the borders between reality and fiction, desire and its realisation, invention and propaganda. This chapter engages the question of the extent to which we can affirm the historicity of Frederick II's self-coronation. It addresses the crucial issue of the nature of this gesture, recognised as transgressive by posterity – but, important, not always by its contemporaries – in the context of preconceived ideas about the relationship between the temporal and spiritual.

Roger II's iconography in Palermo and Frederick II's crowning in Jerusalem complete the triple point of divergence of medieval royal coronations: the rulers of the West are to be crowned by the priests, by God or by themselves. This last ritual was prevalent in medieval Iberia, and the rest of the chapters of this book are devoted to some of these royal self-coronations. It is not by chance that this ritual practice began in the thirteenth century, when Europe had overcome that transitional moment of the twelfth century which, in Koziol's words, moves 'between the sacred liturgies of pontifical kings and the political theatre of statist monarchs', and shifts 'toward the sophisticated administrative apparatuses of the later medieval state while still publicly avowing the political morality of the Carolingians'.[99] The practice of self-coronation of Iberian kings seems to respond to this growing influence of the political theatre of the new monarchs and a sophisticated administrative machinery rather than to the sacred liturgies.

The ninth chapter focuses on the practice of self-coronation among medieval Castilian kings and its religious, political and ideological

---

[99] Koziol, 'England, France and the Problem of Sacrality', 124; Dale, 'Inauguration and Political Liturgy'. On this context see Bisson, *The Crisis of the Twelfth Century*.

implications. It takes Alfonso XI of Castile's self-coronation (1332) as a central event, establishing its conceptual genealogy, significance and relevance and deploying Visigothic, Asturian, Leonese and Castilian chronicles as the main sources. The case of Alfonso XI deserves particular attention, as it throws some light on the debate about the allegedly secular kingship of Castilian kings.

The tenth chapter explores the practice of self-coronation in the Crown of Aragon. It centres on Peter the Ceremonious' self-coronation in Zaragoza (1336), where the king implemented a conscious triple strategy in order to ensure that his ceremony, performed previously by his father, King Alfonso IV the Benign, would not remain an isolated gesture but would become tradition. First, he constructed an autobiographical historical account that would serve as the primary version of the event. Second, he fixed the rite of self-coronation by writing a new ceremonial. Third, he propagated an iconographic tradition through images of himself in miniatures, seals and coins, and, above all, of his gesture of self-coronation. Historiography, liturgy and iconography are brought into play by the king so as to perpetuate the memory of his self-coronation and thus ensure, through repetition, its transformation from an isolated event into a consolidated practice and part of inherited tradition.

The eleventh chapter centres on the self-coronation of Charles III of Navarra (1390), a gesture full of both symbolic meanings and juridical implications. The chapter traces the evolution of Navarrese royal accession ceremonies which emphasise two specific characteristics of Navarrese politics: resistance to ecclesiastical mediation and consensualism. The presence of the oath and the gesture of self-coronation in royal accession ceremonies involve both legal effects and a ritual symbolic dimension. This endows them with enormous force, both in semantic content and in the ritual form that their representations take.

The twelfth chapter traces a general vision of the survival of some self-coronations during early modernity, focusing on the tradition of Aragon after Peter the Ceremonious, especially the self-coronation of Ferdinand I (1414) and the cases of Frederick I of Prussia (1701) and Napoleon (1804), and the most recent examples in the twentieth century, as the practice is globalised and dramatised. The crucial question here is to what extent these self-coronations have lost the actual content carried by their medieval precursors, even if they maintain the same ritual forms in a secularised context. Finally, based on the inductive analysis of the previous chapters and the summary of the ritual's evolution during modernity, the conclusion provides closing remarks on the historical, political, religious and symbolic meanings of the practice of self-coronation among medieval kings, using a long-term approach.

1   Self-Coronation As Ritual

The intensive debate in the field of symbolic anthropology in the 1970s and 1980s on the meaning and interpretation of ritual – in which scholars like Geertz, Turner and Douglas became celebrities – seems to have moved to medieval studies in the past two decades. Scholars such as Buc, Koziol and Althoff imported these anthropological theories to medieval studies through their agreements or disagreements around the idea of how medieval rituals must be interpreted – and if they exist at all. Thus, I am aware that I am reopening a Pandora's box when approaching medieval self-coronations using anthropological theory on rituals. Taking into consideration these debates, this chapter clarifies my ideas. The key question here is whether self-coronations may be considered 'medieval rituals'. The answer is clearly yes, not in an essentialist sense, but in self-coronations' actual performance, context and narrative interpretations and their iconographic representations.

What does self-crowning reveal about the operation of ritual? Ceremonies of royal investiture have become a privileged site for historical understanding of medieval symbols and politics since they serve to emphasise the king's authority, the nature of that power, the use of political symbols, the relationship between the king, nobles and prelates, and the sacred idea of monarchy. The words and gestures included in the coronation ceremony (its form) validate its communicated particular message (its content).[1] Louis Marin argues that 'the power-effect of representation is representation itself': the king really is a king in his images, both visual and narrative.[2] The coronation ceremony is therefore more effective as performance than as argument. It gives cultural legitimacy to the practice it represents. It becomes the supreme moment in the association between

---

[1] On the languages of the gesture, see Sergio Bertelli and Monica Centanni, eds., *Il gesto nel rito e nel ceremoniale dal mondo antico ad oggi* (Florence: Ponte alle Grazie, 1995); Marcel Jousse, *L'anthropologie du geste* (Chicoutimi: J.-M. Tremblay, 2011); Wilhelm Wundt, *The Language of Gestures* (Paris: Mouton, 1973); Jean-Claude Schmitt, *La raison des gestes dans l'Occident médiéval* (Paris: Gallimard, 1990); James R. Knowlson, 'The Idea of Gesture as a Universal Language in the XVIIth and XVIIIth Centuries', *Journal of History of Ideas* 26 (1965): 495–508.

[2] Louis Marin, *Le Portrait du roi* (Paris: Minuit, 2001), 11.

the temporal and the spiritual, and the power of symbols naturally emerges in connection with it.³ Analogous to his role as mediator between God and human beings, the king is also seen to mediate between the clergy and the people; for he, who in some respects also belongs to the clergy, bears the image of Christ in his name as the *Christus Domini*.⁴ Proximity to divinity endows the ceremonies of investiture with a performativity that transcends their dramatic power. This explains why coronations have attracted attention among scholars and the general audience, since the meaning of political power may be understood by historians only through its effects, and those effects only by its forms of representation.

Are Medieval Self-Coronations Properly Rituals?

Together with historians' interest in the power of coronations to transform social and political realities through symbols, anthropologists have emphasised coronations' ritual character.⁵ Crucially, one of the key features of coronation rites, what distinguishes them from profane ceremonials or plays, is that rites *produce* something at the moment they are enacted.⁶ The blend of words and gestures in a given rite performed within a given tradition actually produces (or creates the psychological effect of) an improvement in the weather, healing or, in the case of coronations, divine assistance for the king or confirmation of his divine nature. This implies that all the attendants of the ritual are active participants rather than mere spectators. This is what distinguishes ritual from theatre: you participate in ritual but you are a spectator of a play too.

---

³ The contemporaries of these events felt this way too. For instance, the biographer of Louis the Pious, Ermoldus Nigellus, argued for the transcendence of the gesture over the word, because it meant that what would require many written words could be represented and made to happen in an instant. About Ermoldus, see the introduction by Edmond Farral, *Poème sur Louis le Pieux et épîtres au roi Pépin* (Paris: Les classiques de l'histoire de France au Moyen Âge, 1964), v–xiii, and Thomas F. X. Noble, *Charlemagne and Louis the Pious: Lives by Einhard, Notker, Ermoldus, Thegan, and the Astronomer* (University Park: Pennsylvania State University Press, 2009), 119–26. See also Gerhart B. Lander, 'Medieval and Modern Understanding of Symbolism: A Comparison', *Speculum* 54 (1979): 223–56.
⁴ Suzanne S. Cawsey, *Kingship and Propaganda: Royal Eloquence and the Crown of Aragon, c. 1200–1450* (Oxford: Oxford University Press, 2002), 75–95, section '*usurpant officia sacerdotii*: Royal Sermons'.
⁵ For the cultural and political power of rituals, and for a historical-anthropological approach, see Wilentz, *Rites of Power*; Bell, *Ritual Theory, Ritual Practice*; and Catherine Bell, *Ritual: Perspectives and Dimensions* (Oxford: Oxford University Press, 1997). Also see David Cannadine and Simon Price, eds., *Rituals of Royalty* (Cambridge: Cambridge University Press, 1992). Two other overviews of ritual, more generally considered, are: Gilbert Lewis, *Day of Shining Red: An Essay on Understanding Ritual* (Cambridge: Cambridge University Press, 1980) and Brian Morris, *Anthropological Studies of Religion* (Cambridge: Cambridge University Press, 1987).
⁶ John L. Austin, *How to Do Things with Words* (Oxford: Oxford University Press, 1962).

Because of the inclusive nature of ritual, there is no agreement on one single definition of it. The term has a multitude of uses depending on the time and place, the social groups involved or the specific discourses that derive from its practice. The generation of symbolic anthropologists of the last third of the twentieth century – i.e. Turner, David Kertzer and Douglas, among others – was optimistic about finding a definition which would fit with the immense variety of the circumstances of ritual. Essentialism dominated over historicism. Turner thus defined ritual as 'prescribed formal behaviour for occasions not given over to technological routine'. It would thus be narrowly related to the concept of the symbol, 'the smallest unit of ritual which still retains the specific properties of ritual behaviour; it is the ultimate unit of specific structure in a ritual context'.[7] Kertzer, in his turn, identified ritual as 'an analytic category that helps us deal with the chaos of human experience and put it into a coherent framework'.[8] Yet, more recently, anthropologists have acquired a more sceptical view on the possibility of finding a consensual definition of ritual since, as Edmund Leach posits, there is 'the widest possible disagreement as to how the word ritual should be understood'.[9] They have also returned to a comparative analysis of kingship, which offers a unique window into the fundamental dilemmas regarding the nature of power and the function of rituals, as recent studies by David Graeber and Marshall Sahlins show.[10]

In any case, anthropologists generally agree that what really transforms a ceremony into a ritual is its ability to *change* something in the process more than only showing it, a human activity that transcends human experience rather than being immanent to the world. For this reason, I prefer to apply the term *ritual* rather than *ceremony* to self-coronations because it better reveals the nature of what is being enacted: a ceremony 'indicates' while a ritual 'transforms'.[11] Rudolf Strootman concludes that

---

[7] Victor W. Turner, *The Forrest of Symbols* (Ithaca, NY: Cornell University Press, 1967), 19, and Turner, 'Ritual, Tribal and Catholic', *Worship Jubilee* 50 (November 1976): 504–26.

[8] David I. Kertzer, *Ritual, Politics, and Power* (New Haven, CT: Yale University Press, 1988), 9.

[9] Edmund H. Leach, 'Ritual', in *The International Encyclopedia of the Social Sciences*, ed. David L. Sills. 17 vols. (New York: Macmillan, 1968), 13: 521–3. See also on this sceptical approach to the definition of ritual, Jack Goody, 'Religion and Ritual: The Definitional Problem', *British Journal of Sociology* 12 (1961): 142–64; Rappaport, *Ritual and Religion*, 24–7; and Jan A. M. Snoek, 'Defining Rituals', in *Theorizing Rituals*, ed. Jens Kreinath, Jan A. M. Snoek and Michael Stausberg (Leiden: Brill, 2006), 3–14. For the debate around the definition of ritual see Ute Hüsken and Donna L. Seamone, 'The Denial of Ritual and Its Return: An Introduction', *Journal of Ritual Studies* 27(1) (2013): 1–9, and, from very different perspectives, the Heidelberg project on dynamics of ritual: www.ritualdynamik.de/index.php?id=1&L=1 (accessed August 2018), which contains an account of theoretical and practical perspectives on ritual.

[10] Graeber and Sahlins, *On Kings*, 1–14.   [11] Turner, *The Ritual Process*, 53–69.

'ceremony communicates royal ideology to on-lookers; ritual does the same but also has the power to turn men into kings, or gods, elevating them above the others.'[12] Strootman's formula has the advantage of highlighting the complementary nature of the relationship between the concepts of ceremony and ritual, rather than their incompatibility.

With the decline of structural functionalism in the 1970s, anthropologists increasingly interpreted ritual as an expressive, symbolic and communicative act, the meaning of which was to be deciphered by the analyst. Using examples from modern politics, Kertzer holds that ritual ('action wrapped in a web of symbolism') envelops political action and political power and does so for all cultures, challenging the view that political ritual merely served to bolster the status quo in supposedly primitive cultures: 'Politics is expressed through symbolism. ... Symbolism is involved in politics in many ways. In these pages, I focus on just one, ritual.'[13] Based on his experience with modern political rituals, Kertzer compares them with the power of the king in traditional societies:

> The more the king became the sole source of authority, the more a person's status depended on being closely identified with him. In such a setting, the royal rites were potent weapons. Nobles, clerics, and officials struggled mightily to win symbolic expressions of favour in court rites. Because ritual traditions defined [and made visible] the hierarchy of powers, the ruler was able to bring about changes in status simply by departing from precedent. It mattered not at all that the rites were transparent inventions; power holders could not afford to take them lightly.[14]

Thus, due to the centrality of medieval kings in their societies, ceremonies of investiture and, more specifically, royal coronations have been considered one of the key fields of examination by anthropologists, because they generate a complex system of political, cultural and religious symbols. Historians now realise that, as Douglas explains, 'anyone interested in belief, religion, and symbols looks to anthropology for insight.'[15] She is correct. Symbolic anthropologists have argued that *one* single rhetorical figure or symbolic event may convey many meanings – what Geertz defines as 'the art of interpreting the many meanings of a single rhetoric or symbolic event'.[16] They have helped historians approach that hidden

---

[12] Rudolf Strootman, 'The Hellenistic Royal *Court*' (Utrecht: University of Utrecht, doctoral dissertation, 2007, 257).
[13] Kertzer, *Ritual, Politics, and Power*, 3.   [14] Kertzer, *Ritual, Politics, and Power*, 106.
[15] Mary Douglas, *Implicit Meanings*. Second edition (London: Routledge, 1999), 'Preface'.
[16] Sean Wilentz, 'Introduction. Teufelsdröckh's Dilemma: On Symbolism, Politics, and History', in *Rites of Power*, ed. Sean Wilentz (Philadelphia: University of Pennsylvania Press, 1985), 1–10, here 5. The concept of 'thick description', developed in symbolic anthropology, soon found adherents among historians (Clifford Geertz, *The Interpretation of Cultures* [New York: Basic Books, 1973], 3–30).

essential world emphasised by scholars of religion: 'The symbol, the myth, the image, are part of the substance of spiritual life; they can be hidden, mutilated, and degraded, but they can never be eliminated.'[17]

From this symbolic perspective, medieval self-coronations condense social and political polarities. They become a privileged observatory since 'what is distributed through many fields and situations of secular life is condensed into a few symbolic actions and objects.'[18] They are modes of 'exerting power in shifting and ambiguous contexts', where absolute control is not in evidence, and both 'consent and resistance' may be in play.[19] They become a form of currency of social interaction,

a junction box ('switching point') between the external moral constraints of the social order and the participant's internal feelings and imaginative projections. [Ritual symbols] provide condensation of meanings. As vehicles or instruments, such symbols can provide possible restructurings of an individual's self-image, as in a curing ceremony where there is often a symbolic reordering of the patient into a more satisfactory relationship to her or his context than was true before the ritual.[20]

Yet medievalists have long mistrusted the category of 'ritual', a concept created by and associated with modern social sciences, applied to medieval realities. Buc cautions against the use of the concept of ritual for the historiography of the Middle Ages. Pössel asserts that 'the use of analytical category of "ritual" always needs to be justified: why does the historian constitute her subject in this particular way?'[21] The *danger* of applying ritual theory to medieval reality has also been highlighted by Vincent in his article on the pilgrimage experience of England's medieval kings, where he criticises certain essentialist tendencies of symbolic anthropology, beginning with Turner's ideas.[22] Yet other medievalists like Koziol argue that 'ritual is an analytical category in medieval studies,

---

[17] Mircea Eliade, *Images et symbols* (Paris: Gallimard, 1952), 12. See also Maurice Agulhon, 'Politics and Images in Post-Revolutionary France', in *Rites of Power Rites of Power*, ed. Sean Wilentz (Philadelphia: University of Pennsylvania Press, 1985), 177–205, here 201.

[18] Turner, *Forrest of Symbols*, 285.

[19] Bell, *Ritual Theory, Ritual Practice*, 8. On rituals' social functioning, see Nancy D. Munn, 'Symbolism in a Ritual Context: Aspects of Social Action', in *Handbook of Social and Cultural Anthropology*, ed. John J. Honigmann (Chicago: Rand McNally, 1973), 579–612.

[20] William G. Doty, *Mythography: The Study of Myths and Rituals* (Tuscaloosa: University of Alabama Press, 1986), 346.

[21] Pössel, 'The Magic of Early Medieval Ritual', 115.

[22] Nicholas Vincent, 'The Pilgrimages of the Angevin Kings of England 1154–1272', in *Pilgrimage: The English Experience from Becket to Bunyan*, ed. Colin Morris and Peter Roberts (Cambridge: Cambridge University Press, 2002), 12–45, here 12.

despite its obvious anachronism and situatedness in Western post-Reformation and post-Enlightenment culture.'[23]

In the debate around the existence of medieval rituals (and their interpretations), it is crucial that the new generation of historians working on them – i.e. Weiler, Dale, Simon John, Vincent, Jonathan Lyon, Pössel and Simon MacLean, among others – does not excessively theorise on the question. These historians are certainly aware of the debates around the issue, but they appear to take for granted that the ceremonies they are dealing with – ceremonies of knighting, homage, crown-wearing, acclamations, anointments and coronations – are rituals, and they call them this way. They assume that 'ritual was part of the day-to-day fabric of political life'[24] and that 'ritual mattered, and thirteenth-century England was no exception', in Weiler's formulas.[25] A medievalist approaching rituals of royal accession is thus persuaded that they were 'instruments used, changed or abandoned according to their usefulness'.[26] Self-coronations were, however, pragmatic rituals deployed by kings at their convenience, and they deserve to be analysed individually, after which a comparative approach will shed additional light on their meaning. Ritual becomes thus a useful category for a longue durée study of medieval self-coronations, if one wants to approach not only *what* happened but also *how* and *why* it happened. The danger of anachronistically and artificially applying sociological anthropological models to medieval rituals might be overcome through a detailed and comparative analysis of a particular ceremony adequately inserted in its long-term development. Here Reinhard Koselleck's distinction between 'natural time' and 'historical time' is very useful, since the latter allows combining different periods of time in a synchronic and comparative approach. The unified and broad notion of ritual provides an anthropological-comparative dimension, a complement to the historical-analytical perspective.

One of the most critical anachronisms to avoid involves applying the modern concept of 'politics' to medieval rituals. Buc puts it plainly:

A reading of rituals that emphasizes the political does violence to the medieval understanding of the rites. Even the term 'political ritual' employed in the title of this lecture is something of a misnomer. For a cultural approach, [Clifford]

---

[23] Buc, *The Dangers of Ritual*, 1, and Koziol, 'The Dangers of Polemic', 367–88, here 375, paraphrased in Pössel, 'The Magic of Early Medieval Ritual', 112. On the anachronism of the concept of 'ritual' applied to medieval studies and its advantages and disadvantages, see Pössel, 'The Magic of Early Medieval Ritual', 111–25.
[24] Björn Weiler, 'Knighting, Homage, and the Meaning of Ritual: The Kings of England and Their Neighbours in the Thirteenth Century', *Viator* 37 (2006): 275–99, here 296.
[25] Weiler, 'Knighting, Homage, and the Meaning of Ritual', 295.
[26] Weiler, 'Knighting, Homage, and the Meaning of Ritual', 299.

Geertz's model, elaborated on Balinese data, seems more adequate than those of functionalists like [Max] Gluckman or [Victor] Turner. First, the coinherence of religion and politics characteristic of South-Indian mentality seems very close to Medieval understandings. Second, like the rituals of Bali, medieval rituals such as the coronation or the royal entry seem to derive their power from vertical references to an eternal order.[27]

Historians of rituals should also overcome the typical dualism between 'politics' and 'religion'. These concepts were actually created during the Reformation and Counter-Reformation, so that they are not properly medieval. As a result of this evolution, anthropologists have produced an anachronistic concept of ritual 'that focused more and more on the social function (integrative or manipulative) of religious beliefs and practices'.[28] This artificial approach influenced certain sociologists who, in the 1970s, proposed a distinction between secular political ceremonies and magic-religious rituals.[29] Nevertheless, recent ritual studies no longer validates this false dichotomy between politics and religion and has tended clearly towards the idea that rituals are 'not limited to religion: [they are] equally important to secular contexts, to civic and civil life'.[30] In this vein, Buc stresses the complex textual and hermeneutical nature of the evidence and warns against reading the description of the ceremonies by contemporary chroniclers under the light of a present-oriented anthropological analysis. We cannot reduce the extraordinary symbolic power of these ceremonies to a fixed set of ritual building blocks constructed independently from the context or in an anachronistic projection of modern anthropological notions onto medieval contexts:[31]

Medieval understandings of ritual did not focus on society or politics. ... The Augustinian notion of the *bond of peace* or *bond of charity* (*vinculum pacis, vinculum caritatis*), through a number of media including seventeenth-century Jansenism, did transmute itself into early Sociology's *social bond* (*vinculum sociale, lien social*). Yet this does not allow us to project the sociological concept back into the mentalities of the early and high Middle Ages. In those earlier eras, considerations of salvation, heavenly exemplarity, and providential history, but not social integration, constituted the main focus of understandings of rites.[32]

---

[27] Philippe Buc, 'Political Ritual: Medieval and Modern Interpretations', in *Die Aktualität des Mittelalters*, ed. Hans-Werner Goetz (Bochum: Winkler, 2000), 255–72, here 269.
[28] Buc, '1701 in Medieval Perspective', 123.
[29] Robert E. Goodin, 'Rites of Rulers', *British Journal of Sociology* 29 (1978): 281–99, and Stephen Lukes, 'Political Ritual and Social Integration', *Sociology* 9 (1975): 289–308.
[30] Hüsken and Seamone, 'The Denial of Ritual and Its Return'.
[31] Philippe Buc, 'Noch einmal 918–9. Of the Ritualised Demise of Kings and of Political Ritual in General', in *Zeichen – Werte – Rituale*, ed. Gerd Althoff (Münster: Rhema, 2004), 151–78.
[32] Buc, '1701 in Medieval Perspective', 120–1.

The Context of Self-Coronations

Taking self-coronations as a model for a ritual approach, and trying to proceed historically and anthropologically at the same time, contextualisation becomes a prerequisite for valid interpretation. Contextualisation helps to fix the conventional form of the ritual, its duration, the strength of its own tradition, its eventual variations and its ability to turn itself from a transgression into a convention. This historicist approach to rituals immunises scholars from an essentialist application of anthropological theories, and is the idea at the core of Buc's criticism. The changes within ceremonies of royal accession without ecclesiastical mediation during the longue durée exposed in this book lie within 'not the role or importance of ritual and symbolism, but the wider political context within which one particular type of ritual was employed'.[33] In this approach, anthropologists and historians privilege a different approach to rituals, but do not necessarily exclude each other. Anthropologists tend to focus on the internal structure of the rites and they put each ritual in the context of the total system of the same ritual (in our case, ceremonies of investment), beyond the specific time and place of enactment. As Turner has explained in his analysis of the Ndembu tribe:

Each king of Ndembu ritual, like *Nkula*, has several meanings and goals that are not made explicit by informants, but must be inferred by the investigator from the symbolic pattern and from behaviour. He is able to make these inferences only if he has previously examined the symbolic configurations and the meaning attributed to their component symbols by skilled informants, of many other kinds of ritual in the same total system. In other words, *he must examine symbols not only in the context of each specific kind of ritual, but in the context of the total system* [emphasis added]. He may even find it profitable, where the same symbol is found throughout a wide culture area, to study its changes of meaning in different societies in that area.[34]

Historians, on their part, try to take a detailed approach to the specific context in which the ritual is enacted, being cautious in their comparative comments. Yet both comparative and contextualist approaches are required to properly understand the rites, and I want to rediscover the meaning of self-coronations by locating them in their historical context and in the whole system of rituals of investiture. My approach connects with what Paul Connerton describes as an accurate method for interpreting rites:

To set a rite in its context is seen not as an auxiliary step but as an essential ingredient to the act of interpreting it; to investigate the context of a rite is not just

---

[33] Weiler, 'Knighting, Homage, and the Meaning of Ritual', 296.
[34] Turner, *Forrest of Symbols*, 43.

to study additional information about it, but to put ourselves in a position to have a greater understanding of its meaning than would be accessible to someone who read it as a self-contained symbolic text. Pursuing this line of thought, many historians have demonstrated that if we are to rediscover the meaning of royal rituals in the early modern period we have to relate them comprehensively to the circumstances in which they were performed.[35]

The evolution from imagined and symbolic to performed self-coronations emphasises the need to contextualise this ritual. Clearly, the symbolic self-coronations in ancient Persia and the late Roman motif of the hand of God do not possess the same symbolic meaning of those performed by medieval and early modern Christian kings. We see the same ritual (or variety of ritual), but the meaning is very different in each case because, in the end, a rite is always connected with a dogma or, when this does not exist, with a myth, and these are always-changing historical realities.[36] Examples of self-coronations are generally located in medieval Iberian kingdoms and in early modern Northern Europe rather than in France, Germany and England. In those European kingdoms, self-coronation was not practised at all, with the possible exceptions of Richard I of England and the intriguing story of the auto-investiture of King Cnut, clearly seen as opprobrium. Mediterranean kingdoms, including Castile, the Crown of Aragon, Navarra and Sicily, experienced intensive cultural transactions with other religions and civilisations such as Islam and Byzantium. Thus, the contextualisation of ritual should encompass both the ritual's specific action field and the general cultural frame in which symbols are coherently seen as 'clusters of abstract meaning' of one total ritual system (to use Turner's phrase).[37] Yet I have tried to add a third field of contextualisation, the 'historical-genealogical', to locate rituals in particular political and cultural historical traditions – for instance, the specific tradition of each Iberian kingdom, the kingdoms of Sicily and Jerusalem and the Byzantine tradition.

The Dramatisation of Self-Coronations

In addition to the contextual approach, there is also an obvious analogy between ritual and drama to which we should attend. Peter the Ceremonious, Frederic Hohenstaufen and Martin of Aragon's self-coronations, for instance, became real dramas in which the participants

---

[35] Paul Connerton, *How Societies Remember* (Cambridge: Cambridge University Press, 1989), 51.
[36] William R. Smith, *Lectures on the Religion of the Semites* (Edinburgh: Adam & Charles Black, 1889), 18.
[37] Turner, *Forrest of Symbols*, 43.

functioned as actors, supporting Geertz's notion of ritual as a 'theatre of power'.[38] Yet the phrase 'power served pomp, not pomp power', argued by Geertz in his *Negara*, is reversed in this context: the pomp of the self-coronation serves the king's desire to consolidate his power. The enactment of rituals includes 'the playing out of roles, the use of rhetoric, audience reactions, performances according to rules, and narrative movement toward a crisis and then its resolution'.[39] Ritual provides a platform on which social roles are symbolically enacted. Such ritual symbols attain their motivational power by fusing emotionally derived impulses to learned social values. Kertzer explains that

> Ritual provides one of the means by which people participate in such dramas and thus see themselves as playing certain roles. The dramatic quality of ritual does more than define roles, however, it also provokes an emotional response. … Symbols provide the content of ritual; hence, the nature of these symbols and the ways they are used tell us much about the nature and influence of ritual. Three properties of symbols are especially important; condensation of meaning, multivocality, and ambiguity.[40]

The dramatic dimension of the gesture of self-coronation increases its ritual effectivity. As Kertzer suggests, when 'the gap between rulers and ruled is greatest, rites of rulers are most highly developed'.[41] Some kings who introduced self-coronations were supported in their decisions by contextual pressures, so that Kertzer's intuition is confirmed: Roger II was at the crossroads of the foundation of a new kingdom seeking the emperor's consent, Frederick II felt the pressure of excommunication by the Pope, the troubled Alfonso XI of Castile was surrounded by numerous aspirants to the throne after a long interregnum period, the adolescent Peter IV of Aragon tried to overcome his nobles' rebellion, and the anxious Charles III of Navarra hoped to lessen the power of *pactism* in his kingdom.

Though ritual is a drama, it is not a play: politics is not a game. Political change is not easy to achieve, so ritual serves as an instrument that medieval sovereigns use, as it seems to transcend space and time – ritual

---

[38] Clifford Geertz, *Negara: The Theatre State in Nineteenth-Century Bali* (Princeton, NJ: Princeton University Press, 1980). See also Georges Balandier, *Le pouvoir sur scène* (Paris: Fayard, 2006).

[39] Doty, *Mythography*, 350. See also Victor Turner, *The Drums of Affliction A Study of Religious Processes among the Ndembu of Zambia* (Ithaca, NY: Cornell University Press, 1981), 274–5. On anthropological perspectives of the dramatic dimension of the ritual see Abner Cohen, *The Politics of Elite Cultures: Explorations in the Dramaturgy of Power in a Modern African Culture* (Berkeley: University of California Press, 1981). On sociological perspectives see Hugh D. Duncan, *Symbols in Society* (London: Oxford University Press, 1972), 155–206.

[40] Kertzer, *Ritual, Politics, and Power*, 11.   [41] Kertzer, *Ritual, Politics, and Power*, 52.

tends to the universal. Yet ritual is also an instrument that expresses these eventualities, and it has the power to innovate within a traditional symbolic frame. In this sense, the identification that Johan Huizinga establishes between 'plays' and 'rituals' is useful in the context of discussion of the ritual of self-coronations.[42] Kertzer further explains his perspective on the ritualising power of the rite:

> Since people need to express their social dependence through ritual, political forces that have control over community rites are in a good position to have their authority legitimized. Through such ritual, authority is dramatized and thereby glamorized. This dramatization not only establishes who has authority and who does not; it also defines the degrees of relative authority among the politically influential.[43]

Self-coronations imply both rite and spectacle, and have to be read in the frame of a coherent system of communication.[44] Ritual is thus a language that implies the narrative of the words and gestures but also the internal plot of the symbols, in an 'aggregation of symbols'.[45] Walter Burkert concludes that 'man's most effective system of communication should be associated with ritual.'[46] Communication studies complements the medieval ritual approach. Certainly, ritual gestures are expressive, involuntary, communicative or mimetic.[47] Yet the self-coronation has a strong deliberative and strategic dimension.

Thus, in my analysis of medieval self-coronations, I am particularly compelled by Althoff's idea of the 'consensual' nature of medieval kingship, and the subsequent 'rules of play' (*Spielregeln*) which are never explicitly acknowledged but which nonetheless govern all aspects of public interaction.[48] Rituals represent the norms of political culture, but also establish and help maintain them. This explains why legitimacy of royal

---

[42] Johan Huizinga, *Homo Ludens* (London: Routledge, 1998), 13–27, especially 20 and 27.
[43] Kertzer, *Ritual, Politics, and Power*, 104.
[44] Gunter Senft and Ellen B. Basso, eds., *Ritual Communication* (Oxford: Berg, 2009).
[45] Turner, *Drums of Affliction*, 2.
[46] Walter Burkert, *Homo Necans* (Berkeley: University of California Press, 1983), 29.
[47] Sergio Bertelli and Monica Centanni, 'Il gesto. Analisi di una fonte storica di comunicazione non verbale', in *Il gesto nel rito e nel ceremoniale dal mondo antico ad oggi*, ed. Sergio Bertelli and Monica Centanni (Florence: Ponte alle Grazie, 1995), 9–28, here 19.
[48] Gerd Althoff, 'Demonstration und Inszenierung: Spielregeln der Kommunikation in mittelalterlicher Offentlichkeit', *Frühmittelalterliche Studien* 27 (1993): 27–50; Althoff, *Spielregeln der Politik in Mittelalter* (Darmstadt: Wissenschaftliche Buchgesellschaft, 1997) and *Die Macht der Rituale* (Darmstadt: Wissenschaftliche Buchgesellschaft, 2003). See also Huizinga, *Homo Ludens*, 29–32; Bernd Schneidmüller, 'Konsensuale Herrschaft. Ein Essay über Formen und Konzepte politischer Ordnung im Mittelalter', in *Reich, Regionen und Europa in Mittelalter und Neuzelt. Festschrift für Peter Moraw*, ed. Paul-Joachim Heinig, Sigrid Jahns, Hans-Joachim Schmidt, Rainer Christoph Schwinges and Sabine Wefers (Berlin, 2000), 53–87, and Alexandru Stefan Anca, *Herrschaftliche Repräsentation und Kaiserliches Selbstverständnis* (Münster: Rhema, 2010), 147–71.

power was not taken for granted in the Middle Ages, as we tend to consider, and why rulers continually searched for practices in order to justify and legitimise their power. Indeed, our knowledge of how medieval kings promoted historical writings, a literature that has been very useful for me as an analogical model, illustrates this strategy.[49] The practice of self-coronation appears as a privileged platform for the analysis of different forms of legitimisation by medieval kings. From this perspective, self-coronations, as 'symbols in action' (Koziol), build political and social reality. Their political and social effect is based on the emotion they raise among the attendants rather than on a rational reaction against a liturgical action.

The Function of the Audience

The idea of the ritual dramatisation raises the complex issue of the audience of the ritual of self-coronations. References survive on the participants' reactions to Peter of Aragon's and Charles of Navarra's self-coronations, but not enough to arrive at substantial conclusions. The former is narrated by the king of Aragon in his autobiographical chronicle and the latter is taken from an administrative document commissioned by the king of Navarra himself. Both accounts logically stress the people's enthusiasm with their kings' accession, even if the kings avoided ecclesiastical mediation in their ceremonies of coronation. But the specific ritual nature of medieval self-coronations does not fit with those other rituals connected with 'ritual communication' and 'rules of the game' as labelled by Althoff.[50] The ceremonies of accession analysed in this book are usually conceived by the kings and their advisors in order to expand their legitimacy and strengthen their power, so that kings controlled most a ceremony which was directed precisely to avoid other mediations. Other medieval rituals like knighting, homage, crowning, agreements of nobles, public penance, begging pardon and those related to the *rex renitens* have their own rules and their particular relationships with the audience.[51]

---

[49] Gabrielle M. Spiegel, *The Past As Text* (Baltimore, MD: Johns Hopkins University Press, 1997); Nancy F. Partner, *Serious Entertainments* (Chicago: University of Chicago Press, 1977).
[50] Althoff, *Die Macht der Rituale*, 18–21.
[51] On knighting and homage see Weiler, 'Knighting, Homage, and the Meaning of Ritual', 275–99; on crown-giving see Weiler, 'Crown-Giving and King-Making', 57–88; on reluctant kings see Weiler, '*Rex Renitens* and the Medieval Idea of Kingship', 1–42; on public penance see Mayke de Jong, 'What Was Public about Public Penance? *Paenitentia Publica* and Justice in the Carolingian World', *La giustizia nell'alto medioevo (secoli ix–xi)*, Settimane, 44 (1997), 863–902, and Maclean, 'Ritual, Misunderstanding, and the Contest for Meaning', 105–8; on ceremonies of pardon see Koziol, *Begging Pardon and*

Knighting and homage, for instance, are acts of symbolic communication, of 'symbolic exchanges in medieval politics', whose success 'depend[ed] on as wide an audience as possible in order to be effective' and they constitute 'means available to convey complex messages to a large audience'.[52] In submission rituals such as penance and *deditio*, 'Althoff's "rules of the game" could not have remained completely clear and distinct', so that they 'could collapse into each other under the right political pressures'.[53] In the self-coronations, dependence on the audience for its efficacy is only subsidiary as the message is relatively simple: all the participants know the political implications of the ceremonies of royal accession and the psychological impact of a coronation without ecclesiastical mediation.

Yet important distinctions emerge among the ceremonies without ecclesiastical mediation themselves. While the ceremonies of accession and crown-bringing enacted by Roger II and Frederick II are seen as opprobrium, the self-coronations performed by Alfonso XI of Castile, Peter IV of Aragon and Charles III of Navarra do not spark controversy. The first group is more assimilated to those acts of symbolic communication in which 'some dispute over their meaning existed, and that this dispute was recorded either by contemporary observers or by the actors themselves',[54] as I discuss in my chapters on Roger II (Chapter 7) and Frederick II (Chapter 8). In the second group, the interpretation of the ritual of self-coronation itself does not pose particular problems for accepting them, as the attendants', observers' and later memorialists' reactions confirm.

Roger II and Frederick II must face that 'dual challenge' Weiler proposed in his study on king-making in the West: 'On the one hand, they needed to gain recognition of an often disputed title, and, on the other, to fend off the unwanted attentions of those who had raised them to their royal dignity.'[55] Iberian self-crowned kings seemed to take these political aspirations for granted, so that they could focus on the establishment of

---

Favor, and Althoff, *Die Macht der Rituale*. To be sure, these scholars also have differences in their approaches to rituals. Weiler, for instance, keeps his distance from Althoff's approaches to ritual and power. 'Althoff deals with power (or might) in the composition of rituals, in how they were performed, and how these power relations controlled the meaning of the act. The present [Weiler's article on homage and knighting], by contrast, uses a concept of power that refers to the wider political context within which ritual acts were performed. The difference is a subtle but important one, without denying or weakening the validity of Althoff's reading'.(Weiler, 'Knighting, Homage, and the Meaning of Ritual', 296.)

[52] Weiler, 'Knighting, Homage, and the Meaning of Ritual', 296.
[53] Maclean, 'Ritual, Misunderstanding, and the Contest for Meaning', 119, and Warner, 'Thietmar of Merseburg on Rituals of Kingship', 58.
[54] Weiler, 'Knighting, Homage, and the Meaning of Ritual', 297.
[55] Weiler, 'Crown-Giving and King-Making', 59.

royal autonomy. Interestingly, the historical sources for the first group come from very different cultural and political backgrounds and convey very diverse interpretations of the rituals enacted by Roger II and Frederick II. These sources are contemporary or near-contemporary and are composed by writers who did not witness the events they recorded, and most of these writers had limited access to the royal court or were foreigners to the kingdoms of Sicily and Jerusalem. The sources for the second group were usually promoted by the same Iberian kings who performed those self-coronations and they convey one basic interpretation of the rituals' meaning and consequences.

Even if self-coronations do not tell us about the role of the audience, they do attest to the kings' self-representation: not necessarily how they were perceived by their subjects but how they or their chroniclers saw themselves. Much of this process of self-representation is 'incidental', as Weiler notes.[56] Yet, precisely because of its contingent and non-explicit character, it helps us understand the nature of kingship, particularly the exercise of power.

Yet this leads to the crucial question of agency, which some historians of medieval rituals have connected to the theme of the audience. Strictly speaking, ritual never *does* anything. As Pössel puts it, the attendants' reactions and interpretations are what provides the ritual with a particular meaning or hoped effects, rather than the actors' actions.

> Hands are washed during the Mass as in everyday contexts, what differs is the intention of the actor. . . . Ritual is not so much a category of action as of intention and perception. The real difference between an 'instrumental' and a 'symbolic' act, between washing one's hands in order to clean them, and washing them although they are already clean, is in the mind, not in the action.[57]

In the end, it is in the minds of rituals' participants where the ritual can do anything and may be efficient.

Even attending to these ideas regarding the participants' function in ritual, I argue that the actor's action and intention remain the decisive factors in the ceremony of self-coronation. I am particularly interested in how self-crowned kings manage to adapt themselves to their historical context but, at the same time, propose some transgressivity in the ritual of self-coronations that makes them examples of social innovation and personal agency. The king has designed the whole ceremony with the help of his advisors and governs its whole progress, controls its meaning and usually promotes subsequent liturgical representations and narrative

---

[56] Björn Weiler, 'Tales of First Kings and the Culture of Kingship in the West, C.A. 1050–C.A. 1200', *Viator* 46(2) (2015): 101–28 (here 101).
[57] Pössel, 'The Magic of Early Medieval Ritual', 117.

interpretations. The agency lies with the king rather than with those who participate in the ritual. It may be argued that we cannot attribute to the inauguration rituals the power to make kings. Other factors play key roles, such as the agreement and support of other figures powerful enough to legitimise the kings' dignity. Certainly, some royal inaugurations require the acclamation of the people as part of the rite, and this is the most essential manifestation of the relevance of the attendants' reaction.[58] Yet this does not apply to self-coronations, in which the king's action dominates the entire ritual performance. To be sure, I am sympathetic with Buc's and Pössel's warning regarding

> the assumption of automatic and absolute ritual competence (at least amongst the political actors) [as] another remnant of the fairy-tale conception of the Middle Ages: the description of medieval actors as able to master the rules of their social life serves as a (homogenous, less complex, more 'natural') contrast to our experience of uncertainty about changing etiquette, resultant embarrassments and faux pas, and the existence of differing ideas of changing social manners and mores within a society.[59]

Nevertheless, part of the objective of this book is to show that, even with these questions of agency and audience, each medieval ritual must be analysed and interpreted within its own particular character and context. Self-crowned kings such as Peter IV of Aragon, Alfonso XI of Castile and Charles III of Navarra aimed to control all the details of their inauguration even if they were aware that the meaning and effects of the ritualised acts were never obvious or fixed, and that the design of a given ceremony did not imply the dominion of its consequences.[60] That is why they tried to control not only their self-coronation's particular liturgy, but also its interpretation. For this reason, I stress the relationship among enacted, narrated, and iconographical rituals – an exploration that ultimately depends on extant sources.

Self-Coronations' Transformative Function

The emotional charge around rituals and their connection to the audience are necessary to attain both the *orectic* ritual function – the ability to move

---

[58] Kantorowicz, *Laudes Regiae*, 77–83.
[59] Pössel, 'The Magic of Early Medieval Ritual', 120.
[60] The king's awareness that he cannot control the whole array of the consequences of the rituals is well documented in the examples analysed in Maclean, 'Ritual, Misunderstanding, and the Contest for Meaning', 97–119; Weiler, 'Crown-Giving and King-Making', 57–88; Weiler, 'Knighting, Homage, and the Meaning of Ritual', 275–99; Koziol, *Begging Pardon and Favor*; and Althoff, *Die Macht der Rituale*, among others.

to action, in Turner's category – and the *alethurgical* one – the ability to *create* a new truth, as Michel Foucault posits.[61] Truth and action, belief and will, join in the practice of self-coronation and provide the king-performer and the participants with formidable social and political weapons. As Myron J. Aronoff explains, the emotional climate created by the ritual moves beliefs and perceptions: 'Ritual not only structures our perceptions and suggests certain interpretations of our experience, but it does so in a setting that makes these perceptions and interpretations particularly salient and compelling.'[62]

Thus, self-coronations are not only observable dramas that convey information to the participants but promoters of behaviours based on a new truth. Turner describes this *orectic* function of rituals in these terms: 'By eliciting emotion and expressing and mobilizing desire, ritual symbols add the orectic dimension to their cognitive function.'[63] Performativity fuses with emotion in order to attain the objectives sought by the kings who decide to perform self-coronations. Susanna Rostas clarifies that performativity is a consciously intensified performance which produces strong aesthetic effects.[64] Taking Rostas' ideas, Pamela J. Stewart and Andrew Strathern conclude that 'performativity has to do with *effects*, while performance refers to ritual action itself'.[65] The search for these effects (and the consequent efficacy) of the ritual by its designers shows that the interpretations of the processes of ritualisation mostly speak to issues of power and empowerment, that ritualisation works to produce a particular set of perceptions, or misperceptions, about reality, and that it produces and legitimises hierarchies of power in society.[66]

But beyond this legitimising power, it is worthwhile to refer to the social transformative dimension of these rituals. Self-coronations are not only about trying to change the participants' minds and perceptions; they also aim towards social transformation. Functionalist anthropologists have traditionally suggested that both myths and rituals 'are important agencies in the transmission of a culture and that they act as brakes upon the speed of culture change', and that they are more adaptive than transgressive, more

[61] I take this concept as coined and explained by Michel Foucault, *On the Government of the Living: Lectures at the College de France, 1979–1980* (New York: Palgrave, 2012), 1–21 (lesson 9, January 1980).
[62] Myron J. Aronoff, *Power and Ritual in the Israel Labor Parti* (Assen: Van Gorcum, 1977), 88.
[63] Turner, *Forrest of Symbols*, 54.
[64] Susanna Rostas, 'From Ritualization to Performativity: The Concheros of Mexico', in *Ritual, Performance, Media*, ed. Felicia Hughes-Freeland (London: Routledge, 1998), 85–103.
[65] Pamela J. Stewart and Andrew Strathern, *Ritual: Key Concepts in Religion* (London: Bloomsbury, 2014), 93.
[66] Catherine Bell's ideas commented on in Stewart and Strathern, *Ritual*, 96.

integrative than disruptive.[67] Yet I argue that medieval and early modern self-coronations demonstrate the power of rituals to change society: they are active agents of social transformation rather than passive spectators of social integration. They go beyond embedding past tradition to accommodate themselves to the contemporary needs of society. Self-coronations usually, although not always, make a new proposal rather than strive to maintain a given tradition. They not only mirror social reality but also shape it.[68]

Self-crowned kings function as a 'heterodoxy of repressed voices that oppose orthodox accounts of the world', in Pierre Bourdieu's words.[69] In a sense, they contest the political power established by ecclesiastical hierarchy – or, more properly, they try to resituate it in its natural context. The practice of self-coronations in medieval Europe demonstrates that ritual can efficiently routinise and normalise social and political change.[70]

The concept of liminality also allows us to comprehend the social transformative dimension of self-coronations.[71] The liminal nature of the rituals of self-coronation allows them to function as a privileged field of social and cultural experimentation and subversion, because of their alleged transgressive nature and the subsequent *effect* of marginality. As indicative of larger social structures, ritual allows the analyst to infer the normative, the regulative and the innovative aspects of the social order by observing anomalies and interstices between classificatory categories in ritual usage. As William Doty explains, 'liminal and marginal situations within cultures are the places where the danger of pollution is most likely to be felt.'[72] Thus, I have approached this study of self-coronations, in the words of Jonathan Z. Smith, as

a means of performing the way things ought to be in conscious tension to the way things are. Ritual relies for its power on the fact that it is concerned with quite ordinary activities placed within an extraordinary setting, that what it describes and displays is, in principle, possible for every occurrence of these acts. But it also

---

[67] Kluckhohn, 'Myths and Rituals', 62.
[68] On the continuities and discontinuities of social order promoted by rituals see Klaus-Peter Köpping, Bernhard Leistle and Michael Rudolph, eds., *Ritual and Identity: Performative Practices As Effective Transformations of Social Reality* (Berlin: LIT, 2006) and Fred W. Clothey, *Ritualizing on the Boundaries: Continuity and Innovation in the Tamil Diaspora* (Columbia: University of South Carolina Press, 2006).
[69] Pierre Bourdieu, *Outline of a Theory of Practice* (Cambridge: Cambridge University Press, 1977), 169.
[70] Apter, 'The Embodiment of Paradox', 227.
[71] Victor Turner, 'Liminal to Liminoid in Pay, Flow, and Ritual: An Essay in Comparative Symbology', *Rice University Studies* 60 (1974): 52–92.
[72] Doty, *Mythography*, 315.

relies for its power on the perceived fact that, in actuality, such possibilities cannot be realized.[73]

This power of self-coronations to reveal the tension between the possible and the real is increased because of the intensification of the agency that the nature of this gesture naturally implies, since the king himself, without ecclesiastical mediation, performs the whole ritual – although always in a sacred context. The challenge of a self-coronation confirms its transformative nature, able to sustain a social and political agenda that creates and shapes social reality. As Christel Lane puts it, 'the culture of every society is in part spontaneously generated by its members and in part consciously shaped and directed by its political elites.'[74]

The sovereign who eschews ecclesiastical mediation in his coronation uses the power of tradition, since the alleged transgressive gesture is made compatible with the orthodox liturgical context that frames the ritual. Thus, the participants in the ritual see a supposed transgressive ceremony performed, paradoxically, in a traditional sacred context. What started as a modest genetic history of a case study – several unconventional and exceptional examples of a supposed transgressive ritual – has finally come to make rather large claims on the essential forms of the whole culture. In this sense, medieval self-coronations provide the ritual of royal investiture with its actual meaning, beyond that assigned by tradition. Robert Merton explains this delicate ritual operation of breaking with traditions of the past in order to fit better with the expectations of the present: 'Activities originally conceived as instrumental are transmuted into ends in themselves. The original purposes are forgotten and ritualistic adherence to institutionally prescribed conduct becomes virtually obsessive.'[75]

The specific nature of self-coronations demonstrates the ritual's ability to revisit social content (the progressive affirmation of the monarchy) with ritual form (the adequacy of the ceremony with this social meaning). Significantly, a medieval self-coronation confirms, paradoxically through its own particular alleged transgressive nature, one of the most fundamental rules classic anthropologists assign to the ceremonial: its ability to portray a symbolic resolution to the conflicts in a given society. As Kluckhohn says, 'ceremonials tend to portray a symbolic resolvement of the conflicts which external environment, historical experience, and selective distribution of personality types have caused to be characteristic

---

[73] Jonathan Z. Smith, *To Take Place: Toward Theory in Ritual* (Chicago: University of Chicago Press, 1987), 109.

[74] Christel Lane, *The Rites of Rulers: Ritual in Industrial Societies* (Cambridge: Cambridge University Press, 1981), 1.

[75] Robert K. Merton, 'Social Structure and Anomie', *American Sociological Review* 3 (1938): 672–83, here 673.

in the society.'[76] Rather than lead to instability and tension, medieval Iberian self-coronations assimilate the ritual to the spirit of its time. Actually, this ability of medieval ritual to adapt itself to the time has been noted by medievalists working on rituals. Koziol detects the same trend in his study of rituals of pardon in medieval Europe, so that they may be used as indicators of social (and political, in the case of self-coronations) change.

It is because of this interaction between rituals and society that changes in the performance and perception of rituals can be studied as indicators of social change, just as historians study changes in the language of social categorization (*milites* and *nobiles*, for example) to understand changes in social organization. And just as social categories varied not only from period to period but also from community to community within the same period, so a ritual like supplication varied with the social organization and cultural attitudes of the political community. Although the language was the same, it had many dialects.[77]

From a more general perspective, anthropologists such as Marshall Sahlins explain the same reality in structural terms, extending this projection from social and political to a cultural sphere so that 'the cultural categories acquire new functional values. Burdened with the world, the cultural meanings are thus altered. It follows that the relationships between categories change: the structure is transformed'.[78] The paradoxical result of this process of continuity and change is that political rituals in the Middle Ages can accommodate both 'the ideal of stability and the reality of change'.[79]

The Symbolic Character of Self-Coronations

This interplay of stability and change leads to another relevant anthropological concept: its connection with the world of symbols. The exercise of power demands symbolic practices. Historians and anthropologists agree on the value of rites, ceremonies and symbols as tools to strengthen images of authority and supremacy for medieval and early modern European monarchies.[80] What Robert Darnton once called 'the symbolic element in history' has entered the mainstream of historical studies.[81]

---

[76] Kluckhohn, 'Myths and Rituals', 78–9.
[77] Koziol, *Begging Pardon and Favor*, 237–8.   [78] Sahlins, *Islands of History*, 138.
[79] Koziol, *Begging Pardon and Favor*, 296.
[80] Lynn Hunt, *Politics, Culture, and Class in the French Revolution* (Berkeley: University of California Press, 1986), 54. I would highlight two key articles on this topic: Geertz, 'Centers, Kings, and Charisma', 150–71, and Jacques Le Goff, 'Is Politics Still the Backbone of History?', *Daedalus* 100 (1971): 1–19.
[81] Darnton, 'The Symbolic Element in History', 218–34.

Historians, who are always searching for empirical signs so as to support their hypotheses, have been fascinated by ritual's capacity 'to make the invisible visible and to form the visible in such a way that a deeper meaning could be discovered in it', as Percy E. Schramm puts it.[82] Thus, they continue to search for historical interpretations of symbols, rituals, images and texts through anthropological methods.

Robert Darnton argues that cultural historians should think of symbols as 'polysemic, fluid, and complex'.[83] Michael Herzfeld posits that rituals lead to the syntax of symbols, and 'symbols do not stand for fixed equivalences but for contextually comprehensible analogies.'[84] Koziol, applying this idea to medieval ritual studies, states that 'ambiguity and contradiction, then, are the very soul of ritual, the secret of its flexibility, the source of its emotional power.'[85] Thus, ambiguity becomes 'not only occasionally helpful; it [is] absolutely essential to the success of rituals',[86] as the self-crowned kings skilfully practised.

Yet ambiguity of meaning does not imply that the ritual vessels are semantically empty. Ritual symbols are never arbitrary or meaningless. They are icons and indicators of political power. Indeed, this ambiguity permits rituals to flirt with continuity and stability at the same time. The practice of self-coronations confirms that rituals are not only instances of repetitive and formal actions that transmit ideologies and preserve social cohesion. Rather, they elicit emotional responses from their participants which often lie beyond rational responses.

Rituals' complex world of symbols leads to occasional misunderstandings by non-initiated or external spectators. The anthropologist Andrew Apter tells us that the more he was invited to the Yorubas' rituals and the more he understood them, his presence became increasingly dangerous, 'since the more I learned, the more I could expose and undo. This threat extended to the deities themselves. On many occasions when I pressed devotees for information, they explained that if they revealed cult secrets, the òrisà would weaken and fade'.[87] Medieval self-coronations are obviously far from contemporary Yoruba enchantments. Yet the engagement with the

---

[82] Schramm, *Kaiser, Könige und Päpste*, 1:23.
[83] Darnton, 'The Symbolic Element in History', 223.
[84] Michael Herzfeld, 'An Indigenous Theory of Meaning and Its Elicitation in Performative Context', *Semiotica* 34 (1981): 113–41, here 130.
[85] Koziol, *Begging Pardon and Favor*, 316. See also Barbara H. Rosenwein, *Emotional Communities in the Middle Ages* (Ithaca, NY: Cornell University Press, 2006) and, for the influx of the senses in liturgical and ritual actions, see Eric Palazzo, 'Les cinq sens au Moyen Âge: état de la question et perspectives de recherche', *Cahiers de Civilisation Médiévale* 55 (2012): 339–66.
[86] Koziol, *Begging Pardon and Favor*, 310; see also Turner, *Forrest of Symbols*, 50–1.
[87] Apter, 'The Embodiment of Paradox', 217.

unknown is similar. Medieval self-crowned kings were aware that they were breaking ritual rules at the risk of undermining their authority. Yet they were convinced of the efficiency of the inexplicit explanation of the meaning of the new ceremony they performed or of what Apter calls 'the logic of secrecy'.[88] Actually, 'undermining' the social cohesion by the king who performs self-coronation could sound contradictory, since the king is at the very core of power. Nevertheless, 'the paradox of sovereignty consists in the fact that the sovereign is, at the same time, outside and inside the juridical order.'[89] Thus, the supposed exceptionality of self-coronations may be explained by this 'inside-outside' nature of royal power. A self-coronation is inherently dangerous for the previously consolidated power because it

> both deconstructs and reconstructs the social order in relation to competing political factions, different ritual centers and shrines, and along latent or emerging corporate lines. If the deconstructive discourse is subversive, deep, and powerful, voicing sectional interests and divisive claims, the reconstructive discourse is official, superficial, and authoritative, restoring – at least in principle – the *status quo ante*.[90]

As Paul Connerton notes, anthropologists 'seek to understand the hidden "point" that lies "behind" ritual symbolism by an act of translation in which the encoded text of the ritual is decoded into another language'.[91] They focus on the ostensible forms of the ceremonies in order to understand the hidden symbolic content of the ritual. This has naturally led them to explore the connection of rituals with other forms of articulating meaning in a structured form, particularly myths (via the Cambridge myth and ritual school), dreams (via Jungian and Freudian psychoanalysis) or literature (via critics such as Northrop Frye and Mikhail Bakhtin).[92]

Roy Rappaport puts the question in terms of the relationship between 'form and substance', which are 'inseparable in any performance of any ritual'.[93] Turner performs a clever analogy between the categories of content and form with linguistic models: 'The language of ritual depends upon "syntactical" rules [content] and possesses a "lexicon" of both verbal and nonverbal terms [form] which may be varyingly arrayed to

---

[88] Apter, 'The Embodiment of Paradox', 217.
[89] Giorgo Agamben, *Homo Sacer: Sovereign and Bare Life* (Stanford, CA: Stanford University Press, 1998), 12.
[90] Apter, 'The Embodiment of Paradox', 224.
[91] Connerton, *How Societies Remember*, 53.
[92] Robert Ackerman, *The Myth and Ritual School: J. G. Frazer and the Cambridge Ritualists* (London: Routledge, 2002); Steven F. Walker, *Jung and the Jungians on Myth* (London: Routledge, 2004); Bell, *Ritual: Perspectives and Dimensions*, 12–16 ('Psychoanalytic Approaches to Ritual').
[93] Rappaport, *Ritual and Religion*, 30.

communicate messages, in the form of ritual processes.'[94] As Catherine Bell argues, 'a ritual that evokes no connection with any tradition is apt to be found anomalous, inauthentic, or unsatisfying by most people.'[95] Self-coronations, both medieval and early modern, break in some sense with that circularity, very typical of the rituals, between the formalism of its language and its mnemonic dimension. The participants in the ritual have deeply interiorised its verbal formulas, so that any change leads to confusion, as in cases such as Frederick II and Peter the Ceremonious' self-coronations. Nevertheless, medieval self-coronations could still create fixation in ceremonial (kings commissioned liturgical ordos), while some early modern rituals were more consciously 'repudiated', as Burke states.[96]

Ricoeur's notion of a 'surplus of meaning' illuminates the relationship between the formalism of ritual language and its mnemonic dimension. Ricoeur has argued that the appropriation of Greek myths depends upon the variable part of the myths, which may be perceived through comparing the diverse dramatic forms in which one myth has been dramatised.[97] Yet this residual meaning, admittedly, is much more difficult to obtain in rituals, whose structure has significantly less potential for variance and change than that of myths. The inertia or 'potential for invariance' of the rituals is probably bigger than that of any other cultural manifestation or representation, because they have a powerful mnemonic device and performative language.[98] The participants thus become naturally convinced that the efficacy of the ritual depends in each case upon the exactitude of the utterance itself, that is the repetition of the gestures and words as following the tradition grasped by the books or ceremonies or the reproduction of a given collective experience.[99] Yet, beyond their apparent

---

[94] Turner, 'Ritual, Tribal and Catholic', 510.
[95] Bell, *Ritual: Perspectives and Dimensions*, 145.
[96] Peter Burke uses the expression 'repudiation of the ritual' in the conclusion of his *The Historical Anthropology of Early Modern Italy* (Cambridge: Cambridge University Press, 1987), 223–38. For a European general vision see Roger Chartier, *The Cultural Origins of the French Revolution* (Durham, NC: Duke University Press, 1991); Edward Muir, *Ritual in Early Modern Europe* (Cambridge: Cambridge University Press, 1997), and Alain Boureau, ed., *Le simple corps du roi. L'impossible sacralité des souverains français – XVe–XVIIIe siècle* (Paris: Les éditions de Paris, 2000).
[97] Paul Ricoeur, *Interpreting Theory: Discourse and the Surplus of Meaning* (Fort Worth: Texas Christian University Press, 1976).
[98] Marc Bloch, 'Symbols, Song, Dance and Features of Articulation', *Archives Européennes de Sociologie* 15 (1974): 55–81; R. A. Rappaport, 'The Obvious Aspects of Ritual', *Cambridge Anthropology* 2 (1974): 3–68.
[99] These performative and transformative dimensions are emphasised in Austin, *How to Do Things with Words*, and, more specifically for rituals, in Ruth H. Finnegan, 'How to Do Things with Words: Performative Utterances among the Limba of Sierra Leone', *Man* 4 (1969): 537–51; Jean Ladrière, 'The Performativity of Liturgical Language', *Concilium* 2

unorthodoxy, the paradox of the self-coronations lies in that they convey to the participants a message in which tradition and innovation are compatible.

The concepts related to the ritual of self-coronation introduced in this chapter – namely, its contextual, symbolic, dramatic, *oretic*, *alethurgical* and performative dimensions – allow us to start analysing the historical forms and interpreting the anthropological meanings of this specific ceremony practised by some kings in medieval Europe.

(1973): 50–62; Stanley J. Tambiah, 'A Performative Approach to Ritual', *Proceedings of the British Academy* 65 (1979): 113–69; Stanley J. Tambiah, 'The Magical Power of Words', *Man* 3 (1968): 175–208.

Part I

Heritage

2 Consecration without Mediation in Antiquity

This chapter examines diverse forms of 'self-coronation' or 'celestial coronation' of sovereigns without priestly intervention in the pre-Christian ancient world, based on evidence indicating the existence of this ritual form of consecration from approximately the tenth century BC in Israel, Egypt, Mesopotamia and Persia, to the Constantinian era of the early fourth century. It explores the meaning of these forms of self-coronation as a means of reinforcing royal authority, arrogating a direct relationship with divinity, free from priestly mediation. Unlike in the post-Constantine age, these coronations do not have any particular transgressive meaning. Based on the duality between symbolic and enacted self-coronations, I distinguish whether we are dealing with a merely iconographic phenomenon or if those images also represent an enacted ritual. This distinction is only verifiable when sources of the iconographic type (coins, stone reliefs, murals and miniatures) have some correspondence with textual evidence (literary or historiographical), something that occurs exceptionally.

The First Traces of Self-Coronations: Israel, Mesopotamia and Egypt

The first indications of royal coronations are found in the pre-Israelite territories of the Canaanites and Ammonites. Some insignias from this period reproduce elements connected to coronations, such as sceptres, crowns, sun discs and breastplates, and even provide evidence for the practice of self-coronation in Amarna.[1] In the coronation ceremonies of pre-Israelite Phoenicia, Ras Shamra and Palestine, and particularly in pre-Israelite Jerusalem, the crown had a special importance, as we know

---

[1] As we read in one of the letters preserved in Amarna: 'He is Lord and he has placed himself as god upon the throne of his father.' Samuel A. B. Mercer, ed., *The Tell el-Amarna Tablets*. 2 vols. (Toronto: Macmillan Company of Canada, 1939), 1:178, quoted in Ivan Engnell, *Studies in Divine Kingship in the Ancient Near East* (Oxford: Basil Blackwell, 1967), 79.

from the account of King David putting on the Ammonite crown.[2] The relevance of the crown as a royal insignia has been confirmed by records from Tell Halaf, one of which refers to the divinity of the prince's crown: 'The crown-prince is my god', reads a male dignitary.[3]

The monarchy in Israel, born in large part because of the pressure of Philistine and Ammonite invasions and directly influenced by the Canaanites, never had a position comparable to that of the sacred monarchies of its neighbouring civilisations with regard to the divine nature of royalty.[4] Precisely because of the influence of neighbouring civilisations, Israel had knowledge of the investiture ceremony towards the tenth century BC, at the time of the establishment of the monarchy. However, what may be specific to the Israelite monarchy is that in its investiture ceremony a distinction was established from very early on between the spiritual sphere (unction) and the temporal sphere (coronation) of the ceremony, both realised separately and successively.

The accounts of King David's various unctions are well known, and constitute the sacred part of the investiture ceremony of the king of Israel.[5] Although considered by many to be unreliable from a historical point of view, these accounts accurately reflect the Israelite concept of royal unction by God.[6] Although the kings of Israel were anointed, and this gave them a sacred dimension, they were never considered 'divine incarnations' like the pharaohs or 'sons of God' like some of the Mesopotamian kings. David certainly acquired an almost priestly nature and role, but even so, worship was always officiated by the hierarchies and genealogies of priests that were being developed independently of the

---

[2] The Canaanite enthronement ritual has been analysed and described in Geo Widengren, 'Psalm 110 och det sakrala kungdömet i Israel', *Uppsala universitets arsskrift* 7 (1941): 1–15: the ascension of the throne, the handing over of the sceptre, the bringing of the gifts, the epiphany of the king-god (after his investment with the holy insignia), the promise sworn by the father-god.

[3] G. Rudolf Meyer, 'Die Personennamen, Ortsnamen, Götternamen und Beamtentitel in den Keilschrifttexten vom Tell Halaf', *Archiv für Orientforschung* 6 (1940): 79–84, here 80.

[4] On these influences from other civilisations of the Near East on Israel, see Sigmund Mowinckel, 'General Oriental and Specific Israelite Elements in the Israelite Conception of the Sacral Kingdom', in *The Sacral Kingship* (Leiden: Brill, 1959), 283–93, and Jean de Fraine, *L'aspect religieux de la royauté israélite* (Roma: Pontificio Istituto Biblico, 1954), 7–54.

[5] The different unctions of King David are narrated in 1 Samuel 16:13 (David among his brothers), 2 Samuel 2:4 (as a king of Judah in Hebron) and 2 Samuel 5:3 (as a king of Israel in Hebron).

[6] Aubrey R. Johnson, 'Hebrew Conceptions of Kingship', in *Myth, Ritual, and Kingship: Essays on the Theory and Practice of Kingship in the Ancient Near East and in Israel*, ed. S. H. Hooke (Oxford: Clarendon, 1958), 204–35, here 208. See also, for a more monographic view, Aubrey R. Johnson, *Sacral Kingship in Ancient Israel* (Cardiff: University of Wales Press, 1955), and Martin Buber, *Kingship of God* (Atlantic Highlands, NJ: Humanities Press, 1990).

royal lineages.[7] Indeed, along with the traditional figure of Moses, the prestige of the priestly figure of Melchizedek was also emerging, even making it into the books of the New Testament, especially Hebrews. The centrality of unction within the actual ceremony of enthronement aptly expresses the importance of the priestly figure as an intermediary – the priestly figures of Melchizedek, Samuel and Zadok (who anointed Solomon).[8] Further, royal investitures in Israel do not appear to have had the sumptuousness of those of the Egyptian, Mesopotamian and Persian sovereigns. All this implies that self-coronations were not practised, among other reasons because of the strong presence of the priestly lines, who always acted as mediators between heaven and earth, especially in ceremonies and rites.

This political theology of unction and royal coronation in Israel runs parallel to what developed in ancient Egypt, although here the sacralisation of royalty operated through a theology that legitimised the divine origin of the pharaoh.[9] This divine nature would materialise in the coronation ceremony in which the divine will manifested itself through a mystic ritual whose ceremonial forms varied over time but which kept the pharaoh himself as the main minister.[10]

Albeit in a rather dispersed fashion, it has been possible to learn some parts of these investiture and coronation ceremonies in Egypt.[11] The king

---

[7] Edwin O. James, 'The Sacred Kingship and the Priesthood', in *The Sacral Kingship* (Leiden: Brill, 1959), 63–70, here 67.

[8] Martin Noth, *The History of Israel* (London: Adam and Charles Black, 1965), 165–224.

[9] Henri Frankfort, *Kingship and the Gods* (Chicago: University of Chicago Press, 1955), 143–214; David O'Connor and David P. Silverman, eds., *Ancient Egyptian Kingship* (Leiden: Brill, 1994); Paul J. Frandsen, 'Aspects of Kingship in Ancient Egypt', in *Religion and Power: Divine Kingship in the Ancient World and Beyond*, ed. Nicole Brisch (Chicago: Oriental Institute Seminars, 2012), 47–73; Joachim F. Quack, 'How Unapproachable Is a Pharaoh?', in *Concepts of Kingship in Antiquity*, ed. Giovanni B. Lanfranchi and Robert Rollinger (Padova: S.A.R.G.O.N., 2010), 1–14.

[10] James H. Breasted, *Development of Religion and Thought in Ancient Egypt* (London: Hodder & Stoughton, 1912); Alexandre Moret, *Rois et dieux d'Egypte* (Paris: A. Colin, 1911), 19ff.; A. M. Blackman, 'Myth and Ritual in Ancient Egypt', in *Myth, Ritual, and Kingship: Essays on the Theory and Practice of Kingship in the Ancient Near East and in Israel*, ed. S. H. Hooke (Oxford: Clarendon, 1958), 15–39, here 32ff.; Engnell, *Studies in Divine Kingship*, 4–5; G. A. Wainwright, *The Sky-Religion in Egypt* (Cambridge: Cambridge University Press, 1938), 86.

[11] On the ceremonial coronation of the pharaohs, see Herbert Walter Fairman, 'The Kingship Rituals of Egypt', in *Myth, Ritual, and Kingship: Essays on the Theory and Practice of Kingship in the Ancient Near East and in Israel*, ed. S. H. Hooke (Oxford: Clarendon, 1958), 74–104 (here 78–84); Alexandre Moret, *The Nile and Egyptian Civilization* (London: Routledge, 1996), 123–6; Alexandre Moret, *Du caractère religieux de la royauté pharaonique* (Paris: E. Leroux, 1902), 75–113; 212ff.; Frankfort, *Kingship and the Gods*, 105–9 and 126–30; Johnson, *Sacral Kingship in Ancient Israel*, 80–9; Alan H. Gardiner, 'The Coronation of King Haremhab', *Journal of Egyptian Archaeology*, 39 (1953): 13–31; and Eva L. Meyerowitz, *The Divine Kingship in Ghana and Ancient Egypt*

was considered to be Horus, the legitimate heir of Osiris, thus being actually identified as a divinity and separated from his people by an insurmountable distance. On the sovereign's entry to power, accession and coronation were distinguished. The accession was automatically confirmed at dawn of the day following the death of the old king. The coronation, by contrast, was held some time afterwards, so as to give time for the preparations but also to find a suitable date. We do not know whether at the moment of accession the king carried or appeared already invested with the standard insignia, above all the crown. In any case, the king received them in the coronation ceremony, in which the temporary disruption of the Two Earths was resolved and the divine transfiguration of the new king was assured.

The most important sources for the coronation ritual of the pharaohs are the inscriptions at Deir el Bahri on the story and enthronement of Queen Hatshepsut, and the accompanying scenes on the temple reliefs.[12] But perhaps the most explicit in terms of the development of the ceremonies of purification and coronation are the inscriptions on the statue of Pharaoh Haremhab, the founder of the nineteenth dynasty at Turin.[13] This source gives an idea of the procedure and represents what the ancient Egyptians regarded as the most significant features of the coronation.

The king was first purified by the gods in a ceremony called the baptism of the pharaoh. He was then taken to the Dual Shrines, or the *Per-wer* and *Per-neser*. The *imy-khant* priest adorned and ornamented the future king. The *imy-khant* represented the royal ancestors, but it seems that he did not perform the proper ceremony of coronation. The inscription tells us, in line 17, that Haremhab was then taken by the major ancient Egyptian deity, Amun, to the palace, where he placed the Blue Crown – which marked the king as the son of Re – on the king's head.[14] This crown seems to coexist at this time with the Red Crown of Lower Egypt and the White Crown of Upper Egypt.[15] Once he was crowned by the goddess, the pharaoh was then acclaimed and publicly honoured.[16]

(London: Faber and Faber, 1960), 117, 204, 210, 222–7. For the Ptolemaic inaugurations see D. J. Thompson, *Memphis under the Ptolemies* (Princeton, NJ: Princeton University Press, 1988), 146–54. For the iconographic development and symbolic meaning of the crow at the same period see Maria Nilsson, *The Crown of Arsinoë II* (Oxford: Oxbow, 2012).

[12] Meyerowitz, *The Divine Kingship in Ghana and Ancient Egypt*, 224–7.

[13] Gardiner, 'The Coronation of King Haremhab'.

[14] 'Behold, Amun is come, his son in front of him, to the Palace in order to establish his crown upon his head' (Gardiner, 'The Coronation of King Haremhab', 15).

[15] On the symbology and meaning of the Egyptian crowns see G. Steindorff, 'Die blaue Königskrone', *Zeitschrift für ägyptische Sprache und Altertumskunde* 53 (1918), 59ff.

[16] See also the Ramesseum Dramatic Papyrus, which has been interpreted as a coronation drama, specifically the scenes 26–32, in Kurt Sethe, *Dramatische Texte zu altägyptische*

The most relevant conclusion of these ceremonies in the context of a discussion of coronations without human mediation is that ancient Egypt experienced a radical divorce between what was represented in the temple scenes – the king being crowned by the deity – and what was eventually enacted in the actual ceremonies. In his study Alan Gardiner, using other information on the coronations, the stela of the reign of Ammenemes II, puts the question in a similar way.

> It is noticeable that in the temple-scenes the *imy-khant* [the priest] is never depicted as the officiant. The officiant there seen is a figure wearing the side-lock of youth, whose leopard-skin identifies him with the setem-priest, and whose designation *In-mutef* 'Pillar-of-His-Mother' shows him to have been a personification of [the deity] Horus, the support of the widowed Isis. What is the relation of the In-mutef to the imy-khant? I should guess that the latter – we have found one plural instance – was a purely secular designation, whereas the former was a religious one.[17]

In addition, all the textual and iconographic evidence confirms that the king functions as the high priest par excellence. Certainly, the priests In-mutef and Sem were key figures in the coronation ritual, acting as mediators. But the ritual allowed no other minister than the king, who purifies, dresses, feeds and protects the god.[18] This actually confirms the well-known fact that priesthoods were often identical with state appointments and that 'nearly every person of rank assumed besides their worldly profession one or more priesthoods.'[19] Another proof of the absolute ritual prominence of the king is that, before each ceremony in which the king was in the presence of the gods, he was purified with water and incense, which renewed him and refreshed his divine condition. This would usually happen in the sacristy (the House of the Morning, *per-duat*), where two priests, covered by masks of Horus and Thoth, would wash and purify him and give him the royal insignia of the crown and sceptre. It says much about the idea of 'self-coronation' and 'self-consecration' that, even at the point when it was necessary to attend to the king, this function was exercised by priests in masks of gods, thus emphasising the king's direct intervention in all that referred to the divine origin of his authority, without human mediation.

Mysterienspielen (Leipzig: Hinnchs, 1928), summarised in Frankfort, *Kingship and the Gods*, 123–39.
[17] Gardiner, 'The Coronation of King Haremhab', 27.
[18] Moret, *The Nile and Egyptian Civilization*, 393.
[19] Adolf Erman, *Aegypten und aegyptisches Leben* (Tübingen: Mohr, 1923), 331. See also Arthur M. Hocart, *The Life-Giving Myth and Other Essays* (London: Methuen, 1952), 216.

Over time, the pharaoh was gradually replaced by a priest in the performance of sacred functions. This conveyed a progressive 'humanisation' of the pharaoh, generated a 'privatisation' of worship, and confirmed the importance of self-coronation in the political theory of Egypt, mirroring the obsequies of the pharaoh, in which, as Samuel Mercer points out, 'the officiating priests and assistants impersonated the gods.'[20] Yet, as Francis Dvornik notes, and this is particularly relevant for this book, Egyptian sovereigns tried to avoid priestly intermediation, which was particularly clear at the moment of their coronation.

> The coronation of the [Egyptian] king was neither more nor less than the realization of the promises given to him by the gods at the time of his conception and nativity. *The gods played the main role in the ceremony.* It was they who performed the purification of the royal candidate. They acknowledged him as he was presented to them by the reigning king or by some of the gods. They assisted at the official publication and proclamation of the name of the new king, and it was they who afterwards handed to him the crowns of Upper and Lower Egypt. When all the mystic rites were completed, the king was finally kissed by the supreme god himself.[21]

Similar doctrines, although developed independently of Egypt, dominated in successive Mesopotamian civilisations. Scholars have given different interpretations to the degree of divinity of Mesopotamian kingship.[22] Yet they agree that, at least in the Assyrian-Babylonian civilisations, the divine or quasi-divine status of the king was confirmed with his enthronement and coronation, which included consultation with the gods, the summoning of the nobles, the assumption of the crown, his proclamation as king, the swearing of the oath, homage and concluding banquets. In addition, numerous scholars agree on the idea of the symbolic death of the man-king and his rebirth as a god through the

---

[20] Samuel A. B. Mercer, 'Divine Service in the Old Kingdom', *Journal of the Society of Oriental Research* 6 (1922): 41–59, here 54.

[21] Francis Dvornik, *Early Christian and Byzantine Political Philosophy*. 2 vols. (Washington, DC: Dumbarton Oaks Studies, 1966), 1:11–12 (emphasis added).

[22] On one hand, Frankfort, *Kingship and the Gods*, 215–344, and Dvornik, *Early Christian and Byzantine Political Philosophy*, 1:36–44, lessen the king's divine condition; on the other, C. J. Gadd, *Ideas of Divine Rule in the Ancient East* (London: British Academy, 1948), Engnell, *Studies in Divine Kingship*, and, more recently, Amélie Kuhrt, *The Ancient Near East, c. 3000–330 BC*. 2 vols. (London: Routledge, 1995), 1:63–70, stress their divine nature. See also Piotr Michalowski, 'The Mortal Kings of Ur: A Short Century of Divine Rule in Ancient Mesopotamia', in *Religion and Power: Divine Kingship in the Ancient World and Beyond*, ed. Nicole Brisch (Chicago: Oriental Institute Seminars, 2012), 33–45; Irene J. Winter, 'Touched by the Gods: Visual Evidence for the Divine Status of Rulers in the Ancient Near East', in *Religion and Power: Divine Kingship in the Ancient World and Beyond*, ed. Nicole Brisch (Chicago: Oriental Institute Seminars, 2012), 75–10; René Labat, *Le caractère de la royauté assyro-babylonienne* (Paris: A. Maisonneuve, 1939), 70ff.

coronation ceremony. The comparison between royal consecration-coronation and priestly consecration-coronation, for which there are abundant sources, is especially interesting.[23]

A Sumerian text describes a coronation in Erech, which took place in Eanna, in the temple of Ishtar in Inanna, the priestess of Erech, and clearly contains a self-coronation formula:

He (the ruler) entered into Eanna. // He drew near the resplendent throne dais. // He placed the bright sceptre in his hand. // He drew near the throne dais of Nin-men-na ('Lady of the Crown'). // He fastened the golden crown upon his head. // He drew near the throne dais of Nin-men-na ('Lady of the Crown'). // Nin-PA, fit for heaven and earth.[24]

The king himself acts as the priest in the ceremony; the priest who leads the procession is limited to confirming the investiture, crying out: 'Assur is king, Assur is king!'[25]

As time went on, the role of the priests gained prominence, as in Egypt, an unmistakable symptom of the progressive lessening of the divine character originally attributed to the monarchy, and the plurality of the forces surrounding the seat of power. The coronation ceremony of the Assyrian kings has been better preserved, and we can confirm this development.[26] Thus, the Assyrian kings retained the functions of chief priest, rather than of divinity, and participated actively in the worship of the gods. Consequently, they were not venerated as gods. This priestly character of the Assyrian kings was clearly expressed in the coronation ceremonial. The king, not the priests, offered the sacrifices to the gods before his coronation. But, as one of the surviving documents explains, one of the priests held up the crown and the sceptre and carried them into the king's presence. Then, he crowned the king and said:

The diadem of thy head – may Assur and Ninlil, the lords of thy diadem, put it upon thee for a hundred years. // Thy foot in Ekur (the Assur temple) and thy hands stretched towards Assur, thy god – may they be favored. // Before Assur, thy god, may thy priesthood and the priesthood of thy sons find favor. // With thy

---

[23] Ethel S. Drower, *The Canonical Prayerbook of the Mandaeans* (Leiden: Brill, 1959), 220ff., and Drower, *The Mandaeans of Iraq and Irak* (Leiden: Brill, 1962), 185ff.
[24] Frankfort, *Kingship and the Gods*, 245–6. See also Hermann Bron and Ursula Seidl, *Schutzwaffen aus Assyrien und Urartu* (Berlin: Philipp von Zabern, 1995), 22.
[25] Engnell, *Studies in Divine Kingship*, 17, and Frankfort, *Kingship and the Gods*, 246–7.
[26] Karl F. Müller, 'Das Assyrische Ritual. I: Texte zum assyrischen Königsritual', in *Mitteilungen der Vorderasiatisch-Ägyptischen Gesellschaft* 41/3 (Leipzig: J. C. Hinrichs, 1937), 8 ff., who is followed by E. O. James, *Myth and Ritual in the Ancient Near East* (London: Thames and Hudson, 1958), 55–6 and 65–96; Frankfort, *Kingship and the Gods*, 246–7; Dvornik, *Early Christian and Byzantine Political Philosophy*, 1:32–35, and Ellwood, *The Feast of Kingship*, 15–19.

straight sceptre make thy land wide. // May Assur grant thee quick satisfaction, justice, and peace.[27]

The prerequisite of priestly intermediation was expressed by the confession that the king had to make on the Day of Atonement preceding the celebration of the festival of the New Year. At that ceremony, he surrendered his royal insignia – sceptre, tiara and crown – to the high priest. The priest then deposited them before the statue of Marduk.

Only after the king had made his confession and penance, had been humiliated by being slapped by the high priest, and had promised to observe all the gods' precepts, were the insignia restored to him, accompanied by the promise of divine protection and victory over his enemies.[28]

Finally, the Hittite peoples of Syria and Palestine, influenced first by Egypt but progressively assimilated into Assyrian culture, developed a belief system that did not assign a strictly divine nature to the sovereign but held that every sovereign and his dynasty received a specific kind of divine protection. The king only became divine after his death, maintaining during his lifetime a merely priestly character, as a mediator between divinity and humanity.[29] In fact, the Hittite king was not only the military leader and supreme judge, but also the priest of the nation's cults. For that reason, he was considered the 'priest of the gods'. The offices of king and priest were thus inseparable in the Hittite kingdoms.[30] However, we have very little evidence specifically relating to the coronation ceremony.[31] It was called

---

[27] Frankfort, *Kingship and the Gods*, 247.
[28] Dvornik, *Early Christian and Byzantine Political Philosophy*, 1:41, who follows Franz M. Böhl, 'Der babylonische Fürstenspiegel', *Mitteilungen der altorientalischen Gesellschaft* 11(3) (1937): 35–49.
[29] Dominik Bonatz, 'The Divine Image of the King: Religious Representation of Political Power in the Hittite Empire', in *Representations of Political Power*, ed. Marlies Heinz and Marian H. Feldman (Winona Lake, IN: Eisenbrauns, 2007), 111–36. Other authors have stressed the divinity of the Hittite kingship: Maurice Vieyra, 'Rites de purification hittites', *Revue de l'histoire des religions* 119 (1939): 112–53, especially 152; Oliver R. Gurney, 'Hittite Kingship', in *Myth, Ritual, and Kingship: Essays on the Theory and Practice of Kingship in the Ancient Near East and in Israel*, ed. S. H. Hooke (Oxford: Clarendon, 1958), 105–21; Dvornik, *Early Christian and Byzantine Political Philosophy*, 1:48–51, but nowadays the idea of the assumption of divinity by the king at the moment of his death is shared by the scholarship: Kuhrt, *Ancient Near East*, 277.
[30] James B. Pritchard, *Ancient Near Eastern Texts* (Princeton, NJ: Princeton University Press, 1958), 394; John Garstang, *The Hittite Empire* (London: Constable, 1929), 96; Hans G. Güterbock, 'Hittite Religion', in *Forgotten Religions*, ed. Vergilius Ferm (New York: Philosophical Library, 1950), 81–109; Oliver R. Gurney, *The Hittites* (London: Penguin, 1952), 153–5.
[31] Gurney, 'Hittite Kingship', 119. See also Bedrich Hrozny, 'Inscriptions "hittites" hiéroglyphiques de Carchemish. Essai de déchiffrement', *Archiv Orientalni* 6 (1934): 207–66, here 227, and Louis Delaporte, *Les Hittites* (Paris: La Renaissance du livre, 1936), 179ff.

the Festival of Enthronement but few details of its development have survived. The most significant is the account in which a prisoner was dressed as the king and handed over to the gods in order to escape a spell, from which some details can be extracted by analogy – such as, for example, the fact that they already used unction and that it was a conventional coronation in that there was no place for self-coronation.

> They anoint the prisoner with the fine oil of kingship, and [he (the king) speaks] as follows: 'This man is the king. To him [have I given] a royal name. I have arrayed him [in the vestments] of kingship. I have crowned him with the crown. Remember ye this: that evil omen [means] short years and short days. Pursue ye this substitute.'[32]

Summarising all the evidence, Amélie Kuhrt concludes:

> The new king was anointed, as part of his role as a priest of the major cults; a gift of anointing oil and royal robes was expected as an appropriate gesture of honour to a new king on his accession. In the course of a formal ceremony, the king and queen sat upon the throne for the first time.[33]

One more piece of data evidences this tendency to the priestly condition of the Mesopotamian kings. A painting was discovered in the royal palace of Mari which represents Zimrilin, the last king of Mari and a contemporary of Hammurabi of Babylon, in which the king touches royal symbols – the circle and the sceptre – held by the goddess Ishtar, who is accompanied by other divinities. It was first thought that this scene represented the goddess presiding over the king's investiture, but specialists finally concluded that the circle and the sceptre appeared in Babylonia only during the first Babylonian dynasty, and that they were exclusive to gods as symbols of sovereignty. Consequently, these symbols could not be assumed by kings at that time. Thus, the Mari painting can represent only a scene from a liturgical ritual in which the king played a prominent role as the intermediary between his people and the divinity. Francis Dvornik concludes that 'two interpretations are possible, first that the king is touching the statue of the goddess and inviting her to take her place in the liturgical procession, second that the king is saluting the goddess in his palace and receiving from her a renewal of his office.'[34]

---

[32] Gurney, 'Hittite Kingship', 118. This document is translated by Albrecht Goetze in Pritchard, *Ancient Near Eastern Texts*, 948, 355. See also Vieyra, 'Rites de purification hittites', 112–53, and Engnell, *Studies in Divine Kingship*, 59.

[33] Kuhrt, *Ancient Near East*, 278. On the origin of the rite of anointing, strictly connected with that of the royal investiture and crowning, see Dvornik, *Early Christian and Byzantine Political Philosophy*, 1:282–3.

[34] Dvornik, *Early Christian and Byzantine Political Philosophy*, 1:66–7. See also Marie-Thérèse Barrelet, 'Une peinture de la cour 106 du Palais de Mari', in *Studia Mariana*, ed. André Parrot (Leiden: Brill, 1950), 9–35.

Self-Coronations in Ancient Persia

The ceremonial act of investiture of the sovereign with a crown in ancient Persia is known through references in classical Armenian authors, sporadic commentaries in Ferdowsi and other early Islamic authors and, above all, through iconographic casts, such as some surviving reliefs, as well as vessels and coins. The most relevant fact for my longue durée research is that Achaemenid 'king of kings' usually crowned themselves, and the Sasanian kings started crowning themselves and then were crowned by a priest.[35] Yet no account or detailed description survives of the whole ceremony, although we do possess some important clues as to how it was carried out, as well as the opportunity to compare these casts with kingly practice in contemporary Iran. In contrast to other times and places, the coronation ceremony there was crucial, and has been preserved throughout the centuries, as the king was transformed into a 'new' sacred person, endowed with magical powers and capable of dispensing justice and prosperity. With the coronation ceremony, the king received a new name, and a fire was lit in his honour that was not extinguished until his death, to be relit three days after his death by the new light of his successor.

The successive Persian kingdoms of antiquity contributed decisively to the idea of sacred monarchy.[36] The doctrine of Zoroastrianism, developed from the sixth century BC with the establishment of the new Achaemenid dynasty founded by Cyrus I through the assimilation of Babylonian civilisation, was imposed as the 'state religion'.[37] Humanity is ruled by a god, Ahura Mazda, the Wise Lord of Zoroastrian religion, and immediately below are Mithra and Anahita. The concept of *farnah* was also developed, a 'royal glory' spread by Ahura Mazda, which is the

---

[35] Some details are presented in Hans-Werner Ritter, 'Herrschaftsantritt und Krönungszeremoniell im Perserreich', in *Diadem und Königsherrschaft* (München: C. H. Beck, 1965), 18–30.

[36] Andrea Piras, 'La corona e le insegne del potere nell'impero persiano', in AA.VV., *La corona e le insigne del potere* (Rimini: Il Cerchio, 2000), 7–29; Geo Widengren, 'The Sacral Kingship of Iran', in *The Sacral Kingship* (Leiden: Brill, 1959), 242–57. On the Babylonian period, previous to the Achaemenid, we do not have sources on imperial coronation, but analogies may be made with the Babylonian New Year Festival for the presence of royal insignia: see Amélie Kuhrt, 'Usurpation, Conquest and Ceremonial: From Babylon to Persia', in *Rituals of Royalty*, ed. David Cannadine and Simon Price (Cambridge: Cambridge University Press, 1992), 20–55.

[37] On Zoroastrianism see Mary Boyce, *Zoroastrians: Their Religious Beliefs and Practices* (London: Routledge, 2001); more specific for this period see Boyce, *A History of Zoroastrianism. Volume Two. Under the Achaemenians* (Leiden: Brill, 1982); Alessandro Bausani, *Persia religiosa, da Zaratustra a Babâ'u'llâb* (Cosenza: Lionelio Giordano, 1999); and Josef Wiesehöfer, *Ancient Persia from 550 BC to 650 AC* (London: Tauris, 2010), 199–216.

fount of conquest, health, wisdom, happiness and fortune for the sovereign. These ideas are most evident in the rituals of imperial investiture.[38] The most important evidence of these ceremonies is iconographic, in the tradition of cave reliefs. We cannot therefore be sure that these images are an exact reflection of the content of the ritual investiture ceremony, but they certainly constitute valuable testimony. The most essential part of the ceremony consisted of the offering of a ring-shaped object, conferring divinity on the sovereign, as can be seen in the celebrated bas-relief of King Darius I (522–486 BC) in Bisotun.[39]

Although the award of a ring or diadem is not so obvious in Darius I's representations (Figure 5) as in the relief showing Ardashir I at Naqsh-e Rostam (Figure 7), the figure of the 'investment ring' is essential, as this iconography would persist for centuries, passing intact into the rich stone-relief iconography of the Sassanid dynasty.[40] The two chief hypotheses on the symbolism of the ring are, first, that it might represent the concept of *farnah* (the favour of God that gave the king an aura of royal glory and showed he had the right to rule) and, second, that it could symbolise the passing of power from the divinity to the sovereign.[41] For the purposes of our inquiry, the most significant element is that the transmission of sovereignty

---

[38] A. Shapur Shahbazi, 'Coronation', in *Encyclopedia Iranica* (Costa Mesa, CA: Mazda, 2002 (1993), VI.1:277–9; Maria Brosius, 'Investiture. I. Archaemenid Period', *Encyclopedia Iranica* XIII:180–2; Vesta Sarkhosh Curtis, 'Investiture. II. The Parthian Period', *Encyclopedia Iranica* XIII:182–4; Jenny Rose, 'Investiture. III. Sasanian Period', *Encyclopedia Iranica* XIII:184–8. For the Archaemenid period see, Pierre Briant, 'La roi est mort: vive le roi! Remarques sur les rites et rituels de succession chez les Achéménides', in *La religion iranienne à l'èpoque achéménide*, ed. Jean Kellens (Gent: Irana antiqua, 1991), 1–11.

[39] Louis Vanden Berghe, *Reliefs Rupestres de l'Iran ancien* (Bruxelles: Les Musées, 1983), 10–11 and 115–16; Margaret C. Root, *The King and Kingship in Achaemenid Art* (Leiden: Brill, 1979), 58–61.

[40] A. Shapur Shahbazi, 'An Achaemenid Symbol I', *Archaeologische Mitteilungen aus Iran* 7 (1974): 137–8. Mary Boyce is more cautious about the function of this eventual investment ring, and she uses the expression 'winged circle' to convey the idea of the multiple symbolic functions of this sign. In some representations a divine figure emerges from this winged circle, usually showing pre-eminence over Darius, who appears below (see particularly Boyce's comments on the Bisotun [Behistun] relief, in *A History of Zoroastrianism*, 2:94–6 and 100–1). Yet in other representations in a number of carvings at Persepolis the simple winged disc appears without a figure, which is precisely what in the future will be considered the 'investment ring' (Boyce, *A History of Zoroastrianism*, 2:102–5). Boyce concludes: 'The figure in the winged circle thus appears as superhuman, raised as it always is above the human plane, hovering protectively with the ring of divinity in his hand; and the winged disc also appears on high, and is shown repeatedly as an object of veneration' (Boyce, *A History of Zoroastrianism*, 2:103). For the continuity of the iconography of the Achaemeninan winged circle in future periods of Persian empires see Mary Boyce and Frantz Grenet, *A History of Zoroastrianism*. 3 vols. (Leiden: Brill, 1991), 3:102–3.

[41] On these hypotheses, see for the first Louis Vanden Berghe, 'Les scènes d'investiture sur les reliefs ruperstres de l'Iran ancien', in *Orientala Iosephi Tucci Memoriae Dicata*, ed.

Figure 5 Relief depicting King Darius facing a group of men, roped together, representing rebels defeated by the king. The figure at the top is the god Ahuramazda in a winged disc. The relief is carved into a rock face at Behistun, Bisotun, Iran. © www.BibleLandPictures.com / Alamy Stock Photo.

from heaven to earth happened directly from the divinity to the sovereign, without priestly intervention. The concession of sovereignty to King Darius by Ahura Mazda is also confirmed by inscriptions found in Persian, Elamite and (late Akkadian) Babylonian sources.[42] Darius declares in one of these cuneiform inscriptions his direct appointment by the divinity.

A great God is Ahuramazda, who created this earth, who created yonder sky, who created man, who created happiness for man, who made Darius king, one king over many, one lord over many.... Ahuramazda... saw this earth in commotion, thereafter he bestowed it upon me, he made me king. I am king. By the grace of Ahuramazda I set it in its place.[43]

Beyond these representations, how did the investiture ceremony of the Achaemenid kings really unfold? The maintenance of certain iconographic

---

Gherardo Gnoli and Giuseppe Tucci. 2 vols. (Roma: Istituto italiano per il Medio ed Estremo Oriente, 1988), 3:1511–31, and Boyce, *A History of Zoroastrianism*, 2:103; for the second see Gherardo Gnoli, 'Politica religiosa e concezione della regalità sotto gli Achemenidi', in *Gururajamañjarika. Studi in onore di Giuseppe Tucci*, ed. Giuseppe Tucci. 2 vols. (Napoli: Istituto universitario orientale, 1974), 1:23–88.

[42] Pierre Lecoq, *Les inscriptions de la Perse achéménide* (Paris: Gallimard, 1997), 187–217.

[43] Boyce, *Zoroastrians*, 55.

models over time implies a degree of reliability in the reliefs as a picture of the way the investiture ceremonies developed. The investiture of Cyrus I (652–600 BC?) as king of Babylon most likely followed traditional Babylonian practices, though influenced by the coronation custom of the Assyrian kings and by that of the neighbouring Elamite and Median kings.[44] The rite followed by subsequent kings would show some variations, as we can compare through Greek and Byzantine literary testimonies which have allowed scholars to launch hypotheses on how the ceremony developed, especially that of the first two Achaemenid sovereigns, Cyrus II (559–529 BC) and Cambyses II (529–522 BC), held in Babylon. The ritual of coronation was the ceremonial projection of the idea that the Persian kings were chosen by 'the great god', as an inscription in Behistun shows, and it was applied with success by Cyrus in Babylon in the name of Marduk.[45] After completing the forty days of mourning inaugurated by the death of his predecessor, the new sovereign could be crowned. During the ceremony, he received official insignia: the vestments, a special shoe, the sceptre and the seal.

We have data from Cambyses II's investiture. Leo Oppenheim has interpreted the difficult passage – an inscription with broken lines and words – of the *Nabonidus Chronicle* in which Cambyses' investiture is described. That passage says that Cambyses 'went to the temple' and the priest of Nabu gave him the sceptre as soon as he reached the temple. In the second part of the ritual,

the new king, provided with the royal symbol, was to lead the god who had just bestowed legitimacy upon him in a procession – and eventually to the temple of Bel. Whatever the physical performance of this act implied ... it represents a unique privilege for the Babylonian king to come into some form of direct contact with the image of the god, be this Marduk on the occasion of the annual New Year's festival, or Nabu on the occasion of the ceremony under discussion.[46]

These ceremonies are related to the connections of the Achaemenid dynasty with Babylonian and Egyptian coronation rites. When Cambyses entered Egypt, his condition as conqueror would supposedly be enough to establish his authority there as ruler. But, as K. M. T. Atkinson argues:

---

[44] Heleen Sancisi-Weerdenburg, 'The Zendan and the Ka'bah', in *Kunst, Kultur und Geschichte der Achämenidenzeit und ihr Fortleben*, ed. Heidemarie Koch and D. N. Mackenzie (Berlin: AMI suppl. 10, 1983), 145–51, here 150, and Amélie Kuhrt, 'Babylonia from Cyrus to Xerxes', in *Cambridge Ancient History*, ed. John Boardman, N. G. L. Hammond and D. M. Lewis. 14 vols. (Cambridge: Cambridge University Press, 1988), 4:112–38.

[45] K. M. T. Atkinson, 'The Legitimacy of Cambyses and Darius As Kings of Egypt', *Journal of American Oriental Society* 76 (1956): 166–77, here 167.

[46] Leo Oppenheim, 'The Babylonian Evidence of Achaemenid Rule in Mesopotamia', in *The Cambridge History of Iran*, ed. Ilya Gershevitch. 7 vols. (Cambridge: Cambridge University Press, 1985), 2:529–87, here 556.

There are clear indications that Cambyses did not himself think this to be enough. He was anxious to vindicate his claim in the eyes of native Egyptians also, as the only hope of gaining willing acceptance in place of resentful acquiescence. ... From the record of a contemporary Egyptian official inscribed in the next reign we have evidence that he formally adopted the title 'Descendant of Re' (Masuh-ra), and conformed to the practice of all pious earlier kings in the offering of libations and performing of sacrifices in person in the temple of Neit at Sais. The prostration of Cambyses before the goddess in her temple on this occasion has been interpreted as part of a formal ceremony of coronation according to the Egyptian tradition.[47]

Atkinson concludes that this ceremony was an important part of Cambyses' policy of making himself legitimate in Egypt beyond his position as conqueror.

Self-coronation or self-investiture ceased to be practised with the accession of King Darius in 522, as apparently the king worshipped the main Achaemenid deity, Ahura Mazda, and received the royal insignia, especially the crown, from the priests.[48] The testimony of the Bisotun inscriptions and of some Greek chroniclers, particularly Herodotus and Plutarch, speak of the difficulties involved in his accession to the kingdom, considered by some to be illegitimate, which would explain the necessity to resort to the priests as mediators of his consecration. This is interesting and plausible, but no absolute evidence overall survives for Achaemenid investiture practices – and Greek sources such as Herodotus and Plutarch wrote some centuries after the events. In any case, the subject matter of the aforementioned Bisotun bas-reliefs (Figure 5), which depict a self-coronation, does not coincide with this account of coronation by priests. The possible explanation for this contradiction is that the iconography of those reliefs reflects rather an ancestral practice, the self-coronation practised by Darius' predecessors. The iconography of the reliefs would therefore be more determined by the continuity of iconographic tradition rather than the actual rite followed by the monarch himself in his coronation.

Alexander's victory over Darius III and the subsequent incorporation of the Achaemenid kingdom into the Alexandrine empire fostered contact between the Greek and Persian cultures, particularly in the oriental

---

[47] Atkinson, 'The Legitimacy of Cambyses and Darius As Kings of Egypt', 168.
[48] Plutarch says that Darius' successor went to Pasargadae to 'receive the royal initiation at the hands of the Persian priests' (Plutarch, *Artaxerxes*, 3:1–2), but modern scholars are sceptical regarding the historicity of this source, particularly in Plutarch's interpretation of the decreasing influence of the god Ahura Mazda (Brosius, 'Investiture', 181–2). It seems that Plutarch makes references to a sort of mystic ritual of initiation, previous to the ceremony of coronation (see Shahbazi, 'Coronation'). See also Boyce, *A History of Zoroastrianism*, 2:209.

Figure 6 Relief depicting Ares, the god of war, crowning the honouree after a military victory, third quarter of the fourth century BC. Acropolis Museum, Athens, Greece, piece EAM 2947. © Acropolis Museum, 2011. Photo: Socratis Mavrommatis.

concept of the divine election of the sovereign. While the Persians believed in the divine origin of power, but not in that of the monarch himself, the Macedonian kings were considered of divine origin, at least as sons of divinity.[49] We have iconographic evidence that the crown was a symbol known by the Greeks during the fifth and fourth centuries BC (Figure 6), although whether they used it for ceremonies of investment remains a mystery.

Nevertheless, at some point the crown would be replaced by the diadem, a royal emblem specific to Asia, consisting of a simple strip of white material tied around the head, with the two ends hanging down over the

---

[49] Biagio Virgilio, *Lancia, diadema e porpora. Il re e la regalità ellenistica* (Pisa: Istituti editoriali e poligrafici internazionali, 1999); Ernst Badian, 'The Deification of Alexander the Great', in *Ancient Macedonian Studies in Honor of Charles F. Edson* (Thessaloniki: Institute for Balkan Studies, 1981), 27–71.

back of the neck. During the time of Alexander the Great (336–323 BC), the diadem appears repeatedly as an iconographic motif, above all on coins, which would have broad resonance beyond the Macedonian borders.[50] The Hellenistic kings, who derived the legitimacy of their kingship from Alexander, adopted it from him.[51] In contrast, the key royal insignia of the Persians in the time of Alexander was the upright tiara.[52]

Unfortunately, we have no direct sources on the development of the coronation ceremony of the Hellenistic kings.[53] Roland Smith categorically asserts that the diadem 'was not like a crown, and there was no coronation'.[54] However, given the diadem's importance as an iconographic motif, it is difficult to maintain that there would have been no ceremony planned for its solemn imposition. To be sure, records survive of the new king being acclaimed by the army, with the subsequent formalisation of the pact by an oath, and it would not therefore be surprising for it all to be formalised in an investiture ceremony.

The best-known Hellenistic inauguration is the coronation of Antigonos Monophthalmos in 306, as described by Plutarch, which does not mention the imposition of a diadem. This could mean that Antigonos was probably already wearing a diadem when he came out of the palace to greet the crowd.[55] It is possible that some ritual took place in private, or that a ceremony was enacted in the presence of a selected audience, in which the king would crown himself. Actually, as Rudolf Strootman suggests, in the Hellenistic world, when a king was crowned by another, instead of crowning himself, this indicated that illegal kingmakers or rivals were putting a pretender on the throne.[56] This is interesting for the aims of this book, since it shows that self-coronations are not

---

[50] Hans-Werner Ritter, 'Alexander der Grosse und das Diadem', in *Diadem und Königsherrschaft* (München: C. H. Beck, 1965), 31–78; Hans-Werner Ritter, 'Die Bedeutung des Diadems', *Historia* 36 (1987): 290–301; R. R. R. Smith, *Hellenistic Royal Portraits* (Oxford: Clarendon, 1988), 34–8. On the symbolic meaning of the diadem in the Hellenistic world from the late fourth century BC to the first century AD, and the intensive historiographical debate around it, see Strootman, *Hellenistic Royal Court*, 366–72.

[51] Hans-Werner Ritter, 'Die Rolle des Diadems bei der Begründung der Hellenistischen Königreiche', in *Diadem und Königsherrschaft* (München: C. H. Beck, 1965), 79–169; E. A. Fredricksmeyer, 'The Origin of Alexander's Royal Insignia', *Transactions of the American Philological Association* 127 (1997): 97–109, here 97.

[52] Fredricksmeyer, 'The Origin of Alexander's Royal Insignia', 100.

[53] For Hellenistic's court ceremonies see the convincing portrait of Rolf Strootman, *Courts and Elites in the Hellenistic Empires* (Edinburgh: Edinburgh University Press, 2014), 251–347.

[54] Smith, *Hellenistic Royal Portraits*, 37.   [55] Strootman, *Hellenistic Royal Court*, 230.

[56] Strootman, *Hellenistic Royal Court*, 272, where he provides examples of Hellenistic kings being crowned by others. See especially the narration of Demetrios' coronation, using a diadem that had already been sent by his father Antigonos Monophthalmos (Strootman, *Hellenistic Royal Court*, 281–2).

necessarily subversive acts of sovereignty. Rather, they may be orthodox and conventional gestures, depending on the political circumstances of the moment. Yet after this private ceremony, the most public part of the ceremony would take place, in which the king would present himself to his subjects, a practice analogous to events in the paleo-Byzantine era.[57]

After the Hellenistic era, the sources on coronation ceremonies in Arsacid (Parthian) Persia, though Greek, are more precise and reliable thanks to their chronological proximity.[58] The key gesture, definitively sanctioning the ascent to power of the new sovereign, involved placing the crown on the head of the new monarch. The evidence for these investitures comes to us also via coins. One of the coins depicts the investiture of Phraates V (c.2 BC–AD 4), son of Phraates IV. The king appears together with two deities, each of them holding a diadem in his right hand. Some have identified them as a *nike* putting the crown on the king's head and a *tyche* that is also crowning him, although he might be bringing other insignia.[59] Others show his wife receiving the investiture directly from a deity. This unmediated coronation is confirmed in some first- and second-century coins in which the king appears to be crowned by a deity.[60] They are clearly scenes of coronation by a deity, although we do not know if this motif was transposed into reality in the ceremonies, where the king could put the crown on himself, symbolising that he had received it directly from a deity. However, the written sources contradict it, as Plutarch (*Crassus*, 21.7) writes that the honour of putting the crown on the king's head fell to the Surena family. Plutarch wrote some centuries after the events, but his version is confirmed by the Armenian sources, in which the Surena, one of the seven most influential lines of Arsacid Persia, reserve the privilege of crowning the king.[61]

The Sassanid dynasty (AD 226–651) recovered the splendour and prestige of the Achaemenid period. We know their coronation ceremony through some indirect testimonies: the Islamic chronicles of the tenth century such as the *Annals of Tabari* and the *Chronicle of Bal'ami* and, from

---

[57] Virgilio, *Lancia, diadema e porpora*, 69–75; Andreas Alföldi, *Caesar in 44 v. Chr. Studien zu Caesars Monarchie und ihren Wurzeln* (Bonn: R. Habelt, 1985), 105–32; Strootman, *Hellenistic Royal Court*, 276; Ginnasi, *L'incoronazione celeste nel mondo bizantino*, 9; Simon R. F. Price, *Rituals and Power: The Roman Imperial Cult in Asia Minor* (Oxford: Oxford University Press, 1984), 212–13; Glen W. Bowersock, *Hellenism in Late Antiquity* (Ann Arbor: University of Michigan Press, 1990).

[58] Curtis, 'Investiture. II'.

[59] Ginnasi, *L'incoronazione celeste nel mondo bizantino*, 13.

[60] David Sellwood, *The Coinage of Parthia* (London: Spink, 1980), figs. 58.6, 72.1, 74.2 and 79.17.

[61] Curtis, 'Investiture. II', 183; Erich Kettenhofen, 'Die Arsakiden in den armenischen Quellen', in *Das Partherreich und seine Zeugnisse* ed. Josef Wiesehöfer (Stuttgart: F. Steiner, 1988), 305–55, here 329.

the start of the eleventh century, the celebrated *Shâhnâmè* by Ferdowsi (who died in 1020), with a decidedly literary value but which can also be used to complement other sources.[62] Up to the mid-fifth century, iconographic and documentary evidence confirms that the Sassanid kings had recovered the rite of self-coronation. From the third century on, the Sassanid kings were usually shown on their thrones with a crescent moon as a second crown above the first.[63] The Sassanids believed that the *Xuarra* (a concept that is a cognate of *farr* and *kvarr*), symbolised by the royal diadem, was conferred by divinity, which implied a consecration of the monarch.[64]

Some reliefs survive of the investiture of the founder of the dynasty, Ad Ardashir I (224–40), which took place in 226.[65] The first of the scenes, kept in Fruzabad (Iran), shows Ohrmazd (the name of Ahura Mazda in the mid-Persian context) and the emperor in profile, each facing the other. The former hands the latter a diadem, with three other figures present and a small altar. This image has been reproduced often as a numismatic motif.[66] The second, preserved in a cave relief in Naqsh-e Rajab (Iran), is similar, also representing the investiture of Ardashir I by Ohrmazd through the handing over of a ring of sovereignty by the god. The third, also in a cave relief but this time in Naqsh-e Rostam (Iran), shows the monarch Ardashir I and the deity Ohrmazd in a new iconographic motif, both on horseback, with the king on the left-hand side being handed the ring of sovereignty by the god (Figure 7). This iconographic model clearly differs from the Achaemenid model and would establish itself among Ardashir's successors.

[62] Rose, 'Investiture. III'.
[63] Hans Peter L'Orange, *Studies on the Iconography of Cosmic Kingship in the Ancient World* (Oslo: Aschehoug, 1953), 37–42, fig. 17–18.
[64] 'According to this theory of government [of Khosraw I Anushirvan, 531–79], success in war showed the favour of God and gave the king an aura of royal glory (*farr* or later *kwarr*) that showed he had the right of rule' (Michel Axworthy, *Iran* [Oxford: Oxford University Press, 2017]), 21.
[65] See particularly Bruno Overlaet, 'A Man Created God? Kings, Priests and Gods on Sasanian Investiture Reliefs', *Iranica Antiqua* 48 (2013): 313–53; Roman Ghirshman, 'Les scenes d'investiture royale dans l'art rupestre des Sassanides et leur origine', *Syria* 52 (1975): 119–29; Berghe, 'Les scènes d'investiture', 1511–31; H. Von Gall, 'The Figural Capitals at Taq-e Bostan and the Question of the So-Called Investiture in Parthian and Sasanian Art', *Silk Road Art and Archaeology* 1 (1990): 99–22; Barbara Kaim, 'Investiture or Mithra: Towards a New Interpretation of So Called Investiture Scenes in Parthian and Sasanian Art', *Iranica Antiqua* 44 (2009): 403–15; Matthew P. Canepa, *The Two Eyes of the Earth: Art and Ritual of Kingship between Rome and Sasanian Iran* (Berkeley: University of California Press, 2009), 11–13; Shahbazi, 'Coronation', 277–8; Rose, 'Investiture. III', 185; Dorothy G. Shepherd, 'Sasanian Art', in *Cambridge History of Iran* (Cambridge: Cambridge University Press, 1983): III.1: 1055–1112, here 1055.
[66] Robert Göbl, *Sasanian Numismatics* (Braunschweig: Klinkhardt & Biermann, 1971), 17–24.

Figure 7 Relief depicting King Ardashir I receiving the ring of power from the divinity Ahura Mazda, third century. Relief in Naqsh-e Rostam, Iran. © Interfoto / Alamy Stock Photo.

Here there is some disagreement among scholars, with some asserting that the person handing over the diadem is a deity (Ohrmazd, Ahura Mazda) and others swearing that it is a priest.[67] Should the first view prevail, we would have one of the clearest precedents yet of the iconographical 'heavenly investiture' that would subsequently spread over the Byzantine world and of the ritual self-coronations of the modern Iranian kings themselves. Lending weight to the attempt to identify the relief figure with the divinity Ahura Mazda is the fact that it has been depicted with some iconographic motifs specific to this Persian divinity: long hair and beard, a tower-like crown and the *barsom* held aloft in his left hand.[68] King Ardashir appears with a long pointy beard, his hair crowned with

---

[67] The defenders of the first option are summarised in Ginnasi, *L'incoronazione celeste nel mondo bizantino*, 15; on the second option see Overlaet, 'And Man Created God?', 325–6. There seems to be major agreement on the first – that the god rather than the priest is represented: Wiesehöfer, *Ancient Persia*, 160. Mary Boyce argues clearly that Ohramazd himself gives Ardashir 'the diadem of sovereignty' (Boyce, *Zoroastrians*, 107).

[68] On the contrary, the presence of the *barsom* is what leads some critics, such as Overlaet, 'And Man Created God?', 321–2, to believe that he functions as a priest rather than as a divinity: see also Maneck F. Kanga, 'Barsom', in *Encyclopedia Iranica*, ed. Ehsan Yarshater (London: Routledge, 1989), 3:825–7.

a characteristic spherical hat (*korymbos*) created for purely decorative purposes.[69]

Of course, the fact that both figures (divinity and king) are shown on the same level and at the same size, mounted together on horseback, implies a declaration of the divinity of the king, or at least of his being no different in stature from the divinity. This might also be interpreted as being the king and a priest, both of the same human dimension, albeit one of high dignity. But the first hypothesis is more certain, given the fact that some key iconographic details connected with the divinity (such as the *barsom* mentioned earlier) are excluded in subsequent iconographies, precisely confirming its role in identifying one of the figures as Ahura Mazda, and given that this ceremony developed specifically towards giving greater ritual prominence to the priests.

Bruno Overlaet argues that the other figure appearing in the scene is not the divinity Ahura Mazda but a priest, exactly the person who would have officiated the investiture ceremony in reality and who would have placed the crown on the king's head. He maintains that celestial visions are never shared by the audience – as in the case of Moses' visions on Mount Sinai, where he was alone, or those of Bernadette Soubirous, who, even when surrounded by people, was the only one capable of seeing and speaking with the Virgin.[70] As other people appear in the relief, and there is thus an audience to witness the scene, this celestial vision of the king could not have occurred, and it was a priest who invested him with the crown. However, in his argumentation Overlaet identifies the iconographic motif with the reality of the officiated ritual, when this is not necessarily the case considering the massive iconographic presence of 'visions' in antiquity, and priests are shown differently in these Persian rock reliefs.

Indeed, we know from written sources (such as the *Codex Manichaicus Coloniensis*)[71] that Ardashir's son Shapur crowned himself, which would be compatible with the presence of the divinity as an iconographic motif. An identification is thus created between 'heavenly self-coronation' from an iconographic point of view and the 'self-coronation ritual' from a ceremonial point of view, which might serve as a hypothesis, though it is not demonstrable and might never be fulfilled: a ritual in which the king

---

[69] Jenny Rose, 'Sasanian Splendor: The Appurtenances of Royalty', in *Robes and Honor: The Medieval World of Investiture*, ed. Stewart Gordon (New York: Palgrave, 2001), 35–56 (38 for *Korymbos*); see also on the Sassanid crown K. Erdmann, 'Die Entwicklung der sasanidischen Krone', *Ars Islamica* 15/16 (1951): 83–123.

[70] Overlaet, 'And Man Created God', 325.

[71] W. Sundermann, 'Shapur's Coronation: The Evidence of the Cologne Mani Codex Reconsidered and Compared with Other Texts', *Bulletin of the Asia Institute*, N.S. 4 (1990): 295–8, here 295.

has practised self-coronation corresponding to a scene with a divine presence.[72]

The image of the investiture of Shapur I (240–72), Ardashir's son and successor, has also been preserved in the form of several cave reliefs. Perhaps the most representative of them all is an equestrian depiction of the king receiving the diadem from the divinity, in a cave relief preserved at Naqsh-e Rostam, in the style of the equestrian representation of his father – Ardashir – and Ohrmazd referred to earlier.[73] Shapur I had been crowned by his father, but when he ascended to the throne he crowned himself – he is referred to as 'placing the great diadem on himself'.[74]

There are also signs of coronations in which the Sassanid kings were crowned by members of the Surena family and later by the active ritual function of the *mobad*. These signs come from sources clearly constructed from the point of view of the clergy, and even in this way, they leave open the question of *who* performed the coronation.

That night they will set the crown and throne in the audience-room and the groups of noblemen will take up their positions in their own places. The *mobad* (head of the Zoroastrian clergy) with *herbads* (other religious 'officials') and nobles, the illustrious and the pillars of the realms, will go to the assembly of the princes. They will say: 'We have carried our perplexity before God Almighty and He has deigned to show us the right way and to instruct us in what is best.' The *mobad* will cry aloud saying: 'The angels have approved the kingship of such-a-one, son of such-a-one. Acknowledge him also, ye creatures of God and good things be yours!' They will take up and seat him on the throne and place the crown on his head.[75]

Nevertheless, Sassanid Persia has bequeathed other iconographic examples of self-coronation, such as the relief scene of Shapur II's

---

[72] Ten out of twenty-eight Sasanian rick reliefs have been commonly interpreted as showing a royal investiture, and I follow this argument (Eric De Waele, 'L'investiture et le triomphe dans la thématique de la sculpture rupestre sassanide', in *Archaeologia iranica et orientalis: miscellanea in honorem Louis vanden Berghe*, ed. Léon de Meyer et al. (Gent: Peeters Presse, 1989), 811–23; and J. K. Chosky, 'Sacral Kingship in Sasanian Iran', *Bulletin of Asia Institute* 2 (1988): 35–52. But Kaim, 'Investiture or Mithra', 403–15, argues that the presence of the ring does not necessarily imply the performance of an investiture, since the ring may be interpreted as a *mithra* rather than a crown, the symbolic expression of a contract or covenant, warranted by the divinity. He concludes: 'It appears reasonable to assume that not the moment of enthronement itself, which seems to be less important for dynastic monarchies with strictly defined rules of succession, but the covenant (*mithra*) rather constituted a topic readily dealt with by and illustrated in art of ancient Iran' (411).
[73] Berghe, *Reliefs Rupestres*, 70–1, and Overlaet, 'And Man Created God?', 341.
[74] Following Bal'ami's testimony, quoted in Shahbazi, 'Coronation', 277. See also Sundermann, 'Shapur's Coronation', 295.
[75] Wiesehöfer, *Ancient Persia*, 170. See also Mary Boyce, *The Letter of Tansar* (Rome: Istituto italiano per il medio ed estremo oriente, 1968), 62.

(309–79) investiture at Taq-e Bostan (Iran).[76] Here for the first time two deities appear, each of them to the side of the central figure of the sovereign, who is about to receive the diadem from Ohrmazd to his left. The figure to his left is another deity, Mihr, easily recognisable by his great radial crown.[77] The scene explicitly expresses the belief that power had a divine origin.

Until the early fifth century, sovereigns continued the ancient Sassanid tradition of self-coronation. However, the sources through which these rituals have come to us also have some inconsistencies. Bal'ami's account, for example, relates that Shapur I was crowned by Ardashir, but the three accounts agree that there was no priestly figure presiding or, at least, attending to the king at the moment of coronation. The same may be said of the coronations of Ardashir I, Bahrâm II, Narseh and Yazdegerd I. The investiture of Bahrâm V (421–38) definitively formalises the coronation ceremony with priestly mediation, the *mowbedân mowbed*, the highest priestly authority, presiding from this point on, thus finally sacralising the ceremony, but without abandoning the custom of self-coronation by the king.

Around 491, significantly, the custom of involving the patriarch of Constantinople as the officiating minister of the coronation began. Without denying this relevant conjunction an influence on either of the rituals in Byzantium and Persia, the results of the particular development of each one seem to respond to their own particular context.[78] To be sure, the coronation of 491 is in very specific circumstances, because the heir to the Persian throne happened to be in Constantinople, at the Byzantine court.

However, the chronicler Ferdowsi himself points out that some Persian successors crowned themselves with their own hands: Hormozd III, Qobâd I, Khosrow I, Qobâd II, Sahrabarâz and Yazdegerd III. Finally, Tabari relates in his chronicle that Bahrâm V himself put the crown on his own head.[79] It is clear that the discrepancies in the sources make it difficult to state with any certainty which kings practised self-coronation and which were assisted by the priest. In any case, it is still more evident that the custom of self-coronation was known and practised by the Sassanid kings, as there would be no other explanation for the profusion of references to it

---

[76] Ginnasi, *L'incoronazione celeste nel mondo bizantino*, 22, fig. 34.
[77] Guitty Azarpay, 'The Role of Mithra in the Investiture and Triumph of Sapur II', *Iranica Antiqua* 17 (1982): 181–7. See also Guitty Azarpay, 'Crowns and Some Royal Insignia in Early Iran', *Iranica Antiqua*, 9 (1972): 108–16.
[78] Shahbazi, 'Coronation', 278; Canepa, *The Two Eyes of the Earth*, 13 and 234.
[79] Ginnasi, *L'incoronazione celeste nel mondo bizantino*, 24, who takes it from Ferdowsi, *Le livre des Rois*, ed. Jules Mohl (Paris: Imprimerie Nationale, 1876–8) (vol. V–VII on Sassanides) and Tabari, *Geschichte der Perser und Araber zur Zeit der Sasaniden*, ed. Theodor Nöldeke (Leiden: Brill, 1973).

Figure 8 Self-coronation of Shah Mohammad Reza Pahlavi, Palace of Golestan, Teheran, 26 October 1967. © Bettmann / Contributor, Getty Images.

in the sources themselves. Although these accounts were written some centuries after the events, their coinciding in certain images corresponding to the theocratic ideology of the monarchy in Persia makes them reliable as regards the ideas conveyed, although not all the historical events described.

The exuberance of the royal investiture ceremony in Sassanid Persia, as well as the particular practice of self-coronation, decisively influenced subsequent periods, reaching Islamic and even contemporary Persia, in addition to the influence that it had beyond its borders, in Byzantium and Central Asia. Indeed, the continuity of tradition implied in the self-coronation of Shah Reza Pahlavi (1925–41) in 1926 and of his son Mohammad Reza Pahlavi (1941–79) in 1967 (Figure 8) is further testimony, along with the aforementioned reliefs, of the self-investiture of Persian kings.[80] They may equally have modelled their investitures on

---

[80] For Reza Pahlavi investiture's in 1926 detailed narration see Abbas Milani, *The Shah* (New York: Palgrave Macmillan, 2011), 29–39, and Victoria Sackville-West, *Il più personale dei piaceri. Diari di viaggio. Persia 1926–1927* (Milano: Garzanti, 1992), 99–115. For his son Mohammad Reza Pahlavi see Milani, *The Shah*, 321–2, and *Programme of the Coronation of His Imperial Majesty Mohammad Reza Pahlavi Aryamehr*, s.l., 1967.

Napoleon, but the iconography of the Pahlavis does deliberately echo that of Sassanid and Achaemenid Iran.

In this chapter I have tried to find proof of the growing presence of the investiture and coronation ceremonies in the images and narrations that have been preserved, such as cave reliefs, coins, murals and historical texts. This proliferation proves that the inauguration rite of the sovereign was gaining importance throughout antiquity. The emerging awareness of the historic moment of the sovereign's ascent, and not just of his military victories or his passage, implies a greater complexity in the inauguration ceremonies, and a larger role for the insignia used, especially the crown. A natural consequence of the consolidation of this ceremony among the monarchies of ancient civilisations was the multiplication of the ritual forms in which it appeared.

Some authors have argued that iconographic coronation scenes in antiquity should be understood solely as a sort of apotheosis of the ruler rather than an illustration of a given event.[81] But it is also perfectly defensible to hold that these illustrations showcase the most representative moments in the lives of the monarchs, of which investiture would certainly be one.[82] Aligning with one or other of these opinions is relevant. The first implies that, in principle, the images of an event should be analysed independently of its supposed occurrence. The second allows the representations (in reliefs, on coins and in miniatures) to be attached to a ceremonial reality – that is, for the existence of an iconographic historicism or realism, and for the possibility of using these images as documentary sources of what really happened. These images necessarily imply, regardless of whether they had a ceremonial reality, the unequivocal message of consecration-without-mediation of the sovereign, a resistance to priestly mediation. This trait would pass on, intact, to the Christianised world.

---

[81] Shepherd, 'Sasanian Art', 1983.   [82] Berghe, 'Les scènes d'investiture', 1511–31.

3   The Hand of God

The iconographic motif of the hand of God, developed during late antiquity, connects with the idea and practice of self-coronation. It is particularly essential to this book since it evidences the transition between the pagan and Christian worlds. It extends throughout antiquity, leading to a peculiar exchange between the pagan, Jewish and Christian religions and cultures.[1] This iconography was originally spread through pagan antiquity thanks to the cult of Sabazios.[2] But it was soon expanded to the Jewish world as well. It is a very particular iconographic theme, arising from the encounter between imperial Rome and the incipient Christian religion.[3] The hand of God soon acquired rich symbolism in the context of early Christianity: it was a symbol of the agency of God, who creates and sustains life, protects and frees believers and raises and crowns the chosen.[4] In the more specific context of the 'hand that crowns', it also conveys the early Christians' analogy of the perseverance of believers as that of an athlete, with the difference that

---

[1] Jonathan Bardill, *Constantine: Divine Emperor of the Christian Golden Age* (Cambridge: Cambridge University Press, 2012), 379–80; André Grabar, *Christian Iconography: A Study of Its Origins* (Princeton, NJ: Princeton University Press, 1968), 26 and 40; Sabine G. MacCormack, *Art and Ceremony in Late Antiquity* (Berkeley: University of California Press, 1990), 123–4; Patrick Bruun, 'The Consecration Coins of Constantine the Great', *Arctos*, n.s. 3 (1954): 5–35; Orange, *Studies on the Iconography of Cosmic Kingship*, 184–7; Kantorowicz, 'Oriens Augusti', 119–49. On the ceremonial effects of the symbolic use of the hand see Sergio Bertelli and Hope Maxwell, 'Imposizioni di mani e gesti regali', in *Il Gesto nel rito e nel ceremoniale dal mondo antico ad oggi*, ed. Sergio Bertelli and Monica Centanni (Firenze: Ponte alle Grazie, 1995), 104–39. For a general view of symbolism in the context of Christian iconography see Martin Kirigin, *La mano divina nell'iconografia cristiana* (Vatican City: Pontificio Istituto di Archeologia Cristiana, 1976), especially 126–9.

[2] Orange, *Studies on the Iconography of Cosmic Kingship*, 184–7; John D. MacIsaac, 'The Hand of God: A Numismatic Study', *Tradition* 31 (1975): 322–8; André Grabar, 'Un Médaillon en or provenant de Mersine en Cilicie', *Dumbarton Oaks Papers* 16 (1951): 27–49; Richard Brilliant, *Gesture and Rank in Roman Art* (New Haven, CT: The Academy, 1963); André Grabar, 'Recherches sur les sources juives de l'art paléochrétien', *Cahiers Archéologiques* 14 (1964): 53–7.

[3] MacIsaac, 'The Hand of God'.   [4] Kirigin, *La mano divina*, 96–130.

the Christian receives an imperishable crown, a crown of life, a crown of glory from the hands of God.[5]

A Transitional Iconography between the Pagan and Christian Worlds

The first expression of the 'hand of God' in a Roman context appears in the mid-third century, in the Jewish Dura Europos synagogue representing various scenes of Moses on Mount Horeb and of Ezekiel.[6] One of them shows Abraham with a knife in his hands, preparing to sacrifice his son Isaac, who lies on the altar. The scene shows the dramatic moment when God, represented by a hand in the upper part, intervenes to prevent the sacrifice of Isaac and to provide Abraham with material for the sacrifice, a ram that appears by his side.[7] The hand of God appears, in the top-right corner, as a symbol of divine providence, under which everything is ordered and everything comes about as a result of divine power and authority.

Other Jewish representations of the hand of God are preserved in some amulets in which a hand appears among other schematic signs.[8] It is the case of the striking depiction of the sacrifice of Isaac in the Beth Alpha synagogue, in which the hand of God interrupts the sacrifice of Isaac that Abraham is about to enact, offering him a ram hanging directly from a tree, in a clear echo of the Dura mural.[9]

The first Christian manifestation of the hand of God appears around the mid-fourth century, a century after the oldest surviving Jewish one in the Dura murals. It connects this iconographic motif with the Jewish

---

[5] This image appears in several passages of Saint Paul's (1 Corinthians 9:25) and Saint Peter's (1 Peter 5:4) letters. See Christopher Walter, 'The Iconographical Sources for the Coronation of Milutin and Simonida at Gracanica', in Walter, *Prayer and Power in Byzantine and Papal Imagery* (Aldershot: Variorum, 1993), 183–200, here 187, who notes that the Christian iconography of the hand of God contrasts with the Iranian tradition of the god putting the diadem into the hands of the king, as we have seen in Chapter 2 in the funerary centre of Naqsh-e Rostam.

[6] Kirigin, *La mano divina*, 52–5; André Grabar, *L'art de la fin de l'antiquité e du moyen âge*, (Paris: Collège de France, 1968), 791–4.

[7] Erwin R. Goodenough, *Jewish Symbols from the Greco-Roman Period*. 3 vols. (New York: Pantheon, 1953), 1:227–32; vol. 3, image 602; Michael I. Rostovtzeff, A. R. Bellinger, C. Hopkins and C. B. Welles, eds., *The Excavations at Dura-Europos: Preliminary Report of Sixth Season of Work, October, 1932–March, 1933* (New Haven, CT: Yale University Press, 1936), 347, 355, Plate 49; MacIsaac, 'The Hand of God', 323–4; Grabar, *Christian Iconography*, 40.

[8] Goodenough, *Jewish Symbols from the Greco-Roman Period*, 2:224; vol. 3, images 1024, 1040, 1041. On the value of these Jewish amulets see Goodenough, *Jewish Symbols from the Greco-Roman Period*, 2:214ff.

[9] Goodenough, *Jewish Symbols from the Greco-Roman Period*, 1:246–8; vol. 3, image 638.

assimilation of the pagan cult of Jupiter Sabazios, who in some inscriptions is given the title Pantocrator in order to emphasise the supernatural power and majesty of the creator and ruler of the world.[10] Hence the iconographic motif of diverse votive hands covered in a variety of symbols becomes popular as a representation of the hand of God blessing and protecting the faithful. Indeed, explicit mentions of the hand of God even appear in the New Testament: 'Etenim manus Domini erat cum illo' ('The hand of the Lord was with Him' [Luke 1:66]); 'Et nemo potest rapere de manu Patris mei' ('No one is able to snatch them out of the Father's hand' [John 10:29]); 'Et erat manus Domini cum eis' ('The hand of the Lord was with them' [Acts 11:21]); 'Et nunc ecce manus Domini super te' ('The hand of the Lord was upon you' [Acts 13:11]). Christians adopted the notion of the 'hand of God' as a sign and symbol of divine intervention in the world through the influence of the customs absorbed in Syria because of the expansion of Judaism in those lands. In any case, its assimilation would be tardy; scholars have found no proof of this motif being deployed as a Christian symbol before the fourth century. It does not appear, for example, in the frescoes of the ancient Roman catacombs, despite the sacrifice of Isaac (well suited to the use of that motif) figuring in some of them.

Subsequent images of the hand of God in a Christian context are a *repoussé* relief on a Monza ampulla, showing the Ascension and the Pentecost. The scene seems standard, but beneath the feet of the enthroned Christ, ascending to heaven, is a hand of God (representing the Father) and a dove (representing the Holy Spirit). Below these two figures, and as though appealing to them, appear the twelve apostles, in a scene which undoubtedly depicts the Pentecost, but to which the hand of God has been added.[11]

Textual evidence for the use of the religious iconography of the hand of God comes from Saint Paulinus of Nola, who, in his epistle xxxii to Severus, describes other representations where the Trinity appears depicted in the same way: the Father as the hand of God, the Son as the lamb with the cross, the Holy Spirit as a dove. These representations seem to confirm that the hand of God motif comes from the evangelical scene of the baptism of the Lord.

Erwin R. Goodenough notes that the exchange between the Jewish and Christian motifs occurred naturally, above all in the scenes referring to passages in the Old Testament.[12] The decisive step, which would endure for many centuries, is the use of these Jewish and Christian motifs by fourth-century emperors, starting with Constantine. Constantine must have been

---

[10] Henri Leclercq, 'Main Divine', in *Dictionnaire d'archéologie chrétienne et de liturgie*, ed. Fernand Cabrol and Henri Leclercq. 15 vols. (Paris: Letouzey et Ané, 1931), 10:1206–9.
[11] Grabar, *Christian Iconography*, 114; MacIsaac, 'The Hand of God', 324.
[12] Goodenough, *Jewish Symbols from the Greco-Roman Period*, 1:248.

inspired by the Dura murals to incorporate the hand of God as an iconographic motif into the religious imagery of the empire. The emperor had a special interest in the iconography of Jerusalem and in the Jewish tradition in general for its manner of understanding Christianity through the figure of Christ. Hence the introduction of the monogram of Christ, as well as the hand of God containing evident political meaning, connected with the idea of the self-coronation. The new medallions and coins carry the motif of the emperor represented as majesty, and the hand of God from on high. This composition represents an idea that would remain largely anchored in Western and Eastern Christian iconography: that of the Christian empire as a reflection and projection of the heavenly empire, the emperor on earth receiving his power from the emperor on high, 'the Cosmocrator'.[13]

The first representation of the hand of God in Roman numismatics appears some decades later, well into the fourth century. It is on a Constantinian medallion, dated around 330, in which the emperor appears being crowned by a hand that comes from above (see Figure 9).

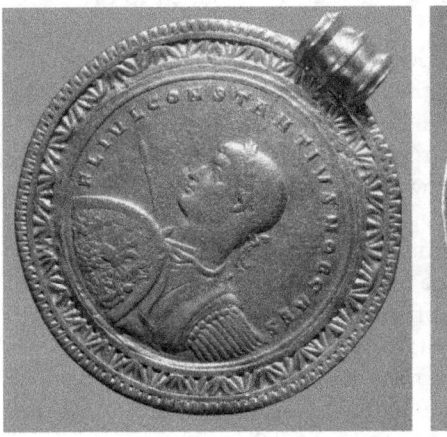

Figure 9 Constantine being crowned by the hand of God. Constantius II Medallon, revers, Kunsthistorisches Museum, Vienna, Münzcabinett, circa 330, KHM 1754/19. © Kunsthistorisches Museum, Vienna.[14]

---

[13] Grabar, *Christian Iconography*, 40–1.
[14] The inscription says, in obverse: 'FL IVL CONSTANTIVS NOB CAES Flavius Iulius Constantius Nobilissmus Caesar.' Caesar, in contrast to Augustus, means that he was (nobilissimus = most noble) co-emperor of Constantine, who at that time alone held the title Augustus. The reverse says: 'GAVDIVM ROMANORVM [to the] Joy of the Romans.' In the exergue we find MCONS, which means MONETA CONSTANTINOPOLIS or rather CONSTANTINOPOLITANA [produced in] the mint of Constantinople.

This is a multiple of thirty-six solidi-coin (half of a roman pound) which was later set into a bezel with a loop. It came to light in 1797 in the hoard of Szilágysomlyó (today Șimleu Silvanei in Romania). The reverse shows Constantine Magnus with the first known depiction of the *manus dei* (hand of God). He is flanked by his sons Constantine II, at the right being crowned by Victory, and Constantius II, at the left being crowned by Virtus. This exceptional coin is believed to have been issued for the inauguration of Constantinople as the new capital in AD 330. The obverse, however, shows Constantius II Caesar. Thus it is likely that similar pieces had been issued also in the names of Constantine I and Constantine II, which are unknown or lost today.

The representation of the emperor being crowned is not new, and it could have taken some analogies with the tradition of investing the emperor with certain insignia (*insigne regium*), especially the 'diadem' (*capiti diadema*) Tacitus mentions in his *Annales*.[15] Previous examples depict the emperor receiving the crown from a deity, for instance from Victoria, a scene that dates back to the time of Augustus, who is shown on the coins being crowned by Victoria, or Trajan, shown being crowned by Jupiter at the famous Arch of Trajan at Benevento.[16] At the same time, researchers have found multiple iconographic evidences in coins and reliefs of the emperors from the first to the fourth centuries crowned with a radial crown, a pagan symbol scholars have already analysed.[17]

However, the innovation in this iconography lies in the way the figure crowning the emperor appears in the upper part of the coin in the form of a *hand* descending from heaven and emerging from a cloud. It is obviously a representation of the Christian God, or at least of scriptural tradition, as the motif appears clearly described in certain biblical passages such as Ezekiel 1:4, Matthew 17:5 and Luke 9:34 (all of them perhaps coming from Exodus 19:16, 'God as lawgiver and master of the world order'). It conveys two of the main consequences of the conversion of Constantine: the Hellenistic and Roman concepts of *Basileus* were enriched by Jewish notions of messianic kingship and the conviction of the person of Christ as the Son of God.[18]

---

[15] The mention of the royal insignia and the diadem appears in Tacitus, *The Annals of Imperial Rome*, trans. Michael Grant (London: Penguin, 1961), 347 (Book XV, paragraph 29).

[16] J. Rufus Fears, *Princeps a Diis Electus* (Rome: American Academy, 1977), 222, plate I. 3, and 232, figure 19. The emperor is shown at the left, holding a thunderbolt and a spear and being crowned by Victoria, also standing to the left.

[17] See especially Bardill, *Constantine*, and Ginnasi, *L'incoronazione celeste nel mondo bizantino*, 28–36.

[18] Dvornik, *Early Christian and Byzantine Political Philosophy*, 1:278–402; Walter, 'The Iconographical Sources', 187–90.

Yet, more specifically, this image symbolises many of the ideas outlined in Chapters 2, 3 and 4. Constantine is represented as receiving his authority directly from God, as he is crowned by a hand emerging from a cloud. His sons, Constantine II and Constantius II, appear in subordinate positions, in terms both of location within the image (on either side) and of size (smaller than Constantine). They are also crowned by the allegorical figures of Virtus and Victoria, who belong to the traditional repertoire of imperial art. The novelty here is the hand appearing from the cloud. What is more, Constantine is crowned with a circlet, closer to the Persian and Hellenistic investiture ring than to the traditional laurel wreath. Although the image does not allow us to see with total clarity, it appears that Constantine is being crowned with that diadem, while his sons receive the traditional laurel wreath. Again, the iconography of the hand of God, as applied to the emperor, substitutes the abundant pre-Christian images in which the emperor appears being crowned by a pagan deity. As Sabine MacCormack concludes, this image represents 'a daring synthesis of Christian future and pagan past, the latter represented in the figures of Virtus and Victoria who crown the Caesars. This image presents an integrated, well-balanced and artistically beautiful image of Christian empire, an empire which, although converted, preserved traditions of the past'.[19]

Although scholars such as Andreas Alföldi maintain that the hand of God motif is pagan and it is used here for the first time as a Christian symbol without another intermediation,[20] it seems evident that Christian symbolism was based rather on Jewish traditions, with Constantine perhaps receiving it from Christianity itself. The circumstance of the representation is the founding of Constantinople, and its inscription ('Gaudium Romanorum') and proclamation of a 'new order' establish a necessary connection with the highest. Eusebius of Caesarea had this image in mind when he wrote, around this time, his *Historia Eclesiastica* 10.4.6.[21]

The Mersin Medallion is dated some years later, but also around the 330s, and the emperor is shown being honoured by a celestial hand. The subsidiary figures are personifications of the sun and moon, on either side of the emperor, in his military pomp, who receives authority directly from God, as *Cosmocrator*.[22] The next example commemorates the death of

---

[19] MacCormack, *Art and Ceremony in Late Antiquity*, 191–2; Ott, *Krone und Krönung*, tafel I.
[20] Andreas Alföldi, 'Insignien und Tracht der römischen Kaiser', *Mitteilungen des deutschen archäologischen Instituts. Römische Ableitung* 50 (1935): 55–6.
[21] MacIsaac, 'The Hand of God', 324.
[22] André Grabar, 'Un Médaillon en or provenant de Mersine en Cilicie', 36–40. On the connections between the divine and imperial dressed in military pomp see Ernst

Constantine in 337, with him ascending to heaven in a chariot towards the hand of God.[23] In the fully Christianised era a coin appears with the imperial stamp of Arcadius. J. D. MacIsaac argues that 'the fact that the Manus Dei is now found on the obverse of the coin is very important, for while deviation or artistic license on the reverse types was not uncommon, the "Imago" of the imperial person verged on the sacred.'[24]

The use of the hand of God also implies that divine authority legitimises the election of the prince, who now succeeds by heredity and not by election. Christians are thus called upon to legitimise the hereditary practice. In the early fifth century, this iconography begins to be applied to female members of the imperial house such as Honoria, Galla Placidia, Eudocia and Eudoxia. The symbol seems to vanish under Valentinian III, being replaced by the aureole ('nimbus'), a pagan symbol that turns into a Christian sign of divine favour and protection.[25]

However, the Roman hand of God was adopted in Byzantium when the usurper Basiliscus tried to establish his dynasty during the reign of Zeno. His wife, Zeonis, would copy the representations that had adorned the coins of the early fifth-century empresses. Finally, the hand of God developed a variety of iconographic forms in medieval Europe: for example, the well-known Exarchate mosaics of Ravenna show the *manus dei* over the saints of the Old Testament, while the imperial family is nimbate,[26] and an icon painting is the usual motif for the scene of the baptism of Christ in Byzantine miniatures.[27] The motif became completely Christianised, in this case well supported by the scene narrated in the Gospels, with the manifestation of the Trinity: the voice of the Father heard from heaven, the Son being baptised and the Holy Spirit appearing in the form of a dove. From the sixth century on, the voice of the Father would materialise iconographically with the hand of God, a motif the Christians adapted from contemporary Jewish art, as with Constantine's medallions.[28]

The theme of the hand of God would survive the collapse of the western Roman Empire, and we have traces of it in Frankish and Carolingian royal and imperial iconographies, especially in representations of Charles the Bald being crowned by a hand from above (see Figure 22). This motif is also relevant after the fall of the western Roman Empire because it would become

---

H. Kantorowicz, 'Gods in Uniform', *Proceedings of the American Philosophical Society* 105 (1961): 368–93, here 386–7.

[23] Grabar, *Christian Iconography*, figure 99.   [24] MacIsaac, 'The Hand of God', 326.
[25] Grabar, *Christian Iconography*, 117–18.   [26] MacIsaac, 'The Hand of God', 328.
[27] Kurt Weitzmann, *Studies in Classical and Byzantine Manuscript Illumination* (Chicago: University of Chicago Press, 1971), 272–272, figures 261, 262.
[28] Grabar, *Christian Iconography*, 115, figure 276.

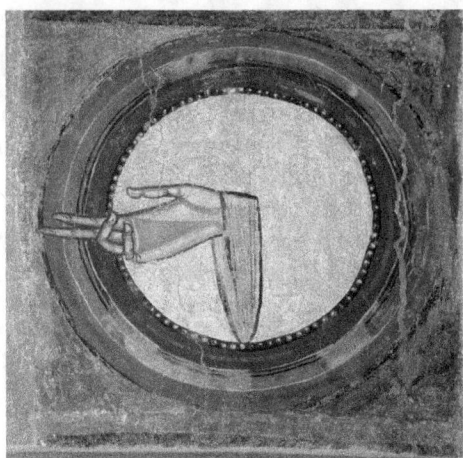

Figure 10 *Master of Tahüll*, the hand of God as an isolated motif. Fresco from the Church of Sant Climent de Taüll, Catalonia, Spain. © Museu Nacional d'Art de Catalunya (Barcelona, 2019).

a recurrent iconographic motif in Romanesque art, clearly connected with the symbolic meaning recognised by the audience (see Figure 10).

Symbolically, the hand of God would have direct genealogical consequences in recurrent images of kings and emperors being crowned directly by Jesus Christ, as in the ivory table depicting Constantine VII being crowned by Jesus Christ kept in the Pushkin State Museum (Figure 14) and the mosaic of Roger II of Sicily in the church of Maria dell' Ammiraglio (the Martorana) in Palermo (Figure 24).[29] There is a parallel between this iconographic motif and the sovereign's wish not to be subordinated to any earthly authority (including priestly), as there was a parallel between the relief depictions of the Persian sovereigns being crowned by the deity and their ritual self-coronation.

The Personalisation of the Crowning Deity in Late Antiquity

The hand of God exemplifies how iconography may function as an instrument for the Christianisation of pagan symbols. As MacCormack notes: 'When the empire became Christian, substitutes had to be found for the pagan deities who had crowned the emperor, although the more

---

[29] Ginnasi, *L'incoronazione celeste nel mondo bizantino*, figure 120; Weitzmann, *Studies in Classical and Byzantine Manuscript Illumination*, 243–4.

neutral images of the emperor being crowned by Victoria were retained.'[30] At the same time, the iconographic language used to stress the majesty of the sovereign varied, although it was, generally, based on the king's frontality compared with the other 'secondary' actors in the scenes depicted, who habitually appear in profile or looking sideways.[31] Viewed in a long-term perspective, the depictions of the deity crowning the sovereign, developed from the majestic and hieratic figures of the Persian reliefs to the delicate hand of God of late imperial coins and Jewish and Christian murals, may function as iconographic prefigurations of the magnificent figures of a humanised Jesus Christ crowning the Christian kings analysed in Chapters 4 (Byzantium) and 7 (Roger II of Sicily). There was thus a development from the hand of God to the person of God, which also had an end.

The iconography of the emperor crowned by the hand of God was not further elaborated or even continued in early Byzantium. This line of thought in art was brought to its conclusion on a set of ivories of the late ninth and early tenth centuries which show the emperor crowned by the Virgin or Christ; divinity here is no longer represented by a symbol but is present in person.[32]

It is therefore not surprising that coronation by Jesus Christ became an important motif in medieval art.[33] This particular iconography, as developed in the medieval West, stemmed from the diverse forms of self-coronation experienced during antiquity, in the pagan and Christianised worlds, analysed in Chapters 2, 3 and 4. However, it has proved more difficult for me to launch a hypothesis with regard to the *meaning* of these forms of self-coronation. Whether they had a purely iconographic existence or whether they were performed ceremonially, it is no easy task to decide if these representations or rituals were realised primarily to justify a sovereign who was insecure in his legitimacy, as would be the case with usurpers in late antiquity.[34] Neither is it clear whether the aim of self-coronation was to downplay the role of the preceding king and thus establish an imaginary break with his line, although this is certainly true with the most clear-cut cases of self-coronation that are usually found in Persia at the start of each of the dynasties – but this could also be related to a natural change in the iconographic models.

[30] MacCormack, *Art and Ceremony in Late Antiquity*, 188–9.
[31] R. Howard Bloch, 'Frontality: The Imperial Look from Christ the Pantocrator to Napoleon', *MLN* 126 (2011): 44–59.
[32] MacCormack, *Art and Ceremony in Late Antiquity*, 257.
[33] Grabar, *L'Empereur dans l'Art Byzantin*, 112–24; Hans Peter L'Orange, *Apotheosis in Ancient Portraiture* (Oslo: Ascheoug, 1947), 110–29.
[34] François Paschoud and Joachim Szidat, eds., *Usurpationen in der Spätantike* (Stuttgart: Steiner, 1997).

But self-coronation might be also considered, paradoxically, a sign of sovereign weakness in late antiquity. Indeed, we know that from the third century, the concept of the divine election of the emperor underwent consolidation precisely because of this perceived weakness.

In the latter half of the third century, no emperor lived long enough to establish a dynasty, and the concept of divine election could sanction the rule of one who had been chosen in fact only by his soldiers. The concept that Jupiter had really bestowed power, dramatically portrayed on the coins issued to the troops, could also serve to establish an aura of sanctity around the emperor. The *auctoritas* of the imperial office never stood lower than it did immediately after the capture of Valerian. Gallienus, or rather his mint officials at Cyzicus and Antioch, was forced to use the ideology of divine election in order to disassociate the new emperor from his dishonoured father, to whom the gods had denied the charismatic power of victory. Aurelian then further developed divine election into a powerful propaganda tool through which he could restore the authority of the imperial office.[35]

In fact, the theology of election was gradually displacing the theology of victory, which, with all its military implications, had been fundamental for the royal mythology and ideology of the Hellenistic monarchies. The Roman republic would also be based on the theology of triumph, founded in the right of the auspices and solidly set within the public institutions. However, the panegyric literature of the late republic was assimilating the concept of the charismatic leader of a supernatural character whom the gods had provided with divine fortune and grace merited by his virtue. Victory in battle was not so much a virtue of the sovereign himself, but a clear manifestation of the grace resulting from his divine election. So it was that political theology carried within it the seed of a later concept of the emperor as divinely elected, vicar and vice-regent of the gods.[36]

In consequence, as J. Rufus Fears argues, divine election emerged as an absolutist doctrine, as clearly demonstrated by the predominance of divine investiture, mostly through the iconography of the hand of God, in numismatic propaganda.[37] From the 'divine election' (*Princeps a Diis electus*) of the late Roman emperors to the election of the sovereign 'by the Grace of God' (*Dominus gratia Dei*) in the early Middle Ages was but a short step, resulting from the fusion of the imperial doctrine of divine election with the models found in Old Testament narratives of kingship, and then with the Christian doctrine of sovereigns as instruments chosen

---

[35] Fears, *Princeps*, 305.
[36] Fears, *Princeps*, 319. Jean Gagé, 'Théologie de la victoire impériale', *Revué Historique* 176 (1933): 1–43.
[37] Fears, *Princeps*, 306.

by God to rule in earthly matters.[38] This doctrine was to dominate the post-Constantinian world for many centuries. It did not, however, emerge from nowhere, but rather was the result of a complex evolution in which Israelite doctrines converged with those of the Egyptian, Mesopotamian and Persian civilisations, consolidated by the complex theory and practice of the Roman emperors.

Indeed, the concept of the divine election of the Roman emperors, inherited and adopted by the Christians, meant that the ceremonies of pagan imperialism were not lost, passing to the papacy and rulers of Byzantium and both the Eastern and Western kingdoms of medieval Europe. This also meant, from the ceremonial point of view, a reduction in the cosmic symbolism that was so typical of the ancient world in favour of one that combined the anthropological with the divine in a Christianised world. The iconography of the hand of God and then the representation of the figure of Jesus Christ unequivocally depicted with his body, recognised as perfect God and perfect man as required, would be two successive images of this evolution.

---

[38] See some of the forms developed as a consequence of this religious and cultural encounter in Allen Brent, *The Imperial Cult and the Development of Church Order* (Leiden: Brill, 1999); Arnaldo Momigliano, ed., *The Conflict between Paganism and Christianity in the Fourth Century* (Oxford: Clarendon, 1963); Ramsay MacMullen, *Christianity and Paganism in the Fourth to Eight Centuries* (New Haven, CT: Yale University Press, 1997); Glen W. Bowersock, 'From Emperor to Bishop: The Self-Conscious Transformation of Political Power in the Fourth Century A.D.', *Classical Philology* 81 (1986): 298–307. For a critique of the artificial distinction between the sacrality of pagan kings and Christian royal sanctity see Janet Nelson, 'Royal Saints and Early Medieval Kingship', in *Sanctity and Secularity: The Church and the World*, ed. Derek Baker (Oxford: Blackwell, 1973), 39–44.

4 Symbolic Self-Coronations in Byzantium

Coronations in Byzantium embody extraordinary ritual and ceremonial significance, a field in which many of the political ideas related to the divine origin of the power of the emperors converged. The ceremony to invest the emperor was one of the most effective ways to make this political and symbolic reality tangible, in particular through the visual power of the moment of the coronation.[1] Paradoxically, however, it was in Byzantium that the custom of having the ecclesiastical hierarchy (i.e. the patriarch of Constantinople) officiating at the coronation was introduced. At a symbolic and a visual level, this diminished the idea of the divine origin of the emperor's authority since it introduced a *mediator* between Jesus Christ and the emperor at the moment the transfer of power was solemnised. Complementary to this ceremonial reality, in the late ninth century, with the enthronement of the Macedonian dynasty, an attempt was made to mitigate the symbolic effects of the Church's intervention by means of the introduction in Byzantium of a particular iconographic motif, known by scholars as the symbolic coronation (André Grabar) or the heavenly coronation (Andrea Torno Ginnasi).[2]

This chapter takes these premises as its starting point and engages in a comparative analysis of the reality of church intervention in the ceremony of the imperial coronation and the fiction of the crowning of the emperor directly by Christ and his angels and saints, as established in the

---

[1] The historical sources for the coronation in Byzantium: Jacob Goar, *Euchologion sive Rituale Graecorum* (Graz: Verlagsanstalt, 1960); Ruth Macrides, J. A. Munitiz and Dimiter Angelov, eds., *Pseudo-Kodinos and the Constanticopolitan Court: Offices and Ceremonies* (London: Routledge, 2013). The *Book of Ceremonies* commissioned by Constantine VII was edited in Johann Jacob Reiske, ed., *Constantini Porphyrogeniti imperatoris, De cerimoniis aulae Byzantinae libri duo* (Bonn, 1829–30). English translation in Ann Moffat and Maxeme Tall, eds., *The Book of Ceremonies* (Canberra: Australian Association for Byzantine Studies, 2012).

[2] Grabar, *L'Empereur dans l'Art Byzantin*, 112–22; Ginnasi, *L'incoronazione celeste nel mondo bizantino*. See also Miguel Cortés, 'El tema de la coronación simbólica en el arte bizantino de la edad de oro', *Erytheia* 9 (1988): 133–41.

iconographic motif of heavenly coronation. These two situations refer to both a historical and a symbolic reality, and each requires specific treatment from a historiographical viewpoint. In fact, the iconographic motif of the heavenly coronation refers in turn to the concept of the self-coronation which is indebted, moreover, to the specific iconography of the *manus dei* analysed in the previous chapter.

To be sure, the continuity with the Roman Empire and the preservation of its tradition is the foundation of political theory and practice in Byzantium. This greatly influenced two aspects related to the subject of imperial coronations. First, Byzantium lacked a right of succession as such, having inherited the Augustan conception of the empire as magistracy. This makes the performance of a ceremony that privileges the assumption of imperial office by the new sovereigns particularly important, independently of their having received the title by heredity, election, acclamation, or usurpation. Second, the relationship between the church and the state involves particular and complex problems, embodied in the role of the Constantinople patriarchy in the royal investiture ceremonies. In this respect, Photius' words on the patriarchy are particularly expressive, as he defines this office as 'the living and animated image of Christ'.[3] It is therefore unsurprising that the patriarchy should have such an obvious ceremonial relevance in Byzantium.

Regarding the sources, the access we have to the investiture ceremonies mostly comes from narrative (literary or historiographical) and iconographic sources rather than institutional or legal documents. Thus, our access to the ritual of Byzantine emperors' coronations is, for the most part, built on rather precarious but nonetheless fascinating foundations.

Church Mediation in the Imperial Coronation: The Function of the Patriarch

The custom of the royal investiture officiated by the patriarch of Constantinople as ordinary officer was introduced in Byzantium in Marcian's and Leo I's coronations in the mid-fifth century.[4] This

---

[3] Photius, *Eisagogé o Introduccuión al derecho*, ed. Juan Signes and Francisco J. Andrés Santos (Madrid: Consejo Superior de Investigaciones Cientificas, 2007), 293 (title III, number 1).
[4] The function of the patriarch as the minister of imperial coronation is examined in Wilhelm Ensslin, 'Zur Frage nach der ersten Kaiserkrönung durch den Patriarchen und zur Bedeutung dieses Aktes im Wahlzeremoniell', *Byzantinische Zeitschrift* 42 (1943–9): 101–15. On the tardive introduction of the anointment see Christopher Walter, 'The Significance of Unction in Byzantine Iconography', *Byzantine and Modern Greek Studies* 2 (1976): 53–73; Gilbert Dagron, *Emperor and Priest: The Imperial Office in Byzantium* (Cambridge: Cambridge University Press, 2003), 60 and 267–76; Miguel Arranz,

variation in the rite, which emphasised the mediating role of churchmen during the ruler's reception of power, adopted different forms in Byzantium from the fifth to fifteenth centuries, depending on the political circumstances of the time, the way the emperor came to power, and the personality of the ruler being invested. Indeed, over the course of the thousand years of its existence, it has been possible to document only three exceptions to this traditional form of coronation. First, the usurper Nicephorus Bryennius crowned himself, though this exception is not particularly significant, as Nicephorus was never officially considered an emperor, as his uprising failed. Had he succeeded, however, it is likely he would have organised an 'orthodox' coronation, since military victory automatically implied political legitimacy. Second, John Cantacuzenus gave notice of his rebellion by placing the crown on his head with his own hands. However, when he officially ascended to the throne, the patriarch crowned him in the traditional manner, as he was keen to receive church acceptance. In this case, the self-coronation was clearly subversive in its significance and seen as opprobrium. However, as soon as the political situation stabilised, the emperor himself agreed to a coronation in the traditional manner, in which he received the crown from the patriarch Isidore. Thus, Cantacuzenus and Isidore became the source of each other's power, the first by propitiating the election of the second, and the second by crowning the first.[5] The final example of self-coronation was at the time of the last emperor, Constantine XI, who was crowned by a layperson but his proclamation as emperor was never actually put into effect.

These three exceptions confirm the relevance acquired by the intervention of the patriarch in the royal investiture and its ritual relevance. From Marcian and Leo I onwards, the coronation implied religious consecration and was a ritual with powerful symbolic connotations whereas authors differ on the eventual constitutional consequences of the ceremony. It is also evident that the crowning by the patriarch was an anomaly in relation to the Roman tradition, even among Christian emperors, and to a certain extent in relation to the Persian tradition. Prior to these dates, Marcian and Leo I's predecessors would, in accordance with Roman tradition, have received the crown from a senior military officer or an official. They would then have been lifted up on a shield and acclaimed by the army, the people and the Senate. The

---

'L'aspect rituel de l'onction des empereurs de Constantinople et (des tsars) de Moscou', in *Roma. Costantinopoli, Mosca* (Roma: La Sapienza, 1981), 407–15.

[5] Peter Charanis, 'Coronation and Its Constitutional Significance in the Later Roman Empire', *Byzantion* 15 (1940–1): 49–66, here 54, 62–3; Steve Runciman, *Journal of Hellenistic Studies* 58 (1938): 127 (book review).

introduction of the patriarch as the ordinary officer of the coronation would also have been aided by the constant spread of the belief in the divine origin of imperial authority, an idea that was firmly established in Byzantium due to its Hellenistic legacy and its proximity to Persia. Even though the idea of God as the source of imperial power was not new – it dates back to the third century if not earlier – Marcian was the first emperor to name God, the Senate and the army as the three elements responsible for his election. Whereas the Senate and the army could act for themselves through visible representatives, God could only be represented by his priests, so the solution of the crowning by the patriarch made sense from this perspective as well.[6]

Even though authors differ on this point, it seems that Marcian was the first to introduce the crowning ceremony by the patriarch in 450.[7] Marcian would have turned to the patriarch to legitimise his proclamation, which had been called into question since it was made without the consent of the emperor ruling in the West, Valentinian III. Marcian had flouted the old constitutional principle that entitled the emperor on the throne to choose his peer in the East or his successor in the West. This could have been plausible grounds for Marcian to turn to the patriarch, thereby gaining legitimisation from an authority other than himself, one who was closer and more respected by virtue of his spiritual standing and his natural prestige in Byzantium itself since he symbolised, as the bishop of New Rome (*Nea Roma*), its imperial tradition.[8]

---

[6] Charanis, 'Coronation and Its Constitutional Significance in the Later Roman Empire', especially 53–4.

[7] Other authors argue that the first emperor crowned by the patriarch was Leo I in 457. On Marcian's and Leo I's coronations see Wilhelm Sickel, 'Das byzantinische Krönungsrecht bis zum 10. Jahrhundert', *Byzantinische Zeitschrift* 7 (1898): 511–57, especially 517 and 539; Friedhelm Winkelmann, 'Zur Rolle der Patriarchen von Konstantinopel bei den Kaiserwechseln in frühbyzantinischer Zeit', *Klio* 60 (1978): 467–81; Arthur E. R. Boak, 'Imperial Coronation Ceremonies of the Fifth and Sixth Centuries', *Harvard Studies in Classical Philology* 30 (1919): 37–47; Kantorowicz, *Laudes Regiae*, 78–9. Yet Frank E. Brightman, 'Byzantine Imperial Coronations', *Journal of Theological Studies* 2 (1901): 359–92, especially 377, argues that the first coronation with ecclesiastical assistance was for the emperor Phocas in 602; Gilbert Dagron expands the chronology towards the age of Constans II of Byzantium in 641 (*Emperor and Priest*, 80–2). See also Panayotis Yannopoulos, 'Le Couronnment de l'empereur à Byzance: rituel et fond institutionnel', *Byzantion* 61 (1991): 71–91, especially 86–9; Peter Charanis, 'The Imperial Crown Modiolus and Its Constitutional Significance', *Byzantion*, 12 (1937): 189–95; John B. Bury, 'The Constitution of the Later Roman Empire', in *Selected Essays*, ed. Harold Temperley (Cambridge: Cambridge University Press, 1930), 103; Louis Bréhier, *Les institutions de l'empire byzantine* (Paris: A. Michel, 1949).

[8] Dvornik, *Early Christian and Byzantine Political Philosophy*, 2:828. See also Francis Dvornik, *The Idea of Apostolicity in Byzantium and the Legend of the Apostle Andrew* (Cambridge, MA: Harvard University Press, 1958) and Peter Charanis, 'Imperial Coronation in Byzantium: Some New Evidence', *Byzantina* 8 (1976): 37–46.

The coronation of Leo I in 457 is the first coronation recorded in the *Book of Ceremonies*.[9] The string of events that took place during his ascent to the throne is illustrative of the various actors who generally took part in this kind of ceremony. Following his election at the Senate, the crowd that had gathered at the Field of Mars (Campus Martius) proclaimed Leo as emperor. Popular proclamation was based on the legitimacy of the senators, military officers and court officials, the three groups who were entitled to elect the emperor. Leo was then led to the tribunal where Bousalgus, a *campiductor* (a high-ranking official), placed a soldier's chain around his neck while Olympius, another *campiductor*, placed another chain around his right arm. While there, Leo also donned the imperial robes and placed the diadem on his own head, a highly revelatory act, as the emperor ceded this prerogative to the patriarch during the religious part of the ceremony.[10] Indeed, Gilbert Dagron comments that this is the true moment of the imperial coronation – which would, therefore, make it a self-coronation in its strictest sense – rather than the one that took place later in Hagia Sophia at the hands of the patriarch, which would instead be a confirmation of the emperor's imperial investiture.[11] Armed with a lance and shield, he received the homage of the officials in order of rank. He then addressed the people, styling himself *autokrator*, *Caesar*, *Victor* and *Augustus* forever, appointed by God and elected by soldiers. The second part of his proclamation took place in Constantinople, where he visited a number of places, among them Hagia Sophia. In the

---

[9] Constantine Porphyrogennetos, *The Book of Ceremonies*, ed. Ann Moffatt and Maxeme Tall (Canberra: Australian Association for Byzantine Studies, 2012), Book I, Chapter 91, 410–17. In the mid-tenth century, Constantine VII Porphyrogenitus ordered the compilation known as the *Book of Ceremonies* (*De ceremoniis aulae Byzantinae*) and, at some point, passages written centuries earlier by Peter the Patrician, Justinian's master of ceremonies, were included (John B. Bury, 'The Ceremonial Book of Constantine Porphyrogennetos', *English Historical Review* 22 [1907]: 209–27, 417–39; Constantine N. Tsirpanlis, 'The Imperial Coronation and Theory in *De Ceremoniis Aulae Byzantinae* of Constantine VII Porphyrogennitus', *Kleronomia* 4 [1972]: 63–91). Consequently, Peter's accounts of the coronations of emperors in the fifth century are quite reliable, as they are much closer chronologically than other ceremonies included in the *Book of Ceremonies*. The book places coronations at the start of the section on civil ceremonies and the promotion of dignitaries, meaning that they are deliberately distanced from the section on religious ceremonies despite the considerable role played by the patriarch (Dagron, *Emperor and Priest*, 57). A distinction is also drawn between an 'old ceremony', carried out during the fifth century, which began with a military parade at the seventh milestone from Constantinople, the Hebdomon, and a 'new ceremony', used from the late fifth century, which was centred on the Hippodrome and Hagia Sophia. See Raymond Janin, *Constantinople Byzantine. Développment urbain et repertoire topographique* (Paris: Archives de l'Orient Chrétien, 1964), 446–9.

[10] Boak, 'Imperial Coronation Ceremonies of the Fifth and Sixth Centuries', 38.

[11] Dagron, *Emperor and Priest*, 61, 63, 81.

church, he placed his crown on the altar in the presence of the patriarch Anatolius.

In this laconic account of the coronation of Leo I, authors have discussed whether it was the patriarch who put the crown on the emperor's head during the ceremony, and hence whether he was indeed the first emperor crowned by the patriarch. However, most scholars agree on the remarkable circumstance that the emperor must have taken the crown off when he entered a holy place. And, in this sacred space, it was the patriarch's task to place the crown back on his head so that he could remove it with God's blessing. Edward Gibbon, who expresses doubts as to whether Leo I was truly crowned by the patriarch, though this is supported by the consolidation of this custom among Leo I's immediate successors, singled out the historic relevance of this moment from the point of view of royal ceremonies.[12] Gibbon based his assertion on the testimonies of Theodore Lector and Theophanes, who stated that Leo was crowned by the patriarch Anatolius. However, Peter the Patrician's account, included in Constantine VII's *Book of Ceremonies* in the tenth century, refers solely to the presence of the patriarch at the ceremony, and not to the role he played.

Beyond the debate concerning the actions of the patriarch, it is also important to note the military dimension of Leo I's coronation. This included many of the more traditional symbols and ceremonies, such as that of Julian the Apostate in Paris in 360 narrated by Ammianus Marcellinus, and it was clearly distinguished from the sacred part.[13] This distinction was repeated in the proclamation of Anastasius I in 491, though the entire ceremony was now held within the walls of the city of Constantinople.[14] The civil and military investiture took place first. Anastasius I was raised on a shield (a very traditional gesture with clear military overtones of Germanic origin) and the *campiductor* placed the chain around his neck, a tradition of Celtic origin in this case.[15] Then came the religious part of the ceremony, but still outside the church: the emperor returned to the *triklinos*, where the patriarch Euthymius pronounced a *Kyrie eleison* and then invested him with the *chlamys* (imperial

---

[12] 'This appears to be the first origin of a ceremony which all the Christian princes of the world have since adopted, and from which the clergy have deduced the most formidable consequences' (Edward Gibbon, *The Decline and Fall of the Roman Empire* [London: Dent, 1993], chapter 36).
[13] On the Germanic origins and military implications of Julian's coronation, its later influence and the Ammianus' narration see Ginnasi, *L'incoronazione celeste nel mondo bizantino*, 34–5, and Brightman, 'Byzantine Imperial Coronations', 365–6.
[14] Porphyrogennetos, *The Book of Ceremonies*, Book I, Chapter 92, 417–25.
[15] The *campiductor* was a military chief: Boak, 'Imperial Coronation Ceremonies of the Fifth and Sixth Centuries', 38.

robes) and placed the crown on his head. The increasingly active presence of the patriarch does not yet imply institutional recognition of the role of the church in the emperor's investiture, though it was given the task of guaranteeing the new sovereign's doctrinal orthodoxy. The real coronation still took place in a civil and military setting, though it was no longer a self-coronation, as in the case of Leo I, but a coronation by the *campiductor*. This pattern was also repeated in the proclamation of Justin I, who was crowned by the patriarch John II in 519.[16]

The coronations of Leo I, Anastasius I and Justin I consolidated the coronation model of the *autokrator*, the emperor proclaimed as the sole ruler. Interestingly, a parallel ceremony developed in the fifth century, which had its origins in the late Roman empire and which would later be taken as the model among the Visigoths and then among Frank and Carolingian monarchs: the ceremony for those who were associated with the throne as co-emperors while the ruling emperor was still alive.[17] In these instances, it seemed natural for the reigning emperor, rather than the patriarch (who served as a qualified witness), to carry out the coronation. This fact confirms that the function of the patriarch (even when, in the first group of coronations for a sole emperor, the *autokrator*, he placed the crown on his own head) did not have any legal effects, at least during the early centuries of the existence of the Byzantine Empire.

This occurred in the fifth century with the crowning of Leo II by Leo I in 473 and of Zeno by Leo II in 474.[18] Leo I fell seriously ill and decided to name his grandson, who had already been proclaimed Caesar, as co-Emperor Leo II. In this case, the military ceremony took place in the customary manner: the people and the legates from various parts of the empire gathered at the Hippodrome, where the soldiers called out to the emperor. He appeared, escorted by senators, and the crowd urged him to crown his grandson co-emperor. The Caesar appeared, placed himself to the left of the emperor, while the patriarch Acacius remained to his right, and recited a prayer prior to the coronation. The precedence given to the emperor, who appears in the centre, with the patriarch to one side, is significant. Following the prayer, the emperor took the crown and placed it on the head of the Caesar, who was then proclaimed Augustus.

In the case of the proclamation of an emperor when the throne was still vacant, the right of nomination came from two sources: the senators and

---

[16] Porphyrogennetos, *The Book of Ceremonies*, Book I, Chapter 93, 426–30.

[17] Christopher Walter, 'The Coronation of a Co-emperor in the Skyllitzes Matritensis', in *Actes du XIVe congrès international des etudes Byzantines*, ed. Mijail Berza and Eugen Stanescu (Bucharest: Editura Academici Republicii Socialiste Romania, 1975), 453–8.

[18] Porphyrogennetos, *The Book of Ceremonies*, Book I, Chapter 94, 431–2.

the soldiers. The people of Constantinople did not have a recognised right to proclaim the emperor, but they were present at the part of the ceremony held at the Hippodrome, divided into their factions of Blues and Greens, as at horse races – a ritual with strong influence at least from the age of Justinian I.[19] When the candidate was presented to the people, they could acclaim him or express their disapproval, but we have no grounds to suppose that the people could force a rejection of the proclamation of an emperor once he had the support of the senate and the military. The most common belief was that God chose the emperors, the army proclaimed them, the people acclaimed them, the Senate nominated them and the patriarch blessed them. Yet the importance and relevance of the different agents of the coronation – army, Senate and people – and their power of legitimating, changed depending on each period, and there are no general rules for this.[20]

These ceremonies were maintained without any substantial variation from the fifth to ninth centuries. Yet the investiture of Basil I, the founder of the Macedonian dynasty, signalled a major change and rested on his status as a 'victorious ruler' rather than as a 'legitimate heir'. His investiture took the form of a 'triumph' rather than of a coronation, properly speaking, since it took place after his glorious return to Constantinople following his victories at Tephrike and Germanikeia in 878–9.[21] This detail is important to my research, as Basil was the first to introduce the theme of the 'heavenly coronation' into Byzantine iconography, combined with the ritual reality, since the role of the patriarch Photius during the ceremony of his proclamation of co-emperor by Michael III is emphasised by the chronicler Symeonis Logothetae.[22] Basil most likely encouraged this iconographic motif, prompted by the fact that he had not ascended to power by the traditional route, based on the custom of the hereditary succession, but through military triumph. Moreover, once established in power, and making the most of his military prestige, he organised a second coronation, perhaps attempting

---

[19] Alan Cameron, *Circus Factions: Blues and Greens at Rome and Byzantium* (Oxford: Clarendon, 1976).

[20] On this evolution see especially the epigraph 'Popular Acclamation and Imperial Accession', in Anthony Kaldellis, *The Byzantine Republic: People and Power in New Rome* (Cambridge, MA: Harvard University Press, 2015), 102–17. This complex and varied evolution is summarised by Kaldellis with the formula that 'the succession was not a legal issue; it was a political one' (*The Byzantine Republic*, 115).

[21] Michael McCormick, *Eternal Victory: Triumphal Rulership in Late Antiquity* (Cambridge: Cambridge University Press, 1986), 154–7 and 169.

[22] The chronicler tells us that just before Michael III crowned Basil 'according with the tradition', the patriarch had removed the crown from Michael III's head and put it on the altar to say the usual prayers: Stephanus Wahlegren, ed., *Symeonis Magistri et Logothetae Chronicon* (Berlin: Walter de Gruyter, 2006), 253, chapter 131, lines 381–9.

to rise above the crime of assassinating his patron, Michael III, whom he overthrew. This second coronation, however, was conducted in the traditional manner, just as the ancient emperors had done.[23]

The key point of all these examples is that, until the late fifth century, the essential part of the proclamation was the military ceremony, held in a civil space and drawing on the tradition begun in the second half of the third century. The second part of the ceremony, held in a sacred place, was of lesser importance. The emperor removed his crown on entering the sacred place, resulting in the patriarch re-crowning him during a ceremony, generally at the end of the Mass. As the military part of the ceremony gradually disappeared, the natural outcome was that the function of the patriarch, who was without question responsible for the coronation in the sacred space, gradually grew in symbolic and constitutional significance.

From Symbolic to Real Meaning to the Patriarch's Mediation

The gradual union of church and state, which began in the reign of Marcian and culminated during the age of Justinian I, influenced the increasing prominence of the patriarch in the proclamation ceremony. His role evolved from being merely of symbolic significance to one with greater legal and constitutional implications. In the West, the political weakness of the city of Rome meant that this marriage between the church and the state was less likely to occur. In Constantinople, however, the political strength of the city paralleled the consolidation of the Constantinople patriarchate against its main competitors, Antioch and Alexandria, above all after the Council of Chalcedon in 451, significantly a date between the coronations of Marcian and Leo I, the first emperors to turn to the patriarch's mediation for their crowning.

As a result, it is easier to understand the increasing importance of the role of the patriarch of Constantinople, the churchman with the highest standing within the empire as the intermediary between God and the person who would henceforth govern 'by the grace of God'. In Byzantium, this never meant that the patriarch of Constantinople took precedence over the emperor, as confirmed by the fact that when a co-emperor or an empress was crowned, it was the emperor who placed the crown on his or her head. Nevertheless, the symbolic aspect of these rituals meant in practice that the patriarch came to wield considerable de facto authority, particularly from the time when the emperor was called upon to make an explicit declaration

---

[23] Dagron, *Emperor and Priest*, 74. See also Norman Tobias, *Basil I: Founder of the Macedonian Dynasty* (Lewiston: Edwin Mellen Press, 2007).

Figure 11 Constantine VII being crowned by the patriarch of Constantinople. Codex Graecus Matritensis Ioannis Skylitzes, Skylitzes Chronicle, Byzantine Italy, eleventh and twelfth centuries, *Synopsis of Histories* by John Skylitzes. Biblioteca Nacional de España manuscript Graecus Vitr. 26–2, folio 114 verso – Codex Graecus, Madrid. © Biblioteca Nacional de España.

of Christian faith, confirmed by the patriarch. It seems that this occurred for the first time at the coronation of Anastasius in 491, as the patriarch Euphemius required a written oath of the new emperor. Anastasius swore to maintain and defend the faith and not to introduce doctrinal innovations into the holy church of God.[24] At the beginning, these oaths were only occasionally required of emperors: Anastasius was probably required to do it because of his reputation for heterodoxy, and in the next centuries we have only the instances of Phocas, who was required to do it by the patriarch Cyriacus in 602, and Leo III, who was required to do it by the patriarch Germanus in 716. Yet after the ninth century, the custom was revived as a permanent part of the ceremony when Michael I requested it of Nicephorus in 811.[25]

---

[24] Peter Charanis, *Church and State in the Later Roman Empire: The Religious Policy of Anastasius I* (Madison: University of Wisconsin Press, 1939).
[25] Charanis, 'Coronation and Its Constitutional Significance in the Later Roman Empire', 57–60; Brightman, 'Byzantine Imperial Coronations', 374.

These details have led historians to wonder whether the participation of the patriarch in the coronation of the Byzantine emperors had solely a religious and spiritual significance or whether it also implied legal and constitutional changes. Wilhelm Sickel was the first to consider the issue in depth. He arrived at the conclusion that the introduction of the patriarch in the coronation ceremony never had any legal effect. By placing the crown on the emperor's head, the patriarch was simply acting as the representative of the electorate – the magistrates, senators and soldiers – and was not legitimised as a source of authority. Consequently, the coronation did not have any ecclesiastical significance either, and the emperor could do without it if he so wished. For scholars of Byzantium in the German school, Marcian was essential to the question, as he conferred on the patriarchs the privilege of crowning the emperor, meaning that the emperor himself could remove the crown.[26] Not long after, however, a number of influential authors postulated that the decisive participation of the patriarch in the ceremony introduced the new constitutional principle that professing the Christian faith was an essential condition for taking up the imperial office. This implied not only that the new emperor had been chosen by the army, the Senate and the people, but also that he was accepted by the church.[27]

Scholars generally agree with the Byzantine idea that the emperor received his power from Christ – as confirmed by the iconography of the heavenly coronation – and that the emperor's coronation by the patriarch represented the sacrament whereby the ruler was connected with God. However, they differ on the degree to which the emperor needed to be crowned by the patriarch. This debate is important in

---

[26] Sickel, 'Das byzantinische Krönungsrecht', 511–57; Boak, 'Imperial Coronation Ceremonies of the Fifth and Sixth Centuries', 37–47; Georg Ostrogorski and Ernst Stein, 'Die Kroenungsordnungen des Zeremonienbuches: chronologische und verfassungsgeschichtliche Bemerkungen', *Byzantion* 7 (1932): 185–233. Similarly, Steve Runciman concludes that even though the patriarch's intervention in the coronation ceremony could on occasion be extremely important, above all when there were doubts regarding the candidate's moral capacity, in fact the patriarch was politically and constitutionally the emperor's servant: Steve Runciman, *The Byzantine Theocracy* (Cambridge: Cambridge University Press, 1977).

[27] John B. Bury, *History of the Eastern Roman Empire from the Fall of Irene to the Accession of Basil I* (London: Macmillan, 1912); G. M. Manojlovic, 'Le people de Constantinople', *Byzantion* 11 (1936), 617–716; Peter Charanis, 'Coronation and Its Constitutional Significance in the Later Roman Empire', *Byzantion* 15 (1940–1): 49–66. More specifically, Peter Charanis argues that whereas in the Christianised Roman Empire the idea that the church was the only source of sovereign authority never quite took root, the oath of faith the patriarchs in Constantinople required of emperors implied that the church was constitutionally more important and that it could even have a right of veto in the case of heterodox emperors (Charanis, 'Coronation and Its Constitutional Significance in the Later Roman Empire', 59).

relation to the issue of self-coronations, since it is a matter of seeing to what extent the emperor was capable of *surmounting* the position of the churchmen as mediators, in this case represented by the patriarch of Constantinople. I argue that the most important aspect of this debate lies in the gradual introduction and consolidation of a ceremonial gesture that was faltering at first but that developed into a custom over time that eventually came to have the standing of law. Rather than an essentialist stance, I assume a historicist view. The emperors from the fifth to the eighth centuries valued the patriarch's intervention in symbolic rather than constitutional terms. From the ninth century, significantly at the time when the iconography of the crowning of the emperor by Christ was developing, the mediating function of the patriarch was not just symbolic but necessary. Thus, while the function of the patriarch in the coronation evolved from the symbolic to the real, the function of Christ in the coronation evolved from the simply theoretical to the iconographic. It appears that the emperor felt the need to emphasise the intervention of Christ, creating a specific iconography to this end, just when the real effects of the patriarch's intervention were becoming firmly established and, crucially, the iconoclastic interlude ended.

The testimony of contemporary writers reveals the growing sacred dimension of the imperial coronation ceremony. When the patriarch began to intervene in the ceremony in the mid-fifth century, the military and lay parties involved did not undergo any change, and on many occasions the coronation did not even take place in a sacred venue. As time passed, however, the soldiers and profane elements became less and less important, giving way to a fully sacred ceremony that was usually held in Hagia Sophia. In addition, the fact that the patriarch did not play a part in the coronations of co-emperors or emperors' spouses but was present and said the expected prayers is further evidence of his function as a de facto guarantor, though his presence did not have legal or institutional consequences but rather symbolic ones. Neither should we forget the parallels, as Panayotis Yannopoulos has analysed, that exist between the ceremony of the imperial coronation and the ceremony to ordain bishops, which further underscores its religious dimension.[28]

Some scholars have linked the introduction of the custom of the crowning of the emperor by the patriarch with the Persian custom (see p. 82), which, after centuries in which self-coronation had dominated the ceremony, moved to coronation by the Magian high priest, precisely during the time of Marcian and Leo I. The diadem itself was imported from Persia via the Hellenistic tradition, so it is not beyond the bounds of

---

[28] Yannopoulos, 'Le Couronnment de l'empereur à Byzance', 71–91.

reason that these symbolic exchanges might have taken place. Persian and Byzantine priests acted as representatives of their religion but also of their class.[29]

The evolution of the function of the patriarch at imperial coronations, and the rise in the sacred dimension of this ceremony, is in keeping with the idea that the authority of the Byzantine emperor derived from God. From the time of Julian the Apostate, the coronation ceremonies had been notably military in character in both Rome and Byzantium. Towards the twelfth century, Manuel I decided that his coronation, conducted on the mountains of Cilice by his father, John II, with the agreement of the army, had not been sufficient and he wanted to be crowned emperor once again by the patriarch in Constantinople (1143). The idea of God as the source of imperial power attained its highest expression in the religious dimension of the coronation ceremony. The patriarch did not exercise a political but a priestly function, as he consecrated the emperor and served as the instrument of divine will. This idea of 'consecration' helps to explain the expression Leo III used, that the ruler in Byzantium was both 'priest and emperor'.[30]

Imagining Coronation without Mediation: The Iconography of the Heavenly Coronation

The desire to emphasise the divine origin of the emperor's authority, and hence the wish to reinterpret the ecclesiastical intervention, entered Byzantium via images rather than rituals. Thus, imperial self-coronation through images has been termed by authors as symbolic coronation (Grabar) or heavenly coronation (Ginnasi). This is an iconographic theme that appears in reliefs and paintings and on coins, and that expressively represents the concept of divine royalty in figurative terms. Its spread conveys one of the most representative signs of the ideological premises of the Byzantine autocracy.

As Ginnasi has analysed in detail, there are precedents for this iconography in pharaonic Egypt and Sassanid Persia, which spread into the Hellenistic world and from there to Rome and Byzantium.[31] Rome

---

[29] Sickel, 'Das byzantinische Krönungsrecht', 511–77; John B. Bury, *The Constitution of the Later Roman Empire* (Cambridge: Cambridge University Press, 1910), 11; Tsirpanlis, 'The Imperial Coronation and Theory in *De Ceremoniis Aulae Byzantinae*'.

[30] Dagron, *Emperor and Priest*; George P. Majeska, 'The Emperor in His Church: Imperial Ritual in the Church of St. Sophia', in *Byzantine Court Culture from 829 to 1204*, ed. Henri Maguire (Washington, DC: Dumbarton Oaks, 1997), 1–11.

[31] An excellent synthesis of these precedents appears in Ginnasi, *L'incoronazione celeste nel mondo bizantino*, 1–26.

received from the Hellenistic world and from imperial Rome the well-established idea of the divine fundament of royalty, expressed so graphically by the iconography of the heavenly coronation. This iconography was prevalent during the time of the Macedonian emperors from the ninth century onwards. It also spread to the West, initially through the miniatures in Ottonian books and later through the Norman monarchy of Sicily.

The divine origin of the authority of the Byzantine *basileus* could eventually have entailed the development of rites or images that reflected this reality. In the sphere of rites, the patriarch's monopolisation of the role of mediator between heaven and earth prevented a direct expression of this reality; in contrast, in the realm of images, there was no occurrence of this restriction through mediation and so the heavenly iconography emerged naturally. Grabar argues that just as the emperor conferred authority on an official through a symbolic gesture or an appropriate insignia, so Christ (or an angel or saint of his by direct delegation) invested the *basileus* with his power as *autokrator* by means of the symbolic gesture of blessing and investiture with the insignia of the crown.[32] Once the theme of the heavenly coronation had emerged, it was passed on to the next generations as a well-established iconographic type, though with interesting variations that I examine in the following pages. Fictional images of heavenly coronations (Figure 14) coexist with referential representations (though these are very few in number) in which imperial proclamations by the army and the populace are represented, usually expressed in scenes of the *elevation* of the king, or those coronations performed by the patriarch himself (Figure 11). However, the imaginary representations of the emperor being crowned by Christ acquire a force and symbolic meaning difficult to surpass due to their formal expressiveness and their reference to content well rooted in the theory underpinning the divine origin of the authority of the Byzantine emperors.

One notable feature of this new iconographic type is the deliberate elimination of the patriarch in the scene of the coronation. The abstract and symbolic nature of the images has made possible to restrict what is represented to its essential meaning: the idea of the direct transmission of power by God. As Grabar comments, 'the *iconographic type* of the symbolic coronation was not established

---

[32] Grabar, *L'Empereur dans l'Art Byzantin*, 112. The iconographic motif of the coronation of the emperor by Christ or his saints has led to a debate on the 'theocratic' or 'theocentric' character of the Byzantine emperor: see Kaldellis, *The Byzantine Republic*, 166, and Apostolos Spanos and Nektarios Zarras, 'Representations of Emperors as Saints in Byzantine Textual and Visual Sources', in *Hybride Kulturen im mittelalterlichen Europa*, ed. Michael Borgolte and Bernd Schneidmüller (Berlin: Akademie Verlag, 2010), 63–78.

until the eleventh century, that is to say, the era when the *rite* of the coronation was fixed definitively as an *ecclesiastical* ceremony presided over by the patriarch.'[33] More or less deliberately, the emperors may have seen the use of this iconographic type as a counterweight to the growing influence of the patriarch, who had also begun to employ the *professio fidei* as an indispensable requisite for investing the *basileus*. In this way, the images of the coronation of the emperor by Christ, or his angels or saints, would surmount, in a solemn manner and in an abstract and symbolic language, the stark reality of the patriarch's increasing influence in imperial investiture ceremonies. The iconography of the hand of God, introduced into official Roman iconography by Constantine or Constantius II (Figure 9), seems a clear precedent for the iconography of the heavenly coronation.[34]

Back in the early sixth century, Justin I (518–27) revived the iconography of the hand of God on coins. A coin minted in Nicomedia shows Justin I in profile as he receives a crown from a divine hand, seen above in the centre.[35] This representation is especially expressive given that Justin was raised on a shield and crowned by the patriarch John II.[36] The hand of God also appears in the upper part of a small coin minted with the image of Constantine V (741–75) accompanied by his son, the future Leo IV.[37] As an iconoclastic emperor who was strongly opposed to anthropomorphic representations of Christ, Constantine V went back to the old iconographic type of the hand of God. However, this is still not a heavenly coronation – though it is very close to this iconographic type – but a translation, in figurative terms, of the special divine protection given to the emperor. In any event, this rudimentary image from the eighth century anticipates the elegant compositions of John I Tzimiskes (tenth century) and of John II Comnenus (twelfth century), in which the hand of God is prominently shown in order to reflect more clearly the blessing of the imperial figure.[38]

Significantly, the hand of God is shown in a gesture not only of blessing but also of placing the crown on the emperor's head. This double action has the quality of combining special divine protection for the person of the emperor on an individual basis (the blessing) with confirmation of the

---

[33] Grabar, *L'Empereur dans l'Art Byzantin*, 113.
[34] MacCormack, *Art and Ceremony in Late Antiquity*, 191–2.
[35] Ginnasi, *L'incoronazione celeste nel mondo bizantino*, 52 (figure 78).
[36] *The Book of Ceremonies*, ed. Moffatt and Tall, 426–30. See also Alexander A. Vasiliev, *Justin the First: An Introduction to the Epoch of Justinian the Great* (Cambridge, MA: Harvard University Press, 1950), 68–82.
[37] Ginnasi, *L'incoronazione celeste nel mondo bizantino*, 65, figure 89; Grabar, *L'Empereur dans l'Art Byzantin*, plate 30, 15.
[38] Grabar, *L'Empereur dans l'Art Byzantin*, plate 28, 6.

divine intervention in the investiture by giving the emperor the main attribute of his power (the coronation). The joint action of the blessing and the heavenly coronation may also have a precedent at a formal level in the Roman emperors of the fourth and fifth centuries, who are crowned by a Genius or the divine hand.

In addition to the hand of God, developed by the emperors of the Constantinian era, another clear precursor of the heavenly coronation by Christ was the numismatic formula in which the emperor Justinian II (685–95 and 705–11) is associated with Christ, with each of them represented on one of the two faces of the coin, minted around 692–5.[39] Moreover, in a donation document of the Church of St. Demetrios of Thessaloniki, Justinian II is described as 'crowned by God', a situation perfectly reflected by the image on the coin.[40] A century and a half later, we find a similar numismatic type, minted in the time of Michael III (842–67), on which the figure of the emperor appears on the reverse and the figure of Christ, shown with long hair and a beard, on the obverse. The inclusion of the face of Christ in association with the imperial portrait acquired an ideological value of far-reaching impact from that time onwards. The reappearance of the Christological motif in the time of Michael III, after a century and a half, evidently led to the emergence of the motif of the heavenly coronation during the Macedonian dynasty. However, the new iconographic motif of the heavenly coronation, over and above the formal appearances with its precedents (the hand of God and Christoform coins), is extremely diverse in its content and symbolic meaning. Just as the crown of laurels revived by Constantine and his successors represents the reward of piety and above all the triumph of the Christian emperor, so the diadem with which the *basileus* was crowned by Christ, the Virgin or an angel represents a sacred symbol of his power.[41]

Against this backdrop, the end of the iconoclastic period and the founding of the Macedonian dynasty ushered in a golden age of heavenly coronation iconography that stretched from the second half of the ninth century to the early eleventh century. The first known example of the Byzantine heavenly coronation is a representation of Basil I crowned by the archangel Gabriel in the presence of the prophet Elijah.[42] Some scholars see the commissioning of this scene and the choice of these two

---

[39] Ginnasi, *L'incoronazione celeste nel mondo bizantino*, 61, figure 84.
[40] Alexander A. Vasiliev, 'An Edict of the Emperor Justinian II, September, 688', *Speculum* 18 (1943): 1–13, especially 5–7.
[41] On the theory and practice of Constantine policy see Bardill, *Constantine*.
[42] Ginnasi, *L'incoronazione celeste nel mondo bizantino*, 75–9; Andrea Torno Ginnasi, 'L'incoronazione imperiale nella produzione artistica dell'età macedone', in *Bisanzion fuori da Constantinopoli*, ed. Mauro della Valle (Milano: CUEM, 2008), 109–90; Ott, *Krone und Krönung*, 61–2, 77–80, 101–4; Jonathan Shepard, 'Crowns from the Basileus, Crowns from Heaven', in *Byzantium: New Peoples, New Powers*, ed. Miliana Kaimakamova

patrons as connected with the political circumstances of the time. The arrival of a usurper emperor and the desire to launch a new era required the emergence of a new ideology to be compatible with the revived old traditions.[43] Moreover, it is very significant that Basil I is the first protagonist in this iconographic revolution, as he was the prime mover behind the advent of post-iconoclastic art. In addition, coronation ceremonies acquired their full religious pomp at this time, perhaps because of the new emperor's need to legitimise a position that was compromised from the point of view of an interrupted dynastic tradition.[44]

This first image of the heavenly coronation is in a manuscript of homilies by Gregory of Nazianzus, produced between 879 and 883. The first miniature shows the classic image of the Christ Pantocrator, the second person of the Holy Trinity, that is to say, God with a human face, whose portrayal concludes the recent victory over iconoclasm. In another image – the most interesting one as regards the subject of the heavenly coronation – the ruler appears on a plinth alongside two other figures.[45] To his right (our left), the prophet Elijah offers the emperor the royal standard of the Constantinian tradition (*labarum*), while to his left, the archangel Gabriel places the crown on his head.

According to the inscription preserved with the miniature, Basil is being crowned by the archangel as the 'governor of the cosmos', thereby clearly expressing the political theory underpinning this new iconography: the celestial origin of imperial power and the appropriateness, therefore, of his divine legitimacy.[46] In addition to the long-established explanations concerning the evolution of the iconography, some authors also believe that some particular circumstances of the time may account for the appearance of this new iconography. Basil's rapid ascent to the throne and the two crimes he committed in order to take power – the murders of Caesar Bardas and his own protector, Michael III – would have compelled him to find extraordinary measures to legitimise his rule. The prophet Elijah was an extremely prestigious figure as he had ascended to heaven without experiencing death. In addition, the emperor

---

and Maciej Salamon (Wydawnicze: Historia Iagellonica, 2007), 139–60; Catherine Jolivet-Lévy, 'L'image du pouvoir dans l'art byzantin à l'époque de la dynastie macédonienne (867–1056)', *Byzantion*, 57 (1987): 441–70; Tania Kambourova, 'Du don surnaturel de la couronne: images et interprétations', *Zograf* 32 (2008): 45–58; Dagron, *Emperor and Priest*, 193–9.

[43] Francis Dvornik, *The Photian Schism: History and Legend* (Cambridge: Cambridge University Press, 1948), 9–18; Shaun Tougher, *The Reign of Leo VI (886–912): Politics and People* (Leiden: Brill, 1997), 70–8.

[44] McCormick, *Eternal Victory*, 154–69.   [45] Dagron, *Emperor and Priest*, 192–9.

[46] Leslie Brubarker, *Vision and Meaning in Ninth Century Byzantine* (Cambridge: Cambridge University Press, 1999), 147–200, especially 158.

Figure 12 Leo VI being crowned by the Virgin Mary. Berlin, Bode Museum, Inventory 2006. © Skulpturensammlung und Museum für Byzantinische Kunst, Staatliche Museen zu Berlin – Stiftung Preußischer Kulturbesitz. Photo: Antje Voigt, 2019.

is crowned by one of the known celestial princes – the archangel Gabriel – who guarantee the supremacy of the forces of good over evil. In 866, Basil had been crowned emperor by Michael III, who was assassinated by Basil himself a year later. Basil then organised a second coronation in the church of the Asomatoi, dedicated to the archangels Michael and Gabriel, thereby making it known that his power came directly from God via his archangels.[47]

---

[47] Dagron, *Emperor and Priest*, 198. McCormick, *Eternal Victory*, 156–7, locates this second coronation in the context of a triumphal entry. On the role of angels in coronation Byzantine scenes see Walter, 'The Iconographical Sources', 190–200.

This image marked the start of the three generations of the Macedonian dynasty – Basil I, Leo VI and Constantine VII – and associated the court of heaven with the imperial family. The prophet Elijah and the archangels Gabriel and Michael are the patrons who appear most frequently in this type of iconography of the real coronation, along with the Virgin Mary, until it culminated in the time of Constantine VII, when Jesus Christ himself crowns the ruler. Decades after the manuscript of Basil I, a similar composition shows the coronation of Leo VI (886–912), in which he is crowned by the Virgin in the presence of the archangel Gabriel.

The three figures are shown at half-length on a beautifully worked piece of ivory, the purpose of which remains a subject of debate among scholars (Figure 12).[48] Three figures appear in one of the scenes: the Virgin Mary in the centre, the emperor to the left and the archangel Gabriel – an already familiar figure in the Byzantine iconography of imperial coronations – to the right. In a very unusual gesture, the Virgin adds a pearl to the crown that is already on the emperor's head. The royal status of the protagonist is confirmed by the traces of purple that survive on the ivory, as well as the tone of the inscriptions around the triptych, the content of which, as Kathleen Corrigan observes, was used in the prayers recited by the patriarch at the emperor's coronation ceremony.[49] So it is no longer an angel, as in the case of Basil I, who crowns the emperor but the Virgin Mary, the queen of the angels. The choice of the Virgin as the intermediary took on a special significance and was later even added as an image on the reverse of coins issued by later emperors, as in the case of Leo VI himself.[50]

The third step in the evolution towards the iconography of the heavenly coronation – after the coronation of Basil by the archangel Gabriel and of Leo VI by the Virgin – is the famous ivory piece that shows Jesus crowning an imperial couple.[51] This ivory is framed by an extensive scene that surrounds a beautiful ivory box which, significantly, shows the story of

---

[48] Kathleen Corrigan, 'The Ivory Scepter of Leo VI: A Statement of Post-iconoclastic Imperial Ideology', *Art Bulletin* 60 (1978): 407–16; Anthony Cutler, *The Hand of the Master: Craftsmanship, Ivory, and Society in Byzantium* (Princeton, NJ: Princeton University Press, 1994), 200–1, and Gudrun Bühl and Hiltrud Jehle, 'Des Kaisers altes Zepter – des Kaisers neuer Kamm', *Jahrbuch Preußischer Kulturbesitz* 39 (2002): 289–306.

[49] Corrigan, 'The Ivory Scepter of Leo VI', 409; Ginnasi, *L'incoronazione celeste nel mondo bizantino*, 80–1.

[50] On the cult of the Virgin in Byzantium, see Niki Tsironis, 'From Poetry to Liturgy: The Cult of the Virgin in the Middle Byzantine Era', in *Images of the Mother of God: Perceptions of the Theotokos in Byzantium*, ed. Maria Vassilaki (Aldershot: Ashgate, 2005), 91–102. See also Leslie Brubaker and Mary Cunningham, eds., *The Cult of the Mother of God in Byzantium* (Farnham: Ashgate, 2011).

[51] Ginnasi, *L'incoronazione celeste nel mondo bizantino*, 82–5.

David, as well as the origin of the custom of the coronation. Even though the work was originally attributed to Basil I, recent research attributes it to Leo VI, based primarily on the inscriptions that surround the entire band between the base and the upper part of the ivory box.[52] The imperial couple crowned by Christ does not seem to be specific historical figures, but instead represents an idealised standard, which proved extremely effective, since later Byzantine iconography closely imitated it. This ivory piece may be regarded as a crucial landmark in the history of the heavenly coronation, since it is the first scene that translated Byzantine theocratic thinking into iconographic terms thanks to the gesture of the crowning of the emperor by Christ's own hands. However, as Ginnasi remarks, the private function of the ivory box, used solely for domestic purposes by the emperors, means that it is still impossible to draw conclusions. Thus, its symbolic and political message was extremely important while its dissemination was still very limited.[53]

Another topic associated with the heavenly coronation is the numismatic representation of the emperor Alexander (912–13) being crowned by St John the Baptist (Figure 13). On one side of the coin, Christ is shown sitting on his throne; on the other, the emperor is being crowned by a figure turning slightly towards him. Even though various hypotheses have been put forward concerning the identity of the figure performing the coronation, who could be Saint Alexander or the patriarch Nicholas I, all the iconographic evidence – long beard, long hair, tunic with numerous folds and a cross in his left hand – make it more likely that it is St John the Baptist.[54] In addition, evident parallels emerge between the gesture of the coronation depicted on this coin and the extraordinary painting held in the New Church of Tokali Kilise in Turkey, in which John the Baptist is shown crowning Christ.[55]

Just as the symbolism surrounding the figure of Gabriel, the messenger, and the Virgin, the universal mediator, made them ideal choices for the figures crowning the emperor, John the Baptist had notable attributes that made him conceptually suited to this rite too. He baptised the Saviour, a clear allusion to priestly and royal anointment. Because of his action, the divinity of the Saviour was manifested through the voice of the Holy Spirit. Thus, the ceremony to invest the emperor reveals his divine origin, analogously taking the form of a kind of epiphany, since the glory of the

---

[52] Anthony Cutler and Nicolas Oikonomides, 'An Imperial Byzantine Casket and Its Fate at a Humanist's Hands', *Art Bulletin* 70 (1988): 77–87.
[53] Ginnasi, *L'incoronazione celeste nel mondo bizantino*, 85.
[54] Nicole Thierry, 'Le Baptiste sur le solidus d'Alexandre (912–913)', *Revue Numismatique* 34 (1992): 237–41.
[55] Henry Maguire, 'Style and Ideology in Byzantine Imperial Art', *Gesta* 28 (1889): 217–31, here 226–7; Maria G. Parani, 'The Romanos Ivory and the New Tokali Kilise: Imperial Costume As a Tool for Dating Byzantine Art', *Cahiers Archéologiques* 49 (2001): 15–28.

emperor is revealed by his parallels with Jesus Christ, as they are both touched by the hand of John the Baptist.[56] In addition, some scholars have also emphasised the semantic identity and symbolic parallels between the rites of the baptism of Christ and the coronation of the ruler: the figure of Christ baptised by John the Baptist is simply replaced by that of the emperor, meaning that every investiture of the ruler acquires a sacred meaning and dimension.[57]

John the Baptist was, moreover, a key figure in Byzantium because of his baptism of Jesus. The transposition of this ceremony to the heavenly coronation of the emperor by John the Baptist symbolises the superiority of the consecrated (the emperor) over the consecrator (the patriarch), just as Christ was superior to the saint who consecrated him. Kantorowicz discovered a beautiful antiphon (*Laudes Regiae*) used in certain ceremonies in the West but which is of Eastern origin and which confirms this: 'The knight baptises the king, a serf the lord, St. John the Saviour.'[58] It also seems highly significant that the scene of the baptism of Christ, along with the scene of the sacrifice of Isaac, is the source from which the iconography of the hand of God naturally developed in late antiquity.[59]

Alexander's main innovation was the support used, since this was the first representation of a full heavenly coronation (not only the hand of God but a full body of a celestial figure) shown on a coin, one of the chief manifestations of all things 'official' and an extremely effective vehicle for disseminating a particular idea devised by the powers that be.[60] Alexander was responsible for finally introducing the iconography of the emperor crowned by Christ himself.

The numismatic programme begun by Alexander was continued by Romanus I Lecapenus (920–44). The complex investiture of Romanus I, who came to power at the end of a period of tremendous political instability in Byzantium (913–20) following the death of Alexander, would have prompted the new emperor to seek different formulae for consolidating his

---

[56] For the Byzantine emperor's coronation as epiphany see Ernst Kantorowicz, '*Oriens Augusti – Lever du Roi*', *Dumbarton Oaks Papers* 17 (1963): 117–77, here 149–62.

[57] Robin M. Jensen, *Living Water: Images, Symbols and Settings of Early Christian Baptism* (Leiden: Brill, 2011); Ioli Kalavrezou, 'Helping Hands for the Empire: Imperial Ceremonies and the Cult of Relics at the Byzantine Court', in *Byzantine Court Culture from 829 to 1204*, ed. Henri Maguire (Washington, DC: Dumbarton Oaks, 1997), 53–79, here 72–5.

[58] '*Baptizat miles regem, servus dominum, Johannes Salvatorem*' (Kantorowicz, *Laudes Regiae*, 142).

[59] Weitzmann, *Studies in Classical and Byzantine Manuscript Illumination*, 272–3.

[60] Vangelis Maladakis, 'The Coronation of the Emperor on Middle Byzantine Coinage: A Case of Christian Political Theology (10th–mid 11th C.)', in *Numismatic, Sphragistic and Epigraphic Contributions to the History of the Black Sea Coast* (Varna: Acta Musei Varnaensis, 2008), 342–59.

Figure 13 Solidus issued by Alexander I (912–13), showing him being crowned by Christ. Dumbarton Oaks Byzantine Collection (BZC.1948.17.3002). © Dumbarton Oaks Byzantine Collection.[61]

legitimacy, notably the introduction of the scene of his coronation due to the direct intervention of Christ. The fact that the second emperor to use this iconography was, strictly speaking, a usurper with no dynastic legitimacy highlights his need to avoid any temporal intermediation and to exploit to the full the available legitimising sources. However, while the appearance of the iconography of the crowning by Christ may have initially been connected with the need for imperial legitimacy, it was soon developed into a consolidated iconography. At this point, it became naturally divorced from a context of political difficulties and acquired its full and specific symbolic meaning, one strictly related to the theory of the divine origin of imperial power.

This complete consolidation of the heavenly coronation and its dissociation from political instability were confirmed by the proclamation of Constantine VII (945–59), the son of Leo VI. Constantine needed to reaffirm his authority because of political instability at the moment he became emperor.[62] He had a beautiful ivory panel made for his investiture. The emperor is shown being crowned by Christ as the *autokrator*, with both figures standing under a baldachin structure.[63] The emperor is

---

[61] Maladakis, 'The Coronation of the Emperor on Middle Byzantine Coinage', 346.
[62] Ginnasi, *L'incoronazione celeste nel mondo bizantino*, 89.
[63] E. Pilnik, 'Ivory with Constantine VII Porphyrogennetos Crowned by Christ', in *Byzantium, 330–1453*, ed. Robin Cormack and Maria Vassilaki (London: Royal Academy of Arts, 2008), 397–8; Kurt Weitzmann, 'The Mandylon and Constantine Porphyrogennetos', *Cahiers Archélologiques* 11 (1960): 163–84.

Figure 14 Ivory table depicting Constantine VII being crowned by Christ. State Pushkin Museum of Fine Arts, II 2b 329, Moscow. © Pushkin Museum of Fine Arts, Moscow.

clearly submissive to the Saviour, from whom his power proceeds, as his head is slightly bowed, his hands are shown in the position for praying and he is placed lower than Christ (Figure 14).

There are no longer any mediators in the scene – Gabriel, the Virgin or John the Baptist. Instead, Christ officiates at the coronation: Jesus himself sanctions the investiture of the emperor. To the left of the emperor's head, an inscription reads 'Autokrator', which, according to some scholars, signals the ceremonial recognition of the reclaiming of the diadem by the Macedonian dynasty after the throne had been usurped by another family for a few years.[64]

This ambitious iconographic programme implemented by Constantine VII should have been accompanied by effective literary labours, since the liturgical and ceremonial book *De ceremoniis aulae Byzantinae* was drawn up during his reign. This work, which was to exert considerable influence later on, explicitly expresses in a number of places the divine source of power, in particular in the passages concerning the emperor's coronation ceremony. Some of the expressions that appear in this treatise make unambiguous reference to the heavenly coronation: 'Glory to God for the crowning of your head'; 'You have been crowned emperor by his hand, so let him guard you for many years in the purple.'[65] Constantine VII took pains to ensure that the representation was not simply archetypal in nature but indicated that it should be a personal portrait, with character and personality.[66] It is no coincidence that when the ritual dimension of the role of the patriarch as a mediator in the imperial coronation increased in importance, so too the iconic dimension of Christ's function as a direct agent in the imperial coronation was consolidated. This fundamental manifestation of the heavenly coronation demonstrates, once again, the imaginary nature of the *iconographic* coronation in comparison with the real character of the *historical* coronation. While the figure is idealised, being crowned by Christ himself, the reality was that his coronation was performed in 911, when he was just five years old, by his father, Leo VI, who was keen to ensure his succession.

An iconographic type that also developed during this period is the coronation at the same time of the emperor and empress, who are shown dressed in robes befitting the most solemn ceremonies.[67] One characteristic

---

[64] Ginnasi, *L'incoronazione celeste nel mondo bizantino*, 90.
[65] Gyula Moravcsik, ed., *De Administrando Imperio by Constantine Porphyrogenitusk*, trans. Romilly J. H. Jenkins (Washington, DC: Dumbarton Oaks, 1967).
[66] Weitzmann, 'The Mandylion and Constantine Porphyrogennetos', 180–1.
[67] On the Byzantine emperors' vestments see Elisabeth Piltz, 'Middle Byzantine Court Costume', in *Byzantine Court Culture from 829 to 1204*, ed. Henri Maguire (Washington, DC: Dumbarton Oaks, 1997), 39–52.

Figure 15 Romanus II of Byzantium and his wife, Eudocia, being crowned by Christ. Constantinople, ivory, c. 945–9. Bibliothèque Nationale, Cabinet des Médailles. Paris. © Bibliothèque Nationale de France.

example is the elegant marble piece in the same style as that depicting the coronation of Constantine VII by Christ, though in this later piece it is Constantine's son, Emperor Romanus II (959–63), who is being crowned by Christ, who, in a similar gesture, also crowns Romanus's first wife, Bertha of Italy, who took the name of Eudocia (Figure 15).

This model returns to the structure of the coronation of the imperial couple (pp. 114–5), though now in a completely official and public context.[68] Christ is shown in a clearly elevated position in the centre of the composition, crowning the emperor and empress, Romanus and Eudocia, who are richly apparelled and stand on a lower stage. This motif spread into the West, as demonstrated by the beautiful tablet of the coronation of Otto II (973–83) and the Byzantine princess Theophanu by Christ, with traces of a purple background, in which Christ is shown with enhanced majesty, framed by a baldachin and standing on a stool (Figure 20).[69]

Other coronations in which Christ is shown crowning two figures are those of Constantine X (1059–67) and his daughter Eudocia, and that of Michael VII (1071–8) and his wife, Maria of Alania. The same compositional structure appears on two lead seals, also attributed to Otto II, corroborating the spread of this dual model to the West.[70] These joint coronations are reminiscent of an iconographic type that appeared in the mid-fifth century in the wall paintings of one of the side chapels of Saint John Lateran, which show Christ crowning two people. The figure of Christ appears in the centre, flanked by the two smaller, symmetrical figures being crowned by him. The identities of these two figures remain in doubt, but the model itself of the three figures, with Christ in a prominent central position crowning the other two, was adopted by later iconography, above all in the version of the coronation of the emperor and empress characteristic of the tenth and eleventh centuries.[71]

The final major depiction of a heavenly coronation during the Macedonian era shows the crowning of Basil II (976–1025) (Figure 16). The work, an early eleventh-century miniature in a psalter preserved in Venice, is a veritable manifesto of the Byzantine political theology regarding the ruler.

---

[68] Ginnasi, *L'incoronazione celeste nel mondo bizantino*, 93–5. See also the different interpretation of Ioli Kalavrezou-Maxeiner, 'Eudokia Makrembolitissa and the Romanos Ivory', *Dumbarton Oaks Papers* 31 (1977): 305–25, and the hypothesis of the eventual marriage symbolism in Christopher Walter, 'Marriage Crowns in Byzantine Iconography', in Walter, *Prayer and Power in Byzantine and Papal Imagery* (Aldershot: Variorum, 1993), 6:1–17.

[69] Ginnasi, *L'incoronazione celeste nel mondo bizantino*, 95–7, figure 123; Jonathan Shepard, 'Western Approaches (900–1025)', in *The Cambridge History of the Byzantine Empire, c. 500–1492*, ed. Shepard (Cambridge: Cambridge University Press, 2008), 549–59.

[70] Percy E. Schramm, *Die deutschen Kaiser und Könige in Bildern ihrer Zeit 751–1190* (Munich: Prestel, 1983), 194–5, 343. For the connections between Byzantium and the Ottonians see Shepard, 'Western Approaches', 537–59.

[71] Francesca Romana Moretti, 'I pannelli dipinti Della capella "cristiana" nell'area dell'ospedale San Giovanni', *L'orizzonte tardoantico e le nuove immagini*, ed. Maria Andaloro (Turnhout: Brepols, 2006), 419–24.

Figure 16 Illustration from the psalter of Basil II, showing the armed emperor being crowned by the archangel Gabriel. Biblioteca Nazionale Marciana, Venice. cod. gr. 17, f. 3 r. © Biblioteca Nazionale Marciana, Venice, Italia.[72]

---

[72] Ginnasi, *L'incoronazione celeste nel mondo bizantino*, 105–7, figure 136; Jonathan Shepard, 'Equilibrium to Expansion (886–1025)', in *The Cambridge History of the Byzantine Empire, c. 500–1492*, ed. Shepard (Cambridge: Cambridge University Press, 2008), 522–6.

The emperor is shown in the centre on a podium, dressed in armour, a sword in his left hand.[73] Above him is a half-length Christ Pantocrator holding a crown. However, the archangel Gabriel, who appears to the left and above the emperor but below Christ, performs the coronation itself. Opposite Gabriel, on the left and at the same height, is the archangel Michael, who is giving Basil a long lance that extends as far as the floor and which they both hold. The scene is completed by six military saints, arranged in two columns of three saints, with one column below each of the archangels, flanking the emperor. Below Basil's feet are eight prostrate figures, presumably his Bulgarian enemies, one of whom is pinned down by the lance.[74] It is difficult not to see in this image a model of the traditional iconography of the resurrection of Christ, with the Roman soldiers asleep at his feet and the angels looking down from up above.

The scene is laden with rich symbolic meaning. The four hierarchical levels – Jesus at the apex, the archangels on the second level, the emperor and military saints on the third and the submissive figures on the fourth – are emphasised by the different background colours: gold for the holy figures and the emperor, and green for the lower area occupied by the submissive figures. The archangel Gabriel appeared earlier in Byzantine iconography – he was shown crowning Basil I and Leo VI and was remembered by Constantine VII when he told his son Romanus II that Constantine the great had been crowned by an angel – an account included in *De Administrando Imperio* (*On the Governance of the Empire*). The archangel Michael is traditionally associated with the military, as he is the declared prince of the heavenly host, the vanquisher of evil forces.[75] The political power conveyed by Gabriel is complemented by the military might conveyed by Michael, eloquently supported by the figures of the military saints associated with the emperor. Ginnasi concludes that the miniature of Basil II, the Byzantine emperor most renowned as a military figure, constitutes the perfect figurative counterpart to the theocratic idea of Constantine VII.[76] Thus, sovereign power and military supremacy remain two allied values of royalty, as originally narrated in the book of Samuel. When Samuel anointed Saul, he did so saying these words: 'Has

---

[73] See the interesting parallels with the late Roman representations in military context in Kantorowicz, 'Gods in Uniform', 368–93.

[74] Anthony Cutler, 'The Psalter of Basil II', *Arte Veneta*, 30 (1976): 9–19; Cutler, 'The Psalter of Basil II, Part II', *Arte Veneta*, 31 (1977): 9–15.

[75] On the devotional function of the heavenly court in Byzantium, especially the archangels Michael and Gabriel, see Henry Maguire, 'The Heavenly Court', in *Byzantine Court Culture from 829 to 1204*, ed. Maguire (Washington, DC: Dumbarton Oaks, 1997), 247–58, and Henry Maguire, *The Icons of Their Bodies* (Princeton, NJ: Princeton University Press, 1996).

[76] Ginnasi, *L'incoronazione celeste nel mondo bizantino*, 107.

not the Lord anointed you to be prince over his people Israel? And you shall reign over the people of the Lord and you will save them from the hand of their surrounding enemies.'[77]

The iconographic motifs described are related in one way or another with the heavenly coronation. The emperor is crowned by saints, angels, the Virgin or Christ. They reappeared in various forms and on different supports (coins, panels, pieces of ivory, paintings, lead seals and reliquaries) in the periods after Basil II, from the last Macedonian (1025–81) to the Comnenus emperors (1081–1204).[78] During these two centuries, however, there were no substantial innovations in the artistic forms or symbolic meaning of the heavenly coronation. The themes were taken from earlier periods in accordance with the ideological needs and intentions of the time. The crowning of Baldwin in May 1204 ushered in a completely new period from the point of view of the practices, iconographies and ideologies of royal coronations given that the Latin influence now prevailed, though the new emperors still sought to legitimise themselves in their new context.[79]

Eastern and Western Iconographic and Ritual Traditions

The motif of the heavenly coronation proved so powerful in Byzantium that, apart from the miniatures in the Madrid Skylitzes (Figure 11), there are very few images of an emperor or member of the imperial family being crowned by a living person: in Byzantium, the images are not historical, heuristic or documentary but ideological, archetypal and imaginary.[80] This evolution is in keeping with the different iconographic trends in the two sides of the empire. In the West, a realistic iconographic conception developed, in which the illustrations matched the historical reality of the rites performed; in the East, an iconography of an ideal and symbolic type

---

[77] 1 Samuel 10:1.
[78] On the iconography of the heavenly coronation during the Macedonian and Comnenus periods, see Ginnasi, *L'incoronazione celeste nel mondo bizantino*, 109–65.
[79] Stefan Burkhardt, 'Court Ceremonies and Rituals of Power in the Latin Empire of Constantinople', in *Court Ceremonies and Rituals of Power in Byzantium and the Medieval Mediterranean*, ed. Alexander Beihammer et al. (Leiden: Brill, 2013), 277–90; Georg Ostrogorsky, 'Zur Kaisersalbung und Schilderhebung im spätbyzantinischen Krönungszeremoniell', *Historia: Zeitschrift für Alte Geschichte*, 4 (1955): 246–56; Theresa Shawcross, 'Conquest Legitimized: The Making of a Byzantine Emperor in Crusader Constantinople (1204–1261)', in *Byzantines, Latins, and Turks in the Eastern Mediterranean World after 1150*, eds. Jonathan Harris, Catherine Holmes and Eugenia Russell (Oxford: Oxford University Press, 2012), 181–220.
[80] Christopher Walter, *Art and Ritual in the Byzantine Church* (London: Variorum, 1982), 119.

emerged, in which the images, based on an imaginary model, did not necessarily coincide with the historical truth of the rites carried out.

Both the Eastern and Western models take their basic ideas from the narratives of kingship in the Old Testament. Nevertheless, the heavenly and symbolic coronation in the East implies the recognition of a holy monarchy, in which power came directly from Christ and in which even ecclesiastical circles were subject to the emperor's rule. The historical and ritual coronation in the West implies the recognition of a temporal monarchy, in which power also came directly from Christ but in which the relationship with the church was more problematic because neither of them were truly subordinate to the other. The result of this was that, over time, the civil realm and the ecclesiastical sphere remained independent of each other in the West, in a way that did not occur in the East. Indeed, it is highly significant that in the West an anomaly should have developed in the usual rite of coronations (self-coronations), which even historically excluded priestly mediation. In the East, the historical experience was transferred to iconographic representation by substitution, implying the church was subordinate to politics; in the West, this transfer of the historical to the iconographic occurred by separation, implying the independence of the two spheres.

The direct intervention of Christ in iconographic depictions symbolises in Byzantium the reality of the formulae employed in the ritual acclamations and the coronation ceremonies, which refers to the fact that the emperors are 'crowned by God' or 'crowned by Christ', as is mentioned on several occasions in the *Book of Ceremonies*.[81] Even in those images in which the Virgin, an angel or a saint crowns the emperor, descending from the top of the representation, is the hand of God who gives his blessing and approves the coronation. The written and ritual idea of the direct transmission of power from Christ to the emperor is thus iconographically corroborated, even though the reality meant that the patriarch's intervention in the coronation was increasingly important. The iconography of the coronation represents, therefore, an ideal type in contrast with the stark reality of the church's mediation in the investiture ceremony.

In the Byzantine case, then, the idea of the self-coronation was reflected iconographically in an imaginary manner, but precisely because of that it is no less 'real' than that of the ceremony itself. Imperial art was given the task of translating into a visual and symbolic and not necessarily referential language the values and ideology that prevailed in each specific

---

[81] Grabar, *L'Empereur dans l'Art Byzantin*, 117.

political period concerning the source of its power.[82] The only preserved representations that refer to an external reality are the miniatures inserted in the manuscript known as the *Madrid Skylitzes* (Figure 11). They paradoxically include the sole iconographic-imaginative representations known to have survived of the historical-eventual practice of the coronations: the custom of raising the emperor on the shield, the patriarch crowning the emperor and the emperor crowning the co-emperor.[83] Some scholars have even drawn a connection between the scene on the celebrated ivory of the coronation of Constantine VII by Christ and the miniature in the Madrid manuscript that shows the patriarch placing the crown on his head.[84] However, the symbols should not be regarded as mere icons with no external referentiality but as signs that have an impact on the implicit reality they depict. This symbolism implies a typical Byzantine trend, which is very different to the Western tradition in terms of the distance between historical reality – the mediation of the patriarch in the emperor's coronation ceremony really performed – and the imaginary reality of the emperor's power received directly from Christ.

---

[82] Michael McCormick, 'Analysing Imperial Ceremonies', *Jahrbuch der österreichischen Gesellschaft für Byzantinistik*, 35 (1985): 1–20, especially 9–10.

[83] On the manuscript of Madrid, *Cronica Skylitzes*, and the ceremonies it contains, see Ginnasi, *L'incoronazione celeste nel mondo bizantino*, 66–72; Sebastián Cirac Etopañán, *Skylitzes Matritensis. Reproducciones y miniaturas* (Madrid: Herder, 1965); Walter, 'The Coronation of a Co-emperor', 453–8; Walter, 'Raising on a Shield in Byzantine Iconography', *Revué des études Byzantines* 33 (1975): 133–75; Vasiliki Tsamakda, *The Illustrated Chronicle of Ioannes Skylitzes in Madrid* (Leiden: Alexandros, 2002).

[84] Grabar, *L'Empereur dans l'Art Byzantin*, 112 and 117; Annemarie Weyl Carr, 'Court Culture and Cult Icons in Middle Byzantine Constantinople', in *Byzantine Court Culture from 829 to 1204*, ed. Henri Maguire (Washington, DC: Dumbarton Oaks, 1997), 81–100, here 85.

5 The Sacralisation of Carolingian Accessions

The transition from paganism to Christianity created new liturgies of ceremonies of accession and new iconographic programmes in the West, as it happened in Byzantium. With the progressive fusion of the rites of unction and coronation in the Carolingian monarchy from the mid-eighth century, the royal investiture ceremony was sacralised and liturgified. Ceremonial liturgification and iconographic Christification are the two main processes in the consolidation of the ideology and practice of Western monarchies from the eighth century. They substitute for (or, perhaps more accurately, are transferred from) the pagan and theocentric models of pre-Carolingian ceremonies and rites.

This chapter focuses on an important aspect that completes the narrative of ritual and symbolic self-coronations through different ages. Carolingian ceremonial practices are highlighted here not only because they develop the basic ceremonies of royal accession which will become prevalent in medieval Europe and will pass to early modern monarchies. The main formative period for the ideology and rituals of medieval royalty in the West lies between the mid-eighth century and the mid-ninth century. The crucial nature of this period for royal investiture rituals is confirmed by the fact that the prayer recited at the moment of coronation by the last Bourbon, Charles X, in 1825, is essentially the same as the prayer used by his predecessor Charles the Bald, ten centuries earlier, at his coronation as king of the Lothringians in 869. Hence the importance of the Carolingian institutions, traditions and ideology, and the reason they merit their own section in this study.[1] Yet, more crucially for this book, they mark a clear divergence between the rituals of accession enacted in Central and Northern Europe, and in the imperial projections in the kingdoms of Sicily and Jerusalem (in which any attempt of liberation from ecclesiastical mediation will be seen as a transgression), from

---

[1] Janet L. Nelson, 'The Lord's Anointed and the People's Choice: Carolingian Royal Ritual', in *Rituals of Royalty*, ed. Frans Theuws and Janet L. Nelson (Cambridge: Cambridge University Press, 1992), 137–80. For this section, see the different contributions in Becher, *Die mittelalterliche Thronfolge im europäischen Vergleich*.

those performed in the Iberian kingdoms, where self-coronations will become conventional rituals of accession or, at least, will be used without question when the context demands it.[2]

Sacralisation: The Fusion of Anointment and Coronation

The ceremonies of the inauguration of a sovereign were independent of the church during late antiquity and even after the fall of the western empire. The ceremonies were purely civil or military acts in both Rome and Byzantium, as well as in some of the early Germanic kingdoms, where the people and the soldiers, and later the magnates, consolidated the rite of ascension by acclamation and the raising of hands.[3] The process began to change when the establishment and consolidation of the idea of divine sovereignty from which kings received their power required the recognition of another higher power, or at least of a mediating one.

---

[2] I am aware that are many differences within the French, English and German models themselves, although I cannot examine them in detail here. For instance, whilst French and English prelates 'were more likely to dispute their own rights of precedence in a king's ceremonies than to dispute the sanctity of the ceremonies conferred' (Koziol, 'England, France and the Problem of Sacrality', 127), 'imperial inauguration was a theatrical production in which two main actors shared the stage and competed for the limelight' (Dale, 'Inauguration and Political Liturgy', 213). Dale makes, in addition, an interesting distinction between the emperors, who neglect 'the imperial liturgy developed by the papal curia in Rome' in their inaugurations in Aachen, and the German monarchs, who 'continued to make lively use of inauguration liturgy to emphasize, in the face of papal opprobrium, the divinely ordained nature of the rule' (Dale, 'Inauguration and Political Liturgy', 213). See also Dale, *Inauguration and Liturgical Kingship*; Johanna Dale, 'Conceptions of Kingship in High-Medieval Germany in Historiographical Perspective', *History Compass* 16(6) (2018): 1–11; Andreas Büttner, *Der Weg zur Krone. Rituale der Herrschererhebung im spätmittelalterlichen Reich* (Ostfildern: Thorbecke, 2012) and Marion Steinicke and S. Weinfurter, eds., *Investitur- und Krönungsrituale: Herrschaftseinsetzungen im kulturellen Vergleich* (Cologne: Böhlau, 2005). Timothy Reuter challenges the assumption that Germany, with its king-emperors, was somehow different from England and France (Timothy Reuter, 'The Medieval German Sonderweg? The Empire and Its Rulers in the High Middle Ages', in *Kings and Kingship in Medieval Europe*, ed. Anne J. Duggan [London: King's College London Centre for Late Antique and Medieval Studies, 1993], 179–211). Nicholas Vincent convincingly argues in favour of the sacral nature of England's medieval kings, so that 'the status to which English kings or queens aspired is supposed, as early as the eleventh century, to have been established on a very different basis from that accepted in France, Spain or Germany. Through to the sixteenth century and beyond, continental kingship remained an essentially "sacral" phenomenon. In England, by contrast, the "sacrality" of English kings was fatally undermined by one undeniable event: the Norman Conquest of 1066' (Vincent, 'Royal Sacrality in England', 2).

[3] Kantorowicz, *Laudes Regiae*, 77. For a more general perspective on the borrowing between Germanic and Roman notions of kingship see Myers, *Medieval Kingship*, 15–58.

Following its practice in Israel, the first precedent for royal unction known in an already Christianised world is the anointing of King Wamba, king of the Visigoths in Spain, by the archbishop of Toledo in 672.[4] It is not entirely clear what inspired this ritual. The rite of unction may have originated in Gaul independently of the Visigothic kingdom, given that the common model was the Bible, a source fully available to all. Unction may even have been based on the ceremony of baptism, with the post-baptismal chrismation of the initiate's head performed by the bishop, rather than on the biblical model.[5] However, apart from its significance for the creation of a more recent precedent than the kings of Israel, Wamba's unction is an apparently isolated event.

The anointing of Pippin the Short in 751 in the west Frankish kingdom by the papal legate Saint Boniface in Soissons was inspired by the biblical anointing of kings by priests and prophets. Just as Wamba's anointing had been relatively isolated from contemporary political or religious circumstances, Pippin the Short's significantly coincides with the introduction of the rite of anointing the priest's hands in his ordination. The introduction of this particular rite, in both royal and priestly investitures, incorporated a Christian sanctity that had won its fight against the pagan rites introduced by native German royalty.[6] Pippin had replaced the last Merovingian king and therefore needed greater legitimacy not only from the Frankish aristocracy, but also from the clergy. Thus contemporary accounts recall the ceremony as the parallel events of both 'the consecration of bishops' and 'the recognition of princes'.[7] In the ideology of sovereign investitures, unction represents the sacralisation of the regal figure. The only substantial difference from episcopal consecration is the use of chrism for the bishop and blessed oil for the king.[8] Royal unction, which anoints the head, arms and shoulders, combines the baptismal ritual (where head, chest and shoulders are anointed) with the episcopal (in which head and hands are anointed), but is clearly distinguished from them.[9] Kantorowicz points out the importance of the introduction of this

---

[4] Roger Collins, 'Julian of Toledo and the Royal Succession in Late Seventh-Century Spain', in *Early Medieval Kingship*, ed. Peter H. Sawyer and Ian N. Wood (Leeds: University of Leeds, 1979), 30–49, especially 44–9.
[5] Nelson, *Politics and Ritual in Early Modern Europe*, 249–50; Jackson, *Ordines coronationis*, 1:23.
[6] Yet some authors have argued that it was a process of substitution rather than innovation, of transference rather than creation *ex nihilo*: Francis Oakley, *Empty Bottles of Gentilism* (New Haven, CT: Yale University Press, 2010).
[7] Nelson, 'The Lord's Anointed and the People's Choice', 151.
[8] Schramm, *Kaiser, Könige und Päpste*, 3:73–4. On the ceremony of unction, see the section 'Anointing Formulas', in Bouman, *Sacring and Crowning*, 107–26.
[9] Cyrille Vogel and Reinhard Elze, eds., *Le pontifical romano-germanique du dixième siècle*. 3 vols. (Vatican City: Biblioteca Apostolica Vaticana, 1963–72), 1:252–4.

rite to the investitures of Frankish kings: 'with Pippin's anointment the royal inauguration was shifted, once and for all, to the sacramental or at least liturgical sphere. ... Thus the inauguration of a king had been passed on, with certain restrictions, to the hands of the clergy.'[10] Josef Fleckenstein confirms this:

> The anointment, which bestowed upon him a new, a spiritual legitimation, was the decisive step in the Christianisation of the kingship. Through it, the ruler entered into an immediate relationship to God, and as God's representative he exercised his rulership as a God-given office.[11]

Once the royal unction had been introduced, the participation of the episcopate becomes essential for the creation of the king and the future performance of his duties. The upshot of this was that, from then on, no king of the Franks, or of the succeeding Carolingians, Capetians and Ottonians, possessed the royal title until they were effectively anointed and crowned.[12]

From the anointing of Pippin in 751 up until the anointing/coronation of Charles the Bald in 848, the Pope or the reigning emperor himself served as the ordinary ministers at the coronations of Carolingian emperors. In the latter case, there was a tradition imported from Byzantium in which the sovereign emperor would crown his heir, whom he would join from that moment as co-emperor. Thus, Pippin himself, anointed by the papal legate in 751, had been crowned shortly afterwards by Pope Stephen II in Saint-Denis in 754, along with his sons Charlemagne and Carloman.[13] Charlemagne was solemnly crowned by Pope Leo III in Rome, on Christmas Day 800, with a ritual corresponding to an imperial crowning rather than the royal.[14] Charlemagne himself invested his son

---

[10] Kantorowicz, *Laudes Regiae*, 78.

[11] Josef Fleckenstein, 'Rex Canonicus: Über Entstehung und Bedeutung des mittelalterlichen Königskanonikates', in *Ordnungen und formende Kräfte des Mittelalters* (Gottingen: Vandenhoeck & Ruprecht, 1991), 197. See also Jackson, *Ordines coronationis*, 1:1.

[12] Andrew W. Lewis, 'Anticipatory Association of the Heir in Early Capetian France', *American Historical Association* 83 (1978): 906–27, and Jean-François Lemarigner, *Le gouvernement royal aux premiers temps capétiens (987–1108)* (Paris: J. Picard, 1965), 25–6.

[13] Philippe Buc, 'Warum weniger die Handelnden selbst als eher die Chronisten das politische Ritual erzeugten – und warum es niemandem auf die wahre Geschichte ankam', in *Die Macht des Königs. Herrschaft in Europa vom Frühmittelalter bis in die Neuzeit*, ed. Bernhard Jussen (München: Berck, 2005), 27–37.

[14] For Charlemagne's coronation see Robert Folz, *Le couronnement impérial de Charlemagne. 25 décembre 800* (Paris: Gallimard, 1964); Rudolf Schieffer, 'Charlemagne and Rome', in *Early Medieval Rome and the Christian West*, ed. Julia M. H. Smith (Brill: Leiden, 2000), 279–95; Davis Valenti, 'L'iconografia del potere imperial: Carlo Magno come "Novus Constantinus". L'iconografia del potere', *Ikon* 5 (2012): 115–38; Janet L. Nelson, 'Warum es so viele Versionen von der Kaiserkrönung Karls des Grossen gibt', in *Die Macht des Königs*, ed. Bernhard Jussen (Munich: C. H. Beck, 2005), 38–55. On the conceptual implications of the imperial title rather than ritual developments of the ceremony see Henry Mayr-Harting, 'Charlemagne, the Saxons, and the Imperial

Louis the Pious in 813, before his death, in a church in Aachen, without the support of any bishop, in a ceremony in which Louis put the crown on his own head. If we believe the biographer Thegan's narration, Louis' would be the first European self-coronation.

> When the above-mentioned emperor understood that the day of his death was approaching – for he was very old – he summoned his son Louis to himself, along with his whole army, bishops, abbots, dukes, counts, and minor officials. He held a general assembly with them peacefully and honourably at the palace at Aachen, urging them to be faithful to his son and asking every one, from the greatest to the least, if it was agreeable to them that he give his dignity, that is, the imperial office, to his son Louis. They all responded joyfully that this was the counsel of God in this affair. That done, on the next Sunday he put on his regalia, placed a crown on his head, and processed forth decked out and adorned with such distinction as befitted him. He reached the church that he himself had built in a higher place than the other altars and was dedicated in honor of our Lord Jesus Christ. He ordered that a golden crown, different from the one he was wearing, be placed on that altar. After he and his son had prayed for a long time, he spoke to his son in the presence of the whole multitude of his bishops and magnates. First of all, he urged him to love and fear almighty God, to keep his commands in every way, to lead the churches of God, and to defend them from wicked men. He instructed him always to show unfailing mercy to his younger sisters and brothers and to his nephews and all his relatives. Then he told him to honor priests like fathers, to love the people like sons, to drive haughty and wicked men onto the path of salvation, to comfort monks, and to be a father to the poor. He instructed him to appoint faithful and God-fearing officers who would detest bribes. He was urged to dismiss no one from his office without due judgment and to show himself blameless at all times before God and the whole people. After speaking these and many other words to his son, in front of the crowd, he asked him if he wished to obey his instructions. He responded that he would willingly obey and that, with God's help, he would keep every precept that his father had given him. Then his father ordered him to pick up with his own hands the crown that was on the altar and to place it on his own head, as a remembrance of all the precepts that his father had given him. So he fulfilled his father's command. After this was done, they heard a solemn Mass and went back to the palace.[15]

Coronation of 800', *English Historical Review*, 111 (1996): 1113–33, and Henry Fichtenau, *L'Empire carolingien* (Paris: Payot, 1958), 72–102. For the context of these coronations see Wolfram Drews, 'Ideología y acceso al trono en época carolingia', in *Acceso al trono: Conceptión y ritualización* (Pamplona: Gobierno de Navarra, 2017), 37–62, and Matthias Becher, *Eid und Herrschaft. Untersunchungen zum Herrscherethos Karls des Grossen* (Sigmaringen: Jan Thorbecke, 1993); Myers, *Medieval Kingship*, 114–23.

[15] The English edition of the chronicle of Thegan is presented in Thomas F. X. Noble, 'Thegan, the Deeds of Emperor Louis', in Noble, ed., *Charlemagne and Louis the Pious: The Lives by Einhard, Notker, Ermoldus, Thegan, and the Astronomer* (Pennsylvania: Pennsylvania State University Press, 2012), 194–218, here 196–7 (the narration of Louis' coronation appears in chapter 6).

Thegan is the only source who recounts Louis' self-coronation, and he does seem well informed about the last days of Charlemagne. Yet three other biographers of Charlemagne and Louis (Einhard, Ermoldus and Astronomer) refer to Louis being crowned by his father. Einhard states that Charlemagne, at the very end of his life,

> solemnly assembled all the leaders of the Franks from his whole realms, and with the advice of all of them, he made his son consort in all his kingdom and heir to his imperial dignity. He crowned him and ordered that he be called emperor and augustus. His plan was accepted with great pleasure by all who were present, for he seemed to have been divinely inspired to look out for the well-being of his kingdom.[16]

Ermoldus records at the beginning of his Book 2 that Charlemagne 'placed a golden crown with jewels, the token of empire, on his son's head', reciting at the same time: 'Receive, son, with Christ Himself conferring it, my crown, and receive with it the symbol of empire too. May the One who confers upon you the height of honour also grant you the power to please Him.'[17] The Astronomer explains that Charlemagne spent the whole summer with his son to instruct him 'on those matters that he thought needed discussion, for instance, how he ought to live and to rule, how the realm should be organized and, once organized, maintained'. Then 'he admonished him and finally crowned him with an imperial diadem and informed him that with Christ's help he was going to have the highest power over all.'[18] The *Annales Regni Francorum* recounts that 'he [Charles] then held the general assembly and placed a crown on the head of his son Louis, king of Aquitaine, whom he had summoned to him in Aachen, and he made him his partner in the imperial name.'[19] Henry A. Myers concludes that 'when Charlemagne designated his son, Louis the Pious, as emperor, he saw to it that the coronation took place with no clergy bestowing the crown. In so doing, he showed how to his liking things should have been done on 25 December 800.'[20]

---

[16] Einhard, *The Life of Charles the Emperor*, in Noble, *Charlemagne and Louis the Pious*, 45 (chapter 30).

[17] Ermoldus Nigellus, *In Honor of Louis*, in Noble, *Charlemagne and Louis the Pious*, 144 (book 2).

[18] The Astronomer, *The Life of Emperor Louis*, in Noble, *Charlemagne and Louis the Pious*, 245 (chapter 20). On the Astronomer see Hans-Werner Goetz, 'The Perception of "Power" and "State" in the Early Middle Ages: The Case of the Astronomer's "Life of Louis the Pious"', in *Representations of Power in Medieval Germany, 800–1500*, ed. Simon MacLean and Björn Weiler (Turnhout: Brepols, 2006), 15–36.

[19] *Annales Regni Francorum*, quoted in de Jong, *The Penitential State*, 18.

[20] See Myers, *Medieval Kingship*, 120, who refers to François L. Ganshoff, *The Carolingians and the Frankish Monarchy* (Ithaca, NY: Cornell University Press, 1971), 48.

Louis, in turn, crowned his son Charles in 838. But these coronations lacked any liturgical or ecclesiastical features, as there was no unction or prayers referring to an existing liturgical scheme.[21] The way Thegan describes it ('after this was done, they heard a solemn Mass') shows the intention to separate the liturgical celebration from the ritual of coronation itself.

This shifting foundational period, begun in the coronation of 751, came to an end with the simultaneous anointing and coronation of Charles the Bald by the bishop in 848. This ceremonial innovation implied profound transformations regarding the idea of royal sanctity, as well as in its relationship with the ecclesiastical world.[22] With the fusion of the rites of anointment and coronation, the coronation ceremony of the Carolingian kings was sacralised and *liturgified*, as it stabilised itself. The royal investiture was monopolised by the bishops and began having tangible legal, constitutional and practical consequences for the history of the western part of the empire.[23] The bestowal of the authority of the Frankish sovereigns, and subsequently that of the greater part of Central and Northern European monarchs, would derive from beyond their own sphere of temporal and civil power, and fall under the spiritual and ecclesiastical power of the bishops. The unction was clearly a clerical monopoly: a king might have crowned another king, but the king had never anointed another king. While bishops have crowned kings, emperors have never ordained bishops.[24] The two rites, unction and coronation, were definitively fused after 848, constituting the two essential rites of royal investitures. Thus, royal investitures were definitively liturgified: 'Royal power became ritualized and Christianised', in Michael E. Moore's phrase.[25] As Simon Maclean summarises,

---

[21] Walter Ullmann, *Medieval Political Thought* (Harmondsworth: Penguin, 1965), 74.

[22] Félix Grat, Jeanne Vielliard and Suzanne Clémencet, eds., *Annals of St-Bertin* (Paris: Klincksieck, 1964), 848:66 (English edition: Janet L. Nelson, ed., *The Annals of St-Bertin* [Manchester: Manchester University Press, 1991]); Janet L. Nelson, *Charles the Bald* (London: Longman, 1992), 154–5, and Janet L. Nelson, 'Kingship, Law and Liturgy in the Political Thought of Hincmar of Rheims', *English Historical Review*, 92 (1977): 241–79; Guy Lanoë, 'L'Ordo de couronnment de Charles le Chauve a Sainte-Croix d'Orleans (6 Juin 848)', in *Kings and Kingship in Medieval Europe*, ed. Anne J. Duggan (London: King's College London Centre for Late Antique and Medieval Studies, 1993), 41–68.

[23] Nelson, *Politics and Ritual in Early Modern Europe*, 135. See also Dominique Alibert, 'Sacre royal et onction royale a l'époque carolingienne', *Cahiers de l'Institut d'Anthropologie Juridique* 1 (1998): 19–37, and Alibert, 'Procéder au sacre royal à l'époque carolingienne', *Cahiers de l'Institut d'Anthropologie Juridique* 13 (2006): 85–95.

[24] On the sacral function of bishops in this period see Ludger Körntgen and Dominik Wassenhoven, eds., *Patterns of Episcopal Power: Bishops in 10th and 11th Century Western Europe* (Berlin: De Gruyter, 2011).

[25] Michael E. Moore, *A Sacred Kingdom: Bishops and the Rise of Frankish Kingship, 300–850* (Washington, DC: Catholic University of America Press, 2001), 1.

The memory of the king's acquisition of his earthly kingdom, and later his entrance to its heavenly counterpart, was thus preserved at major royal churches, and often celebrated with a large-scale banquet provided for by the income from specially designated states. Such gestures reinforced the relationship between rulers and their ecclesiastical allies and made a conspicuous statement about the political resources of kings. In addition, they drew attention to the anointed character of Carolingian kingship: the ritual itself, based on biblical precedent and the ceremonies for the anointing of bishops, and also thought of as analogous to baptismal unction, was one of the fundamental characteristics of Carolingian rule, giving substance to the dynasty's political theology of a special relationship with God.[26]

This change inaugurates a new era of the ideology of the sovereignty of monarchs, which would henceforward be ecclesiastical in its formation, theocratic by nature and symbolic in its execution.[27] Yet it also created a deep historiographical confusion, since we spontaneously tend to identify any ceremony of ascension which does not fit with the original Carolingian model – projected to the French, English and German realms – as conventional, while others ritual forms such as the self-coronations are seen as non-conventional. This leads to misunderstandings in the application of the concept of 'sacrality' to the ceremonies of accession, which require a contextualised analysis and do not accommodate easily to generalisations.[28] In fact, I argue that conventionality and non-conventionality and sacrality and non-sacrality in rituals are not essentialist categories. Rather, they must be considered within the particular context in which they are performed.

Yet what happened in 848 for this momentous turn to be taken? It is clear that the work of some theologians and liturgists at the Carolingian court, chief among them Hincmar of Reims, had weighed heavily in the process, as they developed the idea of priestly mediation of temporal power.[29] This is an interesting nuance because, as Ernst Kantorowicz

---

[26] Simon MacLean, *Kingship and Politics in the Late Ninth Century: Charles the Fat and the End of the Carolingian Empire* (Cambridge: Cambridge University Press, 2003), 145 (see the section 'The Revolt of Hugh, September 885, and the Origins of "German" Royal Consecration', 144–60). The precedents of the interaction between bishops and kings from the fourth-century Gallic period to the break-up of the Carolingian Empire in about 850 may be followed in Patrick J. Geary, *Before France and Germany: The Creation and Transformation of the Merovingian World* (Oxford: Oxford University Press, 1988), chapter 4, and Moore, *A Sacred Kingdom*.

[27] Ullmann, *The Carolingian Renaissance and the Idea of Kingship*, 86–96, Nelson, 'The Lord's Anointed and the People's Choice', 144–5; Walter Ullmann, *The Growth of Papal Government in the Middle Ages* (London: Methuen, 1961), 445–6.

[28] Koziol, 'England, France and the Problem of Sacrality', 124–48.

[29] Nelson, *Politics and Ritual in Early Modern Europe*, 137–8; Bouman, *Sacring and Crowning*, 103, 107–26; Anneliese Sprengler, 'Die Gebete der Krönungsordines Hinkmars von Reims', *Zeitschrift für Kirchengeschichte* 63 (1950–1): 245–67.

notes, if the role of theologians and liturgists was key in the ninth century, from the twelfth century it was that of the canonists, in an evolution 'from liturgy to legal science'.[30] As Nelson shows,

> pursuing the implications of this subtle contrast, we might observe that where the lawyer deals in conflicts, operating with logic through nice verbal distinctions, the liturgist deals in communications, operating with faith through a symbolic code. In view of these differences, he who consults the early medieval *ordines* should be wary of imposing on the age of liturgy the preoccupations of an age of law.[31]

Some historians consider Hincmar of Reims a key figure in this discussion. He had written extensively on royal unction and its liturgical arrangement, and had declared before the consecration of Charles the Bald that the king had been 'crowned and consecrated to the Lord in the possession of the kingdom [of Lothringia] by the agency of the bishops'.[32] Hincmar further justified the fusion of unction and coronation when, in the specific prayer for the rite of unction, he used the coronation as a metaphor for the unction itself: 'The Lord crowns you with the crown of Glory' (*Coronet te dominus corona gloriae*).[33]

The Priestly Mediation in the Western Investitures

The idea of priestly mediation was slowly but surely incorporated into the theory and practice of the inauguration rites of Carolingian kings from the mid-ninth century. It gradually came to be reflected in both the spoken and written professions of faith and obedience that were being introduced into the West as a precondition of royal consecrations. The theory and the practice of priestly mediation was also becoming assimilated through the growing resemblance between rites of royal inauguration and corresponding episcopal ordinations, as well as through the progressive incorporation of the bishop as the ordinary minister of royal

---

[30] Kantorowicz, *King's Two Bodies*, 87–97.
[31] Nelson, *Politics and Ritual in Early Modern Europe*, 339.
[32] 'Non incongruum videtur istis venerabilibus episcopis, si vestrae unanimitati placet, ut in obtentu regni, unde vos ad illum sponte convenistis et vos ei commendastis, sacerdotali ministerio ante altare hoc coronetur ut sacra unctione Domino consecratur' (Hincmar of Reims on the consecration of Charles the Bald of 869, quoted in Nelson, *Politics and Ritual in Early Modern Europe*, 139).
[33] Alfred Boretius, ed., *Monumenta Germaniae Historica, Capitularia Regnum Francorum*. 2 vols. (Hannover: Impensis Bibliopolii Hahniani, 1883), 2:457, n. 302, quoted in Nelson, *Politics and Ritual in Early Modern Europe*, 295; Janet L. Nelson, 'Hincmar of Rims on King-Making: The Evidence of the Annales of St. Bertin, 861–882', in *Coronations: Medieval and Early Modern Monarchic Ritual*, ed. János M. Bak (Berkeley: University of California Press, 1990), 16–34, especially 22–6; Bouman, *Sacring and Crowning*, 8–9; O'Meara, *Monarchy and Consent*, 69–74.

coronations.[34] This tendency was becoming more firmly established above all in the Frankish, English and German kingdoms, effectively rendering the practice of self-coronation impossible in those kingdoms, though it would be tried out in other southern and eastern kingdoms, such as the Iberian ones.

The bishops thus came to be the visible mediators of divine will and the transmitters of the authority of temporal power, as demonstrated in the figures of Zadok and Nathan anointing King Solomon in the Bible miniature commissioned by Charles the Bald around 875 (Figure 17). This image confirms that Carolingian iconographic models convey the reality of facts rather than the ideal of images, in contrast to the Byzantine tradition, where the iconography of royal investitures displays a greater tendency to idealism and symbolism. This complex miniature is incorporated showing various scenes from the life of Solomon, who appears in the central one, sitting on a throne and wearing a crown. The different scenes show the procession in which the king is led to his royal consecration, the exercise of his wisdom in judgement (1 Kings 3:16–28), the escorting of Solomon mounted on David's mule to Gihon and, notably, his anointing by Zadok the priest and the prophet Nathan (1 Kings 1:39–40). In the consecration scene, in spite of a literal reference to the monarch of Israel, the figure is perfectly recognisable as a Carolingian king. The priest and the prophet signal their successors, the bishops who played an essential role in the coronation of Charles the Bald, as well as the people identified as the 'new Israel', the Franks.[35] This image reflects the new spirit implanted in the royal investitures of the Carolingian kings, which would have so much influence over the future of those rites, especially in France, Germany and England.

---

[34] The analysis of the parallels between the ceremonies of episcopal and royal ordinations is very useful here. On episcopal consecrations see Andrieu, *Les Ordines romani du haut moyen âge*; Michel Andrieu, 'Le Sacre épiscopal d'après Hincmar de Reims', *Revue d'Histoire Ecclésiastique* 48 (1953): 22–73; Albert Houssiau, 'La formation de la liturgie romaine du sacre épiscopal', *Collectanea Mechliniensia* 33 (1948): 276–84; Pierre Battiffol, 'La liturgie du sacre des évêques dans son evolution historique', *Revue Historie Ecclésiastica* 23 (1927): 733–63. See also Romà Barriga, 'La consagració episcopal en el Pontifical de Roda', *Analecta Sacra Tarraconensia* 38 (1965): 3–50, who emphasises the parallelism of the episcopal consecration with the coronation of the queens in the formula 'accipe coronam gloriae' (p. 29), and the analogies of the reception of the pontifical insignia such as the crosier and the ring with the king's reception of the royal insignia such as the sceptre and the crown (pp. 32–6). See also Woolley, *Coronation Rites*, 193–4. For a more general perspective, see the epigraph 'Die königliche Investitur der Bischöfe', in Hagen Keller, 'Die Investitur: Ein Beitrag zum Problem der "Staatssymbolik" im Hochmittelalter', *Frühmittelalterliche Studien* 27 (1993): 51–86, here 61–6, and Henry Parkes, *The Making of Liturgy in the Ottonian Church: Books, Music and Ritual in Mainz, 950–1050* (Cambridge: Cambridge University Press, 2015), 133–57 (epigraph 'Episcopal Liturgy').

[35] Nelson, *Politics and Ritual in Early Modern Europe*, viii.

The Sacralisation of Carolingian Accessions

Figure 17 *The Judgement of Solomon*, as described in I Kings 3:16–28. Solomon is led to his royal consecration (top left) and his anointment (1 Kings 1:39–40) (top right). Bible of San Paolo Fuori le Mura, fol. 188 v. Frontispiece to Proverbs. © Abbazia of San Paolo Fuori le Mura, Roma.

This ritual transformation, and its correlative iconographic reflection, is consistent with what had happened in Byzantium, where the relevant function of the patriarch of Constantinople acquired growing importance in the imperial investiture ceremony from the fifth century on. The investiture ritual was therefore increasingly considered an event with an ecclesiastical dimension and, perhaps more importantly, to have certain legal effects. This would also explain why, prior to the unction/coronation of Charles the Bald in 848, imperial coronations with the Pope or reigning emperor as ordinary ministers had been of a markedly ritual nature, but did not normally have legal effects. This chronology also squares with the one established by Koziol, who moreover bases his interpretation on Carolingian diplomas, enriching the heuristic perspective. He downplays the legal value of unction and coronation during the centuries of Carolingian rule, but points out that as time went on, they acquired a value entailing not only sanction but also legal force.[36] As Kantorowicz argues, legal power is more successful when it is strengthened by the force of aesthetics,

A charter, admittedly, does not become legally 'more valid' if furnished with a gold *bulla* in place of a seal of wax; but the importance of the issue becomes more obvious. This is true also of the laudes [regiae]. They do not imply an increase of the legal force of decision made, but they stress the weight of the decision. This weight is imponderable. But in the imponderables, then and now, the legal power is sometimes more effective than in legally constitutive enactments.[37]

However, the relationship between the constitutional effect (realised in their legal effects) and visual effect (realised in their liturgy) in the investiture ceremonies has to be seen in terms of concurrence rather competition. As Max Weber explains, we should say that these ceremonies were progressively gaining legal rather than charismatic dimension. Yet in a long-term approach, although the legal effect remained ever present, it was the ritual effect that gained in importance. This might explain why many coronation rites have been preserved essentially intact over the past ten centuries, as is the case with those of the English monarchs until the twentieth century and the French monarchs until the nineteenth, while its meaning has obviously changed a lot.[38] Finally, it is the visual effect (the

---

[36] Geoffrey Koziol, *The Politics of Memory and Identity in Carolingian Royal Diplomas* (Turnhout: Brepols, 2012), 66. See also Robert Henri Bautier, 'Sacres et couronnements sous les Carolingiens et les premiers Capétiens', *Annuaire-bulletin de la Société de l'histire de France* (1989): 7–56.

[37] Kantorowicz, *Laudes Regiae*, 83.

[38] For comparisons of coronation practices in England, France and Germany see Dale, *Inauguration and Liturgical Kingship*, and Koziol, 'England, France and the Problem of Sacrality', 124–48.

form) that prevails over the constitutional effects (the content). In fact, with the passing of time, the legal effects have been progressively separated from the investiture ceremony, which is no more than a sanction and confirmation of the legal effects that derive from hereditary succession or election by those holding that authority. This continues today, in the elections, proclamations and ceremonies of royal investiture and presidential proclamations of the majority of European monarchies.

Certainly, alternatives to priestly mediation were sought, such as the sovereign king crowning his successor (a custom with indubitable Byzantine resonances) or simply the king appearing crowned during the investiture ceremony – albeit having to remove it at certain points in the ritual, such as during unction. However, as time went on, the transmission of sovereignty through strictly extra-ecclesiastical mediation (above all the diverse forms of self-coronations) would come to appear clearly anomalous to the rite, as heterodox in its practice, and incoherent in its meaning. Once more, a new rite emerged as a natural expression of a new social reality, confirming that rites are not created or sustained artificially, but reflections of a dynamic social reality. As Bloch and Nelson point out, the 'rex ex nobilitate' engendered the 'rex thaumaturgo'.[39]

Parallel to this consolidation of episcopal mediation, but in a certain sense connected to it, the requirement for written professions was established in Visigothic Spain during the seventh century and also, in the ninth century, in the west Frankish kingdoms, in England and in Byzantium. Specialists have interpreted the consolidation of this practice as a response to the political crisis on the part of bishops, who were becoming more conscious of their own unity and responsibility. Of course, this tendency had an immediate and obvious consequence: a greater involvement of the bishops in temporal and political matters.[40] The synchrony between the introduction of the practice of royal unction and the requirement for written professions of faith becomes clear and shows two sides of the same coin: the increase of ecclesiastical influence in the generation of royal sovereignties.

The Effects of the Liturgification of Royal Investitures

One of the results of the liturgification of the investiture rite from the ninth century is the gradual introduction of liturgical *acclamations*, which

---

[39] Marc Bloch, *Les rois thaumaturges* (Paris: Colin, 1961); Nelson, *Politics and Ritual in Early Modern Europe*, 254.
[40] For the Visigothic and England case see Michael Richter, *Canterbury Professions* (Torquay: Devonshire, 1973). For the Frankish case see Nelson, *Politics and Ritual in Early Modern Europe*, 143–55.

are a transposition and a carrying over of formerly pagan investitures. The *laudes* then appear as the ecclesiastical antitype of pagan acclamations, representing the church's sanction and assent to the coronation. Once again, the ritual and visual effect seems to predominate over the specifically legal, its nature being closer to an act of recognition than to an act of constitution.

The coronation proper – that is, the act of placing the crown on the king's head – was likewise included in the liturgical performance; and the handing over of the royal insignia, ring and sword, sceptre and orb, was also liturgicized until the donning of almost every coronation garment became subject to the rites of the Church. Against the background of this evolution, it appears consistent that the formerly profane electoral acclamations of army and people, senate or magnates, should likewise have been liturgicized or should have found an antitype in the divine service. The acclamation as a constitutive and legal act on the part of the people was supplemented by an ecclesiastico-legal act, namely by an acclamation on the part of the Church. This was precisely the function of the laudes at the coronation: they represent the sanction and assent of the acclaiming Church.[41]

The *laudes* thus mitigated the effects of the reduction or even the elimination of the actual participation of the people that resulted from the introduction of ecclesiastical mediation. As a consequence, the acclamations during the ceremony itself, in the sacred place, known as *laudes regiae*, were perhaps introduced to mitigate the disappearance of popular participation. Although the participation of the people in royal investiture had ceased to have legal effects, popular acclamations at least made a show of their presence, having at least a psychological, visual and ritual effect.[42]

Along with all this development, scholars have further raised the question of the gradual divergence that occurred between the investiture rites of the Western kingdoms and those of Byzantium, beyond their common framework of theology, beliefs and Christian practices.[43] This divergence explains the different perception of self-coronations (anomalies of the coronation rite) in the two spheres: in the West they came to be practised ceremonially and, by contrast, in the East they remained solely at the symbolic-iconographic level. In my judgement, the key to this divergence was their different perceptions on priestly mediation. The introduction of the ceremony of coronation of the imperial heir by the reigning emperor in Byzantium served to alleviate the increasingly active participation of the patriarchate in the imperial coronation ceremony. However, it could not extend its effects very far and soon disappeared from the ceremonial. The patriarchate then assumed the monopoly of the ministry of the ceremony,

[41] Kantorowicz, *Laudes Regiae*, 78–9.
[42] Kantorowicz, *Laudes Regiae*, 79, and Schramm, *A History of the English Coronation*, 169.
[43] Nelson, 'Symbols in Context'; Nelson, *Politics and Ritual in Early Modern Europe*, 259–81.

and could therefore justify the ascension of a usurper, the first member of a new family, or of the emperor who had de facto succeeded a member of his own family but where the formal transaction had not taken place in the lifetime of his predecessor.

Up to this point, the development of East and West appear parallel, given that ecclesiastical mediation began to be imposed in both, patriarchal in the former and archiepiscopal in the latter. However, here the distinction between opposites becomes especially important: political/religious, lay/ecclesiastical and profane/sacred. Respecting each dualism in its own nature enables us to understand that the patriarch becoming the ordinary minister of the coronation (ecclesiastical level) does not imply a sacralisation of the rite (sacred level), given that sacralisation occurs only when the unction is introduced. The figure of the patriarch functions in Byzantium simply as a transposition of the figure of the emperor when crowning his successor in life, and it therefore continues to be an essentially political rite. The Byzantine emperor was also the head of the political and ecclesiastical hierarchies (as is reflected in some Justinian mosaics in Ravenna) and could even conduct various liturgical ceremonies commensurate with priestly dignity.[44] The patriarch would also begin to fulfil those same functions, effectively capturing – above all at moments of interregnum – the heights of the political and ecclesiastical sphere.

Thus, at the moment of coronation, the patriarch transcends his priestly function to enter the political sphere, so making the coronation a *religious* act with political implications, but, paradoxically, without becoming essentially *sacred*, as there is no royal unction. This demonstrates the fact that the Hippodrome, the place where coronations took place during the first centuries of Byzantium, effectively functioned as a place as religious as the Hagia Sophia church, given that both were centres of imperial worship. The difference between the two places did not lie therefore in the political/religious category (as both were religious centres that held political ceremonies), but rather in the sacred (Hagia Sophia)/profane (the Hippodrome). Nelson concludes, using concepts borrowed from modern anthropology, above all in Douglas:

If then the coronation of a Byzantine emperor was a religious act, the contrast between eastern and western practice should no longer be sought in a crude distinction between religious and secular, but rather, in differing conceptions of the sacred and the profane.[45]

---

[44] Edmund R. Leach, 'Melchisedech and the emperor: Icons of subversion and orthodoxy', *Proceedings of the Royal Anthropological Institute for 1972* (1972): 5–14, here, 12–13.
[45] Nelson, *Politics and Ritual in Early Modern Europe*, 269–70, and Mary Douglas, *Purity and Danger* (London: Routledge, 1966).

This distinction has in addition the virtue of explaining the different chronology for the introduction of the rite of unction in East and West, and for its discard: whereas in Byzantium unction did not arrive until the twelfth century, and became consolidated from the thirteenth century on (in a context that was already fully Latinised), in the West it was introduced much sooner, as early as the seventh century in Visigothic Spain, from the unction/coronation of Charles the Bald in the mid-ninth century, becoming gradually more widespread in the royal coronation ceremonials and establishing itself as a permanent fixture, while in some other European kingdoms these ceremonies were not practised at all. This would explain too how in Byzantium there was such a marked divorce between the reality (the coronation enacted by the patriarch) and what was represented (the coronation of the emperor by Christ, the so-called symbolic or heavenly coronation), whereas in the West they would even experience examples of the ritual practice of self-coronation (effectively negating priestly mediation), as in the cases of the fourteenth- and fifteenth-century Iberian kings of Aragon, Castile and Navarra.

Another explanation for the maintenance of the non-sacral framework of the investiture ceremony in the first centuries of the Byzantine Empire might be the persistence of the republican ideology of the *principality* from Augustus to Constantine. Indeed, there is scant evidence for inauguration rituals in the empire from the first to fourth centuries. The survival of republicanism would be evident in the continuity of the theory of the imperial *civilitas*: the emperor had to act as though he was the republican leader, *primus inter pares* of citizens, and therefore no special solemnity was required in his inauguration. This republican tradition was salient in the eastern empire, while the decline of the western empire had the effect, paradoxically, of reviving the Hellenistic monarchical tradition in emerging Western kingdoms and there was thus a greater sacralisation of the royal investiture ceremonies there, and a greater presence of priestly mediation.[46] Once the effect of paganisation had been overcome among the Germanic peoples, a gradual ritualisation and liturgification of the coronation ceremony occurred in the various realms, beginning with Visigothic Spain, thus consolidating its effective sacralisation. Nelson explains this long-term development in these terms:

If the delay in the ritualisation of ruler-making in the empire was caused by the persistence of a rival ideology [paganism], in the post-Roman west a similar and

---

[46] Nelson, *Politics and Ritual in Early Modern Europe*, 262. See also Norman H. Baynes, 'Eusebius and the Christian Empire', *Byzantine Studies and Other Essays* (London: University of London, 1955), 168ff., and Dvornik, *Early Christian and Byzantine Political Philosophy*, 2:706–10 and 848–9.

more prolonged delay occurred for other reasons. One was the barbarians' consciousness of inhabiting, in [Karl] Hauck's phrase, 'late antique marginal cultures'; another was the existence of an ideological vacuum, filled only, I suggest, when barbarian elites had fully appropriated (and in so doing remoulded) Christianity. This happened in Visigothic Spain precociously in the seventh century, in England and Gaul in the eighth and ninth centuries, and in east Francia in the tenth century. The outcome so far as royal inaugurations were concerned was broadly common to all these realms: the local hierarchy took over the essential procedures of king-making, made of them a liturgical rite whose central act was the anointing, preceded by the acceptance of conditions by the new office-holder (a foreshadowing, this, of the later coronation oath) and followed by an investiture with weapons and other insignia, usually including a crown.[47]

This progressive ritualisation and sacralisation of the royal investiture ceremony in the West, in counterpoint to the persistence of its politicisation in Byzantium, helps us to understand the opprobrium created by the self-investitures of Roger II in Palermo in 1130 and Frederick II Hohenstaufen in Jerusalem in 1229. These rituals were seen as a transgression, a variation or even an *anomaly* in the rite, to use the expression coined by the anthropologists.[48] Several reasons explain the reluctance to Roger's and Frederick's investitures, the connection of the papacy in the creation of these kingdoms among them.[49] Yet the level of scandal decreased notably in the Iberian self-coronations by Alfonso XI of Castile in Burgos, Peter IV the Ceremonious of Aragon in Zaragoza and Charles III of Navarra in Pamplona, because of the limited influence of Carolingian ceremonials models there, and the traditional Iberian realms' aversion to any ecclesiastical mediation.

Another way of reading the difference between East and West, and so their different ways of reacting to self-coronations, is that the emperor in Byzantium was 'found rather than made', whereas in the Carolingian and Ottonian monarchies the king was *made by* the sacred ritual of unction. Thus, the ideal of rebirth is intimately related in the West with the conception of royal unction.[50] In the West, the consecration of the king was considered a collective act officiated by the bishop as the clerical guarantee of divine grace. It cannot be mere coincidence that the same period that

---

[47] Nelson, *Politics and Ritual in Early Modern Europe*, 265.
[48] Rappaport, *Ritual and Religion*, 33.
[49] Simon John, 'The Papacy and the Establishment of the Kingdoms of Jerusalem, Sicily and Portugal: Twelfth-Century Papal Political Thought on Incipient Kingship', *Journal of Ecclesiastical History* 68(2) (2017): 221–59.
[50] Nelson, *Politics and Ritual in Early Modern Europe*, 271. The idea of the *rebirth* of the king through the ceremony of investment has been analysed from the anthropology of religion in works such as Mircea Eliade, *Rites and Symbols of Initiation* (New York: Harper and Row, 1958), and from the anthropology of power such as Foucault, *On the Government of the Living*, lesson 20, February 1980.

witnessed the episcopal assumption of royal coronation ministries also saw the bishops' elevation to the status of a corporate social elite of *oratores*. This was how the clerics became separated from laymen through the education system that formed them, the exercise of a specific right, the monopoly of the language of knowledge and, above all, the control of the liturgy.[51] The design and exercise of the liturgy made it possible to redefine relations with the empire, founding an ideology that prevented the Carolingian emperor from legitimising his predominance over the priesthood.[52] This would explain why the coronations of heirs by the emperor were waning in the West in the post-Carolingian era. It is not by chance either that the disappearance of this custom is strictly related, chronologically speaking, and most likely conceptually too, with the addition of the rite of unction in the royal investiture ceremonies in the West.[53]

All this would also be coherent with the belated incorporation of unction in Byzantium, confirming that the ecclesiastical hierarchy was the *longa manus* of the emperor, while the importance of the unction's earlier introduction in the West demonstrates exactly the opposite: that the hierarchy did have some real weight in the essential tension between the temporal and spiritual spheres. For this reason, the practice of ritual self-coronations had a real effect on subsequent politics (basically in their emphasis on the autonomy of the temporal in relation to the spiritual, as in the case of Alfonso XI of Castile, Peter IV of Aragon and Charles III of Navarra), whereas in Byzantium they made little sense, remaining at the level of symbolic self-coronations, on a merely iconographic plane.

And here is where we need to turn to another of the essential sources for the analysis of royal investitures: the function and meaning of the ceremonial *ordines*. During the pontificate of John VIII (872–82) important changes took place in coronation ceremonies of the emperors, as noted in the *Ordines Romani*.[54] Thereafter, in the *ordines* composed at the end of

---

[51] See the chapter 'Vox auctoritatis: The Carolingian Liturgy of Authority', in Ildar H. Garipzanov, *The Symbolic Language of Authority in the Carolingian World (c. 751–877)* (Leiden: Brill, 2008), 43–100.

[52] Ullmann, *Medieval Political Thought*, 58–77.

[53] Nelson, *Politics and Ritual in Early Modern Europe*, 271–2. Jacques Le Goff, 'Note sur société tripartite, idéologie monarchique et renouveau économique dans la chrétienté du IXe au XIIe siècle', *L'Europe au IX au XI siècle*, ed. Tadeusz Manteuffel and Aleksander Gieysztor (Warsaw: Varsovie Panstwowe Wydawn Naukowe, 1968), 63ff.; D. B. Loomis, '*Regnum* and *Sacerdotium* in the Early Eleventh Century', in *England before the Conquest*, ed., Peter Clemoes et al. (Cambridge: Cambridge University Press, 1971), 129ff. See also the confirmation of this idea in the rubrics of the early medieval *ordines* of coronation in Bouman, *Sacring and Crowning*, 165ff.

[54] Percy E. Schramm, 'Die Krönung bei den Westfranken und Angelsachsen von 878 bis zum 1000', *Zeitschrift der Savigny-Stiftung für Rechtsgeschichte. Kanonistische Abteilung* 23 (1934): 235–42.

the ninth century, the ministers for the rites of unction and the coronation are different: the former is administered by three bishops and the latter by the Pope himself. The Pope thus reserves the final part of the ceremony to emphasise that the crown, which comes from God, is mediated solely by the supreme pontiff. In addition, the words accompanying the gesture of coronation (the form of the sacrament), also change, indicating their 'quasi-sacramental' nature (the content of the sacrament): instead of the traditional formulation 'accipe coronam', the formulation now used is 'accipe signum gloriae in nomine patris et filii et spiritus sancti'.[55] As for the unction, there is another change that emphasises the pre-eminence of the priest over the emperor: it is no longer performed with the holy oil of chrism, but with natural oil, which is then applied to the right arm and between the shoulders, and no longer to the head. This change is contemporaneous with the introduction, in Roman liturgy, of the Gallican rite of unction of bishops, applied with holy chrism oil in place of natural oil, and applied to the head and not to the arms or shoulders. Thus only the Gallican rite of episcopal unction, and not that of the king or emperor, is considered a true sacrament.[56]

In conclusion, from the mid-ninth century, there is a liturgification of the ceremony of royal investiture, a historical event of enormous consequence and considerable continuity throughout the centuries, especially in French and English traditions. Attempts of self-coronations were viewed thus in those particular traditions as a transgressive challenge of de-liturgification of the investiture ceremony. Nelson concludes: 'Hincmar made coronation, alongside anointing, permanently part of the ecclesiastical procedures of king-making. In West Francia the "liturgification" of enthronement had followed by about 900.'[57] Although, in dealing with Carolingians, it is always difficult to discern what part of this heritage was specifically Carolingian and what was the fruit of its appellation to classical and biblical tradition, the consolidation of the unction ceremony, coupled with the coronation, bequeathed a sacred character to the kings and emperors, who could not be considered henceforth mere laymen.[58] But the relationship with the Pope and the bishops was not

---

[55] Ullmann, *The Growth of Papal Government in the Middle Ages*, 226–7.
[56] Ullmann, *The Growth of Papal Government in the Middle Ages*, 227–8.
[57] For the meaning and function of liturgical *ordines* for the consecration of kings see Nelson, 'Ritual and Reality in the Early Medieval Ordines'; Janet L. Nelson, 'Ritual and Reality in the Early Medieval Ordines', in *The Materials, Sources, and Methods of Ecclesiastical History*, ed. Derek Baker (London: Blackwell, 1975), 41–52; Nelson, *Ritual and Politics in Early Modern Europe*, 329–39.
[58] Weiler, 'Crown-Giving and King-Making', 86. See also Matthew Innes, 'The Classical Tradition in the Carolingian Renaissance: Ninth-Century Encounters with Suetonius', *International Journal of the Classical Tradition* 3 (1997): 265–82, and Gabrielle M. Spiegel,

symmetrical: while the emperor had to be anointed by the Pope or the bishops, the emperor could not ordain bishops, all of which impeded any attempt at transgression of ecclesiastical mediation.[59] However, things were developing in a slightly different way in the eastern and western parts of the Carolingian empire, leading to a different situation with the establishment of the new Anglo-Saxon and Ottonian dynasties.

'The Reditus Regni ad Stirpem Karoli Magni: A New Look', *French Historical Studies* 7 (1971): 145–74.

[59] Allen Brent, 'The Investiture Controversy: An Issue in Sacramental Theology?', *Ephemerides Theologicae Lovanienses* 63 (1987): 59–89, here 83.

6 Anglo-Saxon and Ottonian Christocentrism

The liturgification and sacralisation of royal investitures during the Carolingian period had ritual-ceremonial and symbolic-iconographic effects. In the Anglo-Saxon and Ottonian period, from the mid-tenth century, this transformation was enriched with new conceptions of kingship, notably the assumption of the *Christus Rex* model. Iconographic messages were consistent with liturgical meanings in Anglo-Saxon and Ottonian theory of Christocentric kingship. These new ideas and practices then spread following a specific liturgical and iconographic programme, leaving generous evidence: royal diplomas, theological and liturgical commentaries, ceremonial investiture ordos and miniatures.[1]

At this time a durable interchange and transference developed between Anglo-Saxon and Ottonian models and meanings.[2] The parallels between the two *ordines* of King Edgar and the Mainz, and the transferences of the *Christus Rex* images, were manifest in the late tenth and early eleventh

---

[1] For this chapter, see especially Ludger Körntgen, 'Zur Ikonographie ottonisch-frühsalischer Herrscherbilder', in *Königsherrschaft und Gottes Gnade. Zu Kontext und Funktion sakraler Vorstellungen in Historiographie und Bildzeugnissen der ottonisch-frühsalischen Zeit* (Berlin: Akademie Verlag, 2001), 178–277; Körntgen, 'Das Bild des Königs und das Bild Christi', in *Königsherrschaft und Gottes Gnade*, 297–321; Robert Deshman, *Eye and Mind: Collected Essays in Anglo-Saxon and Early Medieval Art* (Kalamazoo: Western Michigan University, 2010); Deshman, 'Christus Rex', 367–405; Kantorowicz, *King's Two Bodies*, 42–86; Mayr-Harting, *Ottonian Book*. See also Percy E. Schramm, 'Das Herrscherbild in der Kunst des frühen Mittelalters', *Vorträge der Bibliothek Warburg* II (1922–3), 1: 145–224, and Lothar Bornscheuer, *Miseriae Regum. Untersuchungen zum Krisen- und Todesgedanken in den herrschaftstheologischen Vorstellungen der ottonisch-salischen Zeit* (Berlin: De Gruyter, 1968).

[2] Deshman, 'Christus Rex' (section 'The Relations between Anglo-Saxon England and Ottonian Germany', 390–404); Timothy Reuter, 'The Making of England and Germany, 850–1050: Points of Comparison and Difference', in Reuter, *Medieval Polities and Modern Mentalities* (Cambridge: Cambridge University Press, 2006), 284–99. On the debate on the parallels between tenth- and eleventh-century Anglo-Saxon and Ottonian see Ludger Körntgen, 'Introduction', in *Patterns of Episcopal Power: Bishops in 10th and 11th Century Western Europe*, ed. Ludger Körntgen and Dominik Wassenhoven (Berlin: De Gruyter, 2011), 11–16, who argues that, beyond the accuracy or eventual artificiality of this resemblance, 'we do not compare something given but we use the comparative approach in order to get something' (13).

centuries in Anglo-Saxon England and Ottonian Germany. Both territories share a strong Christocentric character, perceptible in the heavy emphasis on Christ's priestly kingship in the miniatures of illuminated books. Christ is invested with attributes of kingship and priesthood in order to increase his resemblances to his temporal image, the terrestrial king. This interchange of ceremonial and iconographic models between Anglo-Saxon and Ottonian motifs should not be seen in terms of the direction of the influence or the degree of originality. Rather, it must be conceived as 'a complex political and artistic dialogue existing between the two countries. Each nation was independently aware of the heritage while nonetheless being influenced by more recent innovations in the other'.[3]

The New Ceremonials: Fixing Liturgification

In the second half of the tenth century, an important consolidation occurred of the ecclesiastical mediation in the rituals of investiture on both sides of the Carolingian states. This evolution may be clearly observed through the liturgical sources, especially the Ottonian ordo of Mainz or Ratold (around 980) and the Anglo-Saxon ordo of King Edgar, known also as the 'English Second Recension' (end of the tenth century).[4]

The ordo of Mainz is particularly detailed on the new ideas of kingship promoted by Ottonian rulers on the relationship between Christ and the emperor.[5] We find in this ordo the theoretical foundations of the motifs of Christological and ruler imagery developed at the time.[6] The king is the *vicarius* and the *typus Christi*. He is anointed following the example of Christ and bears his name. The source of the temporal ruler's authority is Christ's royalty. As Christ is the ruler of the heavenly kingdom, the king is the ruler of the terrestrial kingdom by communion with Christ. Christ is the *Rex Regum*, king of kings. This title has deep meaning since it implies that the Ottonian rulership was imperial in nature.

---

[3] Deshman, 'Christus Rex', 403.
[4] A discussion of parallels and differences between these ordos and among other ceremonials of the tenth to twelfth centuries, and their content and form, is presented in Dale, *Inauguration and Liturgical Kingship*, 50–115.
[5] Jackson, *Ordines coronationis*, 1:27–8; Vogel and Elze, *Le pontifical*, 1:246–59, 266–9.
[6] On the theory of kingship and the liturgical developments of the ordo of Mainz see Henry Parkes, *The Making of Liturgy in the Ottonian Church: Books, Music and Ritual in Mainz, 950–1050* (Cambridge: Cambridge University Press, 2015), 94–100; Dale, *Inauguration and Liturgical Kingship*, chapters 2 and 3; Schramm, *Kaiser, Könige und Päpste*, 3:59–107; Deshman, 'Christus Rex', 387–8. See also Eric Palazzo, *Les sacramentaires de Fulda. Étude sur l'iconographie et la liturgie à l'époque ottonienne* (Münster: Aschendorff Verlag, 1994).

The quasi-sacerdotal character of the ruler is emphasised in the ordo by the fact that, just as Christ is the mediator between God and man, so the king is the mediator between the clergy and the people. While the bishops are the shepherds of souls *in interioribus*, the king participates as the episcopal minister *in exterioribus* as a *defensor* of the church and the *regnator* and *executor* of the kingdom.[7] Nevertheless, the ordo carefully reserved the priestly privilege exclusively for the clergy, and only the clergy can *make* the ruler – and there is no double direction in this attribute, since the ruler cannot make priests.

This particular point will have notable ceremonial implications, fixing the German tradition of the ecclesiastical mediation of the rituals of unction and coronation within the ritual of royal investiture. The quasi-sacerdotal nature of Ottonian kingship, as well as the evident spiritual pre-eminence of the higher clerical orders over the ruler, is accurately depicted in the portrait of Henry II in the Uta Lectionary. In that image, Christ wears the stola in the fashion of the bishop or priest, but Henry II wears his like a deacon, a lower clerical order that does not possess priestly powers.[8] The decisive role of the ecclesiastics as mediators between Christ and the kings was iconographically and theoretically established at the end of the tenth century, and this will have prolonged ritual and symbolic consequences, particularly in the territories of Germany, France and England.[9]

The liturgical developments and symbolic meanings of the Ottonian ordo of Mainz parallel the almost contemporary Anglo-Saxon ordo of King Edgar, which was conceived for the king's investiture in 973.[10] This ordo confirms the analogies between Christ and the king, and the mediator function of the ecclesiastics. Thus, beyond its evident synchrony, the parallels between the *ordines* of Edgar and Mainz are evident. They strengthen the model of Christ-centred kingship and stress the idea that the king mediates between the clergy and the people just as Christ does between God and man. Ottonian and Anglo-Saxon ruler theology are

---

[7] Vogel and Elze, *Le pontifical*, 255–9.   [8] Deshman, 'Christus Rex', 388.

[9] Timothy Reuter questions the stereotype of 'Reichskirchensystem', which leads to the assumption that the Ottonian ruler recruited his ecclesiastical staff for political tasks, in order to control the system: Timothy Reuter, 'The "Imperial Church System" of the Ottonian and Salian Rulers. A Reconsideration', *Journal of Ecclesiastical History* 33 (1982): 347–74.

[10] For the ordo of Edgar, see J. Armitage Robinson, 'The Coronation Order in the Tenth Century', *Journal of Theological Studies* 19 (1918): 56–72; Ward, 'The Coronation Ceremony in Medieval England'; Paul L. Ward, 'An Early Version of the Anglo-Saxon Coronation Ceremony', *English Historical Review* 57 (1942): 345–61. On the connections among Anglo-Saxon iconographic programme, monastic ideas and Edgar's coronation ordo see Robert Deshman, '*Benedictus Monarcha et Monachus*: Early Medieval Ruler Theology and the Anglo-Saxon Reform', in *Eye and Mind*, 104–36, here 135.

closely linked by the content of these two almost contemporary ceremonials. With little differences, 'the Edgar *ordo* derived many of its most emphatically Christ-centered features from the slightly earlier Ottonian Mainz *ordo*.'[11] These ideas of Christ-centred kingship were explicitly stated in the council celebrated around King Egfrid's royal anointing in 679.[12]

These two ordos served as the foundation of the development of coronation rites in the next centuries in Germany and England. During the Ottonian era some small variations in the rite of royal investiture can be seen, although none of them would amount to an essential change. The use of the liturgical *ordines* involved certain continuity and consolidation of the rite.[13] The ceremonial of Otto I clearly illustrates how the central moment of the ceremony's sacredness occurs at the precise moment of coronation.[14] The diadem symbolises the glory of the sanctity assigned to the sovereign with the coronation. The king participates in the priestly ministry *in exterioribus* (recalling the denomination of Constantine as *episkopos tôn ektôs*).[15] He also appears as the representative of Christ on earth given that, in the final part of the coronation, the king is proclaimed *mediator Dei et hominum* ('mediator between God and men').[16]

Ritual narrative sources from this time function as a complement of the liturgical ordos. Widukind of Corvey narrates the coronation ceremony of Otto I (936).[17] Widukind describes the entrance procession to the church, the anointing and the imposition of the crown: all the gestures of ecclesiastical power are recognised as necessary and legitimate, confirming the regal dignity that had previously been acknowledged through a ritual pact with

---

[11] Deshman, 'Christus Rex', 402.
[12] On this council, see Frank M. Stenton, *Anglo-Saxon England* (Oxford: Oxford University Press, 1971), 214ff., and William A. Chaney, *The Cult of Kingship in Anglo-Saxon England* (Berkeley: University of California Press, 1970), 252ff.
[13] Vogel and Elze, *Le pontifical*, 3:59–103.
[14] Giovanni Isabella, 'Modelli di regalità a confronto. L'ordo coronationis region di Magonza e l'incoronazione regia di Ottone I di Widukindo di Corvey', in *Forme di potere nel pieno medioevo (secc. VIII–XII). Dinamiche e rappresentazioni*, ed. Giovanni Isabella (Bologna: Clueb, 2006), 39–56.
[15] Eusebius Caesariensis, *De vita Constantini*, ed. Friedhelm Winkelmann (Berlin: Akademie, 1991), 128, Book IV, Chapter 24.
[16] Vogel and Elze, *Le pontifical*, 1:257–8, rr. 22–6.
[17] Widukind, *Rerum gestarum Saxonicarum libri tres*, 2.1, ed. Han-Eberhard Lohmann and Paul Hirsch, *Monumenta Germaniae Historica*, SSrG 60 (Hannover: Hahniani, 1935), 63–6. See also Hagen Keller, 'Widukinds Bericht über die Aachener Wahl und Krönung Ottos I', *Frühmittelalterliche Studien* 29 (1995): 390–453. For the question of the narration of the Ottonian rites and their preservation in collective memory see Warner, 'Ritual and Memory in the Ottonian Reich', 255–83, Körntgen, *Königsherrschaft und Gottes Gnade*, 121–36, and Warner, 'Thietmar of Merseburg on Rituals of Kingship', 53–76. A critical edition of Thietmar's chronicle appears in *Die Chronik des Bischofs. Thietmar von Merseburg und ihre korveier Überarbeitung*, ed. Robert Holtzmann (Berlin: Weidmannsche Verlagsbuchhandlung, 1955).

the magnates.[18] A century later, the coronation of Henry II (1014) introduced other changes resulting from the adoption of a new ordo whose formulations had been inserted into the Romano-Germanic pontifical of Mainz around 980.[19] This new era is clearly marked by a greater need for priestly mediation. The papal origin of imperial authority is emphasised through a number of ceremonial details: the emperor is called 'electus'; the emperor has to kiss the Pope's feet; the Pope proclaims the emperor as a son of the church; the emperor's faith is assessed via an official exam (*scrutinium*) by the Lateran bishops; and finally, the Pope inducts the emperor into the office of cleric, but not priest, investing him with the tunic, dalmatic, cope and mitre. Ullmann concludes that this new ordo constitutes the bridge between the age of Stephen II, initiator of the papal hierocratic ideology, and the orders of subsequent coronations that would consolidate this ideology through careful ceremonials carrying a strong symbolic charge and involving a growing episcopal participation and mediation in the imperial and royal investiture ceremony.[20]

Anglo-Saxon Images: Representing Christification

An intensive iconographic Christological programme spread in Anglo-Saxon and Ottonian territories, in addition to the mentioned *ordines*.[21] Anglo-Saxon developments were pioneers here, mostly because of the work of Bishop Aethelwold (963–84).[22] He commissioned a luxurious

---

[18] Isabella, 'Modelli di regalità', 54.
[19] Jackson, *Ordines coronationis*, 1:27–8; Vogel and Elze, *Le pontifical*, 1:246–61, 266–9.
[20] Ullmann, *The Growth of Papal Government in the Middle Ages*, 253–61; G. Lanoé, 'Les ordines de couronnment (930–1050): retour au manuscrit', in *Le Roi de France et son royaume autour de l'an mil* (Paris: Picard, 1992), 66–72; Vogel and Elze, *Le pontifical*, 1:246–69; Eric Palazzo, 'La liturgie du sacre', in *Le Sacre Royal a L'epoque De Saint-Louis*, ed. Jacques Le Goff, Eric Palazzo, Jean-Claude Bonne and Marie-Noël Collette (Paris: Gallimard, 2001), 37–89; Stefan Weinfurter, 'Authority and Legitimation of Royal Policy and Action', in *Medieval Concepts of the Past: Ritual, Memory, Historiography*, ed. Gerd Althoff, Johannes Fried and Patrick J. Geary (Cambridge: Cambridge University Press, 2003), 19–38; Hagen Keller, 'Die Investitur: Ein Beitrag zum Problem der "Staatssymbolik" im Hochmittelalter', *Frühmittelalterliche Studien* 27 (1993): 51–86.
[21] I am going to focus here on the active iconographic programme promoted by Anglo-Saxon bishops, but their textual production related to their own episcopal function is also prominent: Joyce Hill, 'Two Anglo-Saxon Bishops at Work. Wulfstan, Leofric and Cambridge, Corpus Christi College MS 190', in *Patterns of Episcopal Power: Bishops in 10th and 11th Century Western Europe*, ed. Ludger Körntgen and Dominik Wassenhoven (Berlin: De Gruyter, 2011), 145–61. For the concept of kingship in the Anglo-Saxon period see William A. Chaney, *The Cult of Kingship in Anglo-Saxon England* (Manchester: Manchester University Press, 1970) and J. M. Wallace-Hadrill, *Early Germanic Kingship in England and on the Continent* (Oxford: Oxford University Press, 1971).
[22] Robert Deshman, *The Benedictional of Aethelwold* (Princeton, NJ: Princeton University Press, 1995).

Figure 18 Maiestas Domini. London, British Library, MS Add. 49598, fol. 70 r. © The British Library Board.

Benedictional, kept in the British Library of London, from his cathedral scriptorium at Winchester. An image of the enthroned Christ with a gold diadem upon his head opens the text (Figure 18).

This image marks a decisive landmark in the consolidation of the Christological analogy of the kingship, since this Anglo-Saxon initial appears to be the earliest known representation in which Christ wears either a royal diadem or crown. This crucial symbolic shift merits a little historical digression, because one may reasonably question the originality of these representations of a crowned Christ in late tenth-century Anglo-Saxon iconographies and in the eleventh-century Ottonian versions.

The concept of the kingship of Christ was one of the oldest in Christianity, and one conveyed in literary and artistic representations.[23] The representations of Christ as king began to appear in the fourth century. Christ was depicted engaged in imperial ceremonies and associated with imperial attributes.[24] Yet these representations emphasised the theme of victory rather than the fact of kingship, so that the proper attribute in which Christ was crowned was the wreath or fillet rather than the royal diadem or crown. Sometimes the wreath was given by the hand of God, a representation which connects with the discussion in Chapter 3. In addition, in early Christian art the wreath also served as a symbol of triumphal martyrdom.[25] But in the tenth- and eleventh-century Anglo-Saxon and Ottonian portraits, Christ is depicted with a diadem, which was the insigne par excellence of temporal rule from the Hellenistic period.[26] For the early Christian artists and audience, to represent Christ wearing the diadem on his head would have associated him directly with temporal rulership and thus diminish his omnipotent heavenly kingship. Indeed, as Deshman notes, 'early Christian artists were content to imply rather than state the kingship of Christ.'[27]

This tradition was continued by Byzantine artists in the Greek East and by Carolingians in the Latin West. The Carolingians used the Old Testament as the predominant model of temporal kingship – the royal office was inspired primarily by stories of kings such as David and Solomon –

---

[23] For the origins of the idea of the kingship of Christ in early Christianity, crucial to understanding this chapter, see Per Beskow, *Rex Gloriae: The Kingship of Christ in the Early Church* (Stockholm: Almqvist & Wiksell, 1962).
[24] Grabar, *L'Empereur dans l'Art Byzantin*, 189ff.; Johannes Kollwitz, *Das Bild von Christus dem König in Kunst und Liturgie des christlichen Frühzeit* (Paderborn: Schöningh, 1948); see also Kantorowicz, 'Gods in Uniform'.
[25] On the distinction between tiaras, wreaths and diadems, and their evolution, see Percy E. Schramm, *Sphaira, Globus, Reichsapfel* (Stuttgart: Anton Hiersemann, 1958); and Klaus Wessel, 'Kranzgold und Lebenskronen', *Archäologischer Anzeiger* (1950/1): 103–14.
[26] Ritter, *Diadem und Königsherrschaft*, 1–127.   [27] Deshman, 'Christus Rex', 375.

rather than Christ himself. And when Christ was portrayed crowned, the attribute was a wreath (the symbol of victory) rather than a diadem. Yet by the ninth century wreaths had become anachronistic as symbols of kingship. Kings usually wear crowns, as the ninth-century Utrecht Psalter shows. In its illustration of Psalm 71, the kings of Tarshish wear proper crowns, while Christ wears the triumphal wreath suspended over his head.[28] So the late tenth-century Anglo-Saxon and Ottonian iconographic programme of Christ represented wearing a crown became an innovative strategy, presented at first in Crucifixion and Ascension images. The innovation of turning the wreath into the crown is mitigated for the sensation of continuity provided by the conventionality of the themes of the Crucifixion and Ascension. But the decisive change is done and, as Deshman concludes,

> The new Anglo-Saxon and Ottonian iconography shifted the emphasis decisively from Christ the Victor to Christ the King, from a Late Antique to a fully medieval concept of the Cosmocrator. The age-old reluctance to represent Christ directly wearing the diadem, the insigne of temporal rulers, was finally overcome in order to make more explicit than ever before the kingship of Christ.[29]

This evolution led to Christ the King becoming once more the predominant model of medieval rulers.[30] With these Anglo-Saxon images of Christ depicted with a crown and the gesture of majesty, the new iconographic and ritual programme foregrounded the analogy of Christ to the temporal ruler, as the temporal ruler resembled Christ.

The Anglo-Saxon Benedictional of Aethelwold was also pioneering in depicting one of the earliest representations of the Magi as crowned kings.[31] The tradition of the Magi has its basis in the Gospel passage of the Three Wise Men who adored Jesus after his birth, but there is no mention of their royalty until the second century. Early Christians connected Psalm 71:10 ('The kings of Tarshish and of the isles shall bring presents') with the Three Wise Men of the Gospels.[32] This iconography is known as *aurum coronarium* because it echoes the Roman ceremony in which citizens of the empire and of the neighbouring subordinating provinces offer a gift (usually a gold diadem) to the emperor. Ultimately, this was the adaptation of an ancient Hellenistic rite of rulership which represents a symbolic acknowledgement of the imperial supremacy of the Roman ruler. This ritual was transferred to early Christian iconography through the motif of the Magi giving a diadem or wreath to Christ, usually found in sarcophagus reliefs. Deshman

---

[28] Deshman, 'Christus Rex', 377, figure 21.   [29] Deshman, 'Christus Rex', 377.
[30] Deshman, 'Christus Rex', 389; see also Kantorowicz, *King's Two Bodies*, 42–86.
[31] Gilberte Vezin, *L'Adoration et le cycle des Mages dans l'art chrétien primitif. Étude des influences orientales et grecques sur l'art chrétien* (Paris: Presses Universitaires de France, 1950), 71ff.
[32] Vezin, *L'Adoration*, 31.

concludes that 'by presenting a diadem and other gifts the Magi enacted an *aurum coronarium* that literally paid tribute to the imperial supremacy of Christ.'[33]

Considering these pagan and early Christian precedents, the miniature of the Benedictional of Aethelwold seems to be the first representation of the Magi presenting a diadem to Christ from early Christianity. The Magi are crowned as kings so that the imperial significance of their presentation of diadems to Christ makes explicit Christ's royalty as 'the king of the kings' (*Rex Regum*). Thus, the Anglo-Saxon iconography of the Magi is added to those of the crowned Christ in the Benedictional promoted by Bishop Aethelwold and the Ottonian version promoted by Archbishop Egbert of Trier, such as the Maastricht cross, the Codex Egberti[34] and the Poussay Lectionary in Paris.[35]

A number of later Anglo-Saxon works adopted the new iconography of the crowned Christ during the late tenth and early eleventh centuries.[36] This entire iconographic and liturgical programme is actually complemented by the intriguing story of King Cnut's self-investiture, which I refer to in the Introduction of this book (pp. 5–7). Cnut's removal and consequent presentation of his crown to Christ is considered by Deshman as

> an actual occurrence that provides a concrete, real life parallel in Anglo-Saxon history to the religious iconography in the English Benedictional where the crowned Magi present diadems to Christ in an *aurum coronarium*. ... The continuation of this imperial rite in the contemporary devotional customs of medieval rulers must have contributed to the genesis of the new iconography of the Magi-kings in Anglo-Saxon and Ottonian art. ... When Cnut gave his own crown to be placed on the head of Christ, he could hardly have found a more direct and graphic way of demonstrating how the ideal of the ruler as the temporal imitator and image of Christ fostered the new iconography of *Christus Rex*.[37]

The crown symbolises the virtuous acts of the king in his life, which legitimises his kingship and enables him to win the crown of glory and eternal rulership with the heavenly monarch. This ideal of royal virtue was

---

[33] Deshman, 'Rex Christus', 380. See also Theodor Klauser, *Aurum Coronarium* (München: F. Bruckmann, 1948), 129–53, and Franz Cumont, *L'Adoration des Mages et l'art triumphal de Rome* (Rome: Tipografia Poliglotta Vaticana, 1932–3), 81–105.

[34] Hubert Schiel, *Codex Egberti: Ms. 24 der Stadtbibliothek Trier: Evangelienbuch* (Basel: Alkuin-Verlag, 1960).

[35] Charles R. Dodwell and Derek H. Turner, *Reichenau Reconsidered* (London: Warburg Institute, 1965), 13ff.

[36] Some examples in Francis Wormald, *English Drawings of the Tenth and Eleventh Centuries* (London, Faber & Faber, 1952), 78ff., n. 54, 56, plates 4a, 28a; Hanns Swarzenski, 'The Anhalt Morgan Gospels', *Art Bulletin* 31 (1949): 77–83, p. 78, figure 9, also 11; Marvin Chauncey Ross, 'An Eleventh-Century English Bookcover', *Art Bulletin* 22 (1940): 83–5, figure 1.

[37] Deshman, 'Christus Rex', 405.

Figure 19 Angels crowning King Cnut as he and his wife, Aelfgifu of Northampton, present the Winchester Cross to the church. The *New Minster Liber Vitae*, Winchester, New Minster, 1031. London, British Library MS. Stowe 944, fol. 6 r. © The British Library Board.

actually iconographically transferred in Cnut's image. In a drawing of the *Liber vitae*, the representation of his virtuous donation is marked by an angel crowning him (Figure 19).

Ottonian Rulers' Portraits and Their Symbolic Meaning

Once the kingship of Christ was established through the iconographic motifs of the *Christus Rex* and the Magi, its transference to ruler portraits by Ottonian artists was simple. The powerful patronage of the Ottonians promoted the making of illuminated manuscripts in centres like Trier, Reichenau, Regensburg and Hildesheim, where new iconographies were created – the enthroned emperor crowned by Christ and the emperor wearing the stola among them.[38]

The reinvention of these iconographies was surely motivated by Ottonian rulers' aim to meld Christ and the emperor. They promoted the transference that Ottoman artists did from the celestial representation of Christ wearing the crown to the temporal representation of the rulers wearing the crown – some of them being crowned by Christ. These patrons and artists were actually involved in the creation of both Christ representations and ruler portraits. This transposition to imperial rulers first materialised in the appearance of the iconography of the Magi-kings. For example, the Chantilly manuscript, commissioned around 983, depicts four crowned personifications of the provinces presenting orbs to the enthroned Emperor Otto II: the transposition of the *aurum coronarium* is thus made explicit.[39]

New subjects and symbologies are added to this first topic. In a Crucifixion miniature in the Uta Lectionary, Christ wears a stola as well as a diadem.[40] Christ is clearly depicted as *Rex et Sacerdos*, in his double royal and priestly insignia – the crown and the stola.[41] The stola, worn only by deacons, priests and bishops, was an unambiguous liturgical vestment and clerical insignia. Christ wears the stola hanging straight down from his shoulders – as do bishops and priests – while Emperor Henry II is depicted wearing the stola the way deacons wear it across the

---

[38] A good summary of this production is presented in Deshman, 'Christus Rex', 368–77.
[39] Deshman, 'Rex Christus', 382.
[40] Erik Cinthio, *Der thronende Christus mit Stola* (Graz: Böhlau, 1962), 285–8.
[41] On Christ's dual office and its derivations in Ottonian iconography and idea of kingship, and particularly on the assimilation of a ruler's coronation to baptism as a guise for the king's assimilation to Christ, see Robert Deshman, 'Otto III and the Warmund Sacramentary: A Study in Political Theology', *Zeitschrift für Kunstgeschichte*, 34 (1971): 1–20. See also Ernst Kantorowicz, 'Deus per Naturam, Deus per Gratia: A Note of Medieval Political Theology', in *Selected Studies* (New York: J. J. Augustin, 1965), 122ff.

chest (Figure 23). There are obvious precedents in early Christianity of the assimilation of the emperor with the sacred orders, especially in Constantine's reign.[42] The Ottonians artists revisited this analogy.

This new iconography promotes the *imitatio sacerdoti* of the emperor, as the enthroned rulers' portraits convey the *imago Christi* (Figure 21). The emperor is seen in majesty, as the earthly type of Christ. His anointment reinforces the priestly office, as depicted in the cycle of miniatures on the Baptism of Christ in the Sacramentary of Ivrea, commissioned about the year 1001 by Otto III's protector, Bishop Warmundus of Ivrea. Interestingly, Henry II was invested with the office of *res canonicus*, providing him with spiritual, quasi-sacerdotal characteristics. Christ's anointment as the messianic king and priest is emphasised by the two different vitals of chrism that John the Baptist holds. Two similar containers of holy oil appear in the miniature of the crowning of a king that illustrates a German coronation ordo in the Sacramentary.

The ruler's unction is clearly associated with that of Christ in the Jordan, so that he receives both royal and quasi-sacerdotal powers when he is anointed in the ceremony of coronation. In all these examples we see that sometimes Christ is adorned with attributes of temporal rulers (the crown), whilst at other times the temporal ruler is enriched with Christological and priestly iconography (the stola, the Majesty enthroned and the Chrism).[43] Both directions of the transference, temporal and spiritual, are impressed in the eleventh-century portraits of Ottonian sovereigns, depicted with clearly Christological resonances.

Beyond its transferences with Anglo-Saxon canons, this programme was strongly influenced by the greater connections established between the Ottonians and Byzantium, especially in the time of Otto II (973–83), who married the Byzantine princess Theophanu in 972. In a celebrated ivory carving, most likely from Italy and housed in the Cluny Museum in Paris, the imperial couple is shown being crowned by Christ (Figure 20).[44] Otto II appears wearing the imperial *loros* (a richly embroidered pendant sash), a garment specific to the Byzantine emperors, and other rich vestments. This image is a clear replica of similar ones that were being created in contemporary Byzantium (Figure 15), and appears to be compensation for the fact that Theophanu had to be crowned by the Pope before marrying

---

[42] Bowersock, 'From Emperor to Bishop'.

[43] Otto III was the first Western ruler to be depicted on his seal enthroned in majesty, appropriating a previously exclusively religious image for royal purposes (Brigitte Bedos-Rezak, 'The King Enthroned, a New Theme in Anglo-Saxon Royal Iconography: The Seal of Edward the Confessor and Its Political Implications', in *Kings and Kingship*, ed. Joel Thomas Rosenthal (Binghamton: State University of New York, 1986), 53–88, here 60; Dale, *Inauguration and Liturgical Kingship*, 244.

[44] Ginnasi, *L'incoronazione celeste nel mondo bizantino*, 95–7.

Figure 20 Holy Roman Emperor Otto II and his wife, Theophanu, being crowned by Christ, engraving after ivory carving, tenth century (C10 Byzantine ivory). © Paris, Musée de Cluny and Musée national du Moyen Âge.[45]

[45] Ginnasi, *L'incoronazione celeste nel mondo bizantino*, 95–7; Mayr-Harting, *Ottonian Book Illumination*, 1: figure 1.

Figure 21 *Otto II in Majesty*, fol. 16 v, Ottonisches Evangeliar, Domschatzkammer Aachen. © Domkapitel Aachen. Photo: Pit Siebigs.[46]

---

[46] On the position of the emperor's hands see Brilliant, *Gesture and Rank in Roman Art*, 204–11, especially the section 'Hand Up' (208–11).

Otto. Byzantium could provide the Ottonians with a notable arsenal of symbols to legitimise and justify their sovereignty as emperors. For a lineage that sought to be considered a 'sacred family', the compilation of these Byzantine symbols of power made them a treasure in themselves – the representation of a king being directly crowned by the deity being one of the most effective.

This image became an important milestone because it was the first specific representation of the moment of coronation since late antiquity in the West. The relevance of this panel lies above all in the political message that it conveys. The concept of temporal power being divinely derived was imported from Byzantium. This concept may have been understood in the East, but was far from being assimilated by the Western lay and ecclesiastical elites. Neither did it have any reflection in ritual practice. However, it represented a clear intention to confirm the imperial autonomy of the Ottonians from the Byzantine emperors. At the same time, the panel showed a marked respect for the dignity of the Byzantine emperors, as attested by the fact that Otto II aimed to be represented with the typical vestments of the Byzantine sovereigns (see the parallel with Figure 15).[47]

This image was also perfectly in keeping with the other image of Otto II in majesty kept in a manuscript known as the Aachen Gospels (Figure 21).[48] The miniature was painted around 973 in the Abbey of Reichenau and shows the enthroned Otto II seated on a throne-bench decked with a roll-shaped cushion, his feet resting on a footstool. The great hand of God descends to crown the emperor. In the Ottonian context, the hand of God descending from a cloud and holding the golden crown that is placed on the emperor's head visually accompanies the prayers recited in the royal investiture rite incorporated by the *ordines* from the coronation of Charles the Bald.[49] They, in turn, integrate the ideology of royalty expounded by Hincmar in the protocol prepared for the consecration of Charles the Bald

---

[47] On the political ideology of the Ottonians see Karl J. Leyser, '*Theophanu divina gratia imperatrix augusta*: Western and Eastern Emperorship in the Later Tenth Century', in *The Empress Theophano*, ed. A. Davids (Cambridge: Cambridge University Press, 1995), 1–27; Pietro de Francisci, *Arcana Imperii* (Milano: A. Giuffrè, 1948), 3:2, 306–34; Hagen Keller, *Gli Ottoni. Una dinastia imperiale fra Europa e Italia (secc. X e XI)* (Roma: Carocci, 2012), 109–28; Roberto Schiavolin, 'Divina dispositio: ordine e governo dell'universo nella politica, nella teologia e nell'arte di ambiente ottoniano', *Esercizi Filosofici*, 2 (2007): 76–106.

[48] Kantorowicz, *King's Two Bodies*, 61–75, figure 5 (Aachen Gospels, c.973). Henry Mayr-Harting dates the image later, circa 996 in the age of Otto III (*Ottonian Book*, 1:60), but argues for the same basic interpretation. See also Schramm, *Die deutschen Kaiser und Könige in Bildern ihrer Zeit 751–1190*, 78ff., and Körntgen, *Königsherrschaft und Gottes Gnade*, 178–211.

[49] Körntgen, *Königsherrschaft und Gottes Gnade*, 280–1.

in Metz in 869, with the words: 'The Lord crowns you with the crown of Glory.'[50] The divine circular aureole circumscribing the hand of God intersects with the oval imperial crown. The emperor's head appears in the space shared by the two aureoles, producing the effect of visual convergence. Of the three planes superimposed on the picture, the upper part is formed by the hands of God, the head of the emperor and the four beasts of the Apocalypse, symbolising the four evangelists. In the centre, to the left and right, at the level of the emperor's feet, two male figures with purple pennants on their shoulders lean forward slightly in a gesture of veneration. The figures appear crowned, perhaps signifying their ducal dignity or symbolising the governors of the *regna* who owe submission to imperial authority. In the lower part, below the emperor's feet, four dignitaries – two archbishops and two warriors – represent the princes of the spiritual and temporal spheres, respectively.

This rich image, loaded with complex meanings, symbolises the emperor elevated to the heavens, having direct contact with divinity, but firmly rooted on earth: almost literally, with his feet on the ground and head in the clouds. Kantorowicz links this iconography with the concept of *imperator ad caelum erectus*, from the Isidorian tradition of Visigothic Spain, subsequently collected by the Anonymous Norman.[51] The glorification of the emperor shown in this image far exceeds any other Western representation, and is comparable only to the cycle of images of the celestial Byzantine coronations of Constantine VII by Christ, dated to the mid-tenth century and, therefore, slightly earlier. But the difference is that, just as those representations left the distinction between the Byzantine emperor and Christ abundantly clear, now the impression is that the Ottonian emperor is identified with Christ (God the Son), while the hand of God is identified with God the Father. We are therefore dealing with a deliberately recreated 'Trinitarian effect' to transmit fundamental ideologies of imperial sovereignty among the Ottonians. Indeed, the emperor appears clad in the *maiestas* of Christ, seated on the throne of Christ, with his left hand open in a clearly Christological gesture, with the mandorla of Christ and surrounded by animals representing the four evangelists.[52] Thus, the emperor was not simply the vicar

---

[50] A. Boretius, ed., *Monumenta Germaniae Historica, Capitularia Regnum Francorum*, ed. A. Boretius. 2 vols. (Hannover, Hahniani, 1897), 2:457, n. 302; O'Meara, *Monarchy and Consent*, 72; Bouman, *Sacring and Crowning*, 8–9; Nelson, 'The Lord's Anointed and the People's Choice', 163–4.

[51] Kantorowicz, *King's Two Bodes*, figure 5; Mayr–Harting, *Ottonian Book*, 1:60, figure 29.

[52] Kantorowicz, *King's Two Bodies*, 63–4.

of Christ on earth, but also truly acting *in persona Christi*, personifying Christ.

It is as though the God-man had ceded his celestial throne to the Glory of the terrestrial emperor for the purpose of allowing the invisible *Christus* in heaven to become manifest in the *Christus* on Earth.[53]

In the image of the enthronement of Otto II, the assimilation of Christ with the emperor is indicated by a literal similarity and radical identification, not just through a physical or facial resemblance between the sovereign and divine archetype.[54] Moreover, the image intuitively represents the emperor's two natures, human and divine, earthly and celestial ('human by nature and divine by grace'), and thus his meta-physiological assimilation with Christ, who is also 'true God and true man'.

The white band, held up by the four animals, which divides the figure of the emperor in two, becomes a symbolic key to the image. The iconography of a cloth band representing the boundary between heaven and earth is pointed out by Percy Schramm.[55] Beyond the many other interpretations of this veil – among them, the symbolisation of the 'veil of the tabernacle' in the Old Testament tradition or that of the separation between the Old and New Covenants – the veil is also deeply connected with the question of royal anointings. In effect, the form of the band suggests a division of the figure of the emperor that is not merely geometric or lineal, but guided by parameters with a strong symbolic component: the emperor's head, chest, shoulders and brachial joints remain in the upper part, while his torso, hands and legs are in the lower part. This reminds us that head, chest, shoulders and brachial joints were the parts in which the emperor was anointed with oil by the priest. The anointed parts of the body referred to the parts that related to Christ ('the anointed'), and therefore to the divine body of the emperor, whereas the rest were considered the common parts of any other man, and therefore reference was made to the emperor's natural body. What, then, of the hands? The fact is that the anointing of the hands, introduced some time

---

[53] Kantorowicz, *King's Two Bodies*, 65.
[54] This impersonification of Christ on the part of the emperor will appear again in the famous scene of the coronation of Roger II of Sicily by Christ in the church of the Martorana of Palermo around the 1140s, commented upon in Chapter 7. There, certainly, two figures, the monarch and Christ, are represented and therefore this assimilation does not occur, but the question of the resemblance, even duplication (*Zwillingsbildung*), between Roger's face and that of Christ has been much commented upon in the specialised literature.
[55] Percy E. Schramm, 'Das Herrscherbild in der Kunst des Mittelalters', *Schriften der MGH*, 13 (1954–6), 199.

before for priestly unction, had still not been introduced for royal unction at the time of Otto II's coronation in Aachen (961) – although it would be introduced shortly afterwards, in the imperial coronation ordo dated around 980–1000.[56] So the division of the veil confirms the 'Christifying' effect of unction and emphasises that the emperor on earth has in common with Christ the two substances: human by nature and divine by grace and consecration.

Finally, this scene differs from the Byzantine versions not only through its visual identification of the emperor with Christ, with whom he is one, but also from the Carolingian representations.[57] The hand of God had certainly been used by the Carolingian monarchs to reflect the direct emanation of the grace of God towards the monarch. In a miniature of Charles the Bald kept in the national library of Paris (painted around 869–70, the period during which he acquired the crown of Lothringia), the emperor is flanked by two bishops (or two popes, possibly Gelasius and Gregory) who turn their hands towards the emperor and who appear to take no active part in the ceremony (Figure 22). They thus seem even more like witnesses than necessary mediators, confirming the theories expounded earlier on the question of priestly mediation in the power of the Carolingian emperors.[58] The hand of God is clearly crowning the emperor, who moreover appears with a halo of sanctity quite separate from the crown. This clearly establishes a distinction between the emperor and Christ, as while holiness is attributed to Charles the Bald, in no sense can he be identified with Christ himself.

With the Ottonians, by contrast, the emperor functions as a substitute for the figure of Christ, and the hand appearing above the picture specifically represents God the Son, Jesus Christ, rather than God the Father. Besides, in the Ottonian miniature of Reichenau, the hand of God that comes from above is not properly crowning, but rather touching, imposing or blessing the crown, as it is already on the sovereign's head. As recorded in the literature, we can never establish with complete certainty

[56] Percy E. Schramm, 'Die Krönung in Deutschland bis zum Beginn des Salischen Hauses', *Zeitschrift der Savigny-Stiftung für Rechtsgeschichte*, 24 (1935): 254ff.

[57] This 'historicist' connection is argued by Stefano Manganaro, '*Stabilitas Imperii*: A Crucial Aspect of Political Thought in the Early and High Middle Ages', in *Renovation, Inventio, Absentia Imperii: From the Roman Empire to Contemporary Imperialism*, ed. Wouter Bracke, Jelle Nelis and Jan De Maeyer (Turnhout: Brepols, 2018), 137–69. On the concepts and practices of empire in the Ottonian period see John W. Bernhardt, 'Concepts and Practice of Empire in Ottonian Germany (950–1024)', in *Representations of Power in Medieval Germany, 800–1500*, ed. Simon MacLean and Björn Weiler (Turnhout: Brepols, 2006), 141–64.

[58] Jean-Claude Bonne, 'Images du Sacre', in *Le Sacre Royal a L'epoque De Saint-Louis*, ed. Jacques Le Goff, Eric Palazzo, Jean-Claude Bonne and Marie-Noël Collette (Paris: Gallimard, 2001), 91–226, here 97.

Figure 22 Charles the Bald being crowned by a hand of God from above. *Sacramentary of Metz*, 1141, Bibliothèque Nationale de France, f. 2 v. © Bibliothèque Nationale de France.[59]

---

[59] Ginnasi, *L'incoronazione celeste nel mondo bizantino*, 73–4; O'Meara, *Monarchy and Consent*, 71–4; Mayr-Harting, *Ottonian Book*, 1:199; Ott, *Krone*, 280, figure 63.

if the hand of God that appears in that representation is that of the Father or of the Son.⁶⁰ But we can make some solidly based inferences. If the Carolingian miniature of Charles the Bald continues the Constantinian tradition (the mentioned medallion of Constantine in which he appears being crowned by a hand of God with a crown clearly separate from his head, Figure 9), the Ottonian miniature of Otto II initiates a new iconographic tradition, in which the emperor is actually identified with Christ – either through substitution as in Otto II's case, or through facial or physical similarity as would become the norm in the later iconographic tradition such as in the case of Roger II of Sicily. Therefore, the concept of sovereignty shown in the miniature of the Reichenau Gospel is clearly more Christocentric than theocentric, and this would prove highly influential not only for subsequent iconographic representations in the West, but also for the effective practice of self-coronations.⁶¹ The theological idea of Christ as 'two natures in one person' is clearly transferred to the sphere of royal authority, projecting that same idea onto the sovereign.

The Ottonian era's iconographic programme confirms the scriptural notion of imperial sovereignty received directly from God ('non est enim potestas nisi a Deo', Romans 13:1). Furthermore, the iconographic programme initiated in the time of Otto II would recur in certain illustrations done during the reign of one of his successors, Henry II. To the hand of God the Father or of Christ we now find the mediations of Peter and Paul, as depicted in the miniatures of one of Henry II's gospels (1007–12), and of his Apocalypse in the early eleventh century. In other representations, two angels participate in the intervention of Christ, descending from heaven with other *regalia*, while two bishops on either side support the emperor's open arms in the form of a cross (sacramentaries of Henry II, between 1002 and 1014).⁶² All of these reinforce the Christocentric nature of the emperor's image.

Particularly important in this regard is a miniature painted in Saint Emmeram of Regensburg Abbey between 1002 and 1003, where a celestial coronation is shown, although now the hand of God has been

---

⁶⁰ Kantorowicz, *King's Two Bodies*, 77.
⁶¹ To complete the discussion on the Ottonian Christocentric royalty see Mayr-Harting, *Ottonian Book*, 1:57–117; Piotr Skubiszewski, 'Ecclesia, Christianitas, Regnum et Sacerdotium dans l'art des Xe et XIe siècles. Idées et structures des images', *Cahiers de Civilisation Médiévale* 28 (1985): 133–79; Mariëlle Hageman, 'Between the Imperial and the Sacred: The Gesture of Coronation in Carolingian and Ottonian Images', in *New Approaches to Medieval Communication*, ed. M. Mostert (Turnhout: Brepols, 1999), 127–63; Andreas Büttner, 'Starrer Text und dynamisches Bild – Eine spätmittelalterliche Miniatur der römisch-deutschen Königskrönung', in *Bild und Ritual. Visuelle Kulturen in historischer Perspektive*, ed. Claus Ambos, et al. (Darmstadt: WBG, 2010), 172–81.
⁶² Bonne, 'Images du sacre', 97.

Figure 23 Crowning of Henry II by Christ. *Sacramentary of Henry II*. Regensburg, 1002–14. Munich, Bayerische Staatsbibl, Clm. 4456, f. 11. © Bayerische Staatsbibliothek München.

substituted, literally, by the figure of Christ, who imposes the crown on the emperor from above (Figure 23).[63]

[63] Mayr-Harting, *Ottonian Book*, 1:67, 180–1 and 194, figure 35; Körntgen, *Königsherrschaft und Gottes Gnade*, 212–35; O'Meara, *Monarchy and Consent*, 81–4. See also Weinfurter,

The emperor's head, shoulders and chest still appear within the oval mandorla framing the figure of Christ and thus, from an iconographic point of view, means the same as in Otto II's miniature, even if a full-bodied Christ now appears. The fact that this represents the *moment* of coronation implies that the legitimisation of Henry II's authority depends on his investiture ceremony, which would also explain the significance, above all from this period on, of the coronation *ordines* (pp. 148–51).

This image also initiates the practice of coronation iconography as a direct reference to the ritual-ceremonial planning, given that some of the acts depicted (e.g. the saints at the king's side take his arms and lead him to the unction and coronation) correspond exactly to what is set out for the ritual in the Germanic coronation ordo, known as the *Pontificale Romano-Germanicum*. The referential nature of the Ottonian images contrasts vividly with the idealistic tendency of the Byzantine representations, in which the divorce between the image (what is imagined ideally as a typology) and reality (what actually takes place as the ritual unfolds – or, at least, what is prescribed in the ceremonial ordo) is very marked.

In addition, the representations collected in the *Sacramentaire de l'évéque Warmundus d'Ivrea*, promoted by Otto III around the year 1000, show diverse images of royal coronations.[64] One of the them portrays a bishop crowning a king, which reflects the reality of the investiture ceremonies being conducted in this period. Yet another, more crucially, depicts the Virgin crowning Otto III, which reflects a symbolic idea rather than a ritual reality. The image shows the Virgin Mary, head of the celestial court and source of power and sovereignty, with the inscription: 'I reward you with the gift of a crown for your good defence of Bishop Warmund.' It encodes the clear message that this link between the Virgin and the emperor is of greater endurance than that represented by a coronation by a pope or a bishop.[65]

'Authority and Legitimation', 19–38 (here 24–8) and John W. Bernhardt, 'King Henry II of Germany: Royal Self-Representation and Historical Memory', in *Medieval Concepts of the Past: Ritual, Memory, Historiography*, ed. Gerd Althoff, Johannes Fried and Patrick J. Geary (Cambridge: Cambridge University Press, 2003), 39–70. For the evolution of the imperial orders see Bouman, *Sacring and Crowning*, 38–49.

[64] Deshman, 'Otto III', 1–20; Schmitt, *La raison des gestes dans l'Occident médiéval*, 118–20. On Otto III's representations see Gerhart B. Ladner, *L'immagine dell'imperatore Ottone III* (Rome: Unione delgli Archeologia, storia e storia dell'arte, 1988). For the context see Knut Görich, *Otto III. Romanus Saxonicus et Italicus. Kaiserliche Rompolitik und sächsische Historiographie* (Sigmaringen: Thorbecke, 1995).

[65] Mayr-Harting, *Ottonian Book*, 1:53 and 88–9; Schmitt, *La raison des gestes dans l'Occident médiéval*, 118–20; Deshman, 'Otto III', 2; Luigi Magnani, *Le Miniature del Sacramentario de d'Ivrea* (Vatican: Biblioteca Apostolica Vaticana, 1934).

This image also takes its lead from the iconographic programme of the hand of God crowning the emperor from above, but now it is the full-body Virgin who appears, slightly higher, and who crowns the emperor – or rather, blesses the crown that has already been imposed. The emperor is depicted leaning towards her in a show of reverence and submission. The general framework of the representation leads one to draw parallels with what Roger II's painter would depict in the mosaic of the coronation of the Sicilian king by Christ in the Martorana church, whose analysis is precisely the next chapter of this book. The answer might lie in its Byzantine influence, but the result is far removed from the archetype.[66] The figure of the emperor lacks the solemnity and hieraticism of the Byzantine representations of the *basileus*, appearing rather rigid though flexible in his stance, with an attitude of submission, prefiguring the scenes of divine investiture that would appear shortly afterwards in the West.

The series of representations of Otto III marks the closing of the whole cycle that began after the fusion of the unction and coronation ceremony which started with Charles the Bald. Stefano Manganaro explains:

At the very beginning, the kingship of Henry I (919–936) was neither sacral nor Christ-centred. Otto I (936–973) marked a turning point, since the anointed king was surrounded by a sacral aura. A relationship with Christ was surely admitted, but, excluding some settings (Mainz, perhaps Cologne), this was not broadly considered as the distinguishing feature of the Ottonian kingship. Partly thanks to Byzantine influences, the relationship with Christ began to deeply characterize the Ottonian kingship from Otto II onwards (973–983). This trend gained *momentum* with Otto III (983–1002), since his kingship was not only Christocentric, but even Christomimetical, allowing an identification between Otto III and Christ.[67] This possibility was not grounded on an unacceptable ontological identity, but it depended on the docile heart of the emperor willing to accept the teachings of Christ. A change of emphasis occurred at the time of Henry II (1002–1024). The relationship between the king and Christ remained important, but also other models – in particular that of Moses – shaped Henry II's ideas and politics, combining the traditional royal duty to be merciful and mild with the harshness of the law.[68]

This complex and heterogeneous itinerary experienced by Carolingians, Anglo-Saxons and Ottonians denotes three decisive characteristics regarding

---

[66] Ginnasi, *L'incoronazione celeste nel mondo bizantino*, 104–5.
[67] For a later evolution of this tendency to Christmimetism and its projections to other places like France and England see Nicholas Vincent, 'Christ and the King: Plantagenet Devotion to Jesus Christ, 1150–1272', *Cristo e il potere: Teologia, antropologia e politica*, ed. L. Andreani and A. Paravicini-Bagliani (Florence 2017), 111–26.
[68] Stefano Manganaro, 'Christo e gli Ottoni. Una indagine sulle immagini di autorità e di preghiera, le alter fonti iconografiche, le insegne e le fonti scritte', in *Cristo e il potere. Teologia, antropologia e politica*, ed. Laura Andreani and Agostino Paravicini Baggiani (Firenze: Sismel, 2017), 53–79, here 79.

the rituals of royal accession. They help demystify some of the already established historiographical categories. First, the inauguration of the normativity of king-making through unction and coronation was established as normative in *certain* Central European kingdoms such as Germany, France and England (and subsequently in the kingdoms of Sicily and Jerusalem), but not necessarily in all the European kingdoms. This ritual tradition has survived until today in England, and lasted until the nineteenth century in the French and German monarchies. But it by no means expanded through medieval Europe, so that this normative character must not be projected onto other European kingdoms. In Hungary, Poland and Bohemia royal unction was adopted by the baptised kings during the eleventh century, but this practice was not necessarily followed by their successors.[69] The royal unction was hardly established among the Iberian kings, since they privileged 'secular' rituals such as the raising on a shield or proper self-coronations rather than the supposed normative formula of the unction plus coronation, as I detail in three corresponding chapters. In Scandinavia, unction was established later, starting in Norway (1163), Denmark (1170) and Sweden (1210).[70] Ireland and Wales established rather different installation ceremonies, and Scottish kings did not receive unction until 1331. As Rudolf Schieffer concludes after his long-term and large-scale comparative analysis of the practice of royal unction in Europe, 'although the royal unction constitutes a characteristic element for pre-modern monarchy, it was not a common factor to constitute Christian kingship throughout the Middle Ages.'[71] This variety of rituals shows that the practice of self-coronation was not necessarily transgressive or non-conventional. Rather, it depended on the context.

Second, the Anglo-Saxon and Ottonian iconographical programme highlights the sacred nature of the kingship and the subsequent kings' dependence on human mediators of an ecclesiastical nature in their assumption of the royal *potestas*. This heightens the sacral nature of kingship but, again, it is not to be taken as a normative for the rest of European kings, since this royal sacrality was actually conveyed in very different forms. It radically contrasts with the Iberian experience, in which its unsacred nature is emphasised using divergent rituals of accession such as the raising on a shield and proper self-coronations. The secular nature of

[69] Knoll, *The Rise of the Polish Monarchy*.
[70] See Line, *Kingship and State Formation in Sweden, 1130–1290*, 388–400, and Sverre Bagge, *From Gang Leader to the Lord's Anointed: Kingship in Sverris saga and Hákonar saga Hákonarsonar* (Odense: Odense University Press, 1996).
[71] Rudolf Schieffer, 'Testamentarische Regelungen zur Integration der Königssöhne westeuropäischer Königsdynastien des Früh- und Hochmittelalters (bis ca. 1300) in die Familienherrschaft', in *Die Mittelalterliche Thronfolge im europäischen Vergleich*, ed. Mattias Becher (Ostfildern: Jan Thorbecke, 2017), 43–80, here 79.

the most part of the ceremonies of royal installation among Iberian kings is compatible with the sacred dimension of a ritual, which is performed in a church and inserted in a Mass.[72] In kingdoms such as Scotland and Portugal, some rituals of accession did not include unction, but they retained a strong religious and sacred element: there was a religious service, and the ceremony took place in a church. Thus, sacrality was experienced in different degrees among European kings, and the rituals performed in accordance with the kings' sacred conditions adopted very different forms.

Third, the process of ceremonial liturgification and iconographic Christocentrism undergone by the Carolingians and Ottonians respectively implied, on one hand, the sacralisation of the monarchy, and on the other, the confirmation of the doctrine of the king's two natures (the natural body and the supernatural body) – a clear Christological analogy. Both doctrines would remain firmly fixed in the ideological body of European monarchies, at least until secularisation from the early modern period. Yet this double meaning of the Carolingian and Ottonian ritual and iconographic coronations would have a double effect on the ceremonies of accession in medieval Europe. The liturgification, along with its corresponding sacralisation of the monarchy, would consolidate the ecclesiastical mediation in French and German realms. Yet Christocentrism would promote the development of symbolic and ceremonial self-coronations analysed in the following chapters. The image of Roger II of Sicily being crowned by Christ, as shown in the mosaic of the Martorana Church in Palermo, is the first clear sign of this evolution, and a formidable example of symbolic self-coronation.

---

[72] See the introductions to Gábor Klaniczay, *Holy Rulers and Blessed Princesses: Dynastic Cults in Medieval Central Europe* (New York: Cambridge University Press, 2007), and Haki Antonsson, *St. Magnús of Orkney: A Scandinavian Martyr-Cult in Context* (Leiden: Brill, 2007).

Part II

Infamy

7 Roger II of Sicily
Imagining Self-Coronation

The iconographic programme developed by King Roger II of Sicily (1095–1154), as depicted in the imposing mosaic in the Martorana church, deserves detailed treatment as the sublimation of the tendency to Christocentrism impressed in the Byzantine, Carolingian, Anglo-Saxon and Ottonian rituals and iconographies discussed in the previous chapters. Roger II of Sicily was Count of Sicily, Duke of Apulia and King of Sicily from 1130. Son of Count Roger I of Normandy, he succeeded his brother Simon to the county of Sicily in 1105, his mother, Adelaide del Vasto, staying on as regent until he began to govern when he reached legal age in 1112. He turned the Norman conquests in the south of Italy into a unified territory raised to the category of kingdom.[1] Roger deserves particular attention in this book because he is the first king who experienced disapproval from his contemporaries because of his royal self-investiture and symbolic self-coronation.

Roger always intended to wear the royal crown, unifying all Norman possessions in Italy, recalling that the leaders of ancient Sicily such as Agathocles had been kings and, therefore, that the capital should move from Salerno to Palermo.[2] The historical fiction created to legitimise a present aspiration appears to have been suggested by his uncle, Henry of Vasto. According to the chronicler Alexander of Telese, who wrote at some point during the 1130s, visions predicted Roger's elevation.[3] He did not claim the throne, but his subjects told him that someone as powerful as he should be king.

With so many successes achieved, all the lands of Beohmond and the whole duchy seemingly in his power, the Prince of the Capuans, the *Magister Militum* of Naples

---

[1] For the historical context of this chapter see Donald Matthew, *The Norman Kingdom of Sicily* (Cambridge: Cambridge University Press, 1992) and Hubert Houben, *Roger II of Sicily: A Ruler between East and West* (Cambridge: Cambridge University Press, 2002).
[2] Houben, *Roger II of Sicily*, 51–2.
[3] A subtle interpretation of this vision, its connection with the problems that arose because of Anacletus' difficult character and its teachings regarding the nature of medieval rituals and the function of narratives of rituals is presented in Buc, '1701 in Medieval Perspective', 106–11.

and all the land up to the borders of the city of Ancona subject to him, and his opponents in war subdued, those close to Duke Roger, and particularly his uncle Count Henry [of Vasto] by whom he was loved more than anyone, began very frequently to suggest to him the plan that he, who with the help of God ruled so many provinces, Sicily, Calabria, Apulia and other regions stretching almost to Rome, ought not to have just the ducal title but ought to be distinguished by the honour of kingship. They added that the centre and capital of this kingdom ought to be Palermo, the chief city of Sicily, which once, in ancient times, was believed to have had kings [who ruled] over this province; but now, many years later, was by 'the secret judgement of God' without them.[4]

Following Count Henry and his close advisors' suggestions, Roger journeyed to Salerno and assembled learned churchmen and other competent princes, counts, barons and others whom he thought trustworthy in order to examine this matter. The expert commission analysed the issue carefully and, as expected, found evidence for an ancient kingship that could be restored, and 'unanimously, as if with one voice, praised [this proposal] and conceded, decided and insisted with mighty prayers' that he ought to be proclaimed king of Sicily at Palermo.[5] As clearly conveyed by Alexander's narration, every step of the proceedings was designed to guard him against accusations of usurpation.

Roger waited for favourable conditions to push for the creation of the new kingdom. In February 1130 there was a schism in the Roman Curia, and the College of Cardinals split. The anti-Norman party, led by Haimeric, elected Gregory Papareschi, a former monk of Cluny, who took the name Innocent II. The other group, many of whom came from the centre and south of Italy, elected Peter Pierleoni, who took the name Anacletus II. Finally, the balance was tipped towards Innocent II, above all due to the support that he received from Bernard of Clairvaux. In addition, perhaps to counteract the Anacletus–Roger axis, the German emperor Lothar III (1133–7), who until then had kept equidistant from the parties of the schism, firmly supported Innocent II.[6]

However, while the schism lasted, Roger II took advantage of the situation and was invested in 1130 as the king of Sicily by Anacletus II, who also granted him the right to designate one of his sons as his successor and to choose the bishop for his unction and coronation ceremony. In doing so, Anacletus II was going against the entire papal tradition, based on the rejection of the Norman presence in Italy and on opposition to the

---

[4] Alexander of Telese, *History of King Roger*, Book II, paragraph 1, in Graham A. Loud, ed., *Roger II and the Making of the Kingdom of Sicily: Selected Sources Translated and Annotated by Graham A. Loud* (Manchester: Manchester University Press, 2012), 77–8.
[5] Loud, *Roger II*, 78 (Alexander of Telese, *History of King Roger*, Book II, paragraph 2).
[6] Mary Stroll, *The Jewish Pope: Ideology and Politics in the Papal Schism of 1130* (Leiden: Bill, 1987).

creation of political units capable of counteracting its political rule in Italy. In return, Roger II lent him his support in his attempt to occupy the papal throne. This is a clear indication of his huge strategic capacity to organise the necessary means to achieve his political ends, a quality which without doubt his grandson Frederick II would inherit.

In his privilege allowing Roger II to be crowned as the king of Sicily, dated 27 September 1130, Anacletus II declared:

> You yourself, to whom divine providence has granted greater wisdom and power than the rest of the Italian princes, have tried splendidly to honour our predecessors and to serve them generously. It is proper [then] to raise up your person and those of your heirs and to adorn them with permanent titles of grace and honour. Therefore we concede, grant and authorise to you, your son Roger, and your other sons following you in the kingdom as you shall decree, and to your heirs, the crown of the kingdom of Sicily, and Calabria, Apulia and all those lands which we and our predecessors have granted and conceded to your predecessors the dukes of Apulia, namely Robert Guiscard and his son Roger, to hold and rule this kingdom in perpetuity, and to have by hereditary right all royal dignities and regalian rights.[7]

We do not know for certain if this privilege was accompanied by a genuine royal election or the corresponding investiture ceremony. In any case, a formal ceremony of investiture may have finally occurred on 25 December 1130. Roger had summoned all his nobles and vassals a few weeks before to the ceremony, which probably took place in Palermo. Shortly before, he had been acclaimed by a popular assembly, as had happened in Salerno in September. Roger needed public signs to confirm his legitimacy as king. Pope Anacletus proclaimed 'that you and your heirs shall be anointed as kings and at the appointed times crowned by the hands of those archbishops of your land whom you wish, assisted if you wish by other bishops of your choice'.[8] As generally occurs with the founding kings of a dynasty, or with the creation of a new kingdom, Roger sought for his monarchy the appearance of a legitimate kingdom, supported by the weight of tradition (rather than an artificial creation), that had been restored by the Pope with the consent of the princes and the people.

Roger II's Ritual Coronation

The extraordinary flourishing of historiography in Norman Sicily, in contrast with the relative paucity of sources in the Lombard period,

---

[7] See Anacletus II's privilege to Roger II, authorising the creation of the kingdom of Sicily, 27 September 1130, in Loud, *Roger II*, 304–5.
[8] See Anacletus II's privilege to Roger II in Loud, *Roger II*, 305.

gives us access to diverse versions of Roger II's coronation. The earlier historiographical vacuum caused a certain tendency to emphasise contemporary events rather than the roots of the political legitimacy, so that Roger's coronation details were provided by different chroniclers.[9]

The abbot Alexander of Telese has left an account of the coronation.[10] Though he was not present, he left a detailed description, since he finished the chronicle around 1135, having collected accounts from various witnesses such as Roger's sister, Maltilda, or her husband, Count Ranulf II of Alife.

The duke was led to the archiepiscopal church in royal manner. There he received unction with the Holy Oil and assumed the royal dignity. One cannot write down nor even imagine quite how glorious he was, how regal in his dignity, how splendid in his richly adorned apparel. For it seemed to the onlookers that all the riches and honours of his world were present. The whole city was decorated in an extraordinary way, and nowhere was there anything but rejoicing and light. Throughout the royal palace the interior walls were gloriously draped. The pavement was bestrewed with multi-coloured carpets and showed a flowing softness to the feet of those who trod there. When the king went to the church for the ceremony he was surrounded by dignitaries, and the huge number of horses which accompanied them had saddles and bridles decorated with gold and silver. Copious amounts of the choicest food and drink were served to the diners at the royal table, and nothing was served except in dishes or cups of gold or silver. There was no servant there who did not wear a silk tunic – the very waiters were clad in silk clothes. The glory and wealth of the royal abode were so spectacular that it caused great wonder and deep stupefaction – so great indeed that it instilled not a little fear in all those who had come from so far away. For many saw there more things than they had even heard rumour of previously.[11]

Alexander of Telese might have exaggerated, but there is other, indirect evidence to confirm the solemnity and grandiosity of the ceremony. In his

---

[9] On the contrast between Lombard and Norman historiographies in Sicily, and their influence in twelfth-century Norman chronicles, see Thomas S. Brown, 'The Political Use of the Past in Norman Sicily', in *The Perception of the Past in Twelfth-Century Europe*, ed. Paul Magdalino (London: Bloomsbury, 1992), 204–7.

[10] For a detailed account of Roger II's coronation and a critical analysis of its historical sources see Reinhard Elze, 'Zum Königtum Rogers II, von Sizilien', in *Festschrift für Percy Ernst Schramm zu seinem siebzigsten Geburtstag* (Wiesbaden: Steiner, 1964), 1102–16. See also Houben, *Roger II of Sicily*, 50–9; Graham A. Loud, *The Latin Church in Norman Sicily* (Cambridge: Cambridge University Press, 2007), 150–8; Theo Broekmann, *Rigor Iustitiae. Herrschaft, Recht und Terror imnormannisch-staufischen Süden (1050–1250)* (Darmstadt: Wissenschaftliche Buchgesellschaft, cop. 2005), 123–8.

[11] Alexander of Telese's *Alexandri Telesini abatis Ystoria Rogerii regis Sicilie Calabrie atque Apulie* (Book II, paragraphs 4–6) is quoted in Houben, *Roger II of Sicily*, 55. See also Laura Sciascia, 'Palermo As a Stage for, and a Mirror of, Political Developments from the 12th to the 15th Century', in *A Companion to Medieval Palermo: The History of a Mediterranean City from 600 to 1500*, ed. Annliese Nef (Leiden: Brill, 2013), 299–324, here 300–1.

study of the *laude regiae*, Ernst Kantorowicz argues that the classic legend 'Christus vincit, Christus regnat, Christus imperat', subsequently reflected in the coins of Roger II, might have derived from the acclamations given by the people during his investiture ceremony.[12]

Two other chroniclers mention Roger's coronation in Palermo in 1130: Falco de Benevento and Romuald of Salerno.[13] According to Falco de Benevento, the minister of the unction and consecration was Cardinal Comes of Saint Sabina, sent by Pope Anacletus II, while Prince Robert of Capua placed the crown on the head of the new king.[14] Perhaps the subsequent discrepancies of Roger and Anacletus weighed heavily with Falco, but in any case the proposal that both the unction and the coronation were administered by an archbishop had already been reflected in the privilege with which Anacletus had handed the new kingdom over to him.[15] Falco was an opponent of the king, and readily highlights Roger's cruelty and manipulations of ceremonies. He actually reflected 'Lombard national feeling, which failed to find overt expression in the Norman-controlled areas, and offers and emotional denunciation of Roger II, comparing his atrocities with those of Nero'.[16] Falco's vision contrasts with Alexander's, since the latter praises the Norman against the local Lombards, who are condemned for their violence and cowardice.

Romuald, the archbishop of Salerno, wrote a chronicle which extends from the creation of the world to 1181.[17] This version notes that, once Roger had recovered control of the citadel of Salerno, and had made peace with some barons and Prince Robert of Capua, 'afterwards, on the advice of the barons and people (*baronum et populi consilio*), he had himself anointed and crowned in Palermo as King of Sicily'.[18] Romuald's

---

[12] Kantorowicz, *Laudes Regiae*, 165, n. 41; William Tronzo, *The Cultures of His Kingdom: Roger II and the Cappella Palatina in Palermo* (Princeton, NJ: Princeton University Press, 1997), 127.

[13] On the different interpretations of these chroniclers see Buc, '1701 in Medieval Perspective', 106–7; Brown, 'The Political Use of the Past in Norman Sicily', 191–210.

[14] Falcone di Benevento, *Chronicon Beneventanum*, ed. Edoardo D'Angelo (Florence: Galuzzo, 1998), 108. See also *The Chronicle of Falco de Benevento*, in Loud, *Roger II*, 184–5. On Falco's interpretation of Roger II's reign see Massimo Oldoni, 'Realismo e dissidenza nella storiografia su Ruggero II: Falcone di Benevento e Alessandro di Telesse', in *Società, potere e popolo nell'età di Ruggero II* (Bari: Dedalo, 1979), 257–83.

[15] Reinhard Elze, 'Tre ordines per l'incoronazione di un re e di una regina del regno normanno di Sicilia', in *Atti del congresso internationale di studi sulla Sicilia normanna (Palermo, 4–8 Diciembre 1972)* (Palermo: Istituto di Storia Medievale, 1973), 438–59, here 438.

[16] Brown, 'The Political Use of the Past in Norman Sicily', 198.

[17] Donald J. A. Matthew, 'The Chronicle of Romuald of Salerno', in *The Writing of History in the Middle Ages: Essays Presented to R. W. Southern*, ed. Ralph H. C. Davis and John M. Wallace Hadrill (Oxford: Clarendon, 1981), 239–74.

[18] Romuald of Salerno, *Chronicon sive Annales*, in Loud, *Roger II*, 254, and Romuald of Salerno, *Chronicon*, ed. Carlo A. Garufi (Città di Castello, 1909–35), 218.

narrative of Roger's self-coronation is hardly credible because he is the only chronicler who mentions this particular ritual, and he wrote many years after the fact. Other contextual reasons might explain Romuald's assertion: he was favourable to the Norman kings and he wrote after the conclusion of the schism that had made Anacletus an antipope. Thus, narrating Roger's self-coronation would elide the direct participation of the schismatic Anacletus.

Yet if, in contrast to Alexander of Telese, Falco and Romuald may hardly be qualified as contemporary sources, other accounts coming from France, Germany and Scandinavia have been preserved of Roger's investiture and coronation. They project Roger's coronation as an event that forms part of a Europe-wide textual tradition. They convey an imaginative type which needs to be taken in its narrative context, but which is no less meaningful in terms of the symbolic realities it seeks to transmit.[19]

One such is a narrative preserved in the chronicles of Ernoul and Bernard le Trésorier, written around 1230, which complements, on one hand, Roger II's 'symbolic coronation' at the iconographic level in the Martorana mosaic and, on the other, the real coronation at the ceremonial level in the ordo described by Reinhard Elze.[20] In these chronicles the supposed coronation of Roger II by the king of France is fabricated. The king of France arrives on the island of Sicily, in the city of Palermo, when 'it was not long since the Christians had conquered the island from the Saracens'. In fact, the island had been conquered by Roger, who was lord of Puglia and Calabria. Roger, on learning that the king of France had arrived at the port, went to greet him. He took him to the castle, where he was fêted as befitted a great king. Roger showed the king of France all his jewels, especially a very beautiful crown of gold. Then, cunningly, Roger asked him to put the crown on his head 'to see how it suited him'. The king, lacking malice, and not wanting to disappoint his host, put the crown on his head – an act that he would later regret. When Roger had the crown on his head, he fell to his knees before the king, thanked him profusely and told him that he could not be crowned by a more exalted man than he. The king realised immediately that he had been tricked and went back to France.[21]

---

[19] Fulvio delle Donne, 'Liturgie del potere: le testimonianze letterarie', in *Nascita di un regno. Poteri signorilli, istituzioni feudali e strutture social nel Mezzogiorno normando* (Bari: Adda, 2008), 331–66.

[20] Reinhardt Elze, 'The Ordo for the Coronation of King Roger of Sicily', in *Coronations: Medieval and Early Modern Monarchic Ritual*, ed. János M. Bak (Berkeley: University of California Press, 1990), 168–78, and Mirko Vignoni, 'L'Ordo Coronationis', in *Le rappresentazioni del potere. La sacralità regia dei Normanni di Sicilia: un mito?* (Bari: Caratterimobili, 2012), 76–84.

[21] Louis de Mas Latrie, ed., *Chronique d'Ernoul et de Bernard le Trésorier* (Paris: Renouard, 1871), 13–14, with an Italian edition in Donne, 'Liturgie del potere', 331–2.

Such is the description that Bernard le Trésorier gives of the coronation of Roger II. Bernard wrote circa 1230 and thus hardly qualifies as a contemporary source. It is also possible that he reworked Ernoul's account, which described the events of the years 1101–31. Bernard's story leads us to conclude that the event of Roger II's coronation is more firmly established by the ceremonial than by the chronicles, thus confirming Philippe Buc's distinction between 'narrative rites' and 'historical rites'.[22] The legendary nature of Bernard's account is confirmed by the fact that these chroniclers are undoubtedly referring to King Louis VII of France, whereas in 1130, the date of Roger's actual coronation, the monarch was in fact Louis VI. The account of the meeting between Roger and the king of France would be more like a reminiscence of the meeting that actually took place between the king of Sicily and the king of France, but in 1149, which most certainly meant Louis VII. Moreover, the action takes place in a crusading context – evident from the story's starting point ('it was not long since the Christians had conquered the island from the Saracens'). Some scholars have even been able to trace the genealogy of the historical transmission, which is passed on to the imaginary accounts without mentioning Roger's guile in asking the king of France to put the crown on him.[23]

Bernard's narration echoes in subsequent chroniclers, as there are different versions, such as Francisco Pipino's in Latin. But no one is as similar as an old Norse tradition, circa 1190, which tells the story of King Sigurd of Norway. Sigurd had embarked on a crusade to the Holy Land in 1107–10. Among the adventures told in the narration, the anonymous chronicler recounts the encounter between Sigurd and Roger II in Sicily in which Sigurd crowned Roger.[24] The story was taken up and expanded a few decades later in Snorri Sturluson's *Heimskringla*, which added the decisive detail that Sigurd granted Roger the right that there should always be a king of Sicily, although in the past there had been only counts or dukes.

In spring King Sigurd came to Sicily, and remained a long time there. There was then a Duke Roger in Sicily, who received the king kindly, and invited him to a feast. King Sigurd came to it with a great retinue, and was splendidly entertained. Every day Duke Roger stood at the company's table, doing service to the

---

[22] Buc, *The Dangers of Ritual*, 1–28.
[23] Donne, 'Liturgie del potere', 357–8. See also Erich Caspar, *Ruggero II e la fondazione della monarchia Normanda di Siclia* (Roma: Laterza, 1999), 92.
[24] The passage is also narrated in Theodore M. Andersson and Karl Ellen Gade, eds., *Morkinskinna: The Earliest Icelandic Chronicle of the Norwegian Kings (1030–1157)* (Ithaca, NY: Cornell University Press, 2000), caps. 61–3, 313–25. Weiler inserts the story in the context of crown-giving ('Crown-Giving and King-Making', 78–9).

king; but the seventh day of the feast, when the people had come to table, and had wiped their hands, King Sigurd took the Duke by the hand, led him up to the high seat, and saluted him with the title of king; and gave the right that there should be always a king over the dominion of Sicily, although before there had only been earls or dukes over that country. It is written in the chronicles, that Earl Roger let himself first be called king of Sicily in the year of our Lord 1102, having before contented himself with the title of earl only of Sicily, although he was duke of Calabria and Apulia, and was called Roger the Great.[25]

These accounts also resemble that of Boleslaw I of Poland who, according to a tale told by an unknown Polish cleric who wrote a *Life* of Saint Stanislas, gained the crown by his inherent virtue and humility.[26] Alexander's story also seems, incidentally, strikingly similar to that of the election of Frederick Barbarossa (1152) that survives in Gilbert de Mons' history of the counts of Hainault, written in the early thirteenth century.

After Conrad king of the Romans had died, the princes of Germany assembled to elect a new emperor for themselves, as it is the law and custom, in a town above the river Main which is called Frankfurt.... When all the other princes had been summoned (who had appointed and had, accordingly, given faith), the three [electors] declared that they had yielded the entire election to the duke of Swabia, after he had given securities by faith and oath. With everyone listening and not contradicting, Frederick said that he was born of the blood of emperors and that he knew no one better to rule the Empire, and therefore he chose himself for the height of such great majesty. Therefore, many who had esteemed him rejoiced with greater joy. Certain men grieved because of envy and avarice, but they could not oppose the election by any means. Frederick, who had come with foresight to the assembly of the election with 3000 armed knights, went to the city of Speyer with haste. There he caused himself to be crowned as king, so that no one could resist him further. Then, crowned, he came to the palace at Aachen, where he wore the royal crown, and a little later, when he found the time, he came to Rome and was invested with the imperial crown.[27]

In their aim to justify Roger's decision to create a new kingdom and self-crown as a king, Alexander's, Romuald's and Falco's narratives, more or less accurately, produced legitimising narratives of the new Norman dynasty in Sicily. They tell us more about Roger's later cruelty – encapsulated in the

---

[25] Snorri Sturluson, *Heimskringla, or Chronicle of the Kings of Norway* (London, 1844), Saga xii, chapter viii–ix, 154–5, and Sturluson, *Heimskringla: History of the Kings of Norway*, ed. Lee M. Hollander (Austin: University of Texas Press, 1964), 385. The story is also narrated by Agrip; see *Ágrip af Nóregskonungasǫgum: A Twelfth-Century Synoptic History of the Kings of Norway*, ed. Matthew J. Driscoll (London: Viking Society for Northern Research, 1995), 71–5.

[26] Weiler, 'Crown-Giving and King-Making', 60–1.

[27] Gilbert de Mons, *Chronicle of Hainaut*, ed. Laura Napran (New York: Boydell, 2005), 54–5.

formula of 'tyrannus', hurled against Roger by Bernard of Clairvaux – than about the particular historical circumstances of the events of 1130 and 1131.[28] They also confirm that the real complexity of this situation was that Roger created a title of kingship where none existed before and was not recognised by the other European rulers. In addition, Roger had to deal with the disapproval of a king who received his title from a schismatic pope, who was only recognised by a handful of Roman aristocrats and against the majority of European rulers and churchmen, who sided with his rival, Innocent II.[29] Emperor Lothar III actually travelled to southern Italy in the mid-1130s in an attempt to depose him. Roger reacted to this menace by imprisoning Pope Innocent II, and did not release him until he had confirmed his royal title and Anacletus' privileges.

In the end, Roger II's actions led to condemnation from another source. The Sicilian example served to highlight the censure and opprobrium attached to the act of self-investiture and self-coronation elsewhere. The image of Roger as a usurper spread across Europe, notwithstanding all his efforts, precisely because he claimed a crown that he should not possess. This reveals the resistance of previously established kingdoms to legitimising the creation of a new one. The powerful counts of Barcelona had to arrange a complex matrimonial strategy in order to acquire the title of kings, taken from the neighbouring kingdom of Aragon.[30] Eleventh-century German accounts of Polish and Hungarian rulers are conditioned by this reality, as the kings of England sought to control Scottish access to the full paraphernalia of kingship.

Once Roger was established as king, future narratives on the kingdom of Sicily would focus on the individual kings, not the dynasty as a whole. Here, again, the parallels with other European kingdoms are notable, and particularly in the case of the historiographical Catalan cycle. There, the accession of the House of Barcelona as kings of Aragon in the mid-twelfth century was primarily legitimised as a whole dynasty with the genealogies of the counts of Barcelona (*Gesta Comitum Barchinonensium*) and then with the heroic narrations of each king, beginning with Jaume I's autobiography.[31]

---

[28] Helene Wieruszowski, 'Roger II of Sicily, *Rex-Tyrannus*, in Twelfth Century Political Thought', *Speculum* 38(1) (1963): 46–78. On the nature of Roger's authority as *Rigor Iustitiae* see Broekmann, *Rigor Iustitiae*, 119–208.
[29] I. S. Robinson, *The Papacy, 1073–1198: Continuity and Innovation* (Cambridge: Cambridge University Press, 1990), 69–76, 382–6.
[30] Martin Aurell, *Les noces du Comte. Mariage et pouvoir en Catalogne (785–1213)* (Paris: Publications de la Sorbonne, 1995); Aurell, *Authoring the Past*, 27–38 and 111–32.
[31] On Sicily, see Graham A. Loud, 'William the Bad or William the Unlucky? Kingship in Sicily, 1154–1166', *Haskins Society Journal* 8 (1996): 99–114; on the shift from legitimating the dynasty to the exaltation of each particular king in the crown of Aragon, see Jaume Aurell, 'From Genealogies to Chronicles: The Power of the Form in Medieval

We also have a 'non-narrative' source of the event, a specific ordo for Roger II's coronation that seems more reliable with regard to *what actually happened* (or, at least, *what was supposed to happen*) than any of the accounts mentioned, which confirms the theory that, on many occasions, the narrative account of the rites differs from the event itself. The ordo was designed for the coronation ceremony of Christmas 1130.[32] It was based on the model of the ritual for the coronation of German kings. The tradition established that the metropolitan was to act as the minister 'as once upon a time Samuel anointed King David, so that you are blessed and installed as king over the people, over whom your Lord God has assigned to you lordship and rule'.[33]

The bishop serves as the ordinary minister of a coronation, as unambiguously established in both the Magunza ordo for the coronation of Christmas 1130 and the instructions issued by Pope Anacletus II at the moment of the kingdom's creation in September of that same year. Indeed, the privilege of Anacletus specified that the new king had to be crowned by the hand of the archbishop of the kingdom, any one of those chosen by the monarch himself and by his eventual heirs.[34] As the ceremonial indicates, the ritual begins with a bishop imploring God to make his servant maintain the common weal. God had made the king, and the king has to rule the kingdom corresponding to this gift. So he is asked to ensure that the monarch fulfil his duties as protector of the church and its liberties. The king then lays down his insignia and is escorted to the altar, where he prostrates himself in the form of a cross on the ground, together with the priests. After the king's promise to safeguard the Catholic faith, protect the church and defend and rule the realm with justice, he receives the symbols of royal power. The archbishop anoints him and gives him the royal insignia, the crown among them. Then the archbishop accompanies the crowned king, together with the assembled bishops, to his throne, where he gives him the osculation of peace. The *Te*

Catalan Historiography', *Viator: Medieval and Renaissance Studies* 36 (2005): 235–64. See also Weiler, 'Crown-Giving and King-Making', 69, 2.

[32] Elze, 'Tre ordines', 445–52; Elze, 'The Ordo', 165–78; Weiler, 'Crown-Giving and King-Making', 67–8; Weiler, '*Rex Renitens* and the Medieval Idea of Kingship', 34–5.

[33] Elze, 'Tre Ordines', rubrica 13. See also Mirko Vagnoni, 'Evocazioni davidiche nella regalità di Guglielmo II di Sicilia', in *Hagiologica Studio per Réginald Grégoire*, ed. Alessandra Bartolomei Romagnoli, Ugo Paoli and Perpantonio Piatti (Fabriano: Monastero San Silvestro Abate, 2012), 771–87, here 783–4.

[34] 'Concedit etiam, ut coronentur per manus archiepiscoporum térrea, quos ipse et eius heredes voluerint' (Paul F. Kehr, *Italia Pontificia. Sive repertorium privilegiorum et litteratum a Romanis pontificibus ante annum 1198. Vol. 8, Regnum Normannorum – Campania* (Berlin: Berolini, 1935), 37, n. 137.

Deum Laudamus is sung, and, finally, the archbishop celebrates the coronation Mass.[35]

Roger II's Symbolic Self-Coronation

We do not know to what extent the ceremony of Christmas 1130 followed the ritual prescribed by the ordo. However, it was a liturgical ceremony, and the king was most probably crowned by the archbishop. But perhaps, more than the event of his coronation and its narrative accounts, Roger II is recognised as the promoter of the famous scene of his symbolic coronation by Christ that can still be admired today on one of the side walls of the church of Santa Maria dell'Ammiraglio, also known as La Martorana, founded by the minister of Roger's kingdom known as Admiral George of Antioch.[36] Having decided to submit to instructions received from Anacletus II for the ritual of his coronation, he also decided to act freely when it came to the iconography that would commemorate the event.

The Martorana mosaic is not kept in its original place, as it was designed to adorn the narthex of the church, which was later enlarged into the nave in which the mosaic now stands.[37] The image appears to have been created between 1146 and 1151, its evident Byzantine model linked to the Greek origin of George of Antioch himself. The image in the mosaic, that of a king being crowned by Christ, conveys the megalomania of the Norman king and reflects the development of Carolingian theocentrism in the Christocentrism of the Ottonian era. The sovereign is identified as 'King Roger' in Latin (but, interestingly, using Greek letters) in an inscription in the upper part of the mosaic. He appears clothed in the typical garments of the Byzantine emperor, wrapped in traditional consular dress. The tunic is magnificent, decorated with gold and pearls. The figure of Christ features prominently, higher and larger than the king, placing the Byzantine crown, with its *pendilia*, on the king's head. Roger is shown in a position of prayer, his head tilted slightly towards the Lord and hands raised in supplication, adoration, reverence and submission. The

---

[35] Elze, 'The Ordo', 170–8.
[36] Ernst Kitzinger, *The Mosaics of St. Mary's of the Admiral in Palermo* (Washington, DC: Dumbarton Oaks Collection, 1990), especially 105–8, 189–97, 206–11 and 314–16; Ernst Kitzinger, 'On the Portrait of Roger II in the Martorana in Palermo', *Proporzioni* 3 (1950): 30–5; Rosa Bacile, 'Stimulating Perceptions of Kingship: Royal Imagery in the Cathedral of Monreale and in the Church of Santa Maria dell'Ammiraglio in Palermo', *Al-Masaq* 16 (2004): 17–52; Thomas Dittelbach, 'The Image of the Private and the Public King in Norman Sicily', *Römisches Jahrbuch der Bibliotheca Hertziana* 35 (2003–4): 149–72; Matthias Ecker-Ehrhardt, *Freiheit im Bild. Zu den Herrscherbildern unter Roger II. von Sizilien und ihren Auftraggebern* (München: Utz, 2012), especially 35–56.
[37] Tronzo, *The Cultures of His Kingdom*, 140; Kitzinger, 'On the Portrait of Roger II', 30–5, and Kitzinger, *The Mosaics of St. Mary's*, 106–8.

Figure 24 Mosaic depicting Roger II receiving the crown from Christ. Church of Martorana, Santa Maria dell' Ammiraglio in Palermo, Italy, around 1143. © Image BROKER / Alamy Stock Photo.

king's face looks similar to that of Christ, underlining the identification of the sovereign with Jesus Christ and, therefore, with his double nature, divine and human.

The scene is clearly based on the Byzantine representations of a century before, especially the ivory table kept in the Pushkin Museum in Moscow which shows the emperor Constantine VII (913–59) receiving the crown from Christ (Figure 14). Roger wears a beautiful blue tunic, adorned with various types of crosses, over which is wound a wide band, known as a *loros* in Byzantium, circling his waist and covering his chest in the form of a cross. This is an interesting detail, as that peculiar intersection of the band at the chest was the traditional way the *basileuses* wore their *loros* – as shown in the aforementioned ivory table of Constantine VII's coronation by Christ – but was no longer the style favoured by Roger II's contemporaries. This confirms that the creator of the mosaic used iconographic models from the past rather than ceremonial realities of the present.[38] Thus, the artist based his work on, or was at least inspired by, the marble reliefs of the age of Constantine VII in the mid-tenth century rather than on the way the contemporary Byzantine emperors dressed in the more solemn ceremonies of the mid-twelfth century.

Roger II's appropriation of the glorious past of the Byzantine emperors is also consistent with his programme to be considered the sovereign ruler of his land, and the first king of a restored kingdom. This purpose was reformulated a little later by John of Salisbury in 1168 with the expression *Rex imperator in regno suo* ('the king is an emperor in his own land').[39] Roger II went even further than the Byzantine emperors, for although they had already been represented as being crowned by Jesus Christ, none of them had sought a facial or bodily similarity with Christ. The choice of Christmas for his coronation day was perhaps also connected with this desire to be identified with Christ. Roger was seeking a spontaneous connection between the day of Christ's birth and the emergence of the 'new man' implied for any king by the recognition of his sovereignty, as a direct result of the ritual's efficacy. This seems to me what the choice of that date meant, rather than a supposed commemoration of the date of Charlemagne's coronation. Other authors, rather interestingly, have linked this possible symbolic causal relationship to the Nativity scenes in the Palatine Chapel of Palermo, thus confirming the supreme importance of the Christmas celebration.[40]

---

[38] Ginnasi, *L'incoronazione celeste nel mondo bizantino*, 155–7.
[39] Tronzo, *The Cultures of His Kingdom*, 140–1.
[40] Tronzo, *The Cultures of His Kingdom*, 118.

Rather more difficult to establish is the degree of realism and historical referentiality of the scene in the Martorana mosaic: was Roger II presented to his subjects in the manner depicted in that scene? Ernst Kitzinger argues that such a hypothesis would not be far-fetched, taking into account the enormous number of details the Sicilian ceremonial imported from Byzantium, Roger II's custom of being referred to as 'basileus', and the assimilation of the official title of emperor of the East. However, other, more tangible evidence leads to the conclusion that the iconographic reality cannot easily be transposed into the ceremonial. Firstly, some vestments have been preserved from the time of the Norman kings of Sicily until today and there are no *loros* among them, but other royal items. And the textual evidence, above all related to the coronation ordo of 1130, also denies a strict realism of the portrait.[41]

Roger II is presented *ideally* in conjunction with Christ and in Byzantine imperial vestments, both in the Martorana mosaic and on his coins. But when he was actually presented to his people, he wore the garb of his own land, Sicily, with marked Islamic influence. This double dimension, ideal and real, perfectly projects the two dimensions (supernatural and natural, celestial and earthly, sacred and profane) that Roger II wanted to reflect in his programme of self-representation, and also appears to characterise the level of reality that both would occupy in the mind of the spectator: the former distant and pictorial, the latter present and ceremonial. The iconographic programme of the Royal Palace of Palermo and of the Palatina Chapel, together with the Martorana portrait, clearly demonstrate the efficacy of this project.[42]

This gap between historical reality and representation (referred to here as the vestments) might be of use in transposing this idea to the theological reality that involved the coronation by Christ as an iconographic motif. The act of Christ crowning the king must be seen strictly for its symbolic content, as the spectators were meant to absorb it. However, we must not exclude a more realist look at the Martorana mosaic, as that was how Frederick saw it in his childhood, and he tried to emulate that coronation by Christ with his own self-coronation in Jerusalem. In any case, we should recall Percy Ernst Schramm's interpretation of this as a representation based on a pictorial mould, 'a stereotyped form passed on regardless of whether it corresponds to reality because it was still felt to be suitable in terms of its content'.[43]

---

[41] Kitzinger, *The Mosaics of St. Mary's*, 191.
[42] Some authors have even claimed, on the basis of other iconographic evidence, that Roger II wore Islamic-influenced garb rather than strictly Byzantine or Sicilian clothing (Tronzo, *The Cultures of His Kingdom*, 143–4).
[43] Percy E. Schramm, *Herrschaftszeichen und Staatssymbolik*. 3 vols. (Stuttgart: Hiersemann, 1954), 1:18.

Nevertheless, the artist – and maybe the king himself, whether it was his direct or indirect inspiration – wanted to furnish this representation with explicit symbolic meaning; recent investigations have insisted on the influence of George of Antioch in the development of the political programme and ideology of the mosaic. Both the identification of Roger II with the Byzantine *basileus* and the exalted act of his coronation by Jesus Christ most certainly made an impression on those who saw it at the time – as they continue to do today. Kitzinger concludes: 'Roger allowed himself to be portrayed in the guise of a Byzantine emperor because the Basileus in Constantinople embodied the ideal of absolute monarchic power which he claimed for himself.'[44] Roger is certainly defined with the title of 'rex' in the mosaic, and his notion of royalty fits perfectly with the sense of the mentioned expression 'rex imperator in regno suo' and with his ambition to replace the imperial Byzantine divinity.[45]

The same symbolic potential of the imperial vestments can be assigned to the far from negligible fact of Roger's desire to appear being crowned by Jesus Christ himself. Ernst Kitzinger interpreted the gesture of Roger II crowned by Christ as the pictorial equivalent of the formulation of the 'king crowned by God' (*a Deo coronatus*), which almost literally equates to the idea of self-coronation, or coronation without the mediation of the hand of man. The visual counterpart of the expression *a Deo coronatus*, explicitly shown in the mosaic, involves a rejection of the earthly church as an indispensable intermediary of the transfer of monarchic power.[46] The same king who asked for the mediation of the Pope in his aspiration to be promoted with the kingship dignity, tried to avoid this mediation in symbolic terms. Mirko Vagnoni has concluded that neither the mosaic of the Martorana nor the image of Christ crowning William II in the cathedral of Santa Maria la Nuova in Monreale (Palermo) represent an identification of the king with divinity, but rather they are a representation of the ideological concept of the king crowned by Christ and, therefore, by God, whence his authority derives. The idea of the *a Deo coronatus* would therefore be incompatible with that of the king as the image of God (*Imago Dei*), of the physical identification of the king with Christ (*Christomimetes*) and the identification of the king with the priest (*rex et sacerdos*).[47]

---

[44] Kitzinger, *The Mosaics of St. Mary's*, 195.
[45] Francesco Calasso, 'Origini italiane della formula "Rex in regno suo est imperator"', *Rivista di storia del firitto italiano* 3 (1930): 213ff., and Wieruszowski, 'Roger II of Sicily'.
[46] Kitzinger, *The Mosaics of St. Mary's*, 195.
[47] Mirko Vagnoni, 'Royal Images and Sacred Elements in Norman-Swabian and Angevin-Aragonese Kingdom of Sicily', *Eikón Imago* 2 (2013): 107–22, here 112 and 120.

This whole programme confirms the increasing notion of the weakness of priestly mediation from the twelfth century in Europe. William Tronzo explains this idea in terms of 'iconographic self-sufficiency', meaning that the creator of the mosaic made 'an image that explained the derivation of Roger's power – not from pope or emperor but from God alone – and at the same time demonstrated the fact of *similititudo* – his Essential Christomimetic nature – in purely visual terms. Such an image could thus be understood by anyone – Arab, Norman, Greek, or Latin – not depending on verbal-commentary'.[48] Now the referent is not, however, only the Byzantine emperors (whose garb has been imitated by the mosaicist and applied to the Norman king), but also the Ottonian emperors, who had been frequently portrayed as being crowned by Christ and who had reformulated the theocentric theory of the Carolingians in Christocentric terms.[49]

In addition, the panel clearly privileges a certain facial resemblance between Roger and Christ. Both are represented in an idealised way, with long hair and well-kept beard, a similarity the Byzantines had never aspired to, as is clearly seen in the paradigmatic portrait of Constantine VII being crowned by Christ (Figure 14).[50] Beyond the obvious Pauline resonances to do with the doctrine of the *Ipse Christus* or the *Alter Christus*, and of reflections around the images of the assumption of the Christ figure by substitution in Ottonian iconography, the theme has enormous ideological and theological significance, and a notable influence on future iconographic models. The idea of the sovereign being crowned by Christ had been recovered by the Ottonians (who had for their part borrowed it from the Byzantines) to underline that neither the Pope nor the bishops nor the priests were necessarily the mediators between them and the deity. The theme disappears, not by chance, during the period of the investiture quarrel, from the first third of the eleventh century to the first third of the twelfth. During this period, there was enormous tension among the European sovereigns (who aspired to greater independence from the Pope and were therefore employing every means at their disposal to guarantee their own autonomy in the temporal sphere), and the growth of the idea of papal theocracy, which also sought to preserve for its part the autonomy of ecclesiastical authority in the spiritual sphere. Roger II thus took up Byzantine-Ottonian iconography at a key moment, but,

---

[48] William Tronzo, 'Byzantine Court Culture from the Point of View of Norman Sicily: The Case of the Cappella Palatina in Palermo', in *Byzantine Court Culture from 829 to 1204*, ed. Henri Maguire (Washington, DC: Dumbarton Oaks, 1997), 101–14, here 108–9.
[49] Kitzinger, 'On the Portrait of Roger II', 30ff.
[50] Kitzinger, 'On the Portrait of Roger II', 30–5; Tronzo, *The Cultures of His Kingdom*, 148; Josef Deér, *The Dynastic Porphyry Tombs of the Norman Period in Sicily* (Cambridge, MA: Harvard University Press, 1959), 154–65; Eve Borsook, *Messages in Mosaic: The Royal Programmes of Norman Sicily (1130–1187)* (Woodbridge: Boydell, 1998).

paradoxically, it seemed to go against the desacralising direction that the rest of the European monarchs were taking as a result of the investiture quarrel. The Norman king thus struck a more traditional, even traditionalist, posture, more in tune with Frankish and Ottonian customs (at least until Henry III), and with his contemporaries in Byzantium, even being for some contemporary authors assimilated with the figure of the *rex et sacerdos*.

This interpretation has held up for many decades, in large part due to the authority of those who have maintained it, especially Kantorowicz and Kitzinger. But it is currently being revised by recent historiography, based above all on new trends in art history.[51] The figurative content of the images should be repositioned in its rightful context, with special attention paid to the audience, the place the image is designed for and its social and religious function.[52] In that case, without denying its historiographical interest, the interpretations of the representations of Roger II being crowned by Christ or crowned by St Nicholas as a specific instance of the theories of *a Deo coronatus, rex et sacerdos* and *Christomimetes* would be considered naive generalisations. Certainly, the message of the divine origin of regal power is unequivocal, and the sacredness of the king is further confirmed by the fact of the insertion of the image in a fully sacred and religious context. But the interpretation that the symbolic message of the mosaic entails a characterisation of the king as priest goes against the historical experience of an existing ecclesiastical hierarchy that was really active and influential at the time of Roger II. The Christocentric theory, reflected in iconographic models, had its apogee in the Ottonian era, especially during the reign of Otto II, but was already clearly in decline by the time of Roger II. The fact that in the Martorana mosaic the decision has been made to clearly mark the differences between the king and Christ (an impression reinforced by Roger II's submissive and adoring attitude, as for his different level) thus confirms this. The same could be argued to demystify an overly literal interpretation of the Martorana coronation scene, as Roger was in almost all certainty anointed and crowned by the archbishop in 1130.

Although Theo Broekmann has convincingly explained Roger's implacable action of imposing his authority, this image does not imply

---

[51] Mirko Vagnoni, '*Rex et sacerdos* e *christomimetes*. Alcune considerazioni sulla sacralità dei re normanni di Sicilia', *Mediaeval Sophia* 12 (2012): 268–84, and Tronzo, *The Cultures of His Kingdom*, 118–24.

[52] Jérôme Baschet, 'Introduction: l'image-objet', in *L'image. Fonctions et usage des images dans l'Occident médiéval*, ed. Baschet and Jean-Claude Schmitt (Paris: Léopard d'Or, 1996), 7–26; Jean-Claude Schmitt, 'L'historien et les images', in *Le corps des images. Essai sur la culture visuelle au Moyen Âge* (Paris: Gallimard, 2002), 35–62.

the recognition of the *incarnation* of Roger II as Christ, which would grant him unconditional power over his kingdom in matters both temporal and spiritual, civil as well as ecclesiastical, and thus invest him with absolute sacredness.[53] Among other things, apart from the aforementioned physical similarity, Roger II's actual submission to Christ, so graphically expressed by the artist through the height difference between the figures, as well as in the slight inclination of the king towards Christ and the position of the king's hands showing his homage to Christ, graphically confirms the very diversity of the two figures' natures and so demystifies the supposed theory of *christomimetes* put forward by Kitzinger.[54]

What cannot be denied, however, is that the image carries an enormous symbolic charge, which contemporaries could perceive as such, among other reasons because there is not the slightest allusion to the authority of the Pope, the source of the very same authority with which the kingdom had been legitimately constituted. Nevertheless, as the visual effect of the iconography of Roger being crowned by Christ had great potential, we cannot have any idea of the actual audience it had at that time, since the mosaic was placed in a private chapel rather than in the cathedral or a popular church. The Martorana was founded by George of Antioch as private sacred place with his own chapel and as a mausoleum for his family.

Another analogous interpretation to this, if more plausible, is the extent to which Roger II sought to identify with the idea of empire through a programme in which iconography also played an important role. And here it is worth summoning the image of the king being crowned by St Nicholas. It is a panel originally situated in the ciborium of the high altar of the basilica of St Nicholas in Bari – now kept in the church's museum. The parallels between the two representations are evident – and this image is probably older than the other in the Martorana. Roger is also described as *Rogerius rex*. The model also comes from Byzantium (in this case, from the coins), and the whole representation has the same air. But the differences are greater: the saint has the same size and stands at the same level as the king, and the dress and symbols of power depicted differ. Finally, the combination between the Byzantine and Western styles is more typical of a local artist than the truly Byzantine ones evinced by the Martorana image, as shown by the image of Roger II with Saint Nicholas at the basilica of Saint Nicholas in

---

[53] Broekmann, *Rigor Iustitiae*, 119–208, and for the debate on the sacrality of the kingship in Sicily see Mirko Vagnoni, *Le rappresentazioni del potere. La sacralità regia dei Normanni di Sicilia: un mito?* (Bari: Caratterimobili, 2012).

[54] 'Se è legittimo parlare de un Ruggero *a Deo coronatus*, assolutament non lo è di *christomimetes* e *rex et sacerdos*' (Vagnoni, 'Rex et sacerdos e christomimetes', 277).

Bari. However, these two representations are essentially the same, as they represent the sovereign described as king, but portrayed prototypically as emperor (*basileus*) and being crowned by Christ or a saint rather than an ecclesiastical mediator. They are idealised, hieratic images, and therefore with little expressivity (given that every gesture might be considered grotesque here, as Jean-Claude Schmitt argues),[55] in which the personal features of the king are not reflected but rather a generic identification with the features traditionally ascribed to Christ (without going as far as a *Christomimetes*, as argued earlier) or, even more, to the Byzantine emperors.[56] These two representations also have the virtue of being the only contemporary ones of the king that have reached us, together with some seals and coins, although these do not offer significant information for the iconography of coronations.[57] For this reason, they are reliable evidence of Roger II's intention to assimilate ideologically with the Byzantine Empire, although in reality he is the head of a kingdom.

Thus, the *imitatio Byzantii*, together with his interest in it being the Pope who directly confers the legitimacy of the new kingdom, gave Roger and his successors absolute authority, but also created certain anachronistic effects in these representations. This increases the impression that Roger and his collaborators were trying to avoid by all means – rhetorical, symbolical and iconographical – the condemnation into which the former count fell after his royal self-investiture. To achieve this artificial reputation, the Norman kingdom of Sicily was even conceived of as an empire and, as a consequence, its representatives acquired imperial rank, meaning that the dominion and authority of its sovereign came directly from God – an imperial aspiration which, interestingly, other European kingdoms such as Castile were trying to achieve at that time.[58] The paradox and irony of this ambitious

---

[55] Schmitt, *La raison des gestes dans l'Occident médiéval*, 120: 'tout geste serait ici gesticulation'.

[56] Houben, *Roger II of Sicily*, 117, argues that 'the face with its bifurcated beard and long hair on each side is indeed a faithful portrait of the Norman king' (Émile Bertaux, 'L'émail de Saint-Nicholas de Bari', *Monuments et Mémoires*, 4 [1898]: 61–90).

[57] Rodolfo Spahr, *Le monete siciliane. Dai Bizantini a Carlo I d'Angiò (582–1282)* (Zurich: AINP, 1976); Lucia Travaini, *La monetazione nell'Italia Normanna* (Roma: Nella sede dell'Istituto, 1995); Mirko Vagnoni, 'Epifanie regie nel regno normando-svevo di Sicilia', *De Medio Aevo* 3 (2013): 91–120, here 95–6, and for some successors of Roger II see 106–9.

[58] On the sacral character of the Norman kingdom of Sicily see Mirko Vagnoni, 'Problemi di legittimazione regia: *Imitatio Byzantii*', in *Il Papato e I Normanni*, ed. Edoardo D'Angelo and Consiglio Leopardi (Firenze: Galuzzo, 2011), 175–90; Vagnoni, *La rappresentazioni del potere*, 63–75; Kantorowicz, *Laudes Regiae*, 155–61; Vagnoni, '*Rex et sacerdos e christomimetes*', 268–84; Antonio Marongiu, *Byzantine, Norman, Swabian and Later Institutions in Southern Italy* (London: Variorum Reprints, 1972); Deér, *The Dynastic*

aspiration lies in that Sicily in fact generated an extraordinary mismatch between its historical reality (always at the expense of balance with other powers such as the German kingdom, the pontifical states, the rising kingdom of France and the crown of Aragon, and the house of Anjou) and its imperial aspirations. This would explain the continuous changes of sovereignty that the kingdom would suffer in the following centuries, and why an indigenous monarchy would never become consolidated. The natural amphitheatre that cradles Palermo is an apt metaphor for the tragedy that the island has lived, always dependent on sovereignties imposed from outside. Those who aspired to a universal sovereignty experienced in fact the drama of the permanent imposition of an external sovereignty.

All the images glossed in this chapter aimed to legitimise the divine origin of royal authority, and the aspiration to avoid any ecclesiastical mediation, rather than an explanation of the rite of coronation. These investitures were usually of a symbolic, celestial or mythical nature, as their fundamental aim was the authority of the emperor through an explicit supernatural intervention.[59] The most recent research actually argues in favour of a religious rather than a political reading of the Martorana mosaic. The scene of Roger II being crowned by Christ should be understood as an adoration of the man-God and a sign of the king's aspiration to eternal life rather than an exaltation of the king's authority and sovereignty.[60] Yet the Martorana mosaic-portrait is extraordinarily consistent with Roger II's imperial fiction, and is therefore relevant for research into self-coronations, as a clear exponent of symbolic coronation.

Some historians have argued that the Martorana mosaic inspired Roger's grandson, Frederick II, who must have admired it in the years of his childhood and adolescence in Palermo. Modern historiography has debunked this romantic story. But it makes full symbolic sense if we consider that Frederick II took Roger II as his model in other political and cultural spheres, as there is even evidence of a commission he gave for a fresco for the atrium of Cefalù cathedral (now lost) in which Roger II appeared wearing a crown and royal vestments, with an inscription

Porphyry Tombs of the Norman Period in Sicily; Léon-Robert Ménager, 'L'institution monarchique dans les États normands d'Italie', *Cahiters de Civilisation Médiévale* 2 (1959): 303–31 and 445–68; Paolo Delogu: 'Idee sulla regalità: l'eredità normanna', in *Potere, società e popolo nell'età dei due Guglielmi* (Bari: Università degli Studi di Bari, 1981), 185–215; Glauco Maria Cantarella, *La Sicilia e i Normanni. Le fonti del mito* (Bologna: Patron, 1980).

[59] Bonne, 'Images du Sacre', 91–226, here 96.
[60] Some recent scholars, especially Mirko Vagnoni, are highlighting the convenience of a mosaic's spiritual rather than political reading.

identifying him once more as *Rogerius rex*.[61] Roger II's respect for his Muslim Arab subjects, as well as his attempt to assimilate Arab and Byzantine cultural traditions, evident in the construction and design of his palaces,[62] is at the root of his iconographic programme in that the visual language has a supra-verbal meaning and could be intuitively understood by Arabs, Normans, Greeks and Latins.[63] This whole multilingual, multinational, multi-ethnic and multi-custom tradition is a typical inheritance of the kingdom of Sicily, and would without doubt constitute an inspiration for the universalistic and imperial politics of Frederick II.[64] The next chapter focuses on him, and especially his supposed self-coronation in Jerusalem: Frederick II ritually invented what Roger II iconographically symbolised.

---

[61] See Maria Valenciano and Crispino Valenciano, 'La supplique des chanoines de la cathédrale de Cefalù pour la sépolture du roi Roger', *Cahiers de Civilisation Médievale*, 21 (1978): 137–50, and Hans Martin Shaller, 'Das Relief an der Kanzel der Kathedrale von Bitonto. Ein Denkmal der Kaiseridee Friedrichs II', *Archiv für Kulturgeschichte* 45 (1963): 295–312, who suggests a date between 1226 and 1229. Nevertheless, we should be cautious with this relationship, since the chronology of this image is still uncertain: see Vagnoni, *La rappresentazioni del potere*, 38–40.

[62] Hans-Rudolf Meier, *Die normannischen Königspaläste in Palermo* (Worms: Wernersche Verlagsgesellschaft, 1994).

[63] Tronzo, *The Cultures of His Kingdom*, 149. On the Byzantine influx of the Norman royal iconography see Sulamith Brodbeck, 'Le souverain en images dans la Sicile normande', *Perspective. La revue de l'INHA* 1 (2012): 167–72.

[64] On the legal links between the chancelleries of Roger II and Frederick II see Kantorowicz, 'Mysteries of State', 69–72. On the universalist aspiration see Jeremy Johns, 'The Muslims of Norman Sicily and the Fatimid Caliphate', *Anglo-Norman Studies* 15 (1993): 133–59; Mirella Cassarino, 'Palermo Experienced, Palermo Imagined: Arabic and Islamic Culture between the 9th and the 12th Century', in *A Companion to Medieval Palermo: The History of a Mediterranean City from 600 to 1500*, ed. Annliese Nef (Leiden: Brill, 2013), 89–132.

8 Frederick II of Germany
Desacralising Rituals

Frederick II's legendary self-coronation in the Church of the Holy Sepulchre in Jerusalem, on Sunday 17 March 1229, remains shrouded in ambiguity, where it is difficult to discern the borders between reality and imagination, desire and realisation, invention and propaganda, history and symbolism.[1] Because of the variability and imprecision of the sources, the singular nature of the gesture and Frederick II's complex megalomaniac personality, this crowning ceremony lives in the realm of legend and controversy. But, paradoxically, two modern historians did more to increase this impression of mystery than the medieval sources: Jacob Burckhardt and Ernst Kantorowicz.[2]

In 1860, Burckhardt described Frederick II as the personification of the 'premodern' prince.

> Bred amid treason and peril in the neighbourhood of the Saracens, Frederick, the first ruler of the modern type who sat upon a throne, had early accustomed himself, both in criticism and action, to a thoroughly objective treatment of affairs. His acquaintance with the internal condition and administration of the Saracenic States was close and intimate; and the mortal struggle in which he was engaged with the Papacy compelled him, no less than his adversaries, to bring into the field all the resources at his command.[3]

This anachronistic but authoritative vision prepared the road for future idealisations of Frederick's strategies, a task undertaken by Kantorowicz, who explicitly describes the event as a self-coronation, connecting it with Napoleon's.

---

[1] As Philippe Buc summarises, 'Frederick II, who according to tradition but not fact, had crowned himself King of Jerusalem' (Buc, '1701 in Medieval Perspective', 92).

[2] On the not always accurate influence of modern historiography on the crown-wearing of Frederick II in Jerusalem see Bodo Hechelhammer, *Kreuzzug und Herrschaftunter Friedrich II: Handlungsspielräume von Kreuzzugspolitik (1215–1230)* (Ostfildern: Jan Thorbecke, 2004), 300–1.

[3] Jacob Burckhardt, *The Civilization of the Renaissance in Italy* (New York: Harper & Row, 1958), 24 (original edition from 1860).

The Pope's unforgiving spirit was turned to good account. Thanks to it, it came about that on the 18th of March, the fourth Sunday before Easter, there took place in Jerusalem in the Church of the Holy Sepulchre the most memorable self-coronation of an Emperor that the world was to see till the days of Napoleon. In full imperial State, the banned and excommunicated Emperor – outside the congregation of the faithful – accompanied by followers and friends, crossed the threshold of the sacred edifice. Here, where the first king of Jerusalem, Godfrey of Bouillon, with humble emotion, refused to wear a golden circlet where his Lord had worn a crown of thorns; here, without intermediary of the Church, without bishop, without coronation mass, Kaiser Frederick II, proud and unabashed, stretched forth his hand to take the royal crown of the Holy City. Striding towards the altar of the Sepulchre, he lifted from it the crown, and himself placed it on his own head – an act, whether so intended, of far-reaching symbolism. For thus, on the holiest spot of all the Christian universe, he asserted a king's immediate vassalhood to God, and without the interposition of the Church approached his God direct as a triumphant conqueror. Frederick II made no effort to derive from doctrines and theories a belief in the immediate relationship of God to Emperor – a doctrine fiercely denied by the Popes since the evolution of the Hierarchy – he based it on the miracles of his own career, obvious to all and far-renowned, which proved as nothing else could do that God's immediate choice rested on his imperial person, if not on his imperial office.[4]

Burckhardt's idealisation of Frederick II as the first *modern* king and Kantorowicz's magnification of the emperor's self-coronation strongly shaped contemporary historiographies and, of course, the popular imagination. They also influenced the next two generations of historians, considering the durable influence of their classical works and their later reception, because of the delay of the English translations from the original German.

Yet a more accurate interpretation has been provided by German historians who, from the 1990s, have revisited the primary sources. Since Frederick's ceremony felt in contempt from the beginning, a good group of testimonies and chroniclers gave their version from the mid-thirteenth century. Most of them recognise that what happened in the Holy Sepulchre that Sunday of Lent was a profane ritual with the crown, rather than a proper (self-)coronation, investiture or ceremony with constitutional effects. Yet these sources also recognise the unconventionality and transgressive dimension of the ritual enacted by Frederick II, and differ in some details. So the crucial question here is not only *what* happened that Sunday of Lent in the Holy Sepulchre, but also the

---

[4] Ernst Kantorowicz, *Frederick the Second (1994–1250)* (New York: Frederick Ungar, 1957), 199. On Frederick II's idealisations see Olaf B. Rader, *Friedrich II. Der Sizilianer auf dem Kaiserthron. Eine Biographie* (München: Beck, 2010), 398–9, and Hellmuth Kluger, *Hochmeister Hermann von Salza und Kaiser Friedrich II. Ein Beitrag zur Frühgeschichte des Deutschen Ordens* (Marburg: N. G. Elwert, 1987), 95–113.

reception of this event in the West and its repercussions for Frederick's reputation. Thus, starting from the difficulties involved in a historical approach to such an event, and based on the authorised historians who have dedicated themselves to this question, this chapter examines its historicity and explores its enormous symbolic potentiality, especially in connection with royal self-investitures and self-coronations.[5] More specifically, I am interested in looking into its alleged transgressive ritual dimension in more depth, as it represents a challenge to our preconceived ideas regarding the relationship between the temporal and spiritual

[5] Historians who have dealt with Fredrick II's self-coronation in Jerusalem are, in chronological order, Ernst Kantorowicz, *Kaiser Friedrich der Zweite* (Berlin: Georg Bondi, 1928) (quoted in the English edition: Kantorowicz, *Frederick the Second*, 197–206); James M. Powell, 'Frederick II and the Church in the Kingdom of Sicily, 1220–1224', *Church History* 30(1) (1961): 28–34; Powell, 'Frederick II and the Church: A Revisionist View', *Catholic Historical Review* 48 (1963): 487–97; Mayer, 'Das Pontifikale von Tyrus und die Krönung der lateinischen Könige von Jerusalem' (specifically 200–10); Percy E. Schramm, 'Krönung und Herrschaftszeichen im Königreich Jerusalem. Kaiser Friedrichs II "Selbstkrönung" und ihre Fortwirkung', in *Kaiser, Könige und Papst. Gesammelte Aufsätze zur Geschichte des Mittelalters* (Stuttgart: Hiersemann, 1971), 4:461–70; Thomas C. van Cleve, *The Emperor Frederick II of Hohenstaufen. Immutator Mundi* (Oxford: Clarendon, 1972), 222–5; James M. Powell, 'Crusading by Royal Command: Monarchy and Crusade in the Kingdom of Sicily (1187–1230)', in *Potere, società e popolo tra età normanna ed età sveva, 1189–1210* (Bari: Dedalo, 1983), 131–46; Kluger, *Hochmeister Hermann von Salza und Kaiser Friedrich II*, 86–122; René Schlott, *Das Rundschreiben Kaiser Friedrichs II. (1194–1250) vom 10.Marz 1229* (Berlin: Grin, 2013); David Abulafia, *Federico II. Un imperatore medievale* (Torino: Einaudi, 1993), 154–8; James M. Powell, 'Frederick II and the Muslims: The Making of an Historiographical Tradition', in *Iberia and the Mediterranean World of the Middle Ages. Studies in Honor of Robert I. Burns S.J. Vol. 1. Proceedings from Kalamazoo*, ed. Larry J. Simon (Leiden: Brill, 1995), 261–9; Andrea Sommerlechner, *Stupor Mundi? Friedrich II. und die mittelalterliche Geschichtsschreibung* (Vienna: Österreichischen Akademie der Wissenschaften, 1999), 303–8; James M. Powell, 'Patriarch Gerold and Frederick II: The Matthew Paris Letter', *Journal of Medieval History* 25(1) (1999): 19–26; Wolfgang Stürner, 'Federico II, re di Gerusalemme', in *Il Mezzogiorno Normanno-svevo visto dall'Europa e le crociate* (Bari: Dedalo, 1999), 159–76; Adrian Boas, *Jerusalem in the Time of the Crusades: Society, Landscape and Art in the Holy City under Frankish Rule* (London: Routledge, 2001), 19–20; Hechelhammer, *Kreuzzug und Herrschaftunter Friedrich II*, 296–306; Christopher Tyerman, *God's War: A New History of the Crusaders* (London: Penguin, 2006), 739–55; Hubert Houben, *Kaiser Friedrich II (1194–1250): Herrscher, Mensch, Mythos* (Stuttgart: Kohlhammer, 2007), 48–53; Knut Görich, Jan Ulrich Keupp and Theo Broekmann, eds., *Herrschaftsräume, Herrschaftspraxis und Kommunikation zur Zeit Kaiser Friedrichs II* (München: Herbert Utz, 2008); Wolfgang Stürner, *Friedrich II. 1194–1250*. 2 vols. (Darmstadt: WBG, 2009), 2:85–169; Rader, *Friedrich II*; Marcello Pacifico, *Federico II e Gerusalemme al tempo delle crociate* (Caltanissetta: Salvatore Sciascia, 2012), 266–82; Marcello Pacifico, 'La coronatio hierosolymitana del 1229', in *Universalità della ragione. Pluralità delle filosofie nel Medievo*, ed. Alessandro Musco (Palermo: Officina di studi medievali, 2012), 245–59. See also Marcus Thomsen, 'Modernität als Topos – Friedrich II. in der Deutschen Historiographie', in *Herrschaftsräume, Herrschaftspraxis und Kommunikation zur Zeit Kaiser Friedrichs II*, ed. Knut Görich, Jan Ulrich Keupp and Theo Broekmann (München: Herbert Utz, 2008), 21–40.

realms, the sacred and the profane, the ecclesiastical and the civil, the church and the state.[6]

The Road to Jerusalem: Dynastic Politics and Crusade Ambitions

Two lines of historical context converge in this story: the evolution of the Latin kingdom of Jerusalem and Frederick's own aspirations to lead the crusade.[7]

A series of more or less fortuitous circumstances led Frederick II to the throne of the Latin kingdom of Jerusalem, starting with the fact that he married the heiress to the kingdom, Isabella II, in 1225 and then assigned himself the role of guardian for their son and heir, Conrad. The emperor's personal involvement in his goal of becoming king of Jerusalem had as much to do with his own development and ambition as sovereign as with the peculiar identity of the Latin kingdom of Jerusalem, founded in 1099 following the conquests of the First Crusade. On one hand, in the 1220s, Frederick was at the apogee of his power, eager for new challenges after having been crowned king of Sicily in 1198 and emperor of the Holy Roman Empire in 1220. On the other hand, the political situation of the Latin kingdom of Jerusalem was in those years precisely the inverse, with its own viability in doubt. The kingdom of Acre (1191–1229) had been founded after the fall of Jerusalem in 1187 and the ensuing years of confusion. Confined to a narrow strip of the Syrian coast with Acre as its capital, the kingdom sustained a precarious existence in those decades, with Beirut and Tyre as its most notable cities, and exercised sovereignty over Tripoli and Antioch.[8] The Latin kingdom of Jerusalem had not been able to overcome its endemic unsteadiness, accentuated by the continuous Muslim threats, the difficulty of achieving a minimum level of stability among the political and social elites, the lack of enthusiasm

---

[6] Gerd Althoff, 'The Variability of Rituals in the Middle Ages', in *Medieval Concepts of the Past: Ritual, Memory, Historiography*, ed. Gerd Althoff, Johannes Fried and Patrick J. Geary (Cambridge: Cambridge University Press, 2003), 71–88, provides examples of changing rites precisely as confirmation of the relevance of the ceremony during the Middle Ages.

[7] For the influence of the evolution of the kingdom of Sicily and its consequences on the relationship between Frederick II and the popes, see Powell, 'Frederick II and the Church'.

[8] On the Latin kingdom of Jerusalem see Joshua Prawer, *Histoire du royaume latin de Jérusalem* (Paris: Éditions du CNRS, 1969–70); Hans E. Mayer, *Kings and Lords in the Latin Kingdom of Jerusalem* (London: Ashgate, 1994); Peter W. Edbury, *John of Ibelin and the Kingdom of Jerusalem* (Rochester: Boydell, 1997); Boas, *Jerusalem in the Time of the Crusades*; Elisabeth Crouzel-Pavan, *Le mystère des rois de Jérusalem (1099–1187)* (Paris: Albin Michel, 2013).

generated by the Pope's calling for new crusades and the perpetual border fluctuations.

This instability grew even more acute at the end of the twelfth century due to the changeability of the royal family. That was the situation of the kingdom around the 1220s, when Frederick II entered the scene. He had contributed to the Fifth Crusade in 1217, promoted by Pope Honorius III (1216–27), sending troops from Germany, though he did not want to commit himself personally, needing to consolidate the situation in his German and Italian territories.[9] Nevertheless, his coronation as emperor of the Holy Roman Empire by Honorius in 1220 stimulated his desire to take part in the next crusade in person. He took the definitive decision in 1223, following a meeting held in the city of Ferentino with Honorius III and John of Brienne, in which his marriage to Isabella II was agreed and thus his eventual accession to the kingdom of Jerusalem as king-consort.[10] However, much to the Pope's unease, Frederick once more delayed his participation in the crusade and the marriage to Isabella II was agreed without his physical presence, by proxy, in Acre, in August 1225.

Shortly afterwards, Isabella II was finally crowned queen by the archbishop of Tyre, at the end of August 1225. She was at that time thirteen. The patriarch of Jerusalem, Gerold of Valence, was supposed to be the proper minister of the ceremony, but he was in Europe at the time.[11] The queen was then sent to Brindisi and the marriage ceremony was held in the cathedral there, in the presence of the two king-consorts (John of Brienne as father and Frederick II as husband), on 9 November 1225. In the ceremony, Frederick declared himself the only king-consort of Jerusalem, stripping of his rights the person who was at that time regent of Jerusalem, his father-in-law, John of Brienne.[12] The latter accepted the reality of the facts, but from that point hostilities opened between father- and son-in-law, and would extend over time with a considerable impact on the Latin kingdom of Jerusalem.

---

[9] On Frederick's original commitment to the crusade, see Hechelhammer, *Kreuzzug und Herrschaft unter Friedrich II*, 77–118, and Stürner, *Friedrich II*, 2:85–90 and 2:126–47, and Guy Perry, *John of Brienne: King of Jerusalem, Emperor of Constantinople, c.1175–1237* (Cambridge: Cambridge University Press, 2013), 89–121.

[10] On Honorious III's ambivalent actions in the tensions between Frederick II and John of Brienne, see Thomas W. Smith, 'Between Two Kings: Pope Honorious III and the Seizure of the Kingdom of Jerusalem by Frederick in 1225', *Journal of Medieval History* 41 (2015): 41–59 (on the marriage between Frederick and Isabella see 43–6).

[11] *Les Gestes des Chiprois* (Genève: J. G. Fick, 1887), chapter 89. On Gerold of Valence see Wilhelm Jacobs, *Patriarch Gerold von Jerusalem. Ein Beitrag zur Kreuzzugsgeschichte Kaiser Friedrichs II* (Aachen: Aachener Verlags- und Druckerei-Gesellschaft, 1905).

[12] On the relationship between Frederick II and his father-in-law, John of Brienne, see Perry, *John of Brienne*, 135–49.

The circumstance of Frederick II's accession to the regency of the kingdom of Jerusalem in 1225 seemed ripe for his eastward expansionist longings. But the situation was complicated when the new Pope, Gregory IX, proclaimed the excommunication of Frederick II in September 1227 in response to yet another delay on the emperor's part in joining the crusade. On 26 April 1228, Isabella II gave birth to a son, Conrad, who would be Conrad II of Jerusalem (and Conrad IV of Germany) and who was the true heir to the kingdom.[13] Some days later, in early May, Isabella II died. Frederick took advantage of the circumstances to put himself forward as regent for his son, Conrad, at least until he reached his majority. Hostilities between Frederick II and John of Brienne intensified. The barons of Jerusalem could have hardly been surprised by the conflict between the two relatives-in-law considering John's involvement in leading a papal army to conquer Sicily against Frederick's interests. Yet this stirred up active opposition in a good part of the native nobility, led by John of Ibelin, who was against Frederick II having the regency of the heir, Conrad II. The kingdom then descended headlong into a long civil war, known as the War of the Lombards, which would drag on until 1243.

Marriage to Isabella II in 1225 made it possible to legitimise Frederick II's regency to the kingdom given the fact that it was squarely in the kingdom's peculiar native tradition by which 'queens make kings', following the recent precedent established by Guy de Lusignan. Yet three years later, when Isabella II died, Frederick was rendered simply guardian of his son and legal heir, Conrad II, a state of affairs he was obviously reluctant to accept.[14] The custom that favoured his accession to the regency had been turned against him, as the death of the queen supposedly dissolved the regency of king-consorts. Two clear precedents were against Frederick's ambitions: Guy de Lusignan and John of Brienne. On the death of his consort, Guy de Lusignan had become sole ruler in 1190, but it was a temporary matter. He abdicated in 1192 in favour of Conrad I. However, Conrad died a few days after taking the office, so that the crown passed to his wife Isabella I (1192–1205). John of Brienne, for his part, had assumed the regency on the death of his wife, Maria the Marquise, in 1212, but with the clear understanding that the legal heir was his daughter Isabella II, also known as Yolande of Jerusalem. Frederick II was therefore aware that on the death of his wife, Isabella II, he as king-consort had to pass the crown to his most direct descendant, namely his son, Conrad IV, but that he might claim the regency during his minority.

---

[13] Conrad was also the king of Germany as Conrad IV (1237–54) and the king of Sicily as Conrad I (1250–4).
[14] Hans E. Mayer, *The Crusades* (Oxford: Oxford University Press, 1988), 233.

This was the situation in early May 1228, after Isabella II's death. Frederick finally left Brindisi on his way to the Holy Land for the crusade on 28 June 1228.[15] Meanwhile, surprisingly, Frederick II managed to regain Jerusalem, thanks to a treaty that he had signed with the Egyptian sultan, Malik Al-Kamil, on 18 February 1229.[16] In exchange, Frederick II promised to help Al-Kamil in his struggle with his nephew Al-Nasir. This was an ephemeral gain, as it barely included a strip of territory allowing defence of the city, which the Khwarazmian Turks reconquered in 1244. Yet the Jaffa Pact triggered the events that would culminate with Frederick II's entrance into Jerusalem. Frederick saw the pact with Al-Kamil as his last chance to conquer Jerusalem, given the lack of support from native crusaders, released by Pope Gregory from the vow of obedience to the excommunicated emperor, and the heightened anti-imperial sentiment not only in the kingdom of Acre but also in Jerusalem itself. Moreover, Frederick had lost the support of Patriarch Gerold of Lausanne and the Knights Hospitaller and Templar, though he could continue to count on the loyalty of Hermann of Salza and the Teutonic Knights, his German and Sicilian subjects, the Pisans and the Genovese.

The Ritual of Crown-Wearing in the Holy Sepulchre

On 16 March 1229, the Christian troops, led by the emperor, entered Jerusalem without too much opposition. His son, Conrad IV, being the legitimate king, Frederick found resistance from the native nobility and the ecclesiastical hierarchy. Yet the great success of the recapture of Jerusalem had given Frederick the upper hand over the other powers embroiled in the Holy Land, and left him in a state of euphoria. Thus, the next day, Sunday, 17 March, he entered the Church of the Holy Sepulchre in order to adore the Holy Sepulchre as he performed a crown ceremony. After the celebration of a Mass and, without any consecration or another ecclesiastical rite, he took the crown, which was laid on the altar, put it on his head and returned to the throne with his royal vestments.[17] Despite its apparent simplicity, this ceremony has become the subject of everlasting polemical and varied interpretations since it was enacted.

On one hand, it seems highly unlikely that Frederick had not carefully planned a gesture of such magnitude and its dissemination, considering that he was, at that time, excommunicated. On the other hand, he was also aware that a proper investiture through self-coronation would be

---

[15] Stürner, *Friedrich II*, 2:143.   [16] Powell, 'Frederick II and the Muslims', 263.
[17] Stürner, *Friedrich II*, 2:158.

considered dishonourable in the West, a defiance of the Pope and an irreverence, taking place as it did in the Church of the Holy Sepulchre. This temple was long considered the centre of Christianity because of its symbolic dimension and it was legitimised in the kingdom itself as the traditional venue for royal coronations since Baldwin II in 1118. In addition, the emperor and his collaborators were well aware that whatever ceremony they performed in the Holy Sepulchre, even the most solemn, would have no juridical, political or practical effects since the royal dignity corresponded to Conrad, Frederick's son. The ceremonial tradition itself made necessary the concurrence of the patriarch of Jerusalem in the ceremony of the investiture, which was not the case. To all this was added the date chosen for the occasion: the third Sunday of Lent, which in the East had the same value as Good Friday, the day the Universal Church commemorates the death of the Saviour on the cross.[18] What is more, the day coincided with the local feast day of the bishop and martyr Alexander. All these circumstances shaped the very essence of the event, so that authorised informants of the ceremony – Patriarch Gerold, Matthew Paris and Roger of Wendover among them – actually reconfigured the interpretation of a simple coronation to appear as a self-investiture and self-coronation. Some of these interpretations were certainly meant to damage the emperor's reputation in the West rather than to provide an accurate report of the actual ceremony.

Europe first learned of Frederick II's crown-wearing and enthronement ceremony from the manifesto *Letentur in Domino et Exultentus Omnes*, written by the Imperial Chancellery for rapid dissemination in the West.[19] This manifest, an expanded version of the sermon preached after the ceremony by the emperor, was produced in both German and Latin.[20] It commemorated the entrance of the Christian troops into Jerusalem on 16 March 1229, ending forty-two years of Muslim rule

[18] The third Sunday of Lent, called *Oculi mei*, was for the Greeks *Adoratio Crucis*, which included a ceremony similar to that of the Latins on Good Friday. There is a certain amount of historical debate about Frederick II's deliberate choice of this day: Schlott, *Das Rundschreiben Kaiser Friedrichs II*, 7; Rudolf Hiestand, 'Ierusalem et Sicilie rex. Zur Titulatur Friedrichs II', *Deutsches Archiv für Erforschung des Mittelalters* 52 (1996): 181–9, here 146.

[19] Max Kerner, 'Letentur in Domino et exutlent recti corde, Zu Inhalt und Dedeutung des Jersusalemmmanifestes Kaiser Friedrichs II. vom 18. März 1229', in *Inquirens subtilia diversa. D. Lohrmann zum 65. Geburtstag*, ed. Horst Kranz and Ludwig Falkenstein (Aachen: Shaker, 2002), 149–72.

[20] As Patriarch Gerold of Jerusalem informed Pope Gregory in a letter: 'Quo facto magister Alemannorum surrexit, et sermonem longum et prolixum primo in Theutonico et postea in Gallico ad nobiles et populum inchoavit, et, sicut nobis relatum fuit, exonerando immo exaltando principem, et ecclesiam salva gratia sua multipliciter onerando' (*Monumenta Germaniae Historica, Epistolae saeculi XIII e regestis pontificum Romanorum selectae*, 'Epistolae Selectae. 1229. 303' [Berlin: Weidmannos, 1887]).

204   Infamy

following Saladin's conquest in 1187. The ritual described in that document was the ceremonial with the crown already practised in both the German and Jerusalem kingdoms.

We entered the holy city of Jerusalem with the Christian army and great joy and we reverently visited the sepulchre of living God as Catholic emperor and the following day, Sunday, we wore the crown ('coronam ibi portavimus') in honour and glory of the supreme King.[21]

From this account it emerges clearly that those who entered the city of Jerusalem on that Saturday in March reverently adored the Holy Sepulchre and that the next day the emperor 'portavit' the crown – the Latin word 'portare' conveys the meaning of 'wearing the crown'. Some historians, Hans Eberhard Mayer and Andrea Sommerlechner among them, have maintained that this word expresses its exact literal meaning (the fact of 'wearing' the crown) and thus does not imply any kind of coronation or, as a consequence, any constitutional effects.[22] The document circulated throughout Europe and was received in the most important chancelleries.[23] Its reception and the testimonies of the witnesses of the ceremony raised a couple of reactions in the West, which are actually the sources extant on the event.[24]

Among these sources, the most reliable account of what happened in the Holy Sepulchre that Sunday of Lent is a letter sent by the imperial counsellor Hermann of Salza (c.1165–1239). Salza was an authoritative witness, having been present at the ceremony, though certainly partisan as a member of Frederick II's chancellery. As Grand Master of the

---

[21] 'Civitatem sanctam Ierusalem intravimus cum ingenti gaudio exercitus christiani et sepulchrum Dei viventis reverenter visitavimus tamquam catholicus imperator ac sequenti die dominico coronam ibi portavimus ad honorem et gloriam summi Regis' (*Monumenta Germaniae Historica, Constitutiones et acta publica imperatorum et regum*, ed. Weiland, p. 166, n. 122).

[22] Mayer, 'Das Pontifikale von Tyrus und die Krönung der lateinischen Könige von Jerusalem', 206, and Sommerlechner, *Stupor Mundi?*, 305, who always refers to 'crowning' between brackets and defines that gesture as 'ambivalent'. See for instance the poem known as *Couronnment de Louis*, in which the poet uses the word 'prendre' as a synonym of 'porter': 'Pren la corone, si seras coronné; Ou se ce non, filz, lessiez la ester' (*Les rédactions en Vers du Couronnment de Louis*, ed. Yvan G. Lepage [Paris: Droz, 1978]), 15.

[23] Schlott, *Das Rundschreiben Kaiser Friedrichs II*, 6. On the manifest, see also Kantorowicz, *Frederick the Second*, 200–5. Kantorowicz included it among 'the most daring' manifestations of the ceremonial of the king's liturgical reception: Ernst Kantorowicz, 'The *King's Advent* and the Enigmatic Panels in the Doors of Santa Sabina', in *Selected Studies* (New York: J. J. Augustin, 1965), 37–75, here 41. On the entrance of Frederick II into Jerusalem and its Hellenistic connections see Kantorowicz, 'Kaiser Friedrich II. und das Königsbild des Hellenisumus (*Marginalia Miscellanea*)', in *Selected Studies*, 276–81.

[24] For a good catalogue of references about the crown-wearing of Frederick in the Holy Sepulchre see Hechelhammer, *Kreuzzug und Herrschaftunter Friedrich II*, 301, and Sommerlechner, *Stupor Mundi?*, 303–8.

Teutonic Knights between 1210 and 1239, he managed to raise the prestige of the order, leading its expansion throughout Prussia and matching the influence of the Hospitallers and Templars.[25] Salza was a diplomat who acted with great tact amidst the tangled relations between the Holy Roman Empire and the papacy. He was genuinely fond of Frederick II and loyal to him, representing him as a mediator at the Roman Curia from 1222. John of Brienne, the man who would become the emperor's father-in-law, knew and respected him. Brienne appreciated Salza for his brave conduct during the Fifth Crusade. This increased the trust between the two knights, a fact that was undoubtedly propitious for the agreement for the marriage between Frederick and Isabella in 1225.

On 15 March Salza wrote to Pope Gregory IX and announced that the king would enter Jerusalem, bringing the crown. The parallel with the scene of Jesus Christ's entry into Jerusalem was clear, although it is perhaps inaccurate to take it literally.[26] Salza conveyed to the Pope that the emperor aimed to 'wear the crown in honour of the king of kings'.[27] This non-presaged the ceremony enacted some days later in the Holy Sepulchre – a rite of 'wearing the crown', rather a proper self-coronation.

Some days after his and the emperor's entrance into Jerusalem, Salza penned the most exact and authoritative description of the events. In a letter to a friend, preserved in the papal registry, Salza affirms that the king (*Dominus Imperator*) went to Jerusalem with the Christian army and, without consecration, took the crown *from* the altar, carried it *to* the throne, sat in the throne and *wore* the crown in the usual way.[28] The prepositions 'from' and 'to' underline the full meaning of the ritual. Mayer, always exhaustive, notes that *sedem* is in the accusative and not the ablative, and thus, preceded by the particle

---

[25] On Hermann of Salza see Adolf Koch, *Hermann von Salza, Meister des Deutschen Ordens: ein biographischer Versuch* (Leipzig: Duncker & Humblot, 1885); Willy Cohn, *Hermann von Salza* (Breslau: M. & H. Marcus, 1930); Kluger: *Hochmeister Hermann von Salza und Kaiser Friedrich II*.

[26] Matthew 21:1–11.

[27] 'Proponit etiam imperator cum omni populo ascendere Ierosolimam et ibi in honore regis rerum omnium ferre coronam, sic enim consultum est ei a pluribus' (*Monumenta Germaniae Historica, Constitutiones*, 2:264; Mayer, 'Das Pontifikale von Tyrus und die Krönung der lateinischen Könige von Jerusalem', 204). On this letter, issued 15 March 1229, see Pacifico, *Federico II e Gerusalemme al tempo delle crociate*, 271–3.

[28] 'Dominus Imperator cum universo exercito Christiano venit Jerusalem et ... in honore regis eterni portavit coronam. ... Non audivit divina, tamen coronam simpliciter sine consecratione de altari accepi et in sedem, sicut es consuetum, portavit' (*Monumenta Germaniae Historica, Constitutiones*, 2:264; Mayer, 'Das Pontifikale von Tyrus und die Krönung der lateinischen Könige von Jerusalem', 204–5).

in, implies directionality.²⁹ This is actually the only eyewitness account of Frederick II's disputed self-coronation ceremony in the Church of the Holy Sepulchre in Jerusalem.

Salza stated that there was some kind of ritual with the crown and that this ritual was performed without any sacred ceremony (*non audivit divina* and *sine consecratione*) accompanying it. The ritual, apart from other ceremonies that may have been enacted but for which there are no details, at least contained a moment in which the emperor took the crown from the altar and carried it towards the throne 'as is the custom'. This phrase recovers its full sense when Frederick II's ritual with the crown is placed in the context of what previous kings of Jerusalem had performed in the same Church of the Holy Sepulchre – that is, ceremonies related to the crown during solemn occasions and without any juridical implications or investiture effects.

At this point, we should discuss how ceremonies of investment worked in the Latin kingdom of Jerusalem from its creation in 15 July 1099, the day in which the crusaders captured the Holy City.³⁰ One week after the conquest, on 22 July, Godfrey of Bouillon was appointed ruler by the crusaders. Yet he did not want to take the title of king of Jerusalem because he felt he was not worthy to be assimilated to Jesus Christ, as narrated in the *Gesta Francorum* (*c*.1101).³¹ Overcoming this reluctance, his brother and first successor, Baldwin, performed the first ceremony of inauguration in the kingdom of Jerusalem. He was anointed and crowned by Patriarch Daimbert in

---

[29] 'Coronam sine consecratione *de* altari accepit et *in* sedem portavit' (Mayer, 'Das Pontifikale von Tyrus und die Krönung der lateinischen Könige von Jerusalem', 205; emphasis added).

[30] These ceremonies are reported, in one way or another, by contemporary chroniclers such as Fulcher of Chartres, Albert of Aachen and William of Tyre, and in the posterior compilation by John of Ibelin. See Mayer, 'Das Pontifikale von Tyrus und die Krönung der lateinischen Könige von Jerusalem', 141–232, and Simon John, 'Royal Inauguration and Liturgical Culture in the Latin Kingdom of Jerusalem, 1099–1187', *Journal of Medieval History* 43(4) (2017): 485–504; Elisabeth Crouzet-Pavan, 'Comment devenir roi à Jérusalem (1099–1187)', in *El acceso al trono. Concepción y ritualización* (Pamplona: Gobierno de Navarra, 2017), 145–66. See also Reinhard Elze, 'Die Krönung der lateinischen Kaiser', in Elze, *Päpste-Kaiser-Könige und die mittelalterliche Herrschaftssymbolik* (London: Variorum Reprints, 1982), chapter 7, and Elisabeth Crouzet-Pavan, *Le mistère des rois de Jérusalem, 1099–1187* (Paris: Alban Michel, 2013). For the specific context of ritual and liturgy of the crusades see Cecilia Gaposchkin: *Invisible Weapons: Liturgy and the Making of Crusade Ideology* (Ithaca, NY: Cornell University Press, 2017).

[31] Jay Rubenstein, 'Holy Fire and Sacral Kingship in Post-conquest Jerusalem', *Journal of Medieval History* 43 (2017): 470–84; John, 'The Papacy and the Establishment of the Kingdoms of Jerusalem, Sicily and Portugal', 247–8; John, 'Royal Inauguration and Liturgical Culture in the Latin Kingdom of Jerusalem', 488–9; Weiler, '*Rex Renitens* and the Medieval Idea of Kingship', 9.

Bethlehem on Christmas of 1100.[32] The ritual of installation of the kings of Jerusalem replicated, from this moment, European and, more specifically, French patterns.

Baldwin's precedent was important since it established the convention that the king of Jerusalem should not be crowned in the Holy City and that it should be done according to the tradition of the Old Testament kings of Israel. The place of coronation, Bethlehem, was symbolic of Old Testament kingship, since David was anointed by Samuel as king of Israel there. Although apparently no explicit connection was made by contemporary popes, some testimonies, such as the letter written by Anselm, the archbishop of Canterbury, to King Baldwin I in 1104, expressed clearly the idea that the kings of Jerusalem should seek to build an image of kingship drawn from biblical and Christological models.[33]

To understand the nature of Frederick II's ceremony in the Holy Sepulchre in 1229, it is relevant to emphasise that Baldwin himself performed some crown-wearings, usually on important feast days.[34] The distinctions between the 'coronations' encompassed in the general ceremonies of royal inauguration and installation ('coronations', *Krönung*) from those non-inaugural ceremonies ('crown-wearings', *Festkrönung*) have been largely emphasised by scholars, and it is particularly relevant here since they had already been performed in the Latin kingdom of Jerusalem – as in Friedrich's own kingdom of Germany.[35] Baldwin performed one of the first crown-wearings precisely in the Holy Sepulchre. The chronicler Fulcher states that Baldwin 'was crowned according to the customs of kings' in the Holy Sepulchre after the Mass, and the *Gesta Francorum* adds that he was adorned 'with a crown and royal vestments'.[36] Another contemporary chronicler, William of Tyre, confirms the tradition of crown-wearing among twelfth-century kings of Jerusalem, as he describes a crown-wearing in 1185 of the child-prince Baldwin V:

Now it is customary in Jerusalem that when the king wears his crown he receives it at the Sepulchre and wears it on his head as far as the Temple where Jesus Christ

---

[32] Fulcher of Chartres, *A History of the Expedition to Jerusalem, 1095–1127*, trans. Frances R. Ryan (Knoxville: University of Tennessee Press, 1969), 148.
[33] John, 'Royal Inauguration and Liturgical Culture in the Latin Kingdom of Jerusalem', 486.
[34] John, 'Royal Inauguration and Liturgical Culture in the Latin Kingdom of Jerusalem', 491–2, 503–4.
[35] For the specific function of the ritual of 'crown-wearing' in Europe, and more particularly in Germany, see Hans-Walter Klewitz, *Die Festkrönungen der Deutschen Könige* (Darmstadt: Wissenschaftliche Buchgesellschaft, 1966). For a more general perspective see Zupka, *Ritual and Symbolic Communication in Medieval Hungary*, 36–45.
[36] John, 'Royal Inauguration and Liturgical Culture in the Latin Kingdom of Jerusalem', 491.

was offered. There he offers his crown but then buys it back. For it used to be the custom that when a mother had her first male child she would offer him at the Temple and buy him back with a lamp or with two pigeons or with two turtledoves.[37]

After Baldwin I's and Baldwin II's (1118) reluctance to be consecrated in Jerusalem, contemporary chroniclers explicitly located Fulk of Anjou's installation ceremony in the Church of the Holy Sepulchre in 1131. This is an important precedent since after that date the kings of Jerusalem no longer hesitated to enact the constituent ritual of coronation in the Church of the Holy Sepulchre. The Latin kingdom of Jerusalem runs here parallel to those of France and England, since they also had fixed sites of coronation – the cathedral of Reims and Westminster Abbey. The Holy Sepulchre had evident sacral symbolism since it was considered the most holy site in all of Christendom. Its election as the sacred place for royal investiture from 1131 and for the performance of other royal rituals 'added an unparalleled dimension to the image of kingship in Latin Jerusalem. It fostered a relationship between the kings and the holiest site in all Christendom, and thereby aligned the monarchy with Christ'.[38]

Fulk's successors Baldwin III (1143), Amalric (1163), Baldwin IV (1174), Baldwin V (1183) and Sibylla and Guy of Lusignan (1186) were also anointed and crowned in the Church of the Holy Sepulchre, in a signalled liturgical drama.[39] Simon John concludes that 'rituals [of royal inauguration in the Latin kingdom of Jerusalem] were intended to harness the liturgical cultural of Jerusalem's habitants, with the aim of building consensus between monarchy and people'.[40] This tradition of the liturgical and consensual nature of the ceremonies of inauguration, well known in other European kingdoms such as France, England and Germany, helps to explain why Frederic II's transgressive gesture in the Holy Sepulchre – no matter its nature – raised public and international contestation.[41] As Nelson and Dale argue, liturgy remained central to the models of kingship that were practised in most European kingdoms in the

---

[37] Quoted in John, 'Royal Inauguration and Liturgical Culture in the Latin Kingdom of Jerusalem', 500.
[38] John, 'Royal Inauguration and Liturgical Culture in the Latin Kingdom of Jerusalem', 502.
[39] John, 'Royal Inauguration and Liturgical Culture in the Latin Kingdom of Jerusalem', 496–502.
[40] John, 'Royal Inauguration and Liturgical Culture in the Latin Kingdom of Jerusalem', 486.
[41] The political use of the liturgy has been extensively explored by Janet L. Nelson in her studies on Carolingian politics and rituals. See also, for thirteenth-century England, Nicholas Vincent, *The Holy Blood: King Henry III and the Westminster Blood Relic* (Cambridge: Cambridge University Press, 2001) and, for thirteenth- and fourteenth-century France, see Cecilia Gaposchkin, *The Making of Saint Louis: Kingship, Sanctity and*

Middle Ages. This being the case, the question arises of why Salza – most probably following Frederick II's indications – chose such an explicit form of transmitting the contents of a supposedly profane ceremony, aware of the surprise, scandal and upset that it would cause among all the chancelleries of the West.

The patriarch of Jerusalem, Gerold of Lausanne (1225–39), reacted immediately to the imperial manifesto and Salza's news. Only eight days after the ceremony, on 26 March, Gerold wrote a letter to Pope Gregory in which he reported that the king, 'wearing the regalia, put the crown in his head ("capiti suo imposuit diadema") in a ceremony enacted at the Church of the Holy Sepulchre'.[42] The patriarch might have invented this information to discredit the emperor in the eyes of the Pope, but too many contemporary sources testify to the fact to assume that Gerold was lying. In addition, his information did not contradict what Salza reported (a ceremony of 'wearing the crown' could also imply the gesture of 'putting the crown in his own head') or other sources, such as a letter from Frederick to Henry III of England, but the moral interpretation of the ritual and Gerold's hostile tone were strikingly different.[43] Although Gerold was not present at the ceremony (he was in fact notable by his absence) and did not enter the city until 19 March, his testimony is reliable as he undoubtedly rushed to receive first-hand information, although we do not know exactly from whom. That information would not have been very difficult to come by, proceeding as it did from both the imperial and anti-imperial camps. The testimonies that have reached us from him confirm that some kind of crown-wearing ceremony took place that day in the Church of the Holy Sepulchre. In addition, the patriarch made Salza's information a bit more specific, using a less ambiguous expression ('capiti suo imposuit diadema') than the 'portavit coronam' used by Salza and the imperial manifest *Letentur in Domino*. Gerold also emphasised the fact that the emperor was dressed solemnly for the occasion ('vestibusque indutus regalibus') and that he demonstratively wore his regalia in Jerusalem.

Crusade in the Later Middle Ages (Ithaca, NY: Cornell University Press, 2008), and see the comparative approach in Dale, *Inauguration and Liturgical Kingship*.

[42] This letter is edited in Carl Rodenberg, ed., *Epistolae selectae seculi XIII*. 3 vols. (*Monumenta Germaniae Historica*), Ep. Saeculi XIII, vol. 1: number 384 (pp. 299–304). It is said there that 'qui summo mane ipso die dominico Sepulchrum intravit, vestibusque indutus regalibus capiti suo imposuit diadema' (p. 303). See also the edition by Dana C. Munro in *Christian Society and the Crusades, 1198–1229*, ed. Edward M. Peters (Philadelphia: University of Pennsylvania Press, 1971), 165–70, and comments in Powell, 'Patriarch Gerold and Frederick II', 20–3.

[43] This letter is presented in Peters, *Christian Society*, 162–5. See Powell, 'Patriarch Gerold and Frederick II', 22, and Pacifico, *Federico II e Gerusalemme al tempo delle crociate*, 281.

Certainly, Gerold could have created this false transposition (from Salza's 'crown-wearing' to his 'self-coronation') so as to discredit the emperor to the native nobility and the people of Jerusalem, and to emphasise the illegitimacy of the ritual Frederick had followed in the Church of the Holy Sepulchre. Yet Salza and Gerold's narrations, different as they were, spread across Europe the idea that what had occurred was a transgressive ceremony with the crown because of its profane nature.

In May 1229, a few weeks after his letter addressed to the Pope, Gerold addressed an encyclical to all believers.[44] He tried to counteract the effects of the imperial manifest *Letentur in Domino*, describing again the events at the Holy Sepulchre that Sunday of Lent, and explicitly noting that the king put the crown on his own head (*suo capiti imposuit diadema*) during a ceremony held there.[45] The basic information of this encyclical is similar to the information contained in the letter Gerold had sent to the Pope, but it contains certain statements which considerably differ from that letter. The differences would be explained by the fact that Gerold's conflict with the emperor was more connected with affairs in the East than with the controversy between Frederick and Gregory IX.[46] The main differences are not in the telling of the story of the ceremony, but in the previous negotiations with the Muslims who allowed Christian troops to enter Jerusalem. While the encyclical maintains that Frederick did not consult anyone about the treaty, Gerold's letter to the Pope describes these discussions in detail, trying to discredit him. This alternative interpretation makes James M. Powell to conclude that the direct author of the letter was not the patriarch since 'this letter contains errors and distortions that Gerold was unlikely to have made.'[47] The version that appears in Matthew of Paris' *Chronica Majora* seems to be a compilation of different documents rather than a single text written by Gerold.[48]

Regarding the ceremony itself, the only substantial difference between the patriarchal encyclical and Gerold's letter to the Pope is the place occupied by the possessive adjective 'suo' in the phrase, which now

---

[44] The letter appeared in Matthew of Paris, *Chronica Majora*, ed. Luard, vol. 57: 3, pp. 179–84. On this letter-encyclical see Powell, 'Patriarch Gerold and Frederick II', 19–26.

[45] 'Dixit enim inter caetera, quod sibi erat sancta civitas restituta; ad quam eum in vigilia Dominicae qua cantatur Oculi mei, cum excercitu Christiano veniret, die sequenti Dominica, satis inordinate satisque confuse, excommunicatus in ecclesia Dominici Sepulchri, in praejudicium honoris ac excellentiae imperialis manifestum, suo capiti imposuit diadema ... non sine peregrinorum confusione maxima et dolore' (Matthew of Paris, *Chronica Majora*, vol. 57: 3, p. 180). See Sommerlechner, *Stupor Mundi?*, 303.

[46] Bernard Hamilton, *The Latin Church in the Crusader States* (London: Routledge, 1980), 258–9, and Powell, 'Patriarch Gerold and Frederick II', 20.

[47] Powell, 'Patriarch Gerold and Frederick II', 24.

[48] Matthew of Paris, *Chronica Majora*, vol. 57: 3, pp. 179–84.

appears before the noun 'capiti' rather than after it. That does not seem to change its meaning in any fundamental way – both formulations emphasise the fact that the king put the crown on *his* own head. The substantive difference with the letter to the Pope is that in the encyclical the tone is not only informative and descriptive but also evaluative, with the patriarch judging the king for the scandal and confusion caused by an excommunicant entering the Church of the Holy Sepulchre and, what is more, crowning himself. The difference in tone between the two documents confirms the objectivity with which the patriarch had informed the Pope a few weeks before, and how inauthentic the patriarch would have been if he had invented the self-coronation event in that report. Now, in the encyclical, Gerold was reacting against the formulation picked up by the manifest that the coronation had been *ad honorem et gloriam summi regis*, as it had been in anyone's book for the glory of Frederick himself and not for that of the 'supreme king', Jesus Christ.

Another source on the event that we have at our disposal is a letter from Pope Gregory to the archbishop of Milan, dated 13 June 1229, in which he states that Frederick II was solemnly crowned in Jerusalem.[49] The Pope had been informed by Patriarch Gerold eight days after the event, and had probably also received news via Salza, who had rushed to give his version of events. Whatever his sources were in addition to Gerold, the Pope held firm to his interpretation: it had been a transgressive ceremony and the gesture merited his full disapproval because it had been enacted 'sollempniter', an adjective not used lightly which confirms the Salza and Gerold sources.

These efforts by the patriarch of Jerusalem and the Pope to denounce Frederick's gesture and damage his reputation were effective. Some time afterwards, the English chronicler Roger of Wendover echoed a papal encyclical that reached England, in which the Pope accused Frederick II of entering the Church of the Holy Sepulchre and of crowning himself 'with his own hand' ('propria manu') before the main altar.[50] Roger

---

[49] 'Et sic idem [Frederick II] in Ierusalem diruta fere penitus et deserta se sollempniter vel potius inaniter coronavit' (*Monumenta Germaniae Historica, Epistolae saeculi XIII*, vol. I, p. 309, n. 390). Sommerlechner, *Stupor Mundi?*, 303.

[50] 'In die annunciationis beate Marie cum esset excommunicatus, intravit ecclesiam Sancti Sepulchri in Ierusalem et ibi ante maius altare propria manu sese coronavit.' Roger of Wendover, *Libri qui dicitur Flores Historiarum*, ed. Henry G. Hewlett, *Rerum Britannicarum Scriptores*, 84.2 (London: Eyre and Spottiswoode, 1887), 364–74. English edition: Roger of Wendover, *Flowers of History*, trans. John A. Giles. 2 vols. (London: Bohn, 1849), 2:527. See Mayer, 'Das Pontifikale von Tyrus und die Krönung der lateinischen Könige von Jerusalem', 206, and Sommerlechner, *Stupor Mundi?*, 306. Roger of Wendover was an English chronicler, probably a native of Wendover (Buckinghamshire), who died in 1236. He was a monk of St Albans Abbey and the first of the important line of chroniclers working at St Albans. On the connections

repeats, with some little variation, the polemic reception that Frederick II's ritual in the Holy Sepulchre received in England. He emphasises the event's self-crowning dimension in order to increase the criticism against the emperor. In addition, Matthew Paris tells us in his chronicle that Stephen, the Pope's chaplain and papal legate in England, arrived in England and accused the emperor of entering the Holy Sepulchre, even though he was excommunicated, and crowning himself with his own hands at the main altar.[51]

Later sources, from several generations after the event, describe the emperor's ceremony with the crown, echoing earlier ones. Yet the formula of 'putting the crown on his head' is not always understood in Gerold's way. The *Estorie de Eracles* reports that, once he entered the Holy Sepulchre, the emperor put a golden crown on the altar and took it and put it on his head without any prelate's assistance.[52] The narration of the self-coronation is again explicit here. Notably, however, at this point the different manuscripts of the chronicle of Eracles offer substantial variations, which once again conveys the ambiguity surrounding everything to do with Frederick II's self-coronation. One of the manuscripts eliminates the three words *si la [la corona] prist* ('he took the crown'), although it concedes the core information: *et la miste su sa teste* ('and he put it on the head').[53] The chronicle of Ernoul and Bernard le Trésorier reiterates twice that the emperor 'wore the crown'.[54] In Germany, the reception was obviously more positive or, at least, neutral. Johannes Ruffus tells us that Frederick carried the crown in the Holy Sepulchre

---

between Matthew of Paris and Roger of Wendover, and the interactions between Paris' *Chronica Majora* and Wendover's *Flores Historiarum*, see Richard Vaughan, *Matthew Paris* (Cambridge, 1958), 21–34; Powell, 'Patriarch Gerold and Frederick II', 25–6; and Björn Weiler, 'Stupor Mundi: Matthäus Paris und die zeitgenössische Wahrnehmung Friedrichs II. in England', in *Herrschaftsräume, Herrschaftspraxis und Kommunikation zur Zeit Kaiser Friedrichs II*, ed. Knut Görich, Jan Ulrich Keupp and Theo Broekmann (München: Herbert Utz, 2008), 63–96.

[51] Matthew of Paris, *Chronica Majora*, vol. 57: 3, pp. 184–5.

[52] 'Et le dimenche de mi caresme s'en entra ou mostier dou Sepulcre et fist metre une corone d'or dessus le maistre autel dou cuer, et puis vint la, si la prist et la mist sur la teste. Onques n'i ot prelat, ne prestre, ne clerc qui i chantast ne riens i deist; et tint le jor grant cort' (*L'Estoire d'Eracles Empereur et la conqueste de la Terra d'Outremer* [Paris, 1859], vol. 2, 1–418, here 374). See Sommerlechner, *Stupor Mundi?*, 306; Mayer, 'Das Pontifikale von Tyrus und die Krönung der lateinischen Könige von Jerusalem', 207. Ernoul formed part of the entourage of Balian of Ibelin, a Jerusalem noble. On this chronicle see M. R. Morgan, *The Chronicle of Ernoul and the Continuations of William of Tyre* (Oxford: Oxford University Press, 1973) and Janet Shirley, *Crusader Syria in the Thirteenth Century* (London: Ashgate, 1999).

[53] See the comments in Mayer, 'Das Pontifikale von Tyrus und die Krönung der lateinischen Könige von Jerusalem', 207.

[54] Louis Mas Latrie, ed., *La chronique d'Ernoul et de Bernard le Trésorier* (Paris: Société de l'histoire de France, 1871), 465.

'to the honour of the Christian people', as Burchard von Ursberg highlights that Frederick organised great celebrations in Jerusalem, the coronation among them.[55] In other cases, such as in Guillaume de Nagis, the deliberate omission of the episode of the Holy Sepulchre may be arguably attributed to an attempt to avoid damaging Frederic II's reputation.[56]

Other chroniclers recount the event during the thirteenth and fourteenth centuries, but they describe it in more neutral terms: Alberich von Troisfontaines, the *Sächsische Weltchronik*, the *Annales Marbacenses*, the *Annales de Waverleia*, the *Annales de Theokesberia*, the *Chronicon S. Medardi Suessionensis*, the *Continuatio Eberbacensis* of Gottfried von Viterbo, the *Annales de Wigornia*, Guillaume de Nangis and Johann von Viktring, among others.[57] Complex versions and interpretations of Frederick II's provocative gesture led to twentieth-century imaginary interpretations of 'self-coronation' by historians such as Kantorowicz, as mentioned at the beginning of this chapter. They probably echoed that other modern self-coronation of Napoleon in Notre-Dame of Paris in 1804 rather than Frederick II's ceremony of crown-wearing itself.

A Ritual of Calculated Provocation That Caused Disapproval

Despite the variety of these interpretations (or precisely because of them), Frederick II's 'wearing the crown' or 'putting the crown on his head' in the Holy Sepulchre poses the problem of the eventual profane and unconventional nature of the ceremony, and the scandal it produced in Europe. None of the descriptions that have reached us of the ritual refers specifically to the ceremonies proper to royal investitures such as the anointing or the knightly armour. This confirms that the essential element was the ritual of wearing the crown from the altar to the throne. In addition, no source notes that the ceremony might have taken place during the course of a Mass, as was the custom. In fact, the astute counsellor Salza had previously persuaded Frederick II not to celebrate Mass during the ceremony in the Holy Sepulchre, as that might further exacerbate the mood of the Pope and the people.[58]

---

[55] Ruffus: 'In Sepulchro Dominico coronam portavit ad honorem populi Christiani.' Burchard: 'Imperator pascha Domini cum multis expensis more regio coronatus procedens Ierosolimis celebravit' (both quotes in Sommerlechner, *Stupor Mundi?*, 306).

[56] Chris Jones, 'The Role of Frederick II in the Works of Guillaume de Nangis', in *Representations of Power in Medieval Germany, 800–1500*, ed. Simon MacLean and Björn Weiler (Turnhout: Brepols, 2006), 273–94, here 280.

[57] Specific references for these sources are given in Sommerlechner, *Stupor Mundi?*, 306–7.

[58] Stürner, *Friedrich II*, 2:158; Pacifico, *Federico e Gerusalemme al tempo delle crociate*, 274.

It is also highly significant that Salza emphasised in his report the fact that 'there was no consecration' in that ceremony. There was an alteration to the established and conventional norm of the royal investitures and the crown-wearing ceremonies in the Latin kingdom of Jerusalem. It affected its sacrality (a profane ceremony performed in a sacred locus) and its liturgy: Frederick performed the ceremony without respecting the traditional ordo known as the Pontifical of Tyre followed by the kings of Jerusalem for their investiture.[59] He knew this ordo well, but was not disposed to follow it, not only because of his own legal incapacity (he was an excommunicant) but also because of the humiliating experience that being crowned by a patriarch or bishop would represent after having been crowned emperor by the Pope. Clearly, having already been crowned king of Sicily (1198) and Holy Roman Emperor (1220), and assuming that the title of king of Jerusalem legitimately belonged to his son, Conrad, the ceremony with the crown performed in the Holy Sepulchre was aimed at increasing his fame rather than seeking legal validity.

In addition, whatever the ceremonial form that the 'liturgy of the crown' performed in the Holy Sepulchre took, Frederick was well aware of the symbolic value of the gesture. He had planned it for the third Sunday in Lent, which in the East had the same value as Good Friday, the day of the death of the Lord. He had performed it in the Church of the Holy Sepulchre, considered one of the centres of Christianity and precisely what made Godfrey of Bouillon forego the coronation to legitimise him as the first king of the Latin kingdom of Jerusalem, because he felt himself unworthy of being crowned in the place where Jesus Christ was crowned with thorns.[60] He also knew that a self-investiture would achieve nothing more than to stir up a native nobility that was already edgy, and scandalise a people prone to religious respect. He was not the legitimate king since the birth of his son, neither was he fit to receive consecration since suffering excommunication by the Pope.[61]

---

[59] Description and historical development and practice of this pontifical are presented in Mayer, 'Das Pontifikale von Tyrus und die Krönung der lateinischen Könige von Jerusalem', 141–232.

[60] 'Dixit se non portaturum coronam auream, ubi altissimus Ihesus Christus passus fuit coronam spineam deportare' (*Annali Genovesi de Caffaro e de'suoi continnuatori*, quoted in Mayer, 'Das Pontifikale von Tyrus und die Krönung der lateinischen Könige von Jerusalem', 208). For a more detailed account and interpretation see Jonathan Riley-Smith, 'The Title of Godfrey de Bouillon', *Bulletin of the Institute of Historical Research* 52 (1979): 83–6; John France, 'The Election and Title of Godfrey de Bouillon', *Canadian Journal of History* 18 (1983): 321–9; Weiler, '*Rex Renitens* and the Medieval Idea of Kingship', 9–10.

[61] Mayer, 'Das Pontifikale von Tyrus und die Krönung der lateinischen Könige von Jerusalem', 209–10.

Finally, in the thirteenth century, a coronation without consecration made no sense, neither did any legal or ecclesiastical consequence stem from it – and perhaps Frederick, aware of this, performed only a ceremony with the crown. The coronation did not *make* the king, as that required unction and consecration, following the tradition of the kingdom of Jerusalem.[62] Since Frederick II and his chancellor Salza knew this, the emperor sought, with that transgressive gesture, an expression of his grandeur, a practical demonstration of his temporal power, which required no spiritual authority or confirmation, rather than a ceremony with supposed juridical effects.[63]

Even considering these adverse political, reputational and legal costs, Frederick went forward with his plans so that his transgressive gesture would echo in Europe, not only in the papal Curia but also in the chancelleries of several European monarchies. He even plotted to spread such a transgressive gesture through the manifest *Letentur in Domino*. In fact, scholars have defended the joint existence of the crown ceremony performed and the manifest *Letentur in Domino* as two parts of a common propaganda strategy on the part of Frederick II.[64]

The influential chronicler Matthew of Paris, active some decades after the event, was one of the most vocal heralds of the scandal produced by Frederick's ritual in Jerusalem. In his report of the event, he included the letter from Patriarch Gerold of Jerusalem to the Pope. Matthew actually closes that chapter emphasising the fact that the ritual enacted in the Holy Sepulchre damaged the emperor's reputation, since he was excommunicated, so that this gesture created great confusion and scandal, especially after the letter that the angry patriarch of Jerusalem wrote to the Pope denouncing the ceremony.[65]

Both the crown-ceremony in the Holy Sepulchre and the *Letentur* manifest mark the start of a phase in which Emperor Frederick II began

---

[62] Mayer, 'Das Pontifikale von Tyrus und die Krönung der lateinischen Könige von Jerusalem', 205; Mayer, *Kings and Lords*, 540.

[63] Mayer notes: 'The barons refused to recognize him as king so the coronation of 1229 had no validity in constitutional law except perhaps as a retrospective legitimization of Frederick's kingship of 1225–8' (Mayer, *The Crusades*, 254).

[64] Schlott, *Das Rundschreiben Kaiser Friedrichs II*, 16–17, who also quotes the historians Albert Brackmann and Otto Vehse.

[65] 'Haec autem epistola eum ad audientiam occidentalium perveniret, non mediocriter famam imperialem obfuscavit, et multorum favorem ademit. Papa autem ad ejus dejectionem diligentius solito insurrexit, et collectioni pecuniae hiavit avidius' (Matthew of Paris, *Chronica Majora*, vol. 57: 3, p. 184). This sentence seems to be a final addition to the mentioned letter by Gerold included in Matthew's chronicle, whose authorship is difficult to attribute either to the patriarch or to the chronicler, but it had the same bad effects on Frederick's reputation in the end (see Powell, 'Patriarch Gerold and Frederick II', 25).

to carry a strong religious-mystical charge.[66] For some, this mystical dimension would reflect the power of God through the emperor. Others considered him a definitive anti-Christ: the excommunicated emperor who usurped the Church of the Holy Sepulchre for his own glory, robbing God of his, precisely the argument Patriarch Gerold used to discredit him. This gesture also heightened the tension between Frederick II and the Church of Rome as it increased his own imperial Roman universalism, influenced perhaps by the Byzantine stamp of the Norman kings of Sicily. If, as king of Sicily, Frederick II had used the kingship as a means of leaving little space for papal pretensions to sovereignty, in Jerusalem he had used the emperorship to proclaim the notion of the ruler called by God to govern all humanity.[67]

Whatever the exact ritual form Frederick II used in his crown-wearing that day, he managed to make it a reality with the words by which the gesture spread throughout the whole of Europe. It echoes even today, confirming the postmodern belief that the word in itself can make facts. The written record was more relevant than the supposed coronation ritual itself. As the medieval scholars declared, *symbolum est collatio formarum visibilium ad invisibilium demonstrationem*: a symbol is the collation of visible shapes for the representation of the invisible or a drawing together of visible forms to demonstrate an invisible thing.[68] With his self-coronation, Frederick wanted to make maximum symbolic use of the visible.

In the end, Frederick's ritual the day after his entry into Jerusalem was an act of calculated provocation. An excommunicated king wearing the crown in the Holy Sepulchre, in the absence of the patriarch of Jerusalem, opposed by the military orders, eyed suspiciously by the aristocracy of Outremer, and fighting off the armies of his former father-in-law in Sicily, was received in the West with the opprobrium the emperor and his collaborators expected. The patriarch's accusation of self-investiture with self-coronation could not surprise anyone, Frederick among them. This makes Frederick's case closer to that of Roger II, whose self-investiture (and consequent symbolical self-coronation in La Martorana) was also seen as opprobrium in Europe. The two great kings involved in the creation and consolidation of the kingdom of Sicily incurred opprobrium. There is an obvious growing fear on the

---

[66] Eberhard Horst, *Friedrich der Staufer. Eine Biographie* (Düsseldorf: Claassen, 1975), 148; Schlott, *Das Rundschreiben Kaiser Friedrichs II*, 18.
[67] Abulafia, *Federico II*, 157.
[68] For the phrase attributed to Hugo of Saint Victor applied to this historical context see Reinhard Elze, 'La simbologia del potere nell'età di Federico II', in *Politica e cultura nell'Italia di Federico II*, ed. Sergio Gensini (Pisa: Pacini, 1986), 203–12.

part of the Pope and the cardinals that these kings' power in Italy would be a threat to the independence of the papacy and the integrity of their own kingdoms. Other European kings, such as the sovereigns in Iberia, seemed to be too far from the Pope to incur opprobrium when enacting self-coronation. These are the kings I focus on in the next chapters.

Part III

Convention

9 Alfonso XI of Castile
From Self-Knighting to Self-Crowning

The Iberian kings of Castile, Aragon and Navarra experimented with several forms of self-coronations from the twelfth to fifteenth centuries. The ritual practices of investiture in these three kingdoms were diverse, but all of them witnessed the turning of self-coronations from transgressive to conventional rituals during that period. The next chapters focus on these symbolic transformations, as well as the explanation and the effects of this radical ritual modification.

While Roger II and Frederick II's self-investitures and their respective symbolical and ritual forms had evident transgressive connotations and were condemned or at least were seen with suspicion, other European kingdoms viewed the act differently. Late medieval Iberian kings, for instance, enacted several ritual self-coronations but their contemporaries did not consider these a transgression of the tradition. Nevertheless, modern historiography and popular opinions have wrongly considered them as heterodox rituals that challenged previously established rules and traditions. Thus, they deserve particular attention, and could throw some light upon the traditional debate on the supposed 'profane' kingship of Iberian kings, and how these ceremonial traditions conditioned the future of the early modern Spanish Empire. More specifically, this chapter focuses on the practice of self-coronation among fourteenth-century Castilian kings and its religious, political and ideological implications.[1] It takes Alfonso XI of Castile's self-coronation as a central event, and

---

[1] For the coronation of the kings of Castile, see Claudio Sánchez Albornoz, 'Un ceremonial inédito de coronación de los reyes de Castilla', in *Estudios sobre las instituciones medievales españolas* (Mexico: Universidad Nacional Autónoma de México, 1965), 739–63, and Luis García de Valdeavellano, *Curso de historia de las instituciones españolas* (Madrid: Revista de Occidente, 1968), 430–2. For a general view of the ideological conception of the Iberian monarchy see José Antonio Maravall, 'Sobre el concepto de monarquía en la edad media española', in *Estudios dedicados a Menéndez Pidal* (Madrid: Consejo Superior de Investigaciones Científicas, 1954), 401–17, Francisco Elías de Tejada, *Historia del pensamiento político catalán* (Sevilla: Montejurra, 1963), José Manuel Nieto Soria, *Ceremonias de la realeza* (Madrid: Nerea, 1993) and José Manuel Nieto Soria, *Fundamentos del poder real en Castilla* (Madrid: Eudema, 1988).

establishes a conceptual genealogy, along with the significance and relevance of this self-coronation.[2]

Alfonso XI's self-coronation and self-knighting make us wonder why he acted in this way, whether there were any precedents for this particular gesture in Castile, and to what extent he was aware of the different rates at which the anointing and coronation ceremonies were introduced into his own kingdoms. It is actually possible to establish a ritual genealogy from Visigothic, Asturian and Leonese kingdoms to the kingdom of Castile, and from Wamba's anointing in 672 to Alfonso XI's self-coronation in 1332, in order to reflect on the precedents for this gesture.

The Origins of Royal Sacralisation in Iberia: King Wamba's Unction

The Visigoths first practised the rite of unction in the second half of the seventh century. It was doctrinally and theoretically based on Isidore of Seville's theories, resolutions of the Councils of Toledo and Bishop Julian of Toledo's historical writings.[3] A century later, the unction ceremony spread from the Visigothic kingdom to the Carolingians, such as Pippine the Short in 751, and then to certain Anglo-Saxon monarchies and to the Byzantine Empire.[4] The anointment as a part of the ceremony of royal investiture would finally arrive in Rome with the anointing of Charlemagne's son Charles, which is also described in the pontifical of Leo III.[5] Thus, Rome did not take this ritual from its own tradition, but from the Frankish kings, who in turn got it from Visigothic tradition.[6]

---

[2] For the relation of Alfonso XI's ceremonies of knighting, anointing and self-crowning see *Crónica del rey Don Alfonso el Onceno*, chapters 120–1; Diego Catalán, ed., *Gran Crónica de Alfonso XI* (Madrid: Gredos, 1977), 506–10.

[3] Collins, 'Julian of Toledo and the Royal Succession in Late Seventh-Century Spain', especially 44–9. The practice of royal anointing and the consequent introduction of the king-making ritual with a liturgical form has to be distinguished from the date at which a fixed rite was established and written down as an ordo, as Percy E. Schramm argues in his study on Anglo-Saxon *ordines*: 'Der Souveränitätsgedanke in den mittelalterlichen Krönungsordines', in *Festschrift Percy Ernst Schramm*, ed. Peter Classen. 2 vols. (Wiesbaden: F. Steiner, 1964), 1:72. See also Janet L. Nelson, 'The Earliest Surviving Royal *Ordo*: Some Liturgical and Historical Aspects', in *Authority and Power*, ed. Brian Tierney and Peter Linehan (Cambridge: Cambridge University Press, 1980), 29–48, here 29.

[4] Louis Duchesne, *Le Liber Pontificalis: texte, introduction et commentaire*. 3 vols. (Paris: E. de Boccard, 1955–7), 38, and the long explanative notes 34–5.

[5] Duchesne, *Le Liber Pontificalis*, 6 and 38, note 35.

[6] On the origins of royal anointing in Frankish royal inauguration rites and the possibility of Irish or Visigothic influence on West Frankish liturgists see Michael J. Enright, *Iona, Tara and Soissons: The Origin of the Royal Anointing Ritual* (Berlin: De Gruyter, 1985); Glauco Maria Cantarella, 'Le sacre unzioni regie', in *Settimane di studio della Fondazione del Centro*

A key event in this story is King Wamba's anointing ceremony in Toledo in 672.[7] The ceremony is narrated in Julian of Toledo's *Historia Wambae*, an exaltation of the Visigothic king that functions as a historical narrative, as an exposition of a *speculum principum* and also as an *exemplum* illustrating doctrinal truths. Historians argue that Wamba (672–80) was the first Visigothic king, and consequently the first European king, to be anointed. Yet other specialists, such as Linehan, posit that Wamba's was not the first royal anointing that Toledo had witnessed, based on his insistence on being anointed at the *sedes antique* – that is, Toledo.[8] Michel Zimmermann argues that the practice of this ceremony could have started in 633.[9] Claudio Sánchez Albornoz asserts that the unction was an established *traditio* among Visigothic kings, but we cannot know from when.[10] In any case, all agree that Julian's is the first description and historical narration preserved of a royal anointing in Spain or anywhere else in the West.[11]

The unction confers on the king the two dimensions of King David's two successive anointings: the internal and constitutive (performed by Samuel), and the external and declarative (performed by Judah's men).[12] The royal unction, theoretically elaborated by Isidore of Seville and performed by Wamba, appears as a sacramental transposition of biblical unction and liturgically adapts the rite of baptismal

---

Italiano di Studi sull'Alto Medioevo (Spoleto: La Fondazione Centro italiano di studi sull'alto medioevo, 2007), 1291–1334.

[7] Julián, Bishop of Toledo, *Historia Wambae*, in *Sancti Iuliani Toletanae Sedis Episcopi Opera, Pars I*, ed. Wilhelm Levison (Turnhout: Brepols, 1976), chapters 3–4. This chronicle was written about 675. A detailed and instructive account of Wamba's inauguration and anointment appears in Suzanne Teillet, *Des Goths à la nation gothique: Les origines de l'idée de nation en Occident du Ve au VIIe siècle* (Paris: Les Belles Lettres, 1984), 607–17. See also Samuele Sacchi, *Modelli di regalità di area iberica durante il VII secolo: tra i concili di Toledo e il pensiero isidoriano* (Pisa: Università degli Studi di Pisa, 'Tesi di dottorato', 2011).

[8] Linehan, *History and the Historians of Medieval Spain*, 56. Wamba is one of the Iberian medieval kings whose figure and personality have generated substantial narrative and legendary accounts; see Aengus Ward, *History and Chronicles in Late Medieval Iberia: Representations of Wamba in Late Medieval Narrative Histories* (Leiden: Brill, 2011).

[9] Michel Zimmermann, 'Les sacres des rois wisigoths', in *Clovis: histoire et mémoire. Vol. 1: Le baptême de Clovis, son écho à travers l'histoire* (Paris: Presses de l'Université Paris-Sorbonne, 1997), 9–28.

[10] Claudio Sánchez Albornoz, 'La ordinatio principis en la España goda y postvisigoda', in *Estudios sobre las instituciones medievales españolas* (Mexico: Universidad Nacional Autónoma de México, 1965), 712.

[11] It seems that other European monarchies started this practice not before the end of the eighth century; see Bloch, *Les rois thaumaturges*, 464ff.

[12] The first, David's unction, is recorded in 1 Kings 16:13; the second is documented in 2 Kings 2:4. See Jean de Pange, *Le roi très chrétien* (Paris: Fayard, 1949); Marc Reydeller, *La Royauté Dans la littérature latine de Sidone Apollinaire à Isidore de Séville* (Rome: École Française de Rome, 1981), 536–9.

confirmation.[13] The Jewish sacerdotal and royal unction now has its parallel with the new Christian-Visigothic episcopal and royal unction.[14]

With this new ceremony of unction, the church becomes the necessary intermediary between God and the new king. Thus the church, as well as the people, confirms the king's authority with the *sacramentum*, which confirms the king's charisma and link with God (*non est potestas nisi a Deo*, Romans 13:1). There begins, then, a certain parallel between bishop and king, and a transference of certain symbols and liturgies (a bishop's anointing among them) naturally emerges. Due to the spread of the ideas of Gregory of Tours, Gregory the Great and, particularly in Hispania, Isidore of Seville, the symbol of *rex-sacerdos* (king-priest) would soon emerge in the Visigothic kingdom. The consecrated king confirms his royal function, while the consecrated bishop confirms his sacerdotal function. This political-theological practice would prove to be an important heritage for the subsequent Iberian dynasties, particularly those of Castile, via Asturias and Leon.

From Asturias to Leon: The Fusion between Unction and Coronation

Historians differ on the interpretation of the effects of the Islamic invasion of Iberia from 711, and on the extent to which that year marks an absolute or relative rupture with tradition. In any case, the political scenario shifted radically, and Christian societies could survive only as structured organisations under the kingdom of Asturias in the West and the Pyrenean provinces in the East. After the eighth century, Castilian kings would feel that they were the successors of the Visigothic kings, following Asturias-Leon-Castile as their main line of tradition.

Critics agree that the most probable restoration of the unction ceremony after the Islamic invasion took place during King Ordoño II's (914–24) enthronement. The reprise of the anointing tradition under Ordoño II at the beginning of the tenth century is one of the clearest links of the Astur-Leonese dynasty with the Visigothic one. Documentary evidence (as distinct from chronicle sources) of other Leonese kings being anointed after Ordoño II, such as Ramiro II (944), Bermudo II (982) and Ferdinand I (1038), also exist.[15]

---

[13] Janet L. Nelson, 'National Synods, Kingship As Office and Royal Anointing: An Early Medieval Syndrome', *Councils and Assemblies* 7 (1971): 41–59, here 52.

[14] The apparition of the episcopal unction remains uncertain; see Pierre Batiffol, 'La liturgie du sacre des évêques dans son évolution historique', *Revue d'Histoire Ecclésiastique* 23 (1927): 733–63, here 745–9.

[15] Claudio Sánchez Albornoz, 'La sucesión al trono en los reinos de León y Castilla', in *Estudios sobre las instituciones medievales españolas* (Mexico: Universidad Nacional

Historians argue that the unction ceremony was also performed before Ordoño II, specifically with Alfonso II (829) and Alfonso III (866), but they give only historiographical evidence from works elaborated some centuries afterwards rather than documentary sources.[16] Yet extant documentary evidence is not sufficiently convincing, since all of it is historiographical. It is always difficult to know which of the sources that mention the anointing of Leonese kings are the most accurate, but in general the documentary sources are more credible than the historiographical ones since the latter are usually more conditioned by the spirit of their own times than that of the times they are dealing with. In any case, based on the historicity of Ordoño II's unction, we can conclude that two and a half centuries after Wamba's unction, this ceremony re-emerged to strengthen the religious and spiritual dimension of royalty.[17]

In the complex identity process that connects the new Christian peninsular monarchies with pre-Islamic Iberia, via Visigothic tradition, the *Chronica de Alfonso III* or *Chronica Visigothorum* is an important link. This text took the tradition of the *Historia Gothorum*, as promoted by Alfonso III (866–910), and created an influential narrative of the battle of Covadonga – a mythical account which reported the first Islamic defeat against Christian troops. The *Chronica de Alfonso III* includes the earliest reference to the restoration of the anointing of Visigothic kings after 711. The author of this chronicle privileges royal unction, since he begins his chronicle with the narration of Wamba's anointing, based on Julian's *Historia Wambae* account. Historians agree that the accounts of Alfonso II's and Alfonso III's anointings are false interpolations in the chronicle, precisely in order to provide Ordoño II with vital precedents for the practice of unction.[18] Authors disagree on the continuity of this practice among Ordoño II's successors, but they agree that it was at least intermittently practised.[19] In any case, all of them concur that the re-

---

Autónoma de México, 1965), 687, and Sánchez Albornoz, 'La *ordinatio principis*', 723–4, where he gives the specific documental and historiographical references.

[16] Sánchez Albornoz provides historiographical evidence for the royal unction of Leon and Castilian kings, in 'La *ordinatio principis*', 724, n. 98, in which Alfonso II and Alfonso III are included, but he seems to contradict himself in Sánchez Albornoz, 'La sucesión al trono en los reinos de León y Castilla', 687, n. 148, where he provides documental evidence that the first king anointed was Ramiro II (944) – that is, after Ordoño II. See also Percy E. Schramm, *Las insignias de la realeza en la edad media española* (Madrid: Instituto de Estudios Políticos, 1960), 1–63.

[17] Thomas Deswarte, *De la destruction a la restauration. L'idéologie du royaume d'Oviedo-León* (Turnhout: Brepols, 2003), 181–3.

[18] Linehan, *History and the Historians of Medieval Spain*, 146–7.

[19] Linehan argues that the unction becomes an exceptional rather than an ordinary practice (Peter Linehan, 'León, ciudad regia, y sus obispos en los siglos X–XIII', *El Reino de León en la Alta Edad Media* 6 [1994]: 409–57, here 423–8 and 433). Deswarte opts for a more permanent continuity of the practice (*De la destruction a la restauration*, 183).

emergence of the royal unction from Ordoño II, and the proliferation of historical narratives stressing its ceremonial relevance, meant an increasing and progressive return to the religious dimension of royalty.

The originality of this period lies in the fact that, for the first time, the ceremony of unction is associated with coronation in Iberia – a century and a half after the unction-coronation of Pippine in 751 in the neighbouring Frankish kingdom. Complementary to this ritual tradition, the first iconographic testimony of the royal crown (*diadema*) in the kingdom of Leon appears in a miniature in Ferdinand I's (1037–65) psaltery.[20] Such iconographic sources proliferated during the first half of the twelfth century, particularly among the miniatures in which the kings of Asturias and Leon were shown with the crown, sceptre and throne as attributes of power.[21] Following this iconographic evidence, historians have argued that the coronation ceremony was associated with unction from the very origins of the Asturian monarchy.[22] But the documentary and iconographic evidence of the presence of the crown does not confirm the existence of a specific ceremony of coronation until the early eleventh century, with Alfonso VII. Synchronically to this ritual innovation, the crown emerges as a relevant sign of royal authority. Two pieces of evidence survive for this: one iconographic and the other documentary.[23]

The miniatures composed at this time assign an unquestionable relevance to the crown. In 1055, the scribe Fructuoso was commissioned by King Ferdinand I to elaborate the *Book of Hours*. He inserted some miniatures. There is a marvellous 'capital' in the form of a rich crown, and the king appears in other miniatures wearing a big crown. This image

---

[20] Fernando Galván Freile, 'La representación de la unción regia en el antifonario de la catedral de León', *Archivos Leoneses* 49 (1995): 135–46, here 143.

[21] Manuel C. Díaz y Díaz, Fernando López Alsina and Serafín Moralejo Álvarez, *Los tumbos de Compostela* (Madrid: Edilán, 1985), in the epigraph 'Láminas I–VI and VII–XXII'; Sánchez Albornoz: 'La *ordinatio principis*', 725. The kings of Leon appear with crowns in the miniatures of the *Codex Vigilamus*, in Fernando I's *Liber Horarum*, in the *Liber Testamentorum* of Oviedo and in the *Libro de estampas* of Leon; see María Elena Gómez-Moreno, 'Las miniaturas del Antifonario de la Catedral de León', *Archivos Leoneses* 8 (1954): 305; Gonzalo Menéndez Pidal, *Sobre miniatura española en la Alta Edad Media* (Madrid: Espasa Calpe, 1958), 9, 33, 45 and 55.

[22] Sánchez Albornoz, 'La *ordinatio principis*', 720; Galván, 'La representación', 143.

[23] Jesús Domínguez Bordona, *La miniatura española* (Barcelona: Gustavo Gili, 1930), vol. 1: *lamina* 26 ('Codex Vigilanus seu Albeldensis' kept in El Escorial, Biblioteca del Real Monasterio, f. 428, about 976, in which appear Chindasuinth, Recceswinth and Egica above, the Leon queen Urraca and kings Sancho and Ramiro in the middle, and three scribes below) and vol. 1: *lamina* 34 ('Diurno de Fernando I', kept in Santiago de Compostela, Biblioteca de la Universidad, f. 3r: the scriba Fructuosus between King Fernando I and Queen Sancha). See also Sánchez Albornoz, 'La *ordinatio principis*', 725, note 100.

sharply contrasts with the *Codice Vigilano*, in which Visigothic kings (Chindasuinth, Receswinth and Egica) and a Leonese queen and kings (Urraca, Sancho and Ramiro) are all represented without a crown: they (the Visigoths) wear a mitre or (in the case of the Leonese) a halo. This image was drawn in 975, some decades before Ferdinand's *Book of Hours*, which could be proof that the crown was not yet consolidated as a sign of authority and majesty – or at least that it had less relevance than the religious symbols of the mitre and halo. It is very important here to note the date the codices, miniatures and images were produced, rather than that of the monarchs whose image is being shown.[24]

Key documentary evidence for the consolidation of the crown as a sign of authority and power in the age of Ferdinand I lies, interestingly, in the ceremony of *de-coronation* he underwent at the end of his reign, in order to die poor and penitent. In a vivid narration, the *Historia Silense* relates that the king called the bishops and abbots and, in a solemn ceremony in which he was full of tears, he turned the royal dress into poor clothes and the crown into sackcloth.[25] Yet the increasing presence of the crown in iconographic and historiographical sources does not confirm the existence of a *ceremony* of coronation. The first ceremony of coronation seems to be that of Alfonso VII in 1111. Certainly, the *Historia Silense*, composed at the beginning of the twelfth century, describes the coronation of Ordoño II, one and a half centuries before that of Alfonso VII. But historians argue that this account is an invention of the chronicler, inspired by the Carolingian precedent reported by Eginhard in his *Vita Karoli*, in order to strengthen precisely the tradition recovered by Alfonso VII. Beyond the evident precocity, given their Visigothic precedents, of Asturian, Leonese and Castilian kings in unction and coronation practices, regarding Alfonso VII as the first Castilian king to be enthroned with a coronation ceremony is a chronology that fits better with the

---

[24] Sánchez Albornoz seems to fall into this anachronism in 'La *ordination principis*', 725, n. 100, giving the same historical value to miniatures produced on very different occasions, and thus in different contexts: 976 (*Codex Vigilanus* of Albelada), 1055 (Fernando I's *Book of Hours* of Compostela), 1126–9 (*Liber Testamentorum*, Oviedo), and twelfth century (*Libro de las estampas*, from Leon), all of them compiled in Domínguez Bordona, *Miniatura española*: 1, *lamina* 26 (*Vigilano*), 34 (*Book of Hours*), 70–5 (*Liber Testamentorum*) and 77 (*Libro de las estampas*). For a more general approach, and particularly the relationship between images and liturgy, see Eric Palazzo, *L'Évêque et son image* (Turnhout: Brepols, 1999), particularly the chapter 'Les sacres et les couronnments', 253–305.

[25] Francisco Santos Coco, ed., *Historia Silense* (Madrid: Sucesores de Rivadeneyra, 1921), 90–1; Justo Pérez de Urbel and Atilano González Ruiz-Zorrilla, eds., *Historia Silense* (Madrid: Escuela de Estudios Medievales, 1959), 208–9. See an English edition of *Historia Silense* in Simon Barton and Richard Fletcher, *The World of the Cid* (Manchester: Manchester University Press, 2000), 9–64.

general tendency of European monarchies, which were tardy in reintroducing this rite.[26]

The *Historia Silense* chronicler's description of Ordoño II tells us that the crown was placed by twelve prelates.[27] Nevertheless, this account is contextually more suggestive of the time when it was written (the beginning of the twelfth century) than the time it describes (the beginning of the tenth century), which would confirm the hypothesis that this episode of Ordoño II's coronation was an artificial intercalation. But, in any case, these ceremonies would have been restored at some time between those two periods.

The coronation of Alfonso VII took place in Santiago de Compostela in 1111, as narrated in the *Historia Compostelana*.[28] The king, still a boy, was anointed and crowned (*aureo diademate coronatum*) by Bishop Gelmírez of Santiago de Compostela, in the church of Santiago.[29] This coronation was urged by the historical circumstances which surrounded it – namely, the minority of Alfonso and the desire of his mother, Queen Urraca, to consolidate his future sovereignty – but this event also served as a relevant precedent for succeeding royal generations.[30] In fact, the coronation of 1111 was followed by a repetition of the ceremony in 1126 (*aureo diademate coronatum*[31]), on the occasion of the death of the king's mother, Queen Urraca, and by the celebration of the imperial king's enthronement in 1135 (*imposuerunt super caput eius coronam ex auro mundo et lapidibus pretiosis*).[32] The recovery of an attribute of royal power (the coronation) used by the Roman emperors and then the Visigothic kings is proof that the temporal dimension of the Asturian and Leonese monarchy was growing all the time.[33] The spread of coronation ceremonials at the beginning of the twelfth century in Iberia, the Ceremonial of Cardeña among them, was a natural consequence of the restoration of this ceremony.[34]

---

[26] Alexander Pierre Bronisch, 'Krönungsritus und Kronenbrauch im Reich von Asturien und León', *Studi Medievali* 39 (1998): 327–66, here 338, 349–58 and 365–6.

[27] Santos Coca, *Historia Silense*, 37–8.

[28] Emma Falque Rey, ed., *Historia Compostelana* (Turnhout: Brepols, 1988), book 1: chapter 66. See also Deswarte, *De la destruction a la restauration*, 206.

[29] Sánchez Albornoz, 'La *ordinatio principis*', 726, n. 106.

[30] Bernard F. Reilly, *The Kingdom of León-Castilla under Queen Urraca, 1109–1126* (Princeton, NJ: Princeton University Press, 1982), 73.

[31] Luis Sánchez Belda, ed., *Chronica Adefonsi Imperatoris* (Madrid: Escuela de Estudios Medievales, 1950), 5.

[32] Sánchez Belda, *Chronica Adefonsi Imperatoris*, 55–6.

[33] On the use of the crown in the Roman Empire see André Chastangol, *L'évolution politique, sociale et économique du monde romain de Dioclétien à Julien* (Paris: Sedes, 1985), 170–4; on the Visigoth kingdom see María R. Valverde Castro, 'Simbología del poder en la monarquía visigótica', *Studia Historica: Historia Antigua* 9 (1991): 139–48.

[34] Francisco de Berganza, ed., Ceremonial de Cardeña, in *Antigüedades de España*. 2 vols. (Madrid: Francisco del Hierro, 1721), 2:681–4. Some hypotheses on the ultra-Pyrenean

Self-Coronation As Usurpation and Censure in Twelfth-Century Castile

The beginning of the twelfth century also witnessed the introduction of a new subject into the narratives: the unorthodox ceremony of self-coronation. Two chronicles (the *Historia Silense*, about 1115, and Bishop Pelagius of Oviedo's chronicle, about 1118) draw an explicit parallel between a certain unexpected and unorthodox rite (self-coronation) practised by the usurper Paul (the enemy of the Visigothic King Wamba, the first king who was anointed five centuries earlier), and the violent King Sancho II, the enemy of his brother Alfonso VI, who eventually succeeded him as the king of Castile.

Pelagius of Oviedo recounts that, in 1072, the usurper-king Sancho II, after having defeated his brother Alfonso VI, 'himself placed the crown on his head in Leon'.[35] Although Sancho II receives some praise in the chronicle, the gesture is unquestionably seen by Pelagius as a sign of usurpation, as Paul, the Duke of Narbonne, who fought Wamba four centuries before, is described in the *Historia Silense* as a usurper for having been named king after having placed the crown on his own head.[36] It is certain that the compiler of the *Historia Silense* knew the account of Paul's self-coronation, fixed some centuries before in Julian's *Historia Wamba*. Julian always defines Paul as 'tyrannus', in contraposition to the religious King Wamba. After reproaching Paul for profaning the old Visigothic treasury in order to take Reccadedus' crown for his own coronation, Julian tells the story of Paul's self-coronation.[37]

The same parallel between the transgression of self-crowned Castilian kings and that of usurping Visigothic kings is expounded by the chronicler Rodrigo Jiménez de Rada, Archbishop of Toledo, who stated in his history

---

origin of this ceremonial and its eventual use in Leon and Castilian coronations is presented in Sánchez Albornoz, 'La *ordinatio principis*', 731–4.

[35] See 'Tunc Sancius rex cepit regnum fratris suis Adefonsi regis, et imposuit sibi in Legione coronam', in *Crónica del obispo Don Pelayo*, ed. Benito Sánchez Alonso (Madrid: Sucesores de Hernando, 1924), 78. For Sancho II's self-coronation see Bronisch, 'Krönungsritus und Kronenbrauch im Reich von Asturien und León', 357; Deswarte, *De la destruction a la restauration*, 206; Linehan, *History and the Historians of Medieval Spain*, 398. Reilly argues that the act of self-coronation was not an act of arrogance but arose from Bishop Pelayo de León's refusal to take part in the ceremony (Bernard F. Reilly, *The Kingdom of León-Castilla under King Alfonso VI* (Princeton, NJ: Princeton University Press, 1988), 63), but this does not seem to be the spirit of the chronicler's annotation, or the meaning of the context in which this gesture is articulated – with Sancho II just having defeated his brother Alfonso after a long fight.

[36] Santos Coco, *Historia Silense*, 5–6; Pérez de Urbel and González, *Historia Silense*, 117.

[37] Julian de Toledo, *Historia Wamba regis*, chapter 26, ed. Levison, 240–1. See also Thomas Deswarte, 'Le Christ–roi: autel et couronne votive dans l'Espagne wisigothique', in *Églises et pouvoirs*, ed. Bruno Béthouart and Jérome Grévy (Boulogne-sur-Mer: Maison de la Recherche en sciences humaines 'Palais Impérial', 2007), 71–83, here 76.

of Spain (about 1245) that Sancho II crowned himself, and in his history of the Arabs that kings had crowned themselves in the Visigothic period.[38]

These two transgressive gestures (Visigothic King Paul's and Castilian King Sancho's self-coronations) are contrasted with the behaviour of Ferdinand I (1037–65), who appears as a legitimate king who respects the rules of accession to power, accepting the crown conventionally, (supposedly) being crowned in 1038 and named king.[39] Thus, the gesture of self-coronation is seen, at least during the twelfth century, as a transgression of a natural receipt of authority, rather than a legitimate practice of kingly autonomy. It is identified as the natural consequence following self-investiture, so it led to substantial criticism.

By the end of the twelfth century, the rites of unction and coronation, though only intermittently practised, were established in Castile. Some authors have argued that this is probably the most important sign of the transition from an elective to a hereditary monarchy.[40] Yet, perhaps more interesting for the aims of this chapter, the balance and intermittency between unction and coronation witnessed by Leonese and Castilian kings from the ninth to the twelfth century (from Ordoño II to Alfonso VII) is a key theological-political event which would profoundly shape the next two centuries.

If the beginning of the twelfth century witnessed the self-coronation narrative turn, things became more radical from the thirteenth century in terms of resistance to ecclesiastical mediation of royal ceremonial practices. From that time on, the chroniclers removed every mention of anointing from their narratives, eventually describing the enthronement ceremonies simply as coronations. They posthumously desacralise the Castilian monarchs. The crown became a symbol of temporal sovereignty, which could be used by the kings independently of the bishops with the rite of self-coronation. In addition, the chronicler Rodrigo Jiménez de Rada suggests, in his narration of Ferdinand I's coronation, that it was to the acclamation of the aristocracy rather than to action by the bishop that Ferdinand had owed his throne.[41]

To be sure, we do not have evidence of coronations or the unction of Alfonso VII's successors, Enrique I (1214–17) and Ferdinand III (1217–52). Neither Rodrigo Jiménez de Rada's chronicle, *La Crónica Latina de*

---

[38] Rodrigo of Toledo, *Historia De Rebus Hispaniae*, ed. Juan Fernández Valverde (Turnhout: Brepols, 1987), chapter 7, epigraph 20: 'sibi trium regnorum imposuit diadema'; Rodrigo of Toledo, *Historia Arabum*, ed. José Lozano Sánchez (Sevilla: Publicaciones de la Universidad, 1974), chapter 9: 'more rerum Gothorum sibi imposuit diadema'. See also Linehan, *History and the Historians of Medieval Spain*, 398 and 392.
[39] Sánchez Alonso, *Crónica del Obispo Don Pelayo*, 71.
[40] Sánchez Albornoz, 'La sucesión al trono en los reinos de León y Castilla', 687.
[41] Linehan, *History and the Historians of Medieval Spain*, 398.

los reyes de Castilla, nor *La Crónica General* say anything about theses coronations.[42] We have only the indirect word of Alfonso X's (1252–84) installation ceremony, which probably consisted of a simple traditional gesture of 'elevation'.[43] Linehan has convincingly argued that Alfonso X's self-coronation in 1252, narrated by Antonio Ballesteros in 1963, based in turn on the Marqués de Mondéjar's 1700s account, was a historiographical creation induced by the specific historical context of Spain at the beginning of the eighteenth century, rather than thirteenth-century historical reality.[44] This is a typical presentist and anachronistic approach, and standard practice in all-purpose historiography.[45]

Finally, Alfonso X's son, Sancho IV (1284–95), was crowned by four bishops at Toledo Cathedral in 1284.[46] Significantly, it was the first coronation in Castile since 1111: Alfonso VII's 1135 imperial coronation was, in some sense, reiterative, or at least bearing an imperial rather than a properly monarchical meaning.[47] Interestingly, during the second half of the thirteenth century, the figure of Wamba was being reconstructed thanks to appropriation by Alfonso X and the spread of the *Poema de*

---

[42] Sánchez Albornoz, 'La *ordinatio principis*', 734.
[43] See the letter from Jofré of Loaysa to King James I of Aragon and the sober narration of Alfonso X's elevation in his own chronicle: Manuel González Jiménez, ed., *Crónica de Alfonso X el Sabio según el Ms. II/2777 de la Biblioteca del Palacio Real* (Murcia: Academia Alfonso X el Sabio, 1999), 4.
[44] Peter Linehan, 'The Accession of Alfonso X (1252) and the Origins of the War of the Spanish Succession', in *God and Man in Medieval Spain*, ed. Derek W. Lomax and David Mackenzie (Warminster: Aris & Phillips, 1989), 59–79, here 60–1. See also Manuel González Jiménez, *Alfonso X el Sabio* (Barcelona: Ariel, 2004), 44–6, and Joseph F. O'Callaghan, *El rey sabio. El reinado de Alfonso X de Castilla* (Sevilla: Universidad de Sevilla, 1999), 48. A biography of Alfonso X is given in Simon R. Doubleday, *The Wise King: A Christian Prince, Muslim Spain, and the Birth of the Renaissance* (New York: Basic, 2015).
[45] As argued in David Lowenthal, *The Past Is a Foreign Country* (Cambridge: Cambridge University Press, 1985); John L. Gaddis, *The Landscape of History* (New York: Cambridge University Press, 2004); Gordon S. Wood, *The Purpose of the Past* (New York: Penguin Press, 2008).
[46] *Crónica de D. Sancho*: 4:1, in *Crónicas de los Reyes de Castilla*, ed. Cayetano Rosell (Madrid: Atlas, 1953), 1:69b; Mercedes Gaibrois de Ballesteros, *Historia del reinado de Sancho IV de Castilla* (Madrid: Revista de Archivos, Bibliotecas y Museos, 1922–8), v–vi. On the political implications of Sancho IV's first coronation see Peter Linehan, 'The Politics of Piety: Aspects of the Castilian Monarchy from Alfonso X to Alfonso XI', *Revista Canadiense de Estudios Hispánicos* 9 (1985): 385–404, here 389–91. Actually, this was the first coronation of Sancho IV since he was probably crowned a second time in Sevilla: José Manuel Nieto Soria, *Sancho IV, 1284–1295* (Gijón: Trea, 2014), 49–51.
[47] During the thirteenth century, chroniclers such as Rodrigo Jiménez de Rada turned Alfonso VII's imperial coronation into self-coronation. Yet I do not take this argument as central, since this historiographical move has evident imperial implications, interested in providing Alfonso's coronation with a strong ecclesiastical dimension rather than a properly royal or monarchical one (Linehan, *History and the Historians of Medieval Spain*, 463–5).

Fernán González.[48] Sancho IV's coronation was a gesture full of political significance, aimed at strengthening the king's legitimacy before his father Alfonso X's other preference in the person of Alfonso de la Cerda. This decision once again contradicts the idea that the coronation had only a secondary symbolic meaning.[49] Sancho IV's son and successor, Ferdinand IV (1295–1312), was not crowned or anointed. His chronicler does not refer specifically to the coronation or anointing ceremonies, but to a more general ritual of enthronement when he was nine years old, in the central altar of Toledo Cathedral, in 1295, which also included the oath.[50]

The archbishop of Toledo was present at the ceremony, but he was only a qualified observer. Things seem to follow, at least for once, a progressive line towards resistance to ecclesiastical mediation. Nevertheless, the line's crooked tendencies soon reasserted themselves. At the beginning of the fourteenth century, Castile experienced another turn in coronation ceremonies, with the appearance of a new ceremonial, complementary to the *Ceremonial de Toledo*, and elaborated around the 1280s. This new ceremonial was probably commissioned by the same Alfonso XI (1312–50) who had relatives in Portugal, and it was elaborated by a Portuguese bishop of Coimbra (1319–33) called Ramon, and written around the 1320s.[51] Alfonso XI followed this ceremonial in his installation, which consisted of the three successive ceremonies of anointing, knighting and coronation – although he turned the coronation by the celebrating bishop into a coronation of himself. This ceremonial confirms that the coronation was at the core of the ceremony, since the part of the text devoted

---

[48] Linehan, *History and the Historians of Medieval Spain*, 483–6.
[49] José Manuel Nieto Soria, *Iglesia y poder en Castilla. El episcopado, 1250–1350* (Madrid: Universidad Complutense, 1988), 59.
[50] *Crónica de Fernando IV de Castilla*, ed. Rosell, chapter 1, *Crónicas de los reyes de Castilla*, 1:93. See also Antonio Benavides, *Memorias de don Fernando IV de Castilla* (Madrid: Real Academia de la Historia, 1860), 1:2, and César González Mínguez, *Fernando IV de Castilla (1295–1312)* (Vitoria: Colegio Universitario de Álava, 1976), 31.
[51] The transcription and some interesting comments on the ceremonial are included in Sánchez Albornoz, 'Un ceremonial inédito de coronación de los reyes de Castilla' 739–63. This ceremonial is usually called *El ceremonial de El Escorial* because it is kept in this monastery. See also Linehan, *History and the Historians of Medieval Spain*, 584–92; Odile Jouini-Bastien, *Libro de las coronaciones. Manuscrit III.3 de la Bibliothèque de l'Escorial*. 2 vols. (Paris: Université de Paris, These de troisieme cycle, 1983–4); José Manuel Nieto Soria, 'Los libros de ceremoniales regios en Castilla y Aragón en el siglo XIV', in *El ceremonial de la Coronación, unción y exequias de los reyes de Inglaterra*, ed. Eloísa Ramírez (Pamplona: Gobierno de Navarra, 2008), 177–94; Eduardo Carrero Santamaria, 'Architecture and Liturgical Space in the Cathedral of Santiago de Compostela: The *Libro de la Coronación de los reyes de Castilla*', *Hispanic Research Journal* 13(5) (2012): 466–86; Olga Pérez Monzón, 'Ceremonias regias en la Castilla Medieval. A propósito del llamado Libro de la Coronación de los reyes de Castilla y Aragón', *Archivo Español de Arte* 83 (2010): 317–34.

specifically to the ceremony was entitled 'how the king is going to be crowned' and only in the end of the paragraph is the anointment mentioned.[52]

Alfonso XI's Self-Knighting and Self-Coronation

Nevertheless, no mention of the self-coronation appears in the ceremonial, so that we have to search for narrative sources. Alfonso's self-coronation is narrated in the *Crónica del rey Alfonso Onceno*.[53] The chronicler explains that the king wanted to be knighted and crowned because he was determined to make his kingdom great.[54] This text allows us to compare the ceremonial rubrics that were supposed to come before Alfonso's actual performance on the day of his coronation.[55] He did not in the event follow the ceremonial he himself had commissioned. Linehan expresses well the contrast between the 'should be', as planned by the ceremonial, and the 'what really happened', as narrated by the chronicle.

Nowhere is the contrast between their two perceptions of the king's place in society, the bishop's and the chronicler's, more startlingly apparent than in their accounts of what ought to have and what really did happen on the occasion of the knighting of Alfonso XI.[56]

Alfonso XI was first knighted by the mechanical arm of the automated statue of Saint James in Santiago (25 July 1332),[57] then anointed at the Monastery of Las Huelgas (Burgos) in August of that same year,[58] in front of the same mechanical sculpture (moved from Santiago to Burgos

---

[52] Sánchez Albornoz, 'Un ceremonial inédito de coronación de los reyes de Castilla', 756.
[53] On Alfonso XI's self-coronation see Peter Linehan, 'The Mechanization of Ritual: Alfonso XI of Castile in 1332', in *Ritti e rituali nelle società medievali*, ed. Jacques Chiffoleau, Lauro Martines and Agostino Paravicini Bagliani (Spoleto: Centro Italiano di Studi Sull'alto Medioevo, 1994), 309–27; María del Pilar Ramos Vicent, *Reafirmación del poder monárquico en Castilla: la coronación de Alfonso XI* (Madrid: Universidad Complutense, 1983); Linehan, *History and the Historians of Medieval Spain*, 584–601.
[54] *Crónica del rey Don Alfonso el Onceno*, chapters 120–1; Catalán, *Gran Crónica de Alfonso XI*, 507.
[55] Ruiz, 'Une royauté sans sacre', 429–53. Ruiz explores this story as the singular manifestation of the Castilian 'royauté sans sacre', which does not claim the healing character of French and English kings, or the backing of the church, in the coronation ceremony. See also Bloch, *Les rois thaumaturges*.
[56] Linehan, *History and the Historians of Medieval Spain*, 592. A very interesting comparison is made between Bishop Ramon's ordo and Alfonso XI's chronicle in Linehan, 'The Politics of Piety', 391–3.
[57] Catalán, *Gran Crónica de Alfonso XI*, 507. For the integration of the chivalrous ceremonial of elevation to knighthood into the coronation ritual of Western European kings see Schramm, *A History of the English Coronation*, 76 and 93ff.
[58] Catalán, *Gran Crónica de Alfonso XI*, 510.

for the occasion⁵⁹), before finally crowning himself in that very ceremony. The automated Saint James (Figure 25) enabled the king of Castile, both in Santiago and in Burgos, to assert his independence of all earthly powers both spiritual and temporal.⁶⁰

Yet the discordance between the El Escorial Ceremonial and the ritual that Alfonso XI followed in his installation ceremonies is particularly striking at the moment of coronation, immediately following his anointing. The chronicler explains that, after the anointment, the bishops blessed the crowns that were in the altar and went back to their sites, and then 'the king ascended to the altar, took the crown of gold and put it on his own head.' Then, the king crowned the queen and they heard the Mass together.⁶¹ Yet the ceremonial had planned the ceremony otherwise, since it supposed the bishop should have put the mitre and then the crown on the king's head (both overlapped) after having been ordained as a knight of Santiago.⁶²

There is no mention of the mitre in the chronicler's account. Linehan argues that mitres belonged to a wider world than Castile had ever known, just as the entire ceremonial evoked scenes that the wider world had not witnessed since the age of Alfonso VII. Alfonso XI (or, rather, the *narration* of Alfonso XI's installation ceremonies) revived practices that the popes had been striving to remove during the previous two centuries.⁶³

---

⁵⁹ Catalán, *Gran Crónica de Alfonso XI*, 507.
⁶⁰ About the automated Santiago and its function in Alfonso XI's knighting and anointment see Linehan, *History and the Historians of Medieval Spain*, 592–3 and 598–9, and Linehan, 'Alfonso XI of Castile and the Arm of Santiago (with a Note on the Pope's Foot)', *Miscellanea Domenico Maffei dicata*, ed. Antonio García y García and Peter Weimar (Goldbach: Keip, 1995), 121–46. The sculpture-machine of Santiago is today still visible in the cloister of the church of the Monastery of Las Huelgas in Burgos.
⁶¹ 'El Rey subió al altar, e tomó su corona de oro con piedras preciosas e de muy gran presçio, e púsola en la cabeça; e tomó él la otra corona, e púsola a la Reyna' (Catalán, *Gran crónica de Alfonso XI*, 510). See also Rosell, *Crónicas de los reyes de Castilla*, 1:233–5. A more sober narration is given in the *Poem of Alfonso XI*: 'El muy noble rey aquel día / su corona fue tomar / la reyna donna María / y la fizo coronar' (Yo Ten Cate, ed., *El poema de Alfonso XI* [Madrid: Bermejo, 1956], 111, chapter 392). This sobriety is compatible with the hypothesis, argued by Diego Catalán, that the poem would be a versified abbreviation of the chronicle: Diego Catalán, *Poema de Alfonso XI. Fuentes, dialecto, estilo* (Madrid: Gredos, 1953), 10 and 16. On this poem see María F. Nussbaum, *Claves del entorno ideológico del 'Poema de Alfonso XI'* (Lausanne: Sociedad Suiza de Estudios Hispánicos, 2012). See also the parallel narration of another chronicle: 'El Rey subió al altar solo, et tomó la su corona, que era de oro con piedras de muy grand prescio, et púsola en la cabeza; et tomó la otra corona, et púsola a la Reyna, et tornó fincar los hinojos ante el altar': Francisco Cerda, ed., *Cronica de D. Alfonso el Onceno de este nombre: de los reyes que reynaron en Castilla y en Leon* (Madrid: Antonio de Sancha, 1787), chapter 100.
⁶² Sánchez Albornoz, 'Un ceremonial inédito de coronación de los reyes de Castilla', 762–3. An analogous tradition of putting the mitre over the crown is documented in Ecclesiastes 45:12.
⁶³ Linehan, *History and the Historians of Medieval Spain*, 601.

Figure 25 The automated statue of Saint James. Monasterio de las Huelgas, Burgos, Spain. Second half of the thirteenth century. © Album / Oronoz.

The custom of placing the crown above the mitre was already apparent in some of the ceremonials of German kings: 'Once the Epistle has been read and the Gradual sung, the emperor processes to the altar, where the supreme pontiff places the clerical mitre on his head and the imperial diadem on the mitre.'[64] The ceremonial of El Escorial probably took this rite from the German tradition.

This idea strengthens my belief that Alfonso XI of Castile's self-knighting and self-coronation were not uncalculated or naive gestures but strategic and premeditated rites through which he aimed to gain autonomy from ecclesiastical hierarchy. Circumstantially, perhaps the effective performance of Alfonso XI's gesture was favoured by the difficult situation of Pope John XXII in Avignon, but in any case this could not have been reason enough to justify or legitimise such a gestural transgression. When Benedict XII replaced John XXII as pope in 1334, he maintained a close watch on Iberian affairs, but he was not able to prevent Peter IV of Aragon's self-coronation in 1336.

After Alfonso XI, his son Enrique II Trastámara (1367–79) was also crowned at the Monastery of Las Huelgas in Burgos. The chronicler says that the king 'coronose allí por Rey' ('he crowned *himself* there as a king') and then he received the homage of the nobles through the kissing of his hands, a feudal tradition that had been restored to the coronation ceremony at some uncertain time before.[65] John I (1379–90) was also crowned and the chronicler used a parallel expression: 'él (the king) se coronó' ('the king crowned himself') although the phrase remains ambiguous because of the Spanish reflexive pronouns' typical polysemy. We have certainly kept a miniature in which the king is crowned by the bishop, but this is not conclusive proof of the ceremony actually enacted, since we know that images and rituals may differ in their content.[66] Whether self-crowned or not, if the restoration of the feudal tradition of the homage of the nobles was a substitute for the former sacred oath, then this would be another sign of the resistance to ecclesiastical mediation in the Castilian monarchy.[67]

---

[64] Elze, *Ordines coronationis*, 66.

[65] Pedro López de Ayala, *Crónica del rey Don Pedro*, ed. Eugenio de Llagunoy Amirola (Madrid: Rivadeneyra, 1875), 540.

[66] Luis Suárez Fernández, *Historia del reinado de Juan I de Castilla* (Madrid: Universidad Autónoma, 1977), 1:26–7; Nieto Soria, *Ceremonias de la realeza*, 28. On the miniature that depicts John I of Castile being crowned by the bishop see José Manuel Nieto Soria, 'El imperio medieval como poder público: problemas de aproximación a un mito político', in *Poderes públicos en la Europa Medieval* (Pamplona: Gobierno de Navarra, 1997), 403–40, here 437, and Nieto Soria, *Ceremonias de la realeza*, 212.

[67] On the feudal tradition of the 'besamanos' (literally, 'hand-kissing') see Sánchez Albornoz, 'La *ordinatio principis*', 734–6. Yet the new studies are stressing the long tradition of the 'besamanos' and its very particular nature; see Álvaro Fernández de

This turn from the religious *sacramentum* to feudal and profane homage, begun at some time in the thirteenth century, would also explain the abandonment of the practice of unction after Alfonso VII, only for it to be restored, paradoxically, by Alfonso XI during the fourteenth century. In addition, authors have argued that the eventual missing of the ritual of unction did not necessarily imply the existence of the belief of the un-sacred nature of Castilian kings.[68] Faith was not failing, and the sacred meaning of the ceremonies remains, but the monarchy was increasing its autonomy more and more with respect to the church, its power in the face of the nobility and its tendency towards autocracy.[69]

Is Spain Different?

Based on its legendary origins in the Visigothic kingdom, Castile experienced the manifestations of some transference in the ritual forms from the temporal to the spiritual, and vice versa, and their different symbolic liturgical meanings, transformations and political uses.[70] Where Wamba wanted to be anointed so as to consolidate his power and authority in the seventh century, Alfonso XI wanted to avoid being anointed in order to gain autonomy from the spiritual sphere and to strengthen his authority in the fourteenth century. Alfonso's self-coronation, and the consequent reduction of the sacralisation dimension of the ceremony, confirms the increasing monarchical aspiration of gaining independence from ecclesiastical hierarchy and the growing tension between both the temporal and spiritual spheres.

Nevertheless, this royal autonomy should not be viewed as a progressive, lineal or teleological evolution. Many breaks and ups and downs occurred in this supposed progression. On one hand, this crooked line demystifies the idea of a supposed theocracy from Visigothic Spain that

---

Córdova, 'Los símbolos del poder real', in *Catálogo de la exposición de Los Reyes Católicos y Granada*, ed. Alberto Bartolomé and Carlos J. Hernando (Granada: Sociedad Estatal de Conmemoraciones Culturales, 2005), 37–58.

[68] Nieto Soria, *Fundamentos ideológicos*, 62–5.

[69] José Antonio Maravall, *La oposición política bajo los Austrias* (Barcelona: Ariel, 1972), 156–7; Sánchez Albornoz, 'La *ordinatio principis*', 737, and Linehan, *History and the Historians of Medieval Spain*, 430. See, contra, José Manuel Nieto Soria, *Los fundamentos ideológicos del poder real en Castilla (siglos XIII–XVI)* (Madrid: EUDEMA, 1988), 62 and 67.

[70] For certain specific aspects of the evolution of the Castilian kingdom, the symbolism of the crown and the evolution of the concept of sovereignty see Manuel García-Pelayo, 'La corona. Estudio sobre un símbolo y un concepto político', in García-Pelayo, ed., *Del mito y de la razón en la historia del pensamiento político* (Madrid: Revista de Occidente, 1968), 13–64.

would survive in the Spanish Habsburg monarchy and largely mark the whole development of Spain until the twentieth-century Franco regime. But it also denies (or at least moderates) the typical Spanish 'special way' ('Spain is different'), in this case the experience of a radical royal autonomy from ecclesiastical mediation (or the 'un-sacred' monarchy) lacking in other classic European monarchies such as those of France and England.[71]

At this stage, we should wonder if these self-coronations were further evidence of the exceptionality of medieval Iberia, as has been argued. Yet the *exceptionalism* of Spanish medieval history is in fact the exceptionalism of the whole Mediterranean culture as opposed to those of Northern Europe. Brian Catlos argues that:

Spanish exceptionalism is, in fact, the Mediterranean norm, viewed as anomalous only when subjected to inappropriate comparisons with distinct developments taking place in the Latin Christian heartlands of northern Europe.[72]

Catlos' point is important to frame the distinction between the north and south of Europe in terms of the development of the ceremonies of royal accession. This divergence is clearly perceptible in the evolution of self-coronations in the early modern period. Here, again, simplifications or generalisations are not a good way to proceed, since some of the Northern European kingdoms would assume the ritual of self-coronation, from Christian V of Denmark (1671) to Charles XII of Sweden (1697), Frederick I of Prussia (1701) and Napoleon (1804) (see chapter 12).

John of Paris, in his defence of *anti-hierocratism*, declared that kings were kings even without unction and that in many Christian countries, such as those of Hispania, the anointing of kings was not practised at all.[73] John Balliol of Scotland and Gerald of Wales provide similar testimonies.[74] Paradoxically, if medieval Spanish kingdoms were identified by their contemporaries for their 'demystification' or 'unsacrality', they fell into the contrary reputation in the early modern ages: as John H. Elliott has put it, 'the sense of global mission [of Habsburg Spain] was

---

[71] As Bloch's classic book showed long ago; see Bloch, *Les rois thaumaturges*.

[72] Brian A. Catlos, 'Christian-Muslim-Jewish Relations, Medieval "Spain", and the Mediterranean: An Historiographical Op-Ed', in *In and Of the Mediterranean: Medieval and Early Modern Iberian Studies*, ed. Michelle M. Hamilton and Núria Silleras-Fernández (Nashville, TN: Vanderbilt University Press, 2015), 1–16, here 11.

[73] John of Paris, *De potestate regia et papale*: chapter 18: 'Unde in novo testamento non legimus quod sacerdotes imungere debeant reges nec etiam observatum in omnibus regibus christianis, ut patet in regibus Hispanorum': Jean Leclercq, ed., *Jean de Paris et l'ecclésiologie deu XIIIe siècle* (Paris: Vrin, 1942), 229. See also Kantorowicz, *King's Two Bodies*, 326, and Linehan, *History and the Historians of Medieval Spain*, 443.

[74] Linehan, *History and the Historians of Medieval Spain*, 390.

complemented by a close identification of throne and altar: the ruler of Spain was the standard-bearer of God's cause.'[75] Once more, the abstract, teleological and aprioristic *grand récit* of the 'process of secularisation' does not work in historical reality.

Because of this variation in the models of unction and coronation among Castilian kings, critics have oscillated between the thesis of sacralisation and profane monarchy. Perhaps they have not stressed enough the ruptures in each of the two eventual developments, focusing instead on the continuities and looking for a lineal evolution. I argue that it would be very useful to apply to this historical problem the hypothesis of political theology, well established in political philosophy but absent from historiographical debate.[76] This could help explain the meaning of the ritual ceremonies of royal installation, and their ability to transfer certain sacred categories to the temporal sphere. This approach avoids the excessive polarisation (sacralisation vs. secularisation) into which the history of symbolic meaning in medieval Castilian monarchy is prone, and allows us to analyse the whole process in terms of eventual and maintained transferences of certain sacred categories to the secular sphere, and vice versa.[77]

This raises the question of why Iberia was different. In this book I point to a very long and rich tradition of self-coronation (or at least of bypassing human mediators) that was deeply engrained in European culture. In a way, the Iberian kingdoms thus emerge at the centre rather than at the periphery of Europe. Yet the question also becomes why this might have been so. Some of the eleventh-century Iberian examples seem to echo parallel cases in Hungary and England, as recorded in twelfth-century texts. According to William of Malmesbury (*c.*1125), King Edgar refused to wear his crown in the tenth century because of his sexual transgressions,

---

[75] Elliott, 'Power and Propaganda in Spain of Philip IV', here 148.
[76] As is well known, Ernst Kantorowicz uses this concept in the subtitle of his study on the theory of the king's two bodies: 'A Study of Medieval Political Theology' (Kantorowicz, *King's Two Bodies*). The concept was coined by the jurist Carl Schmitt at the beginning of the twentieth century: Herrero, *The Political Discourse of Carl Schmitt*, 157–77.
[77] Certainly José Manuel Nieto Soria ('Origen divino, espíritu laico y poder real en la Castilla del siglo XIII', *Anuario de Estudios Medievales* 27[1] [1997]: 43–100, here 97–8) has argued for the hypothesis of *transference* taken from Kantorowicz's idea of 'mysteries of state'. On the other side, historians have sustained the theory of the sacralisation and secularisation of the Castilian monarchy, which sharply contrasts with other European royal dynasties, starting with the neighbours Portugal and Aragon: Ruiz, 'Une royauté sans sacre', 429–53; Linehan, *History and the Historians of Medieval Spain*, 426ff.; O'Callaghan, *El rey sabio*, 47–9; Adeline Rucquoi, 'De los reyes que no son taumaturgos: fundamentos de la realeza en España', *Relaciones. Estudios de historia y sociedad* 13 (1992): 55–83.

and, according to the *Vita of Saint Ladislaus of Hungary* (c.1180), he refused to wear his crown for seven years because he had seized the throne from his elder brother. Yet unction and coronation remained normative in these kingdoms and in most of Europe, and self-coronations were seen as opprobrium, while in Iberia self-coronations became conventional when they were enacted.

This could be explained in part because of the relative absence of the papal influence in Iberia – with the partial exception of the crown of Aragon – if we compare it with other Central and Southern European kingdoms. In the thirteenth and fourteenth centuries, the popes were keen on ensuring that kings abided by the practice of unction and coronation (or at least they seem to have expected that they did). But they could not avoid the conventionalisation of the practice of self-coronation among the Iberian kingdoms, which makes the Iberian case more peculiar. In some cases, there were strong papal objections, which differed in effects. In others, the popes just condoned them or simply ignored them.

The popes responded with disagreement against the apparition of the new kingdoms, especially during the high Middle Ages, when the Southern European kingdoms of Jerusalem, Sicily and Portugal and the Central European kingdoms of Bohemia, Hungary and Poland were created.[78] Each of them had a specific relationship with the papacy, especially with regard to papal recognition. The process of creation and recognition of nascent kingdoms is an essential part of medieval European history, but it does not directly affect Asturias, Leon, Castile, Aragon and Navarra, since these kingdoms were born centuries earlier, in the context of the first Christian expansion against the Islamic territories established in Iberia from the beginning of the eighth century. Consequently, these three kingdoms' relationship with the Pope did not respond to a common strategy, as they did not properly need papal recognition – although it was considered convenient.

This leads to the important question of to what extent the Pope was involved in Iberian affairs. Contrasting with the German kingdom, the Holy Roman Empire and the related kingdoms of Sicily and Jerusalem, Iberian kingdoms did not suffer close papal pressure. This is not the only explanation of the fact that self-coronations could attain conventionalisation in Iberian kings, but I am sure it helped. This is particularly accurate

---

[78] For the Southern European kingdoms see John, 'The Papacy', 223–59; for the Central European kingdoms see Nora Berend, Przemyslaw Urbanczyk and Przemyslaw Wiszewski, *Central Europe in the High Middle Ages: Bohemia, Hungary and Poland, c. 900–c. 1300* (Cambridge: Cambridge University Press, 2013).

for the kingdoms of Castile and Navarra, where the tensions emerging from the proximity of the kingdom of France were more urgent than papal pressure. Yet in the crown of Aragon this tension came, in equal parts, from the kingdom of France and the Pope, as I explain in detail in the next chapter.

10 Peter IV of Aragon's Self-Coronation
A Conventionalisation Programme

Everything was ready for the solemn rite of the anointing and coronation of Peter IV of Aragon (1336–87). The ceremony was set for 14 April 1336 in Zaragoza's San Salvador Cathedral. The celebrant was to be the archbishop of Zaragoza, Pedro López de Luna y Ximénez de Urrea (1318–45), to whom the honour fell as the metropolitan of the kingdom's capital. However, that spring morning a heated discussion took place in the vestry shortly before the start of the proceedings. The king and the archbishop could not agree on who should place the crown on the new monarch's head. As a result, the liturgy was delayed, to the consternation of the assembled throng packing the cathedral.

The ceremony consisted of two essential elements: unction and coronation. The king had no objection to letting the archbishop take the lead in administering the unction, considered a sacrament and proper to the spiritual and sacred sphere. But he demanded that the archbishop desist in his desire to also lead the moment of coronation, which belonged to the temporal sphere. He wanted to crown himself and thus to replicate his father Alfonso IV's gesture at his coronation eight years before in the same place, putting the crown on his own head without the aid of the officiating bishops. For all the archbishop's insistence, the king vigorously refused his requests. At sixteen years of age, the king was having to face his first real test, a foretaste of how complex his reign would be. Ultimately, the young monarch's wishes prevailed, and King Peter solemnly and ceremoniously placed the crown on his own head.

King Peter's self-coronation leaves no doubt as to its importance as a symbolically charged political gesture; it is worthy of critical analysis. Beyond its appearance, it reflects an unspontaneous conflict, full of dramatic implications, which could fit well with Althoff's concept of *Inszenierung* applied to these public scenes. The king and the archbishop were fully aware of the scope, meaning and effects of this variation to the coronation rite, which is why their argument in the vestry was so heated. Furthermore, the importance of King Peter's gesture is not determined by its exceptional nature (he probably imitated the performances of his

Figure 26 Miniature showing King Peter IV of Aragon crowning himself. *Ceremonial de consagración y coronación de los reyes de Aragón*, fol. 19 r. Annex to the *Ordinacions de Cort*, second half of the fourteenth century. Biblioteca de la Fundación Lázaro Galdiano, Reg. 14425. © Museo Lázaro Galdiano. Madrid.

father, Alfonso IV of Aragon, and Alfonso XI of Castile), but by its normative capacity in consolidating a tradition for the future. Beyond the fact that the very act of Peter's self-coronation still deserves more specific attention, critics have already analysed the Aragonese royal ordinations and coronations.[1] Historians and literary critics have also

---

[1] Bonifacio Palacios Martín, *La coronación de los reyes de Aragón, 1204–1410. Aportación al estudio de las estructuras medievales* (Valencia: Anubar, 1975); Bonifacio Palacios Martín, 'El Ceremonial', in *Ceremonial de consagración y coronación de los reyes de Aragón. II. Transcripción y estudios* (Zaragoza: Centro de Documentación Bibliográfica Aragonesa, 1992), 105–33; Ricardo Centellas Salamero, 'Pedro IV. Ceremonial de consagración y coronación de los reyes de Aragón', in *Aragón. De reino a comunidad. Diez siglos de encuentros*, ed. Antonio Angulo (Zaragoza: Cortes de Aragón, 2002), 190–1; Juan Antonio Yeves Andrés, 'De la unción a la coronación. Ceremonial de la consagración y coronación de los reyes y reinas de Aragón', in *Maravillas de la España Medieval. I. Estudios y Catálogo*, ed. Isidro Bango Torviso (León: Junta de Castilla y León, 2001), 95–6; Olga Pérez Monzón, 'De la unción a la coronación. Libro de la coronación de los reyes de Castilla y Aragón', in *Maravillas de la España Medieval*, 97–8; Pérez Monzón, 'Ceremonias regias

highlighted Peter's singular ability to strengthen his authority by many different means, such as the king's moral energy in contrast with his corporal weakness, and his particular and conscious use of writing to increase the administrative efficiency of his extensive kingdom.[2] Considering these scholarly precedents, I want to focus specifically on Peter's role in designing a historiographical, liturgical and iconographic programme that would provide the ceremony of self-coronation with long endurance. Thus, I argue that these representations commissioned by King Peter emerge as a means of continuity and future consolidation of his own political and cultural foundations.

This chapter analyses three of the strategies King Peter implemented so as to ensure that his self-coronation would not remain an isolated gesture but would come to form part of a tradition and become the conventional ritual of royal investiture in the crown of Aragon. The first is Peter's creation of a historical account that would serve as the primary version of the event, his autobiography. The second is the setting of the coronation ceremony rites through elaborating a new ceremonial. Finally, the propagation of an iconographic tradition through images of the king himself – decked with royal insignia – in miniatures, seals and coins and, above all, of the gesture of self-coronation. The king thus deployed historiography, liturgy and iconography in order to perpetuate the memory of his self-coronation and ensure, through repetition, its transformation from an isolated event into a consolidated practice and part of inherited tradition.

The Tradition of the Investiture Ceremonies in the Crown of Aragon

The relevance of Peter's self-coronation (and his unequivocal aspiration in providing this gesture with permanency and endurance) lies in his desire to release himself from ecclesiastical influence in the quest for a more temporal royal authority. Besides, as he explicitly states in the

---

en la Castilla Medieval'; Percy E. Schramm, 'Der König von Aragon. Seine Stellung in Stadtsrecht (1276–1410)', *Historisches Jahrbuch*, 74 (1955): 99–123; Antonio Durán Gudiol, 'El rito de la coronación del rey en Aragón', *Argensola* 103 (1989): 17–40. Closer to the sources but unreliable in some of its information, see Gerónimo de Blancas, *Coronaciones de los serenísimos reyes de Aragón* (Zaragoza: Diego Dormer, 1641).

[2] Ramon d'Abadal, *Pere el Cerimoniós i els inicis de la decadència política de Catalunya* (Barcelona: Edicions 62, 1987); Francisco M. Gimeno Blay, *Escribir, reinar. La experiencia gráfico-textual de Pedro IV el Ceremonioso (1336–1387)* (Madrid: Abada, 2006); Josep Bracóns Clapés, *'Operibus monumentorum que fieri facere ordinamus', L'escultura al servei del Cerimoniós, in Pere el Cerimoniós i la seva època* (Barcelona: Consejo Superior de Investigaciones Científicas, 1989), 209–43.

ordo he commissioned some years after the ceremony, his aim was to separate the temporal sphere from the spiritual. These are the key concepts I use in this chapter, rather than the level of sacrality of the king, which has already been studied and debated.[3] Significantly for our purposes, Peter maintained the ceremony of unction linked to the coronation, in a clear message about the preservation of the sacred in the ceremony, since anointing is obviously more sacralising than crowning.

All indications suggest that Peter the Ceremonious knew the coronations of his father, Alfonso IV of Aragon, and Alfonso XI of Castile, enacted just eight and four years before his own in 1336.[4] Nevertheless, without denying the eventual influence of Iberian tradition, and the more distant kingdom of Sicily, Peter the Ceremonious' gesture is the culmination of a long Aragonese dynastic practice: his self-coronation and the writing of a new ordo for the coronation conclude the cycle of coronations of Aragonese kings.

The first Aragonese king who was crowned, Peter the Catholic, went to Rome in 1204 to receive the diadem from Pope Innocent III, who also conferred upon him the sceptre and received his homage. But this homage to the Pope would constitute a burden for the future kings of Aragon, since it would be a source of obligations, as the same Innocent III reminded Peter the Catholic one year after his coronation.[5] This was dramatically manifested in 1213 in the crisis caused by the crusade against the Cathars. To repel the crusaders, the Cathars turned to Peter II of Aragon for assistance.[6] Peter's sister Eleanor had married Raymond VI of Toulouse, establishing a feudal link and securing an alliance with that strategic county of the south of France. On 15 January 1213, Innocent III wrote to the legate Arnaud Amaury and to Simon de Montfort, ordering the latter to fight against the Cathars. Concerned that Simon had grown too powerful, and aware of his obligations regarding his feudal oath with his vassals, Peter decided to come to the aid of Toulouse. The crown of Aragon, under Peter II, allied with the

---

[3] Teófilo Ruiz has highlighted the un-sacred tendency of peninsular monarchy (Ruiz, 'Une royauté sans sacré', 429–53) as José Manuel Nieto Soria has its sacralisation ('Origen divino, espíritu laico y poder real en la Castilla del siglo XIII').
[4] Ramón Muntaner, *Crònica*, chapter 295, in *Les quatre grans cròniques: Jaume I, Bernat Desclot, Ramon Muntaner, Pere III*, ed. Ferran Soldevila (Barcelona: Alpha, 1971), 936. See Aurell, *Authoring the Past*, 210–12.
[5] See the document of 15 June 1205 collecting Innocent III's demands to Peter the Catholic in Antonio Durán Gudiol, *Colección Diplomática de la Catedral de Huesca*, ed. Durán Gudiol. 2 vols. (Zaragoza: Instituto de Estudios Pirenaicos, 1969), 2:631–2.
[6] Ernest E. Jenkins, *The Mediterranean World of Alfonso II and Peter II of Aragon (1162–1213)* (New York: Palgrave, 2012), 123–57.

county of Toulouse and various other entities. Innocent denounced Peter and ordered a renewal of the crusade. Peter's coalition fought against Simon's troops on 12 September in the Battle of Muret. The crusaders were clearly outnumbered. King Peter was struck down and killed in the battle. The coalition forces, hearing of his death, retreated in confusion. This allowed Simon's troops to occupy the northern part of Toulouse. This event would give rise to the continued tensions between the kings of Aragon and the Pope during the next centuries.

In fact, Peter's son James the Conqueror steadfastly refused to be crowned by Pope Gregory X, because he wanted to liberate the kingdom of Aragon from servitude to Rome. As he confesses in his autobiographical *Llibre dels fets*, he preferred to return to his kingdom without the crown rather than having to pay homage to Rome.[7] His successor, Peter the Great, was the first Aragonese king crowned in Zaragoza, the capital of the kingdom, in 1276, at the same time as his wife, Constanza, and in the presence of the principal nobles and citizens. Although he was crowned by the bishop, he instituted the autonomy of the ceremony, liberating it from Rome.[8]

The question of Sicily (1282–4) would tense even more the relationship between the Pope and the kings of Aragon. Diplomatic negotiations followed the expulsion of the Angevins and French from Sicily.[9] The Sicilian communes turned to King Peter to release them from French dominion. They offered the crown to Peter and his wife, Constance of Aragon, and the couple entered Palermo on 4 September 1282. Sicily was incorporated in the crown of Aragon from then on. The incorporation of Sicily into the crown of Aragon was an event of great consequence for the direction and rate of change in the Catalan-Aragonese court and its political thought and ritual practice – and also at an artistic level, since the royal pantheon in Santes Creus has to be understood as a reference back to the Hohenstaufen pantheon in Palermo.[10] The custom of using political symbols and rituals, from Roger II to Frederick II, greatly influenced later Aragonese kings.

Not by chance, Peter the Great's successor, Alfonso III the Liberal, introduced the oath in the coronation ceremony in Zaragoza in 1286 and,

---

[7] James I of Aragon, *Llibre dels fets*, chapter 538, in Soldevila, *Les quatre grans cròniques*, 183. English edition: *The Book of Deeds of James I of Aragon*, trans. Damian Smith and Helena Buffery (Burlington, VT: Ashgate, 2003).

[8] Bernat Desclot describes the ceremony in chapter 97 of his chronicle (see Soldevila, *Les quatre grans cròniques*, 460).

[9] Coll, *Bernat Desclot*, 3:74.

[10] Marta Vanlandingham, *Transforming the State: King, Court and Political Culture in the Realms of Aragon (1213–1387)* (Leiden: Brill, 2002), 9. See also Barry Charles Rosenmann, *The Royal Tombs in the Monastery of Santes Creus* (Ann Arbor: University of Minnesota, 1991).

more interestingly, explicitly declared that, though he received the crown from the bishop, this did not imply political subordination to Rome.[11] James II the Just (1291–1327) was not crowned in Zaragoza, as his previous coronation as the king of Sicily, received before 1291, made a new ceremony unnecessary.[12]

These disruptions in coronation practice show how inconvenient the ceremony was for Aragonese kings because of their tense relationship with Rome, the question of Sicily and the difficulties in balancing the several branches and multiple territories of the kingdom at that time. Thus, Alfonso the Benign restored the coronation ceremony in 1328, but introduced the original and daring practice of self-coronation.[13]

Alfonso IV's self-coronation is meticulously described by Ramon Muntaner, who probably witnessed the ceremony, in his chronicle.[14] He reports that, before the start of the Mass, the king placed the crown and the sword on the high altar 'with his *own* hands'. The king was anointed with chrism on his right shoulder and arm by the archbishop of Zaragoza. At the end of the Mass, the king unsheathed his sword *himself* and placed it back on the altar, near the crown. Then they began a second Mass and, after a long ceremony, at the moment of the coronation, 'the Lord King *himself* took the crown from the altar and placed it on his *own* head; and when he had done this, the lord Archbishop of Toledo [the king's brother, who had celebrated the second Mass] and the Lord Infante en Pedro [also the king's brother] adjusted it for him.'[15]

---

[11] The coronation is narrated by Ramon Muntaner, chapter 155. The king states that 'non intendimus a vobis recipere tanquam ab Ecclesia romana, nec pro ipsa Ecclesia nec contra Ecclesiam' (Palacios Martín, *La coronación de los reyes de Aragón*, 308). See also Francesc Carreras i Candi, 'Itinerari del rey Anfós II (1285–91), Lo Liberal', *Boletín de la Real Academia de las Buenas Letras de Barcelona* 10 (1921–2): 61–83.

[12] The chronicler Ramon Muntaner writes that 'ab gran benedicció rebé la corona' ('he received the crown with great blessing'), Muntaner, chapter 185, in Palacios Martín, *La coronación de los reyes de Aragón*, 190–1.

[13] Palacios Martín, *La coronación de los reyes de Aragón*, 269–76. See also Palacios Martín, 'El Ceremonial', 104–33. Palacios Martín emphasises that Alfons el Benigne was the Aragonese king who introduced the practice of self-coronation, because other scholars before him wrongly attributed it to Pere el Gran, most probably confusing Pere el Gran (King Peter III of Aragon but Count Peter II of Barcelona) with Pere el Ceremoniós (King Peter IV of Aragon and Count Peter III of Barcelona) – see, for instance, Schramm, *Las insignias de la realeza en la edad media española*, 93–94.

[14] Alfonso IV's coronation is narrated by the chronicler Ramon Muntaner (*Crònica*, chapter 295–8, in Soldevila, *Les quatre grans cròniques*, 939–49). See also Aurell, *Authoring the Past*, 210–21; Palacios Martín, 'El Ceremonial', 104–33; Durán Gudiol, 'El rito de la coronación del rey en Aragón', 17–40; and Schramm, *Las insignias de la realeza en la edad media española*, 93–4.

[15] 'Ell mateix [the king], pres la corona de l'altar e la's posa al cap; e con la s'hac posada al cap, la senyor arquebisbe de Toledo e el senyor infant En Pere e el senyor infant En

Eight years later, in 1336, Peter the Ceremonious would follow similar rituals during his own coronation, but in a context of considerable tension and pressure. He did not even allow his crown to be adjusted by anyone after his coronation.

The King's Autobiography: Setting Down Memory

King Peter wanted to be master of the primary historical account of what had happened on the morning of his consecration and royal coronation. That is why he decided to include the story of his self-coronation in the autobiographical chronicle that he worked on with his collaborators. This narrative strategy fits very well with the tendency of certain medieval rulers to seek control and fix the interpretation of the rituals through written representation.[16] His version of events, constructed with the help of his scribes, goes as follows.

After scrupulously observing the prescriptions for prayer, fasting, personal cleanliness and choice of wardrobe in readiness for the occasion, the King set off for the Cathedral vestry in good time. There he met the celebrant, Pedro López de Luna, and the long list of concelebrants, among them the bishops of Lleida, Tarazona, Santa Justa (Cerdeña), and many priors, canons and various members of religious orders, as well as some knights, most notable among them Ot de Montcada, one of the king's advisors.

Just when the ceremony was due to begin, a loud argument started up in the vestry itself between the king and archbishop. The archbishop asked the king to let him place the crown on his head at the moment of coronation. King Peter refused, as he planned to act in accordance with the custom initiated by his father, Alfonso IV, who had put the crown on his own head without the aid of the attendant

---

Ramon Berenguer adobaren-la-hi' (Ramon Muntaner, *Crònica*, chapter 297, in Soldevila, *Les quatre grans cròniques*, 940). Ramon Muntaner uses a peculiar and rather unusual Catalan verb, *adobar*, in order to emphasise that the gesture of putting the crown on his head was performed by the king himself, and that his brothers only 'adjusted it'. This verb transmits the idea that the archbishop could barely fix the crown or would have little to do once the king had placed the crown on his own head. Notably, the archbishop of Zaragoza was not part of this ritual, even if he was one of the celebrants of the Mass; very interestingly, Peter uses exactly the same verb in the narration of his own coronation, when he prohibits the bishop not only to crown him but also to 'fix' ('*adobar*') the crown after his self-coronation (Pere el Ceremoniós, *Crònica*, 2:10–12, in Soldevila, *Les quatre grans cròniques*, 1025–6), making evident that he knew Muntaner's narration very well.

[16] This is the main point argued in Buc, *The Dangers of Ritual*, especially on 67–79, which has generated an intensive historiographical debate in the past decades, since Buc's approach to the rituals has been contested particularly by scholars on medieval ritual such as Althoff and Koziol (see Isabella, 'Rituali altomedievali', 186).

bishops. In this heated discussion in the vestry, King Peter had the support of his advisor Ot de Montcada, who made the case to the archbishop that the coronation of the monarch 'at the hands of a prelate' would be prejudicial to the crown. However, none of the other courtiers present opposed the archbishop, leaving the king to defend himself practically unaided.

The king had to resist the metropolitan of Zaragoza, face down the suspicion of the other bishops and prelates and overcome the apathy of his own advisors. Moreover, time was pressing: the people present in the nave of the cathedral began to grow impatient with the delay to the ceremony. All the same, he was resolved to withstand the archbishop's demands.

In the face of the king's categorical negative, the archbishop then decided to change strategy, begging the king with great insistence that the king at least allow him to adjust (*adobar*) or set straight the crown in full view of the people, after the king had put it on with his own hands. Pedro López de Luna had witnessed the same action eight years before, when Alfonso IV had allowed the celebrant of that coronation, his brother Juan, the archbishop of Toledo, and his other two brothers, Princes Pedro and Ramon Berenguer, to adjust the crown once it had been put on by the king himself. Alfonso may not have wanted to do this, but he did let them adjust the crown because they were, after all, his brothers. In any case, the impact of the self-coronation was thus somewhat mitigated by the appearance of the archbishop immediately afterwards, as joint architect of the coronation.

With this new request, the king met the opposition of even his own advisors, who tried to persuade him to give in. Further, the archbishop reproached him for dishonouring the whole church with his arrogance, and specifically the archbishopric of Zaragoza, as well as his own kingdom of Aragon. The king then decided to agree to the archbishop's requests, driven above all by the cumulative delay. The procession finally set off for the church, where the ceremony began. But when the moment of coronation arrived, the king went up to the altar and put the crown on himself, forbidding the archbishop to touch it, and setting it straight on his own head. The archbishop was disconcerted but went on with the Mass, feigning normality and solemnity, and fulfilling the remainder of the formalities.

Such is the version of events that appears in the second chapter of King Peter's autobiographical chronicle, known as the *Llibre del rei en Pere* (*Book of King Peter*).[17] Peter recounts these events in his *Llibre* with the

---

[17] The account given here is my paraphrase and summary of the original: Peter IV of Aragon, *Llibre del rei en Pere*, 2:8–12, in Soldevila, *Les quatre grans cròniques*, 1025–6.

simplicity of truth but also with the pride of one who has acted in accordance with his dignity, overcoming adversity. The autonomy that emerges from Peter's historical representation runs parallel with the political sufficiency that emerges from his self-coronation, which is in turn perpetuated through time with the creation of a new iconography. The story demonstrates the power of ritual gestures and symbols, and the control King Peter exercised over them. It reveals his calculated mastery of the situation, even under pressure from his adversaries. At a time when royal succession was dynastic rather than elective – independent both of approval or consecration by the church and of election by the people – Peter the Ceremonious laid claim to the power of symbols.[18]

This is, in fact, the only account that we have of the ceremony, and while it carries a heavily dramatic, subjective and emotional charge, none of the external facts available to us casts any doubt on its historicity. There is little chronological distance between this first historical representation and the event itself. The detailed nature of the account and, above all, the minute description of the king's state of mind, confirm the close relation between the historical event and its narration. The evidence also shows that King Peter was already working on the book of his own deeds and on other historical books that he had commissioned his secretaries to write around 1349, only thirteen years after his self-coronation (*librum gestarum nostrorum*).[19] In any case, we know for certain that the king had finished writing the first three chapters in 1375, from a letter sent to Bernat Descoll, one of his collaborators in the chronicle.[20] Besides, the king's meticulous working method, personally elaborating the drafts that his secretaries passed on to him for the final wording of the finished manuscripts, suggests that the writing of the chronicle had begun many years before.[21]

In the chronicle of his reign, the king was concerned specifically to highlight the moment of self-coronation. He does not even refer in his account to the other rites in the long ceremony, such as the unction or

English edition: *Chronicle: Pere III of Catalonia (Pedro IV of Aragon)*, trans. Mary Hillgarth and intr. Jocelyn N. Hillgarth (Toronto: Pontifical Institute of Mediaeval Studies, 1980).

[18] For the consolidation of late medieval European dynastic monarchy over the sacred or elective see Kantorowicz, *King's Two Bodies*, 330.

[19] On the dates of Peter's *Llibre* composition see Hillgarth, 'Introduction', in *Chronicle. Pere III*, I:53–7. The sentence *librum gestarum nostrorum* refers to a letter from the king to one of his secretaries in the court, Bernat de Torre, in which the king asks Bernat to send the *librum gestarum nostrorum* ('the book of our deeds') to him, in order to continue it (see Antoni Rubió i Lluch, *Documents per l'història de la cultura catalana mig-eval*, vol. 1 [Barcelona: Institut d'Estudis Catalans, 1908], 143).

[20] Rubió i Lluch, *Documents per l'història de la cultura catalana*, 263ff.

[21] Antoni Rubió i Lluch, 'Estudi sobre l'elaboració de la crònica de Pere el Cerimoniós', *Anuari de l'Institut d'Estudis Catalans* 3 (1909–10): 519–70.

the handing over of the other royal insignia such as the sceptre and pommel. Significantly, the narrative centres on the aforementioned argument in the vestry. The king intersperses the ordered account of events with descriptions of his own state of mind. First, he is saddened by the indolence of his advisors.[22] Then he is greatly dismayed at having to confront someone of the archbishop's authority, who is also his priest, on the very day that he was to be most honoured in his life and receive the dignity of royalty.[23] Lastly, aware of his youth, he finds his emotional composure disturbed again when he has to make a final decision, feeling rushed into it by the impending start of the ceremony. It is then that the subtlety and astuteness that are so characteristic of his reign emerge: although he appears to give way to resolve the situation and allow the ceremony to commence, he decides at the moment of truth that he will take the crown himself and dispense with the archbishop's participation.[24] These emotional notes increase the dramatic force of the account and move the reader to the king's side, convinced of his courage and loyalty, as well as of his statesmanlike sense of duty in the face of his new public responsibilities.

Once he has completed his account of the coronation, the chronicler-king focuses on the applause he received from his vassals in the cathedral itself and on his grandiloquent departure on a horse. He was decked out in silver chains, with the sceptre in his right hand and the pommel in his left, both made of gold. The festivities that followed his coronation went on for three days, during which, according to the king's calculations, around ten thousand people came up to the royal table. This last detail is worthy of note, the royal exaggeration contrasting with the strictly realistic tone of most of the chronicle.

To properly understand the importance that King Peter placed on the gesture of self-coronation, we need to turn to the aforementioned account that the chronicler Ramon Muntaner had produced a few years before of his father Alfonso IV's self-coronation. In contrast, Peter the Ceremonious makes only a brief reference to it in his chronicle.[25] Muntaner finished his around 1336, the year Peter was

---

[22] 'Fom fort torbats en nostre cor' (Peter IV of Aragon, *Llibre*, 2:10, in Soldevila, *Les quatre grans cròniques*, 1025–6).

[23] Peter IV of Aragon, *Llibre*, 2:11, in Soldevila, *Les quatre grans cròniques*, 1026. For the closed relationship between King Peter and Archbishop Pedro López de Luna, see Josep Rius Serra, 'L'arquebisbe de Saragossa, canceller de Pere III', *Analecta Sacra Tarraconensia* 8 (1932): 1–62.

[24] Peter IV of Aragon, *Llibre*, 2:11–12, in Soldevila, *Les quatre grans cròniques*, 1026.

[25] Muntaner, *Crònica*, chapter 244–8, in Soldevila, *Les quatre grans cròniques*, 934–43. English edition: *The Chronicle of Muntaner*, trans. L. Goodenough (Nendeln: Liechtenstein, 1967).

crowned. We cannot know for certain if Peter was familiar with this account or if he was present at his father's coronation ceremony, as he was only nine years old at the time. In any case, he was certainly apprised of the splendour of that ceremony, as his chronicle contains a rather mysteriously laconic note that it had been celebrated 'more honorably than any of its predecessors'.[26]

However, it is useful to compare the two accounts, in terms of both form and content. With regard to form, Muntaner's account is marked by his enthusiasm, which deprives it of objectivity and deliberation. King Peter's smacks of authenticity on account of its realism, but is informed by an intensely emotional and subjective authorial presence, inherent in autobiographical writing. As for content, the texts reflect differences in the two ceremonies that require in-depth analysis. Perhaps the most important of these is that the rites of anointing and coronation of King Peter took place jointly in a single Mass, whereas Alfonso's involved the celebration of two Masses, one including the rite of unction and the second the coronation.

At King Alfonso's coronation, the first Mass had been conducted by Pedro López de Luna, who anointed the king; the second was conducted by the king's brother Juan, the archbishop of Toledo, who appears not to have had too many problems recognising the king's right to self-coronation, content to adjust it on his head afterwards. Pedro López de Luna would not have felt humiliated or disregarded in this case, because he did not officiate in that part of the ceremony. In contrast, eight years later, the situation was very different. By merging unction and coronation in a single Mass, Archbishop Pedro would necessarily have to conduct the coronation, and he did not want to play a supporting role. Perhaps he assumed that King Peter would forget the small matter of self-coronation, a practice initiated by his father but without precedent in Aragon. King Peter, however, considered it a matter of no little weight, which explains the tension generated in the vestry.

I therefore posit that the importance of the self-coronation ceremony lies not in what it might say about greater or less 'autonomy' or 'independence' for the king as regards the bishop, but rather a step forward in the differentiation between the spiritual and temporal spheres. The former was expressed in the rite of anointing by the bishop, to which none of the Aragonese kings had posed any obstacle; the latter was expressed in the rite of coronation, which was exactly the point where Kings Alfonso and Peter claimed full autonomy. Significantly, this distinction was chosen as

[26] Peter IV of Aragon, *Llibre*, 1: 43, in Soldevila, *Les quatre grans cròniques*, 1019.

the central point of the introduction to the ceremonial commissioned by King Peter for the coronation rites of his successors.

The Coronation Ceremonial: The Regulation of the Liturgy

In 1353, sixteen years after his coronation, King Peter and his collaborators finished working on a new ceremonial for the rite of (self) coronations of kings.[27] The new ceremonial was an appendix to a very lengthy document entitled 'Regulations Made by His Highness Peter the Third of Aragon on the Governance of All the Officials of His Court', dated 1344. Written in a beautiful Catalan, it constituted the first vernacular version of the texts regulating the running of the royal house and the duties of all its advisors, scribes and officials.[28] Inside these 'Regulations' we find a more specific ceremonial on royal investiture with the title 'Regulations Made by the Most High and Excellent Prince and Lord, Peter the Third, King of Aragon, of the Manner in Which the Kings of Aragon Will Be Consecrated and Crown Themselves'.[29] Even in the title itself, unction and coronation are clearly distinguished and the act of self-coronation is emphasised. The ceremonial of the coronation of kings was complemented by another, shorter one, expounding how queens should be consecrated, and how they should be crowned by their royal husbands.[30]

---

[27] Palacios Martín argues that the ceremonial was produced between 1336 and 1338, or even before the ceremony (Palacios Martín, *La coronación de los reyes de Aragón*, 238–40). Yet this last assertion is difficult to sustain: if the ceremonial had been in existence before the ceremony, the discussion in the vestry would make no sense, since the question of the self-coronation would have been discussed during the process of writing the text, rather than at the ceremony itself.

[28] The *Ordinacions* in Catalan promulgated by King Peter in 1344 are an almost literal translation of the Latin *Leges Palatinae* promoted by King James III of Mallorca. The kingdom of Mallorca was reincorporated into the crown of Aragon after the conquest of the island by King Peter in 1343. This obviously would facilitate this cultural connection. See Françoise Lainé, 'Des *Leges Palatine* aux *Ordinacions* de Pierre IV. Un modèle dérobé', in *Constitution, circulation et dépassement de modèles politiques et culturels en peninsule Ibérique*, ed. Ghislaine Founès and Jean-Michel Desvais (Bordeaux: Presses universitaires de Bordeaux, 2009), 17–56. Yet the *Leges Palatinae* did not refer specifically to the self-coronation rite – which would appear in the appendix in the *Ordinations*.

[29] 'Ordinació feta per lo molt alt e molt excel.lent príncep e senior lo senyor en Pere Terç, rey d'Aragó, de la manera con los reys d'Aragó se faran consagrar e ells mateys se coronaran', in *Ordinacions de la Casa i Cort de Pere el Ceremoniós*, eds. Francisco M. Gimeno, Daniel Gonzalbo and Josep Trenchs (València: Universitat de València, 2009), 241–66. The ceremonial was originally in Aragonese, although the second version, which prevailed in the end, was written in Catalan (Palacios Martín, *La coronación de los reyes de Aragón*, 238).

[30] Gimeno, Gonzalbo and Trenchs, *Ordinacions de la Casa i Cort*, 266–74.

The writing of this new ceremonial and the detailed rubrics it contained again confirmed the importance Peter assigned to the anointing and coronation ceremony, and his conception of the monarchy as the heart and nerve centre of society. The Aragonese king has passed into historical significance with the epithet 'the Ceremonious', which is closely related to his desire to exalt the function of royalty, and particularly to consolidate a written and visual memory of the monarchy. This required a complex of ceremonies, rites and symbols proportional to his authority and the expression of his centrality, as both the very detailed compilation of *Ordinacions* (ordinations) commissioned by him and promulgated in 1344 and his royal nickname itself, *El Ceremoniós* (the Ceremonious), show.[31] Among these ceremonies, coronation was of course one of the most notable. The king himself was directly involved in the writing of the new ceremonial, as shown by the signed revisions that appear throughout the original manuscript, correcting the successive drafts that his scribes would pass to him, or adding some new idea.[32]

The new ceremonial consolidated the crown of Aragon's practice of establishing a ritual for the liturgical celebration of the anointing and coronation of kings.[33] Peter II the Catholic (1196–1213), the first king of Aragon to crown himself, did so in Rome in 1205. It would appear that he followed an imperial ceremonial, adapting it to his royal condition.[34] Following the long reign of James I (1213–76), who preferred not to undergo this ceremony as it would renew the vassalage initiated by his father, the next two crowned kings were Peter III the Great (1276–85) and Alfonso III the Liberal (1285–91). Both followed the 'Pontifical of Huesca', so called because a copy has been preserved in Huesca Cathedral, and were crowned in Zaragoza Cathedral, a tradition that would endure. The original core of the Huesca ceremonial matches a Burgundian ceremonial that must have been written at the end of the thirteenth century.[35] It was used by King Peter as the basis for his 'Regulations'.

The coronation of Alfonso IV the Benign (1327–36) in Zaragoza Cathedral in 1328 produced an important change in the ceremony of anointing and coronation of the kings of Aragon. Up to that time, they

---

[31] Peter's book of ordinations compiles many rites and ceremonies programmed by the king, such as the way of celebrating the feasts (*Ordinacions de la Casa i cort*, 207–33); for this book see also notes 40 and 63.
[32] Gimeno, Gonzalbo and Trenchs, *Ordinacions de la Casa i Cort*, 14–15.
[33] Palacios Martín, *La coronación de los reyes de Aragón*, 229–40.
[34] Palacios Martín, *La coronación de los reyes de Aragón*, 25.
[35] Pascual Galindo Romeo, *El breviario y el ceremonial Cesaragustianos (Siglos XII–XIV)* (Zaragoza: Gasca, 1930), 130, and Schramm, *Las insignias de la realeza en la edad media española*, 130.

had used the Huesca pontifical, adding new ceremonies to it in marginal notes, such as the handing over of the pommel granted to Peter II by Innocent III, or the reception of the order of cavalry. Doctrinal modifications were also introduced, such as the substitution of words alluding to the elective nature of monarchy with others emphasising its hereditary nature. Alfonso IV, by contrast, found himself operating in a different context, in which the European monarchies sought to emulate the pomp of empire in their ceremonies. His coronation was not based on the Huesca pontifical, but on the rather more ostentatious imperial ceremonial of Constantinople, proven by the fact that Alfonso appeared in the vestments of a deacon. His successor and son King Peter would follow this example and embed it as a rule in the ceremonial he commissioned.

Reflecting this tradition of using different rituals in the coronation of Aragonese kings, the ceremonial commissioned by King Peter consists of two clearly differentiated parts: on one hand, a conceptual and theoretical introduction, explaining the meaning of the ceremony, and on the other, the specification of the gestures and words that make up the rite as such.[36] The two parts are distinguished from each other by the grammatical form employed: in the introduction it is the royal 'We', and, in the ritual part, the third person. The first part is expository and discursive, the second enunciative and schematic. Finally – and fascinatingly – the first part is written in Catalan, while the second combines Catalan in the introductory sections with Latin in the strictly liturgical expressions.

The introduction is a brief but ambitious attempt to give theoretical legitimacy to the gesture of self-coronation. King Peter was aware that his desire for the king to crown himself alone contrasted radically with established custom in medieval Europe. It was normal practice at that point for the metropolitan to place the crown on the king's head (*metropolitanus reverenter coronam capiti regis imponant*).[37] Based on the content of both Peter's chronicle and the ceremonial inspired by him, I argue that King Peter considers that the dignity of royalty is such that it bears comparison to that of the kings of the Chosen People, whose line emerged with King Saul, chosen and anointed by Samuel the priest. That justified complete autonomy in the temporal sphere. The dignity can be corrupted by excessive vanity, but also by a disdain for the gifts and rights attributed

---

[36] Introduction in f. 157r–158v (Gimeno, Gonzalbo and Trenchs, *Ordinacions de la Casa i Cort*, 241–4); the ritual in f. 159r–176r (Gimeno, Gonzalbo and Trenchs, *Ordinacions de la Casa i Cort*, 244–66). The ceremonial of the queens' coronations has a similar structure, with an introduction followed by the exposition of the liturgy of the ceremony (Gimeno, Gonzalbo and Trenchs, *Ordinacions de la Casa i Cort*, 266–74).

[37] This example is taken from the twelfth-century Sicilian ordo edited by Reinhard Elze, 'The Ordo', 175.

to the king, as Peter himself sought to make clear in his argument with the archbishop on the morning of his coronation.

In order to legitimise and justify his self-coronation, King Peter explains that the ceremony of consecrating and coronation of kings refers to two different realities:

> We have to deal with two realities very solemn: the first spiritual and the second temporal. Proper to the first is, namely, the holy sacrament of unction, which in the old law was dispensed by the princes among the priests as we read in the Old Testament, in the word of God as spoken by the prophet: 'and thou shalt anoint unto me him whom I name unto thee' [1 Samuel 16:3] ... [the second] is temporal, which is to say, it refers to the crown, by which the earthly princes receive dominion over the people, and of this we have a foreshadowing as can be read in Holy Writ: 'And he brought forth the King's son, and put the crown upon him, and gave him the testimony' [2 Kings 11:12].[38]

Using a scriptural reference chosen to justify the unction was a commonplace in medieval political theology, referring to the God of Israel's choice of David as king in place of the reprobate Saul.[39] God promised to guide Samuel at the moment of choosing a king, who would arise from among the seven sons of Jesse: *et unges quemcumque monstravero tibi* ('and thou shalt anoint unto me him whom I name unto thee'). In fact, when Samuel recognised David, he 'took the horn of oil and anointed him in the midst of his brothers. And the Spirit of the Lord rushed upon David from that day forward' (1 Samuel 16:13). David was not proclaimed king of Israel until some time afterwards, but the unction received went with him as a sign until his actual ascent to royalty and his re-anointing as king of Judah following the death of Saul (2 Samuel 2:4), and eventually of all Israel (2 Samuel 5:1–5). Significantly, church tradition has chosen the latter episode, in which David is anointed as king of all Israel, for the liturgy of the Mass of the Feast of Christ the King, a royal status which David prefigured. So it is hardly surprising that the anointings of David should constitute a model for the legitimisation of medieval monarchy, as did the anointing of the first king of Israel, Saul, also related in the book of Samuel.

> Then Samuel took a flask of oil and poured it on his head and kissed him and said, 'Has not the Lord anointed you to be prince over his people Israel? And you shall reign over the people of the Lord and you will save them from the hand of their surrounding enemies'. (1 Samuel 10: 1–9)

---

[38] Gimeno, Gonzalbo and Trenchs, *Ordinacions de la Casa i Cort*, 242–3.
[39] See the epigraph 'The Unction of David As an Imperial Theme' in Walter, 'The Significance of Unction in Byzantine Iconography', 61–6.

However, the scriptural quotation King Peter chose to justify the 'temporal' part of the ceremony is less known, and refers to the anointing of Jehoash as king of Judah. Jehoash, son of the old King Ahaziah, had been saved by some observant Jews to liberate them from the regent Athalia, who had usurped the kingdom following Ahaziah's assassination, preserving the cult of pagan deities and planning to wipe out the entire royal line. In the seventh year a rebellion took place, led by the Temple priest, who 'brought forth the King's son, and put the crown upon him, and gave him the testimony; and they made him king, and anointed him; and they clapped their hands, and said, God save the King' (2 Kings 11:12). Shortly after, the regent Athalia was killed at sword point in the royal palace and Jehoash was taken 'into the palace, entering by way of the gate of the guards. The king then took his place on the royal throne, and all the people of the land rejoiced. And the city was quiet' (2 Kings 11:19–20).

Of course, this passage was not selected randomly by the king and his collaborators, and it is especially relevant to the coronation ritual. It highlights the act of proclaiming the new king in the Temple portico, with the regent still alive and hiding out in the royal palace. The sign of the new king being proclaimed is not now unction, but the placing of the crown and the insignia (*testimonium*) and, with the regent now dead, his enthronement. The king's intention in choosing this text is, therefore, to emphasise the act of coronation, which on this occasion occurs *before* unction.

The distinction between spiritual and temporal reality forms the basis of the introduction to King Peter's ceremonial. It is the key to understanding the vigour with which Peter defended the appropriateness of his putting the crown on himself, without any mediation by the archbishop. His attitude is a kind of reaffirmation of the Evangelist's maxim, 'Render therefore unto Caesar the things which are Caesar's, and unto God the things which are God's', which lies at the centre of medieval political theology. In the final paragraph of the introduction to the ceremonial, the king again distinguishes clearly between the two parts of the ritual, the spiritual and the temporal:

Just as the kings of Aragon be worthy of receiving the holy sacrament of unction in the city of Zaragoza, capital of the kingdom of Aragon, which gives us our title and principal name, so it is also fitting and reasonable that in that [city] the kings of Aragon should likewise receive the crown and other royal insignia, just as we see the emperors take the principal crown in Rome, the city that stands at the head of their empire.[40]

---

[40] Gimeno, Gonzalbo and Trenchs, *Ordinacions de la Casa i Cort*, 244.

The second part of the document provides a detailed exposition of the rubrics, gestures and prayers for the ceremony. The king must prepare from the preceding week, fasting for three days: Wednesday, Friday and Saturday. On the eve of the coronation he is to bathe, confess, receive Communion and appear before the knights of the realm in vestments specified by the ceremonial, symbolising the chastity and dignity of the king. That same day he must withdraw in prayer in the coronation church. He specifically says a prayer which, because it is written in Catalan (in contrast to the Latin of most of the others in the ceremony), would appear to be the work of the king himself:

Lord God, it has pleased You to choose me as King and ruler of this chosen people, for which I deeply thank You. And as it is a great burden to bear without Your grace and help, I beseech You the favor that in this royal dignity of which I will receive the insignia tomorrow, I will have such a life and do such works as are in Your sight pleasing, worthy and honorable to my crown, and for which I will attain Your glory at my end.[41]

This evening prayer is recorded by King Peter himself in his chronicle. He recounts that, on the eve of the coronation he went up to the altar of San Salvador, bowed before Jesus Christ and his mother and, with great devotion, said some prayers 'that our Lord God put in our hearts, with all the humility we could summon'.[42] Those prayers may be the two brief imprecations that the king inserts in Catalan among the other Latin prayers. The first is the one just quoted; the other appears at the end of his ritual investiture as a knight:

My Lord God, I pray You look favorably on this ordination of knighthood, which I now receive; that I might do such works as to serve You and earn my soul lasting glory, my heart honor and merit, and my royal crown and people growth and security.[43]

After the king had recited the prayer, a squire was to bear the royal arms to the altar and the king was to withdraw to keep an all-night vigil; if he could not, owing to advanced years or other factors, the ceremonial stipulated that the king at least sleep in the vestry or somewhere close to the church.

In considering this exception, the king must have been very aware of the attitude of the knights who accompanied him to the church on the eve of his coronation. Seeing how he tarried over his prayer and how tired he was already, they insisted that he rest and withdraw to sleep in the vestry.

---

[41] Gimeno, Gonzalbo and Trenchs, *Ordinacions de la Casa i Cort*, 245.
[42] Peter IV of Aragon, *Llibre*, 2: 8, in Soldevila, *Les quatre grans cròniques*, 1025.
[43] Gimeno, Gonzalbo and Trenchs, *Ordinacions de la Casa i Cort*, 252.

They had prepared a bed for him there, so that the next day 'he might partake in the festival with great joy'.[44] The king relented, moved by his vassals' consideration for his 'tender' age. By contrast, his vassals passed the whole night in 'high spirits, singing and sport', which certainly contradicts the rule in the ceremonial where the king orders that 'the nobles and knights and other people with whom he [the King] has come stay in the church accompanying and watching over the King's arms [placed at the altar] all night'.[45]

At dawn, the king was to get up and hear a private Mass in one of the cathedral chapels. Then he was to go to a seat of honour prepared for the occasion, until the metropolitan and other officiating bishops called him into the vestry, once they had put on their vestments for the Mass. This suggests that the argument in the vestry must have taken place with all the prelates already dressed for the celebration of the Mass. The king was also in special vestments, wrapped in a dalmatic and with a stole crossed at the chest, as deacons usually are when reading the Gospel at Mass, which is clearly sacralising. Some historians have seen in this attempt to assimilate the king with the deacon an urge not only to 'appear' but actually to 'exercise', robing in the vestments of a deacon and therefore assuming a real hierarchical status, as was envisaged for the coronation of emperors.[46]

The procession of the principal royal insignia – crown, sceptre and pommel – would begin, leading to the foot of the altar. Then long dedications to God and his saints were recited (the *litanies*). These would be proclaimed by the prelates with the king on bended knees as a show of humility – an attitude analogous to that adopted by candidates for ordination as deacons or priests, though they prostrate themselves completely on the floor. After that, things would proceed to the investiture of the king as a knight, if he had not received it before. Here the blessing of the sword took prominence. It had a threefold function: to defend the church against heretics, to protect the poor, orphans and widows, and to maintain justice for his people.[47] The ceremony would then conclude with the king girding himself with his sword 'without the aid of any other person', in a gesture that prefigured the self-coronation and symbolised his autonomy from the ecclesiastical hierarchy in temporal matters. This was a clear allusion to

---

[44] Peter IV of Aragon, *Llibre*, 2: 8, in Soldevila, *Les quatre grans cròniques*, 1025.
[45] Gimeno, Gonzalbo and Trenchs, *Ordinacions de la Casa i Cort*, 245.
[46] Palacios Martín, *La coronación de los reyes de Aragón*, 213–14.
[47] Gimeno, Gonzalbo and Trenchs, *Ordinacions de la Casa i Cort*, 251. This triple function appears almost in the same way in the Catalan text of Muntaner, *Crònica*, chapter 297 in Soldevila, *Les quatre grans cròniques*, 399–940.

Aragonese monarchic tradition, given that James I had done the same thing in his ceremony of investiture as a knight at Monzón.

The ceremony then continued with readings, the profession of faith and the presentation of the candidate, in a way that was also similar to the ordination of the diaconate and presbytery. The presentation fell to the two most honourable bishops, who would endorse the king before the metropolitan, confirming that the kingdom was his by legitimate succession. Next was the unction ceremony, one of the key moments. The metropolitan anointed the king's shoulders and chest with holy oil. Then came the placing of the crown:

This prayer having been said, the King takes the crown from above the altar and he himself puts it on his head without the aid of any other person. And while the King is placing the crown on his head, the Metropolitan utters this prayer: *receive this sign of glory, the royal diadem and crown.*[48]

In the same way, the king went to the altar to take the sceptre with his right hand and the pommel with his left. The coronation ceremony would conclude with the singing of a solemn *Te Deum*, followed by the rest of the Mass and final prayers. At the end of the Mass, the king would leave the church riding solemnly on a white horse, adorned with all the royal insignia – the crown on his head, the sceptre in his right hand and the pommel in his left. Afterwards, he would hold a banquet for all the guests and festivities would begin that would last for at least three days.[49]

The act of self-coronation reinforced the king's autonomy in temporal matters and privileged the role of the crown itself in the ceremony. The ceremonial stresses that, the crown being round, it has no beginning or end, which implies that the king should wear it with the infinite intention of doing good works, and especially of reigning fairly and justly. Kings must wear it on their head, the locus of understanding, which leads to goodwill. It is laden with precious stones, symbol of the virtues that should adorn the life of a king. The crown also furnishes the king with the necessary fear of God.[50] It is, literally, the key emblem among the various iconographic representations commissioned by the king in commemoration of his own self-coronation.

---

[48] Gimeno, Gonzalbo and Trenchs, *Ordinacions de la Casa i Cort*, 259.
[49] Analogies with the French and German traditions can be found in Jackson, *Ordines Coronationis*.
[50] Gimeno, Gonzalbo and Trenchs, *Ordinacions de la Casa i Cort*, 233–44. The chronicler Muntaner also explains the symbolic meaning of the crown in a similar way (Muntaner, *Crònica*, chapter 298 in Soldevila, *Les quatre grans cròniques*, 942).

The Images in the Text: Iconographic Representation

King Peter's self-coronation was not the first during the Middle Ages – neither in Europe nor on the Iberian Peninsula, nor even in Aragon. It was, however, the first and only one to generate iconographic representations. These are preserved today in two of the three versions of the aforementioned liturgical document *De la manera con los reys d'Aragó se faran consegrar e ells mateys se coronarán* (*On the Manner in Which the Kings of Aragon Are Consecrated and Crown Themselves*), commissioned by the king himself at the start of 1353 (see Figures 4, 26, 27, 29, 30).[51] Their pages contain delightful miniatures depicting the moment at which the king of the crown of Aragon – conceived generically rather than individually – places this royal emblem on his own head, dispensing with any civil or ecclesiastical intervention in the handing over of the crown, and receives the blessing of the bishop before a group of lay witnesses.

The image of self-coronation highlights the king's desire to appear as maximum sovereign but, paradoxically, these kinds of images then disappear in Western iconography until the beginning of the nineteenth century and Napoleon's self-coronation. Yet it is possible to find later scenes with a similar meaning, if somewhat augmented by directly linking the king with the divine. This is the case with the frontispiece of the Latin version of the *Llibre de franqueses i privilegis del regne de Mallorca* (*Book of Freedoms and Privileges of the Kingdom of Mallorca*), from around 1337–9,[52] or with one of the panels making up

---

[51] The most ancient manuscript of the *Ordinacions* of King Peter IV appears to be the *Manuscrito de san Miguel de los Reyes*, which belonged to the royal palace of Valencia and would have been written between 1353 and 1357. It is kept in the Biblioteca de la Fundación Bartolomé March, Palma de Mallorca (Ms. 2633). In the illustration, the king is shown kneeling down before the bishop after having taken the insignia: crown on his head, sceptre in his left hand and pommel in right hand. Bohigas argues that this is the most ancient manuscript as the king is represented in his youth; see Pere Bohigas, 'El manuscrit Phillips de les "ordinacions del rei en Pere"', *Cuadernos de Arqueología e Historia de la Ciudad* 10 (1967): 109, and Bonifacio Palacios Martín, 'Estudio histórico de las Ordenaciones', in *El 'Manuscrito de San Miguel de los Reyes' de las 'Ordinacions' de Pedro IV* (València: Scriptorum, 1994), 58. We know from another document that King Peter was still not sure about the ceremonial in 1367 (Rubió i Lluch, *Documents per l'història de la cultura catalana*, 2:216, doc. CCXXII).

[52] Arxiu del Regne de Mallorca. Palma de Mallorca. Còdex núm. 1. The frontispiece was commissioned by the *Jurats* of Mallorca, and James I is represented in a miniature as being crowned by angels; nevertheless, historiography does not coincide with the identification of the king. See Gabriel Llompart and Isabel Escandell, 'Estudi historicoartístic', in *Llibre dels reis. Llibre de franqueses i privilegis del regne de Mallorca*, ed. Ricard Urgell (Palma de Mallorca: Universitat de les Illes Balears, 2010), 111–41. See also Marta Serrano Coll, 'Falsas historias, proposiciones certeras. Dominio visual e imágenes persuasivas en el entorno áulico de la Corona de Aragón', *Codex Aquilarensis* 27 (2011): 191–212, especially 200–4.

Archbishop Don Sancho de Rojas' lovely altarpiece from around 1415–20.[53]

The illustration relating to the second epigraph entitled *De la manera con les reynes d'Aragó se faran consagrar e los reys d'Aragó les coronaran* (*Of the Manner in Which the Queens of Aragon Are Consecrated and the Kings of Aragon Crown Them*) also represents an innovation, as the queen is depicted at the precise moment that her husband places the crown on her head (Figures 27, 30).

According to the iconographic evidence, which contrasts with the miniatures in the three surviving versions of the Aragonese ceremonial, the queens were never shown being invested by their husbands, at least during the Middle Ages. On one hand, when they were proclaimed in the same ceremony as the king, they were shown next to them, as in the imperial models of the tenth and eleventh centuries (Figure 28), during the act of unction, coronation or the later service of Holy Mass.[54]

On the other hand, when the queen had her investiture on a different day than the king, another type of representation emerged in which she was shown kneeling during the unction ceremony, at the moment of coronation or when receiving the blessing, usually by the bishop.[55]

In neither of these cases was the queen's coronation carried out by the king, which reaffirms the exceptional nature of what King Peter the Ceremonious did. In marked contrast, King Peter is shown crowning his wife.

---

[53] The table is shown in the Museo del Prado (Madrid) and commentators have interpreted it as the coronation of King Ferdinand I of Trastámara by Jesus Christ. An introduction to this subject is provided in Marisa Melero Moneo, 'La Virgen y el rey', in *Maravillas de la España Medieval I. Estudios y Catálogo*, ed. Isidro Bango Torviso (León: Junta de Castilla y León, 2001), 419–31.

[54] As shown in the mid-fourteenth-century French *Ordre de la consécration et du couronnement des rois de France*, f. 37v. (Bibliothèque Nationale de France, Lat. 1246), in the *Ceremonial de coronación de los reyes de Castilla y León*, f. 19r. (Biblioteca de El Escorial, Cod. Esc. & III.3) and in different manuscripts of the thirteenth-century *Grandes Chroniques de France*. See François Avril, Marie Thérèse Gousset and Bernard Guenée, *Les Grandes Chroniques de France* (Paris: Philippe Lebaud, 1987); Hedeman, *The Royal Image*; Le Goff et al., *Le Sacre Royal*; Anne H. Hedeman, 'Copies in Context: The Coronatio of Charles V in His Grandes Chroniques de France', in *Coronations: Medieval and Early Modern Monarchic Ritual*, ed. János M. Bak (Berkeley: University of California Press, 1990), 72–87.

[55] See for instance, *Ceremonial de coronación de los reyes de Castilla y León*, f. 24r. (Biblioteca de El Escorial, Cod. Esc. & III. 3), *Pontifical à l'usage du diocèse de Reims*, f. 83 (Biblioteca Apostolica Vaticana, Chigi CVI, 182), *Livre du sacre de Charles V* (at the miniature of Jeanne du Borbon. British Library, Ms. Tiberius B. VIII) or the *Pontifical of Sens* (St. Petersburg, National Library, Lat. Q.v.I, n° 35). See Pérez Monzón, 'Ceremonias regias en la Castilla Medieval'; Edward S. Dewick, ed., *The Coronation Book of Charles V of France* (Rochester, NY: Boydell, 2010); Shane Bobrycki, 'The Royal Consecration Ordines of the Pontifical of Sens from a New Perspective', *Bulletin du centre d'études médiévales d'Auxerre BUCEMA* 13 (2009): 131–42.

Figure 27 King Peter IV of Aragon crowning the queen. *Ceremonial de consagración y coronación de los reyes de Aragón*, fol. 35 v. Annex to the *Ordinacions de Cort*, second half of the fourteenth century. Biblioteca de la Fundación Lázaro Galdiano, reg. 14425. © Museo Lázaro Galdiano. Madrid.

Ideologically, these Aragonese illustrations fall into the tradition that, in the second quarter of the fourteenth century, inspired the *marginalia* which introduced the *Ordo ad injugendum et coronandum regem Franciae* of the *Pontifical à l'usage du diocèse de Reims* (*Pontifical As Used by the Diocese of Rheims*): in the middle of the lower margin, the kneeling king is shown receiving the crown from the hands of a layman, rather than from the archbishop, as the ritual would prescribe.[56]

---

[56] Biblioteca Apostolica Vaticana, Vatican (Ms. Chigi CVI, 182, f. 71r). On the iconography of the coronations of the pontificals see Palazzo, *L'Évêque et son image*, 258–305. Richard Jackson holds this pontifical comes from Cambrai, not from Reims as traditionally believed (Jackson, *Ordines coronationes*, vol. 2, Ordo XXIIA).

Figure 28 A king being crowned and anointed by a bishop. Bibliothèque Nationale de France, MS., LAT. 1246, f. 37 v. *Ordre de la consécration et du couronnement des rois de France*. Circa 1250. © Bibliothèque Nationale de France.

This should be taken as one more proof of the necessary and joint role both ecclesiastics and laymen took in this rite, even at the expense of magnifying the honour and dignity of the latter over the former.[57]

The only illustrations showing the king of Aragon's self-coronation come from the miniatures that adorn two of the three versions of the ceremonial commissioned by Peter the Ceremonious. Done during the second half of the fourteenth century (though certainly no later than 1380), they were meant for the royal palaces of Barcelona, Zaragoza and Valencia.[58] The first manuscript, dated between 1370 and 1380, comes in the final appendix to the sumptuous *Ordinacions de cort fetes per el molt alt senyor en Pere Terç rey d'Aragó sobre lo regiment de tots los officials de la sua cort* (*Court Regulations Set Forth by His Royal Highness Peter the Third, King of Aragon, on the Administration of All the Officials of His Court*). This codex was produced by the royal workshops of Barcelona, as can be deduced

---

[57] Bonne, 'Images du sacre', 208–9.
[58] Facsimile, edition and commentaries in Bonifacio Palacios Martín, ed., *Ordenación y ceremonial de la coronación de los Reyes de Aragón / [2] El 'manuscrito de San Miguel de los Reyes' de las 'Ordinacions' de Pedro IV* (València: Scriptorium, 1994).

from its literary style, the decorative elements and the repetition of the Aragonese arms in its illuminations.[59] One of the most significant moments in the coronation of the king of Aragon is reproduced in the codex's first initial in folio 129 r: the instant at which the sovereign places the crown on his own head (Figure 29).

Thus, the king, standing before the altar in the presence of several people seated on wooden benches, holds aloft a great golden fleur-de-lis crown while facing the metropolitan of Zaragoza, now restricted by the regulations to giving a simple blessing. On a textual level, the autocratic character that the monarchy was assuming was obvious in Peter the Ceremonious' ceremonial. Anything that could sully the image of its sovereignty was eliminated, which is why this miniature illustrated his iron determination in such a clear and graphic way. Dressed in his dalmatic – beautifully and abundantly bordered with gold thread – and sporting loose, well-kempt locks, the sovereign lowers his head to place the crown on it with his own hands, the mark of royalty par excellence.

The second part of the appendix, which begins in folio 147 r, describes how the queens of Aragon were to be crowned. Its initial miniature depicts the moment at which the queen, in the presence of several ecclesiastics – among whom can be seen the archbishop of Zaragoza blessing her – receives the crown from her husband (Figure 30).

This ceremonial entailed innovations as regards the traditional iconography of the coronation of queens, who usually attained regal dignity through the sacrament of marriage: 'betrothals make the queen', in Fanny Cosandey's words.[60] Generally speaking, the images accompanying these liturgies show that the queen was entitled to similar formalities as the king, being not only his wife, but also the mother of the future king (or so they hoped).[61] It is true that, as a sovereign, the queen partook of the sacredness of the monarchy, so she was also anointed, but she acceded to the crown through her spouse, so her subordination to him was a reality acknowledged by various mechanisms – and whereas the king kept the crown for his whole life, she could lose it.

---

[59] Bibliothèque Nationale de France, Paris (Ms. Esp. 99). The hypothesis of this manuscript's chronology is presented in Pere Bohigas, 'L'agrupament de les miniatures del llibre vermell', *Analecta Montserratensia* 9 (1962): 47. See also Françoise Lainé, 'L'image du roi dans le ms. Espagnol 99 de la BNF (c. 1350–1360)', *e-Spania, Revue interdisciplinaire d'études hispaniques médiévales* 3 (2007).

[60] This would explain why the queen's unction was less solemn than the king's. She appears with fewer insignia and her ceremony has less ritual: Fanny Cosandey, *La reine de France. Symbole et pouvoir* (Paris: Gallimard, 2000).

[61] In the French tradition, the queen received a special blessing, since she would be the mother of the future king: Bouman, *Sacring and Crowning*, 151.

266 Convention

Figure 29 Self-coronation of Peter the Ceremonious. *Ordinacions de Cort*, c.1370–80. Bibliothèque Nationale de France, ms. Esp. 99, fol. 129 r. © Bibliothèque Nationale de France.

Figure 30 Peter the Ceremonious crowning the queen. *Ordinacions de Cort*, c.1370–80. Bibliothèque Nationale de France, ms. Esp. 99, fol. 147 r. © Bibliothèque Nationale de France.

This basic principle usually manifested itself at the textual level: among other elements of a legal nature, the queen's ceremonial follows her husband's investiture – she is crowned after the king. However, this generic difference can also be seen at the figurative level given the notable lack, in the European sphere, of representations of the queen compared with those relating to the coronation of kings. In this sense, King Peter's ceremonial also marks a milestone in proclaiming certain parity in this regard, although the equivalence is merely quantitative, not qualitative. The representations of the queen's coronation need to be understood as a manifestation of the regal self-proclamation and, therefore, as a further proof of the political exploitation of the image by Peter the Ceremonious, as it falls to none other than the king to crown the queen. Thus the subordination of the queen to her husband is evident not only in the *incipit* of Peter's ordination ('the Kings of Aragon will crown them [the queens]'), but also in the beautiful illustration that accompanies it. She is crowned by the king in accordance with the ceremonial, before an altar on which liturgical objects have been arranged, wearing embroidered clothing, kneeling and with her hands together in an attitude of prayer. King Peter's narrative (his autobiographical chronicle) supports the idea that he himself enacted this solemnity, explaining that he moved to Zaragoza because he wanted to crown his wife, Queen Sibilia, and to organise a big celebration in her honour.[62]

There are very similar images to these two initials in the second of the codices of the *Ceremonial de Consagración y de Coronación de los reyes de Aragón* (*Consecration and Coronation Ceremonial of the Kings of Aragon*), also from the second half of the fourteenth century (see figures 4, 26, 27).[63] This manuscript is one of the vernacular copies that were made from the Latin original, specifically the one prepared for Zaragoza, and it appears to be incomplete.[64] It lacks the previous document, the *Ordenaciones de corte* (*Court Regulations*) which, by contrast, goes with the other copies intended for Barcelona and Valencia. The shields

---

[62] Peter IV of Aragon, *Llibre*, in Soldevila, *Les quatre grans cròniques*, appendix. The queen receives from the king the crown, the sceptre, the pommel and the ring, called the *medicus*, on the fourth finger of her right hand: see Palacios Martín, *Estudio histórico de las Ordenaciones*, 87. See also Núria Silleras-Fernández, 'Creada a su imagen y semejanza: la coronación de la Reina de Aragón según las Ordenaciones de Pedro el Ceremonioso', *Lusitania Sacra* 31 (2015): 107–25.

[63] Biblioteca de la Fundación Lázaro Galdiano, Madrid (Ms. R. 14.425), f. 19r (for the king's coronation) and f. 35v (for the queen's coronation). See facsimile, edition and commentaries in *Ceremonial de Consagración y Coronación de los Reyes de Aragón* (Zaragoza: Centro de Documentación Bibliográfica Aragonesa, 1992).

[64] Found in Sádaba (Aragon) at the beginning of the twentieth century: Palacios Martín, *Estudio histórico de las Ordenaciones*, 15.

hanging from the borders that frame the writing boxes for the first folios of the coronation of both monarchs might indicate that the codex came from the royal workshops. They are of Íñigo Arista of Aragon and the Cross of St George in the case of the king's coronation, and just of Aragon in that of the queen. At a stylistic level, the drawing of clear analogies between the initials of this manuscript and those of the previous one means accepting the dependence of one on the other.[65]

In emphasising the gesture of self-coronation, these representations show the king's interest in relegating the prelates to a secondary level. This tendency is also highlighted in the representations of the coronations of queens, where the king plays a leading role, magnifying his power to the detriment of the visual statement of his links with the divine. Nevertheless, since unction remains in the ceremony, it is not the ceremony or the kingship which are secularised. It is the authority of confirming or conveying temporal power which is given to the king. As a consequence, the monarchy maintained a marked interest in expressing its connection with the sacred by means of all kinds of textual and iconographic resources: significantly, King Peter set up, with the aim of asserting the sacred origin of his office, a series of mechanisms that affected his own image and that of his insignia.

The iconography of medieval coronations verifies the presence of laymen, whose participation could be justified by the monarch's awareness that his survival rested, in large part, on the recognition of his vassals. Their original witness role, sometimes reduced to mere assent, was giving way to their involvement in one of the high points of the ceremony: their help in the putting on of the insignia which, in the eyes of those present, symbolised the receiving of royal dignity. Yet neither of these topics appears in the miniatures adorning the various copies of the ceremonial of Peter the Ceremonious' coronation. For that reason, they proclaim themselves as the most exceptional graphic source for the autocratic character of the kingdom of Aragon.

King Peter's Ritual Strategies

King Peter had to create new cultural weapons so as to preserve his position in the kingdom of Aragon and in Catalan society. Threatened during his reign by internal insurrections and external competition, he

---

[65] Bohigas argued first that both were composed by the same artist (Bohigas, *L'agrupament de les miniatures del Llibre Vermell*, 47), and afterwards that at least they were made at the same workshop: Pere Bohigas, *Sobre manuscrits i biblioteques* (Barcelona: Abadia de Montserrat, 1985), 114.

emphasised historical language, liturgical gestures and iconographic models in order to protect the reputation of the kingship. These means shaped the perception of interests, developed discursive royal ideology, increased the apparatus of propaganda, highlighted ritual symbolic meanings and led the public to acquire a specific image of the king.[66] Historical, liturgical and iconographic representations emerge as a means of persuasion, a way of reconstituting the social and political world.[67] Ultimately, King Peter's efforts at constructing the memory of his own reign through history, liturgy and images are an operation of self-justification. He *understood* the cultural power of the writing of history, the symbolic attraction of royal ceremonies and the popular efficacy of iconographic strategy. He used historical texts, liturgical rituals and images as a tool for the control of his large kingdom, from 'autography' to authority.[68]

More specifically, King Peter benefitted from the devaluation of late medieval royal coronations, which were affected by the progressive separation of episcopal unction – a true sacrament – from the ceremony of the coronation.[69] The unction continued as an important part of the ordo of the coronation, but possessed less symbolic power than the act of coronation itself. This strengthened the influence of the gesture of self-coronation. It confirms King Peter's idea of the divorce between the spiritual (unction) and temporal (coronation) parts of the ceremony. His aspiration to separate the temporal from the spiritual was made explicit in 1344, by his refusal to pay tribute to Rome for the possession of Sardinia, arguing that no one, not even the Pope himself, was superior to the king in temporal things. Peter rejected papal intervention and denied the pre-eminence of the Pope over Aragon, speaking of 'the superiority which is falsely claimed over the kingdom of Aragon, for which, after God, we recognize and have no superior in

---

[66] Peter the Ceremonious' calculated rhetoric and propensity to propagandistic ceremonies have been analysed in Cawsey, *Kingship and Propaganda* and Vanlandingham, *Transforming the State*.

[67] I borrow some of these concepts from Hunt, *Politics, Culture, and Class*, 24; William H. Sewell Jr, *Work and Revolution in France* (Cambridge: Cambridge University Press, 1980); and John G. A. Pocock, 'The Concept of a Language and the *métier d'historien*: Some Considerations on Practice', in *The Languages of Political Theory in Early-Modern Europe*, ed. Anthony Pagden (Cambridge: Cambridge University Press, 1987), 19–40.

[68] Armando Petrucci notes Peter had an 'alphabetic mentality' (Gimeno, *Escribir, reinar*, 11–13 and 21), which Clanchy assigned to this time: Michael T. Clanchy, *From Memory to Written Record* (Oxford: Blackwell, 1993), 185–90, and Attilio Bartoli Langeli, *La scrittura dell'italiano* (Bologna: Il Mulino, 2000), 40–75. See also Stock, *Implications of Literacy*.

[69] As Kantorowicz suggests, the ceremony of unction would progressively lose rank in the liturgy and receive a different canonical treatment: Kantorowicz, *King's Two Bodies*, 318–24.

temporal things'.⁷⁰ He actually insulted Pope Benedict XII, defining him as 'so avaricious and mean'.⁷¹ This attitude against the Pope illustrates why Peter considered himself one of the 'great lords of the world', and helps us understand his search for autonomy from the ecclesiastical sphere.⁷²

Certainly, the very ceremony of self-coronation remains a sacred liturgy, and must be located in the context of the whole ceremony of the king's installation and unction. This is clear from the ordo that Peter himself ordered to be produced and also from the context of the illustrations in Figures 26, 27, 29 and 30, which are closely contemporary with Peter's self-coronation and thus have an enormous historical value as a source. Yet a coronation ceremony directly officiated by the king increases the impression of the king's autonomy, and even asserts the capacity for a sacred role. To what extent this king's disposition towards a sacred role and to what extent the exaltation of his authority by conveying temporal power through self-coronation led, paradoxically, towards subsequent secularisation in early modern Europe is a very interesting question, but one that would require further research to answer.

I have tried to show that Peter the Ceremonious engaged all manner of symbols in order to consolidate his power. The image of the king, imprinted in the Catalan *imaginaire* for centuries and summarised with his popular nickname *El Ceremoniós*, reveals the efficacy of his strategy. In addition to the three kinds of representation analysed in this chapter, he also projected the construction of sculptures of his ancestors in the royal palace of Barcelona, the restoration of the royal pantheon in Poblet and the carving of the nineteen figures of his predecessors on the new royal coronation sword, being considered the custodian of tradition of the kingdom. His title 'The Ceremonious' refers to his obsessive attention to gestures, rituals, ceremonies and liturgies as platforms of political power. Peter was aware that any policy of consolidation required recourse to the authority of the past. Yet he not only emphasised the collective memory shared by his subjects, but also operated with the symbols that made the emergence of his own authority possible. Many of these gestures illustrate his political power and natural authority as a king. The most impressive of the gestures took

---

[70] Hillgarth, *Chronicle. Pere III*, 'Introduction', 1:77. Part of this strategy is his intention of conveying himself as *rex et sacerdos*, as worked, for the Anjou dynasty, in Darleen Pryds, *The King Embodies the Word* (Leiden: Brill, 2000).
[71] Hillgarth, *Chronicle. Pere III*, 'Introduction', 1:224–5.
[72] 'E així com és acostumat de fer per los grans senyors del món en semblants cases' (Pere el Cerimoniós, *Crònica*, 5:30, Soldevila, *Les quatre grans cròniques*, 1119).

place when Peter was still an adolescent of sixteen, and definitively marked his tendency to autocracy and authoritarianism: his self-coronation. Far from causing a loss of authority among his subjects, this gesture provided the king with an authority which served to prolong his reign; indeed, it was one of the most durable of the Middle Ages. All this confirms Buc's intuition that 'besides blasphemy, medieval political culture feared manipulations of rituals as well as hypocrisy in rituals.'[73] Peter's subjects perceived the dramatism of his confrontation with the bishop, but they appreciated the authenticity of the king and the ritual performed by him.

Fifteenth-Century Aragon: Dramatising Self-Coronations

As a manifestation of this authority, Peter the Ceremonious' act of self-coronation was repeated by his grandson Martin I on 13 April 1399 in Barcelona.[74] Peter the Ceremonious' theatricality is clearly perceptible in Martin I's coronation ceremonies, though these lose part of their ritual content and authenticity, deriving to a clear dramatisation rather than being properly liturgical. Pere Miquel Carbonell (1434–1517) wrote a detailed account fifty years after the event.[75] He tells us that King Martin I went up to the altar, took the crown and put it on his head, and then did the same with the sceptre and pommel. The bishop had blessed the crown, the sceptre and the pommel just before the king's self-coronation.[76]

Interestingly, another of Carbonell's surviving accounts describes a performance, in the main courtyard of the Aljafería Palace in Zaragoza, of a play (or *entremès*, in the Catalan original) which represents the coronation of the king of Aragon. The play emphasises the fact that the king's sovereignty is received directly from the deity, as angels descend from above in the scene to serve the sovereign, offering him celestial gifts and serving him food.[77] To demonstrate this divine aspect of the

---

[73] Buc, '1701 in Medieval Perspective', 119.
[74] The coronation of Martin I has been analysed in Francesc Massip, *La monarquía en escena* (Madrid: Comunidad de Madrid, 2003), 205–20, and Massip, *La Festa d'Elx i els misteris medievals europeus* (Malcan-Elx: Institut de Cultura Juan Gil-Albert, 1991), 123–6.
[75] These notes were recorded by a chronicler in the seventeenth century: *Rúbriques de Bruniquer. Ceremonial dels Magnifichs Conserllers y Regiment de la Ciutat de Barcelona*, Vol. 1 (Barcelona: Impr. d'Henrich, 1912–16), 233.
[76] Pere Miquel Carbonell, *Chròniques d'Espanya [1495–1513]* (Barcelona: Carles Amorós, 1546), fol. 216–23, in Massip, *La monarquía en escena*, 209. Carbonell based his work on the artist Lluís Borrassa's version of the ceremony, which he witnessed.
[77] Carbonell, *Chroniques d'Espanya*, 220.

king's rule, an aerial artefact was used, allowing God's envoy to meet the king through scenic fiction.[78] Francesc Massip argues that in the medieval imagination, and more specifically in the world of spectacle, the devices of scenic fiction were perceived as real events or, at least, as events that were capable of happening to the extent that divine or supernatural interventions were also accepted as real or possible.[79] From a comparative perspective, he concludes, the unfolding of myth in drama is the original matrix of the theatrical experience in the most diverse civilisations.[80]

In 1414, the last self-coronation in medieval Europe took place, when Ferdinand I of Aragon followed to the letter the ceremonial left by his ancestor Peter the Ceremonious, and decided to put the crown on his head himself, relegating the bishop to the background.[81] One of the most detailed and reliable accounts that we have is that of the chronicler Hieronymus Zurita in the mid-seventeenth century, who recounts the events in his *Annals*.

The celebration was ordered, and the coronation ceremony with the greatest pomp and solemnity that was ever seen in these Kingdoms [of the crown of Aragon, namely Aragon, Valencia and the principality of Catalonia], and was the last that there has been until our times [around 1669, when Zurita writes his chronicle], because the Kings and their successors were not crowned with such majesty and triumph as was ordered for the Coronation of this Prince, and as his ancestors saw. ... Beginning to celebrate the Mass, the King took from the altar a Crown of uncommon richness, which he had ordered to be made for his coronation, and put it on his head, and took the sceptre and royal orb and when he was seated on his throne, the Infante Don Alfonso [future Alfonso V of Aragon] arrived, and the King wrapped him in a robe, and put a hat on his head, and

---

[78] Francesc Massip, *A cos de rei. Festa cívica i espectacle del poder reial a la Corona d'Aragó* (Valls: Cossetània, 2010), 92. See also the drama/ritual/historical approach in Francesc Massip, 'El rei i la festa. Del ritu a la propaganda', *Revista de Catalunya* 84 (1994): 63–83, and, for the dramas around the coronation of Ferran I of Aragon in 1414, see Francesc Massip, 'Imatge i espectacle del poder reial en l'entronització dels Trastàmara (1414)', in Massip, *A cos de rei*, 97–120.

[79] Massip, *A cos de rei*, 172. See also José Manuel Nieto Soria, 'La realeza', in Nieto Soria, ed., *Orígenes de la monarquía hispánica: Propaganda y legitimación (ca. 1400–1520)* (Madrid: Dykinson, 1999), 25–62, here 55; Ángel Gómez-Moreno, *El teatro medieval castellano en su contexto románico* (Madrid: Taurus, 1991), 89–97.

[80] Francesc Massip, *El teatro medieval* (Barcelona: Montesinos, 1992), 32.

[81] The coronation of Ferdinand I of Aragon has been analysed in Inez Macdonald, 'A Coronation Service 1414', *Modern Language Review* 36 (1941): 351–68, here 361; Esteban Sarasa Sánchez, *Fernando I y Zaragoza (La coronación de 1414)* (Zaragoza, Ayuntamiento de Zaragoza, 1977); Esteban Sarasa Sánchez, *Aragón en el Reinado de Fernando I (1412–1416)* (Zaragoza: Institución Fernando el Católico, 1986), 82–6; Roser Salicrú i Lluch, 'La coronació de Ferran d'Antequera: L'organització I els preparatius de la festa', *Anuario de Estudios Medievales* 25(1) (1995): 699–759, here 741–3.

a golden rod in his hand, and gave him peace, and the title of Prince of Girona, as his first-born [and successor].[82]

As all available sources indicate,[83] it was a true ritual and dramatic spectacle, which deliberately followed the ritual created by Peter the Ceremonious and continued by his sons John and Martin at a time of dynastic discontinuity, since Ferdinand I belonged to the house of Trastámara instead of the traditional house of Barcelona.[84] The dynasty of the house of Barcelona, which had reigned in the crown of Aragon since 1137 due to the marriage between the daughter of the king of Aragon, Alfonso the Battler, and the count of Barcelona, Alfonso the Chaste, had been supplanted, after three centuries, by the house of Trastámara, originating from Castile. This was made possible through a pact agreed on by representatives of each one of the estates of the crown of Aragon, and is known as the Compromise of Caspe (1412). But the legal decision had to be confirmed by the consolidation of the practice, political legitimisation and popular recognition, because what the king's self-coronation demonstrated here was a desire for a repetition of what had become a family tradition. Thus, interestingly, self-coronation functioned as a guarantor of the custom rather than a transgressive move. The transgressive ritual enacted by Frederick II in Jerusalem, Alfonso the Benign in Zaragoza and Alfonso XI in Castile had been transformed into a way of continuing with tradition.[85]

---

[82] Gerónimo Zurita, *Los cinco libros primeros de la segunda parte de los anales de la Corona de Aragón. Tomo Tercero* (Zaragoza: Herederos de Pedro Lanaja y Lamarca, 1669), 101.

[83] Zurita, *Los cinco libros*, 101, libro XII, capítulo XXIV; Pere Tomich, *Històrias e conquistas*, chapter XLVII, ed. Juan Sáez Rico (València: Anubar, 1970), 128–9; *Crónica incompleta del reinado de Fernando I de Aragón*, ed. L. Vela Gormedino (Zaragoza: Anubar, 1985), 45–9, chapter XXVII; Gerónimo de Blancas, *Coronaciones de los Serenísimos Reyes de Aragón* (Zaragoza: Diego Dormer, 1641), chapter 9, 91–116, in *Cartas del baile general de Valencia, Joan Mercader, al rey Fernando de Antequera*, ed. Margarita Tintó Sala (València: Consejo Superior de Investigaciones Científicas, 1979), 305–18 (self-coronation of Ferdinand I in 314). Some of these chroniclers are based on the chronicler Alvaro García de Santa María, who witnessed the ceremony, but his chronicle is lost in some passages.

[84] Inez Macdonald, *Don Fernando de Antequera* (Oxford: Dolphin Book, 1948), 199–200.

[85] The chronicler Gerónimo Zurita points out that Ferdinand I's successors were not crowned with 'such majesty and triumph'. They also stopped crowning themselves. Indeed, Alfonso the Magnanimous (1416–58), the king who received his insignia from his own father, Ferdinand, in 1414, and John II (1458–79) limited themselves to swearing the *fueros* of Aragon at the cathedral of Zaragoza at the start of their reigns, with a certain solemnity but without the pomp that had marked the coronation of 1414. See Gudiol, 'El rito de la coronación del rey en Aragón', 34.

11 Charles III of Navarra
Juridical Implications of Self-Coronations

Charles III of Navarra performed his self-coronation on 13 February 1390, in a solemn ceremony that took place in the cathedral of Pamplona.[1] Despite its sacred setting, the ceremony had an essentially lay character, as had been the tradition in Navarra since the restoration of the kingdom by García Ramírez in 1134.[2] The civil dimension of Charles III's royal accession ceremonies was made especially manifest at the precise moment of coronation, when the king took the crown himself and placed it on his head, without the aid of the bishop. This gesture demonstrates the autonomy of the monarch in relation to the ecclesiastics, at least insofar as it referred to his authority in matters of a temporal nature. Yet this majestic self-coronation should not be regarded as an isolated or exceptional ritual since it should be interpreted having in mind three factors. Firstly, it responds to the tradition of the other Iberian kingdoms in which the ceremony of self-coronation had been enacted, as clearly perceptible in analogous ceremonies previously performed by the kings of Castile and Aragon. It also reflects the particular idiosyncrasy of the kingdom of

---

[1] The record of the ceremony of Charles III's coronation appears in: Archivo General de Navarra (AGN), *Comptos, Documentos*, Caja 59, n. 10, fol. 1, dated 13 February 1390; AGN, *Comptos. Registros*, 209, fols. 1r–3v, and AGN, *Comptos. Registros*, 210, fols. 1r–3r; Archivo Municipal de Estella, *Fondos Especiales*, n. 15 y n. 65, fols. 68v–73v; Archivo Municipal de Pamplona, Caja 19, n. 167. An edition of the record of the ceremony is presented in Ricardo Cierbide and Emiliana Ramos, *Documentación medieval del Archivo Municipal de Pamplona (1357–1512)*, Vol. 2 (San Sebastián: Sociedad de Estudios Vascos, 2000), 82–6, n. 222, and Merche Osés Urricelqui, *Documentación medieval de Estella (siglos XII–XVI)* (Pamplona: Gobierno de Navarra, 2005), 377–83, n. 143. See also José Yanguas y Miranda, *Diccionario de Antigüedades del reino de Navarra* (Pamplona: Diputación Foral de Navarra, 1964), 202–5; José Ramón Castro, *Carlos III el Noble, rey de Navarra* (Pamplona: Institución Príncipe de Viana, 1967), 203–8; Merche Osés Urricelqui, 'El ritual de la realeza navarra en los siglos XIV y XV: coronaciones y funerales', in *El ceremonial de la Coronación, unción y exequias de los reyes de Inglaterra*, ed. Eloísa Ramírez (Pamplona: Gobierno de Navarra, 2008), 305–21; Fermín Miranda García, 'La realeza navarra y sus rituales en la alta edad media (905–1234)', in *Ceremonial de la coronación*, 253–78; Eloísa Ramírez Vaquero, 'Reinar en Navarra en la baja edad media', in *Ceremonial de la coronación*, 279–304.

[2] José María Lacarra, *El juramento de los reyes de Navarra (1234–1329)* (Madrid: Real Academia de la Historia, 1972), 24.

Navarra, as the culmination of a long ritual trajectory that had begun with the introduction of the civil royal oath in the context of the restoration of the kingdom in 1134. And, finally, and once more, it reacts to a particular need generated in a given context, reinforcing once more the idea of the malleability of the rituals.

To obtain a more complete and realistic vision of this particular ritual, and before discussing Charles III's self-coronation, we should analyse the evolution of the royal accession ceremonies in Navarra, from the investiture of García Ramírez (1134) to Charles III's self-coronation (1390). I highlight five steps in this itinerary of royal accession of the kings of Navarra: the effects of the restoration of the kingdom of Navarra in 1134 against the will of the Pope; Theobald I of Champagne's oath, which took place some years after his accession to the throne in 1234; the reintroduction of the anointment with Theobald II in 1257; Joanna II and Philip III of Navarra's oath and anointment in 1329; and Charles III's self-coronation in 1390.

The Restoration of the Kingdom of Navarra against the Will of the Roman Curia (1134)

The kingdom of Navarra took shape in the eastern Pyrenees, in the context of the first reaction of the Iberian Christian kingdoms against Islam from the mid-eighth century.[3] Accounts of the origins of the kingdom are set in that period and involve the fusion of Muslim and Vascon family lines, the centrality of Pamplona and the figure of Iñigo Arista as founding hero. The kingdom of Pamplona soon found itself pressured by the expansionist tendencies of its peninsular neighbours Aragon and Castile, and was effectively absorbed by them between 1076 and 1134.

However, its status as founding kingdom of the *Reconquista* earned Navarra symbolic wealth and a prodigious sense of identity. This meant that, when the first opportunity presented itself upon the death without issue of King Alfonso I the Battler of Aragon in 1134, the kingdom could be restored and came to be known as the kingdom of Navarra, replacing

---

[3] Ángel Martín Duque, 'La realeza navarra de cuño hispano-godo su ulterior metamorfosis', in *A la recherche de légitimités chrétiennes*, ed. Patrick Henriet (Lyon: Casa de Velázquez, 2003), 225–41; José María Lacarra, *Historia del reino de Navarra en la Edad Media* (Pamplona: Caja de Ahorros de Navarra, 1975), 21–73. For the ritual and *imaginaire* realities of the first times of the kingdom see Luis Javier Fortún Pérez de Ciriza, 'El acceso al trono. La coronación', in *Sedes reales de Navarro*, ed. Luis Javier Fortún Pérez de Ciriza (Pamplona: Gobierno de Navarra, 1991) and Fermín Miranda García, 'La imagen del poder monárquico en el reino de Pamplona (siglos X–XII)', in *VI Congreso General de Historia de Navarra. III. Ponencias* (Pamplona: Eunate, 2007), 73–95.

the kingdom of Pamplona.[4] However, the restoration of the kingdom took place in the face of opposition from the neighbouring kingdom of Aragon and, crucially, the Roman Curia.[5] The illegitimacy of the new monarchy, born outside Alfonso the Battler's will, and perhaps other considerations of geopolitical and strategic order, meant that the Pope did not approve the new kingdom.

The Pope's opposition to the kingdom led to one ritual and one political consequence. From a ritual perspective, the kings had to abandon royal unction (which had perhaps already fallen out of use as early as 1076, with the advent of the house of Aragon), and the ceremonies of accession to the throne were basically reduced to the civil ceremony with the military aspect of raising on the pavis.[6] From a political perspective, groups of nobles took advantage of the unstable situation and supported the new monarch, but made him subject to certain clauses of mutual loyalty agreed upon by means of an oath, which gave him a rather feudal physiognomy from the outset. There was a growing sense that the kingdom of Navarra had emerged from a negotiated relationship between the king and the kingdom (his subjects). The introduction of the oath ceremony in the kingdom of Navarra occurred in this unstable context.

In Navarra, the abandonment of unction and the nature of the restored kingdom as the product of a negotiated pact promoted the introduction of the oath. However, these pledges by the king to his nobles did not necessarily assume a ritual form persisting in the ceremonies of accession to power, but had a legal form through various 'mutual loyalty clauses between the king and the nobles'.[7] It is likely that, in this foundational era, the kings García Ramírez (1134–50), Sancho VI the Wise (1150–94) and Sancho VII the Strong (1194–1234) swore an oath.[8] Yet the ritual formalisation of these pacts between the king and his people and its

---

[4] Ángel Martín Duque, 'Del reino de Pamplona al reino de Navarra', in *Signos de identidad histórica para Navarra, Vol. 1* (Pamplona: Caja de Ahorros de Navarra, 1996), 145–54.

[5] Ángel Martín Duque, 'Singularidades de la realeza medieval navarra', in *Poderes públicos en la Europa Medieval: Principados, Reinos y Coronas* (Pamplona: Gobierno de Navarra, 1997), 299–346.

[6] Fermín Miranda García, 'La realeza navarra y sus rituales', 263–71, and Eloísa Ramírez Vaquero, '¿Irrupción?, sustitución, permanencia. El acceso al trono de Navarra, 905–1329', in *El acceso al trono. Concepción y ritualización* (Pamplona: Gobierno de Navarra, 2017), 241–85, here 255–63.

[7] Lacarra, *El juramento de los reyes de Navarra*, 10.

[8] Martín Duque, 'Singularidades de la realeza', 333, and Lacarra, *El juramento de los reyes de Navarra*, 23. For the introduction of the oath in other medieval European monarchies see, for England, H. G. Richardson, 'The English Coronation Oath', *Transactions of the Historical Society* 23 (4th series) (1941): 129–58; see, for Castile, José Manuel Nieto Soria, 'El juramento real de entronización en la Castilla Trastámara', in *Europa e Itali. Studi in onore di Giorgio Cittolini* (Florence: Firenze University Press, 2001), 371–84, and Ana Isabel Carrasco Manchado, 'Palabras y gestos de compromiso: los reyes castellanos

specification in a legal document (known as the *fuero*) would happen just a century after the establishment of the kingdom. This meant that, from 1234, the oaths had a much denser and more specific content.

The Establishment of the *Fueros* and the King's Oath at the Accession of Theobald I (1234)

In 1234, the succession order was again broken following the death of Sancho VII the Strong. The accession to the throne of Theobald I, from the house of Champagne, unleashed fierce tensions between the faction that had supported his candidacy – a group of nobles headed by the bishop of Pamplona – and those who had opposed it. The situation was aggravated by the king's tendency towards personal rule, accustomed as he was to absolute dominion over his counties, in which he minted coins, summoned the army, dictated laws and judged lawsuits according to his whim. The king quickly earned the mistrust of those who had supported him, both the bishop and the higher-ranking nobles, as well as the *infanzones* and knights of the mid-ranking nobility. The latter had created various juntas, associations or guilds which were originally designed for the defence of the kingdom from the abuses of the great barons, but which also began to assume a role in the defence of the native laws of the kingdom, in the face of growing pressure from the monarchy. These primitive juntas, authorised by Sancho IV the Strong, extended through several *comarcas*, but all converged in the *junta de Navarra*, from which the king designated the representatives who were to govern it. In time, the junta's governing bodies were monopolised by the *infanzones* and their raison d'être was the defence of the rights of the mid-ranking nobility.[9]

Between the accession in 1234 and 1238, the tension grew between King Theobald and the *infanzones* of the junta of the kingdom of Navarra to the point where both parties turned to Rome for mediation. This petition allowed both the king and the *infanzones* to create a detailed catalogue of the contents of the rights and obligations of the king towards his subjects and of the subjects towards the king. These obligations constituted the contents of the oath sworn by the king and the people during the royal accession ceremony of Theobald I, but now

y sus juramentos (siglo XV)', *e-Spania. Revue interdisciplinaire d'études hispaniques medievales et modernes* 4 (2007), online, accessed 25 September 2016; for Aragon see Bonifacio Palacios Martín, *La práctica del juramento y el desarrollo constitucional aragonés hasta Jaime I* (Madrid: Universidad Autónoma de Madrid, 1979) and Ralph A. Giesey, *If Not, Not* (Princeton, NJ: Princeton University Press, 1968).

[9] For the constitution and development of the junta of Navarra see Lacarra, *El juramento de los reyes de Navarra*, 10–14.

they needed to be set out in detail and brought up to date. To this end, on 25 January 1238 Theobald agreed to appoint a commission composed of ten great nobles, twenty knights and ten men from monastic orders and headed by the king and bishop. The towns and cities of the kingdom (especially Estella, Pamplona and Tudela) were not represented, as they had not been in conflict with the king.

According to Theobald I's mandate, the commission's aim would be to put in writing 'those *fueros* that are and must be [defended] between us and them, improving them on the one hand and on the other what we with the bishop and these representatives may have agreed'.[10] The king justified the need to specify the contents of his own commitment to the kingdom, 'as we promised [to the Navarrese knights and gentry] and swore on the day that we were raised up as king of Navarra, on which we returned their "fueros" to them, we now promise again to all that we will preserve them steadfastly always.'[11] Thus the basis for what would be the codification of the *fueros* of Navarra was negotiated between the king and his subjects in the Estella agreement of 25 January 1238.

This declaration magnificently expresses the seriousness with which the Navarrese and their king took the oath that was solemnly declared on the day of accession to the throne which, in this case, had been four years earlier. In addition, from that Estella committee emerged what was known as the 'Old Fuero of the Kingdom of Navarra', the immediate precedent for the subsequent and definitive 'Fuero General', composed of twelve chapters.[12] In the prologue, it announces that it deals with 'how they should raise the king in Spain, and how he should swear to them'. The two main ceremonies of royal accession (the raising up and the oath swearing), each of them enacted by the people and the king respectively, are thus established.

The declaration continues with a brief historical introduction to the kingdom, whose origins go back to the early period of the *Reconquista* (the first half of the seventh century). It relates that when the Moors conquered Spain through the betrayal of the Visigothic king Roderic, only

---

[10] Privilege of Theobaldo I, *Comptos*, Cart. 3, 155–6 (Lacarra, *El juramento de los reyes de Navarra*, 71).

[11] Lacarra, *El juramento de los reyes de Navarra*, 71, doc. 1.

[12] Editions of the *Fuero General de Navarra*: Juan F. Utrilla Utrilla, *El Fuero General de Navarra. Estudio y edición crítica de las redacciones protosistemáticas (Series A y B)* (Pamplona: Gobierno de Navarra, 1987); Ángel Martín Duque, *Fuero General de Navarra. Recopilación arcaica. Códice de la Real Academia de la Historia* (Pamplona: Mintzoa, 2005); Ángel Martín Duque, 'Fuero General de Navarra. Una redacción arcaica', *Anuario de Historia del Derecho Español*, 50 (1986): 781–861; Juan F. Utrilla, *El Fuero General de Navarra* (Pamplona: Fundación Diario de Navarra, 2003). See also José María Lacarra, *Notas para la formación de las familias de Fueros de Navarra* (Madrid: Olórzaga, 1933).

a few nobles managed to take refuge in the Pyrenean and Aragonese valleys of Aínsa and Sobrarbe, lands which formed part of the original nucleus of the future kingdom of Aragon.[13] There were about three hundred nobles 'on horseback', who, seeking advice from other kingdoms, were told to organise around a king who would lead them, but to first make sure that they wrote down their rights to be sworn by the king. Finally, they chose King Pelagius, who fought in Asturias and all over the mountains.

This account, clearly a presentist reading of events that had occurred five centuries earlier, legitimised the crown of Navarra in asserting itself in all the 'monarchies of Spain' and placed it at the origins of the kingdoms of Asturias and Aragon.[14] In the mid-thirteenth century, a new historical image of the kingdom of Navarra was based on a recreation of its origins, in which a *pacted* monarchy was deemed to have been established, the legal foundations of which come from the people rather than the king. The promoters of this reinvention of tradition were the 'rich men' (the old blood aristocracy) and the 'men of the street', the inhabitants of the active boroughs of the towns and cities, dedicated to business and the world of money. Established in a new tradition, nobles and bourgeoisie completed their work with the promotion of new rules (the *fueros*), new legal treatment and a new ritualised ceremonial.

Moreover, this account justifies the idea of popular sovereignty, given that first comes the community of free men consciously asserting rights, and from which monarchical sovereignty therefore proceeds: 'primero las leyes, luego los reyes' ['first the laws, then the kings'].[15] This formula is similar to other European perspectives of the time, such as that used by the *Coutume* ('Custom') of Bayonne: *Abans son pobles que senior* ('the people are before the lord'). There the fear was that the distant king of England on whom they depended might exceed his authority. The *Coutume* uses the argument that it is simpler for small towns to achieve restrictions on the sovereignty of their lords.

The more populous small towns, wanting to live in peace, are those that create lords to contain and subdue the strong and maintain each in his right, such that

---

[13] Antonio Durán Gudiol, *Los condados de Aragón y Sobrarbe* (Zaragoza: Guara, 1988).
[14] Ángel Martín Duque, 'Imagen histórica medieval de Navarra. Un bosquejo', *Príncipe de Viana* 60 (1999): 401–58, and Martín Duque, 'Del espejo ajeno a la memoria propia', in *Signos de identidad*, 21–50.
[15] Giesey, *If Not, Not*. This description, from the thirteenth century, is by Juan Gil de Zamora, *De preconiis Hispanie*, ed. Manuel de Castro y Castro (Madrid: Universidad de Madrid, 1955), 337–8. The thesis of the origin of 'popular sovereignty' in the Iberian monarchies, and especially in Navarra, is argued in Lacarra, *El juramento de los reyes de Navarra*, 18, and Percy E. Schramm, 'Der König von Navarra (1035–1512)', *Zeitschrift der Savigny-Stiftung für Rechtsgeschichte* 81 (1951), 151.

each one might live according to his condition, the poor with their poverty and the rich with their wealth. And in order to assure this in perpetuity, the towns submit to a lord, granting him what he has and keeping what they have. In testimony of this origin, the lord must take an oath to his people before the people do to their lord; and this oath taken by the people to their lord is not valid if the lord does not keep his, for if the lord violates his, the people are not bound by theirs, since the lord is committing falsehood against his people, not the people against him.[16]

The nobles and citizens of the neighbouring viscounty of Bearn established for their part rules that had to be sworn by the viscount on coming into possession of his domain. He was to swear to the barons and then to the whole court that he would be loyal to them, that he would judge the barons with rectitude and without causing prejudice to them.[17] Only after having received this guarantee did the barons and the court swear their oath of fidelity to him, which completely inverted the order of the oath in the French feudal tradition.

Other counties turned to accounts of their remote history to reaffirm the idea of a sovereignty agreed to between the king and his people. In those distant times, in the absence of an available lord, they would generally seek one out in distant lands to augment their prestige if possible. That is what happened in counties near Navarra, such as Bearn, whose inhabitants finally found their lord in Catalonia; in Bordeaux, where the citizens turned to the last son of the king of Castile; and in Auch, where they also looked to Castile to locate their lord.[18]

All this evidence shows that in many counties of southern France and northern Iberia the conviction existed that the prince is subject to law, because his sovereignty does not arise from himself, but from the expressed will of the people to grant it to him for the correct exercise of his office. That is the justification for the custom of the royal oath in Navarra, which would remain in stable use for centuries, down to the present day with the figure of the king of Spain.

The *fuero* agreed upon by the nobles and the king in Estella in 1238 sought to specify the content of the royal oath through clear and precise legal formulas. Two ideas underlie this new pact and help us understand why the nobles were able to acquire so many privileges from the king. In the first place, Theobald I was a foreign king who did not know the laws and customs of Navarra. He was accustomed to the customs of the France of Louis IX, where it was specifically stated that 'the king does not depend

---

[16] Lacarra, *El juramento de los reyes de Navarra*, 34–5.
[17] Pierre Roge, *Les anciens Fors de Bearn. Études sur l'histoire du droit béarnais au Moyen Age* (Toulouse: Privet, 1908).
[18] Lacarra, *El juramento de los reyes de Navarra*, 35.

on anyone, except God and himself.'[19] In the second place, the Navarrese nobles were aware that, traditionally, it had been they who had chosen the king, and not the other way round. Indeed, a century before, in 1134, the line of succession had been interrupted with the death of Alfonso the Battler. As they did not agree with the provisions the king had made in his will, the Navarrese nobles, together with the help of the bishop of Pamplona, themselves chose García Ramírez as successor. Although it was more of a confirmation than an election, this decision made it difficult for the king of Navarra to consider his kingdom as entirely his.[20] The *fuero* of 1238 thus had its basis in the reality that the accession of a foreign king in the kingdom of Navarra had been brought about and made possible by the local nobility.

After this 'account of origins', the *fuero* describes in detail the ceremonies of accession to the throne. Thus, the new political formulations around the pact between king and nobles and their subsequent legal expression also entailed (as it could not be otherwise) the establishment of new ceremonials of royal accession. In contrast to most European monarchies of the time, the *fuero* did not provide for unction or coronation, but rather restored the old Germanic rite of raising upon the pavis.[21] Before being raised up, the king had to swear on the cross and the Gospels that he would maintain the *fueros* or privileges of his subjects, or that he would enhance them, without ever diluting them. The succeeding provisions add the ceremonial of the oath and the raising up. The king was to be raised in an episcopal see and had to stand all night keeping vigil after hearing Mass, making an offering of purple cloth, handing out his coins and then receiving communion; finally he would be raised on a shield by the twelve great nobles of the kingdom and acclaimed by them thrice: 'Royal, royal, royal.'[22] Finally, the king would cast his coins among the subjects present up to an amount of 100 sueldos, 'to make it understood that no other earthly king has power over him', and then gird his own sword. The rite completed, the twelve great nobles of the kingdom would in turn duly swear the oath of loyalty. The ceremony was performed before a cross and some Gospels, and the nobles pledged to defend the person of the king, the land and the people, and to steadfastly preserve their *fueros*. Finally, they would kiss his hand. These ceremonies on the

[19] Pau Viollet, ed., *Etablissements de saint Louis*, Vol. 2 (Paris: Renouard, 1881), 135.
[20] Schramm, 'Der König von Navarra', 123.
[21] Sánchez-Albornoz, 'La *Ordinatio Principis*', 705.
[22] We have seen examples of the raising of the king, a ceremonial practice that some emperors performed during the late Roman period, as recorded by Ammianus Marcellinus and Cassiodorus. This ceremony was also practised upon certain Scandinavian kings' accession, adopting ritual forms such as the raising of the king onto the Mora stone or raising him to a high seat (Line, *Kingship and State*, 394–6).

part of the nobles are clearly an echo of feudal homage paid by vassals to their lord.[23]

The ecclesiastics, for their part, were scarcely involved in the ceremony. The king certainly heard Mass and took Communion, as a show of piety and spiritual preparation. But no prelate participated in the ceremony of royal accession, in which no unction and coronation were scheduled. The king's vigil on the night before belonged in the context of the vigil of arms rather than spiritual preparation. In contrast to the *promissio* that features in French or English imperial ceremonials, and which had been preserved in Byzantium from its beginnings, the Navarrese king did not commit himself to defend the Catholic faith or its churches and ministers.

Indeed, the contents of the *fueros* sworn by the king were free from ecclesiastical mediation. The form of the oath had much more to do with the feudal oath that the lords swore to their vassals than with the oath that the Byzantine emperors, the Visigothic kings, the German rulers and the French and English kings swore to the high clergy, in which they made a profession of faith and promised protection to the church. Because of all of this, the investiture ceremony of the Navarrese monarchs was essentially secular, without ecclesiastical intervention, as might be presumed of a monarchy that had been re-established in 1134 with the support of the emperor but against the wishes of the Roman Curia.

Starting from the ceremonial outlined, and from the historical circumstances prevailing in the kingdom of Navarra from 1134 until 1329, we can conclude that the royal oath was the most essential part of the investiture ceremonies, in contrast with the practice of most European monarchies. The king had to swear the oath before properly receiving the royal investiture, which is to say, before the raising up. Even chronologically, the king's oath came first, then that of his vassals. All these circumstances led Schramm to conclude that the oath of the Navarrese kings involved the broadest and deepest concession made by any sovereign in the medieval West.[24]

Schramm is probably right, but the Navarrese oath has resemblances to other stories narrated by Central European chroniclers. Although not frequent, agreements of oaths between the king and the subjects were set in medieval Europe. In this context, the story of King Álmos serves interesting comparative purposes. The blood oath was established in Hungary around 1200–30 by the ruler Álmos and some of his nobles. Álmos was leading the Hungarians to conquer new lands. Before the campaign began, the seven leaders of the army swore that they and their

---

[23] Utrilla Utrilla, *El Fuero General*, 1:153–4.
[24] Schramm, 'Der König von Navarra', 148.

progeny would always accept Álmos and his descendants as their leader, but on the condition, first, that all plunder would be shared equally, and, second, that Álmos and his successors would always consult and heed the advice of the seven leaders and of their descendants. The story is told in the *Gesta Hungarorum*. Narrating the election of Prince Álmos, the chronicler reports that:

> The seven leading persons [of the Hungarian people], who right up to the present day are called the Hetumoger, not tolerating the pressures of space, having taken counsel among themselves to quit the soil of their birth, did not cease seeking by arms and war to occupy lands that they might live in. Then they chose to seek for themselves the land of Pannonia that they had heard from rumor had been the land of King Attila, from whose line Prince Álmos, father of Árpád, descended. Then, these seven leading persons realized from their common and true counsel that they could not complete the journey begun unless they had a *leader and a master* above them. Thus, by the free will and common consent of the seven leading persons, they chose their *leader and master*, and of the sons of their sons to the last generation. ... These seven leading persons were noble by birth, strong in war, and firm in their faithfulness. Then they said with equal will to Prince Álmos: 'From today we choose you as *leader and master* and where your fortune takes you, there will we follow you.' Then on behalf of Prince Álmos the aforesaid men swore an oath, confirmed in pagan manner with their own blood spilled in a single vessel. And, although pagans, they nevertheless kept true to the oath that they now made among themselves, until they died.[25]

The content of the oath is detailed in the next chapter of the chronicle. The prince has to belong to Prince Álmos' lineage. Goods acquired should be shared by all the nobles. The prince has always to ask advice of the leading persons signing the oath and their successors. If one of the leaders making the oath is unfaithful to the prince, all the leaders have to revenge him, so that the blood of the guilty should be shed, 'just as their own blood had been shed in the oath that they had made to Prince Álmos'. If anyone seeks to breach parts of his oath, he should be put under an everlasting curse. In the end, the Anonymous gives the names of the seven men making the oath.[26]

The clauses of the legendary Hungarian blood oath reflect the concerns of both the king and the aristocracy in the chronicler's time. The seven great men were guaranteed their rights and the oath additionally contains in rudimentary form what became the oft-discussed 'right of resistance' of the nobility, codified in the famous Golden Bull of Andrew II of 1222. As the editors of the text concluded, 'all these notions coincided with the

---

[25] Anonymus, Notary of King Béla, *Gesta Hungarorum*, ed. László Veszprémy, János M. Bak, Martyn C. Rady and Rogerius, Archbishop of Split (Budapest: Central European University Press, 2010), chapter 5, p. 17.
[26] Anonymus, *Gesta Hungarorum*, chapter 6, p. 19.

concerns of the ever more powerful aristocracy of the early thirteenth century, one of the possible intended "audiences" of the retired notary [the chronicler].'[27]

Another parallel narrative is located in Denmark. Sven Aggesen tells the story of one of these pacts, but its duration, in contrast to the Navarra's *fueros*, was ephemeral:

> However, after a long time, a council was held in Lolland, and the rulers decided to divide the kingdom into equal thirds and to confirm the treaty by an oath. But the treaty did not remain firm for long, as the outcome of the arrangement showed. For after the council had been held, the three we have mentioned came together that autumn in the city of Roskilde for a feast, and they dined first with King Sven. The peace and trust between them had been broken.[28]

These historical narratives, spread in Europe from the end of the twelfth century onwards, are narrative echoes of diverse charts of liberties promulgated by European kings from the 1180s to the 1220s. They seem to embody the natural reaction of feudal societies to monarchical impunity. James C. Holt summarises this chain of pacts of concession of liberties to the subjects by the king to alternatively the nobles or the towns:

> In 1183, as part of the Treaty of Constance, the Emperor Frederick Barbarossa ended an unavailing war in northern Italy by granting the towns of the Lombard League a series of liberties which gave them practical independence of imperial rule. In 1188 King Alfonso IX of León, in the midst of a long feud with Castille, promulgated ordinances in the *cortes* of León which conferred important feudal privileges on his vassals. In 1205 King Peter II of Aragon, after costly foreign adventures, drafted, but did not promulgate, important concessions for his subjects of Catalonia. [In 1215 the Magna Carta was promulgated by King John of England.] In 1220 the young Emperor Frederick II bought support for his bid to unite the Empire and the Sicilian kingdom by granting special privileges to the ecclesiastical princes of the Empire. In 1222 King Andrew II of Hungary ended a period of expensive adventure abroad by granting the Golden Bull to his vassals.[29]

The Navarrese *fueros* (1238) would be probably the last link in the chain. Yet what makes the Navarrese case relevant is that it resulted in

---

[27] Anonymus, *Gesta Hungarorum*, 'Introduction', xxv–xvi.
[28] Eric Christiansen, ed., *The Works of Sven Aggesen: Twelfth-Century Danish Historian* (London: University College, 1992), 79–80. The chronicler Saxo Grammaticus tells parallel stories: Saxo Grammaticus, *The Danish History, Books i–ix*, ed. Douglas B. Killings and David Widger (e-book, 2013) (www.gutenberg.org/files/1150/1150-h/1 150-h.htm). On Scandinavian historical literature, especially from 1070 to 1300, see Brigit Sawyer and Peter Sawyer, 'Adam and Eve of Scandinavian History', in *The Perception of the Past in Twelfth-Century Europe*, ed. Paul Magdalino (London: Bloomsbury, 1992), 37–51.
[29] James C. Holt, *Magna Carta* (Cambridge: Cambridge University Press, 1997), 25.

a charter – though the parallels with the Unknown Charter or the mentioned Golden Bull of Hungary seem intriguing. The Unknown Charter was generated in the context of the agreements and disagreements between King John of England and his barons.[30] It consists of a copy of the charter of liberties of King Henry I, followed by promised or proposed concessions by King John. It seems that it was the result of one of the previous stages of the negotiation that finally concluded with the Magna Carta.[31] Thomas Bisson argues that this charter reveals the crisis of power and authority propitiated by King John's arbitrary behaviour. At some point, he had to gain the support of the barons of northern England, first by force granting their unanimous claim of exemption and exhaustion, then by pact in a meeting at Wallingford (1 November 1213) mediated by the legate Nicholas and Archbishop Stephen. The chronicler Coggeshall narrated these dealings, in which 'almost all the barons of England joined together to protect the liberty of the church and of the whole realm.'[32] Since the agreement at Wallingford finally collapsed, King John gathered a lay assembly in Oxford on 15 November 1213, a meeting that turned into an unprecedented confrontation of armed knights and unarmed barons. Bisson concludes that:

> Nothing else is heard of an assembly that would have been even more historic than the lonesome extant summons of knights of the shire that tells of an intention; and if some items in the so-called 'Unknown Charter' conceivably date from Wallingford, the parleys in which they became associated with the Henrician charter of liberties seem to have occurred early in 1215.[33]

The Reaction of Theobald II and the Reintroduction of Unction (1257)

The custom of royal oath-taking restored by Theobald I in 1234 and confirmed by the pacts of 1238 between the king and nobles was simpler than what would be observed by his successors. His son Theobald II

---

[30] See Holt, *Magna Carta*, 308–19 (for the parallels with the Magna Carta) and 418–28 (for its edition and comments). It is called 'Unknown' because it was not known to English historians until J. H. Round discovered it in 1893 (Round, 'An Unknown Charter of Liberties', *English Historical Review* 8 [1893]: 288–94). See also Nicholas Vincent, 'Oaths and Magna Carta', in *Le Sacré et la parole: Le serment au Moyen Âge*, ed. Martin Aurell, Montserrat Herrero and Jaume Aurell (Paris: Garnier, 2018).

[31] The different theories around the 'Unknown Charter' dating are addressed in Holt, *Magna Carta*, 420–3.

[32] Coggeshall, *Annales prioratos de Dunstaplia*, quoted in Bisson, *The Crisis of the Twelfth Century*, 523.

[33] Bisson, *The Crisis of the Twelfth Century*, 523.

swore loyalty to the kingdom on 27 November 1253.[34] The formula of his oath enumerates in detail all the clauses it contained. The king must protect the *fueros* and customs of each social body in the kingdom. He has to avoid the arbitrary customs introduced by his predecessors Theobald I, Sancho the Strong and Sancho the Wise. He has to preserve the rights of the inhabitants of the kingdom, ensuring that no one is imprisoned or has his goods seized unless there is proof of treason or robbery. The king's majority of age is stablished at twenty-one years and he has to be submitted until that age to the *Amo*, a nobleman chosen beforehand by the great nobility, knights and townsmen. Currency should be maintained in circulation for twelve years and, if necessary, he can change it only once during his reign. When the king must be absent from the kingdom, he will have to leave as seneschal in Navarra the *Amo* or another decided on by the twelve advisors of the kingdom.[35]

However, some months after taking the oath, towards the spring of 1254, Theobald II signalled his frustration with the restriction on sovereignty implied by accepting its contents. He then went to the Pope claiming that in order to take possession of the kingdom he had been obliged to swear an oath that he believed to be contrary to the liberties of the church. As a result, he asked Innocent IV to release him from the oath taken in the royal accession ceremony. The Pope authorised the bishop, Peter of Meaux, to do whatever he considered necessary for the salvation of the king's soul, the liberty of the church and the interest of the kingdom of Navarra.[36] Louis IX also supported Theobald, as for him it was inconceivable that the king should have to be bound by laws agreed upon with his subjects. As was well known, the king of France had not only been made the representative of Christ on earth by virtue of his anointing, but he had also attributed with miraculous powers.[37] Moreover, Theobald married Isabella, Louis IX's daughter, on 6 April 1255, which made the French king's mediation in Navarra more powerful. Theobald could also count on the support of Alfonso X of Castile, who was, during those months, negotiating the marriage of his daughter Berengaria with the king of France's firstborn son.

In 1257, Theobald II finally received word from the Pope that he could be anointed by the bishop of Pamplona, in accordance with the customs of other European monarchs. The privilege of unction and coronation

---

[34] On Teobaldo II see María Raquel García Arancón, *Teobaldo II de Navarra, 1253–1270* (Pamplona: Gobierno de Navarra, 1985).
[35] Lacarra, *El juramento de los reyes de Navarra*, anexos II y III.
[36] Lacarra, *El juramento de los reyes de Navarra*, 36.   [37] Bloch, *Les rois thaumaturgues*.

was extended, shortly afterwards, to the queen.[38] To mitigate the anticipated discontent of the Navarrese, the Pope preserved the 'raising' of the king on the pavis, stating that it was to be performed before the anointing and coronation ceremony, which could be officiated by any Catholic bishop in the event of the see of Pamplona being vacant. With the introduction of this ceremony, the king wanted to emphasise that his dignity and authority were not founded on the will of the subjects who raised him as king, but in the assumption of a grace that came from on high, through the mediation of the priest with unction. The gestures enacted in each of these ceremonies – the raising by subjects and the priestly anointing – were indeed a visual reflection of the different political significance of the two procedures: raising from below by the subjects and anointing from above by the priest. This represents one of the most expressive metaphors for what specialists have designated 'ascending theory' (the raising on the pavis by subjects) and 'descending theory' (the anointing with oil on the king's head by the bishop).[39] While the Navarrese barons strove to emphasise the raising and the oath, which expressed the nature of noble election and the king's submission to law, Theobald was concerned with accentuating the divine nature of royalty, with the introduction of unction and coronation by the bishop.

Convergence between the Oath and the Anointing: The Accession of the Counts of Evreux (1329)

All the indications suggest that, ultimately, Theobald II was neither anointed nor crowned, and therefore did not make effective the privilege of unction that he had acquired from the Pope. But the force of legal enactment meant that unction became active in Joanna II and Philip of Evreux's ceremonies of accession to the throne, as explicitly confirmed in the record of their oath, issued in 1329.[40] However, reaching that point involved a lengthy transition.

Theobald's successor, his brother Henry I, was raised on the shield and took the oath in Pamplona on 1 March 1271, but there is no record of either unction or coronation. However, Henry died shortly afterwards, in 1274, ushering in a change of dynasty. He left an eighteen-month-old

---

[38] J. Goñi Gaztambide, 'Regesta de bulas de los Archivos navarros (1198–1417)', *Anthologica Annua* 10 (1962): 253–354, doc. 189, 195, 197.

[39] Walter Ullmann, *Principles of Government and Politics in the Middle Ages* (London: Methuen, 1961).

[40] Lacarra, *El juramento de los reyes de Navarra*, 101–3; Iñigo Mugueta and Pascual Tamburri, 'Coronación juramentada. Navarra 1329', *Príncipe de Viana* 68 (2007): 169–90, here 177.

daughter, Joanna, born to Blanca, who was in turn the daughter of Robert of Artois, brother of Saint Louis and thus totally foreign to the kingdom. The Navarra *Cortes*, made up of members of the three estates, then took the initiative. Following a period of crisis, Philip III of France turned up in Pamplona in September 1276, sacked the city, confiscated most of the assets of the great nobility and governed the kingdom, without having to swear the *fueros* or receive the crown, until 1284. That same year, his son and heir, Philip IV of France, married the heir to the kingdom of Navarra, Joanna I. They both inherited the kingdom in 1285, on the death of Philip III.

Philip IV, who referred to the *plenitudo regiae potestatis*, was not best suited to submit to the system of privileges agreed upon by the nobility and the monarch as reflected in the *fueros*. He had received his royal consecration in the cathedral of Reims, but was aware that this ceremony did not have sufficient legal validity for him to be considered king of the Navarrese. Meanwhile, the Navarrese *infanzones*, knights and citizens had established a firm alliance against the French king's pretensions to sovereignty. It appears that Philip the Fair finally took the oath as king of Navarra before the barons, who had gone to Paris for that very event, between 1298 and 1305. His sons Louis the Stubborn and Philip the Tall did likewise in Pamplona in 1307 and Paris in 1319, respectively. On the death of Philip IV, there were no surviving children. His brother Charles the Bald prepared to reign in Navarra. However, he died in February 1328 without any issue.

After fifty years of dependence on the house of Champagne (1234–74) and fifty-four under the French crown of the Capetians (1274–1328), the Navarrese barons took the initiative at the moment of the French interregnum. A group of eight great nobles, forty-three knights, thirteen representatives of groupings of lesser nobility, representatives of forty-four towns and the viscount of Baigorri met in Puente la Reina in March 1328 and conspired to defend the kingdom of Navarra from whoever was supposed to reign over it and to help each other defend the kingdom. Significantly, the clergy were not present.

The favourite for the succession was Joanna, daughter of Louis the Stubborn, who was married to Philip of Evreux. The count and countess of Evreux jointly swore the oath to the kingdom on 5 March 1329 in the Pamplona cathedral. So, subsequently, did twelve great nobles representing the subjects of Navarra's new monarchs. Two very different records of this oath have been preserved, thus generating diverse interpretations. Some authors have arrived at the conclusion that the first record is that of the actual oath and that the second, rather more extensive, is a collection of the clauses most favourable to the monarch, involving commitment for the Navarrese estates, and which, for that reason, was kept only in the royal archives.[41]

In any case, the two records clearly specify that the oath be taken 'in the form and manner that by all those of the aforementioned kingdom [Navarra] meeting together in Larrasoaña, in the presence of the aforementioned gentlemen, was agreed'.[42] In addition, the first one states that the kings reserved for themselves the 'power to be anointed and to receive the other royal honours according to the privileges granted to the kings of Navarra, excluding the liberties and franchises and other rights of the said kingdom'.[43] So the kings wanted it known that, along with the duty of their oath, they also had the right to be anointed, thus emphasising the sacred status of the monarchy. Around 1329, three ceremonies (the civil ones of oath and raising, and the sacred one of unction) converged in the Navarrese monarchs' rite of accession to the throne.

The Self-Coronation of Charles III the Noble (1390)

Charles II the Bad (1349–87), the son of Philip and Joanna of Evreux, introduced the coronation ceremony in 1350. The introduction of the imposition of the crown did not mean the disappearance of the other three ceremonies practised by their predecessors (oath, raising and unction), resulting in the convergence of four ceremonies in the rite of accession to the throne. The documents of the meetings prior to the 1329 oath certainly used the word 'coronation', but most likely referred to the generic notion of ceremonies of accession to the throne.[44] His son Charles III the Noble (1387–1425) preserved the coronation, but introduced the variation of the self-coronation (1390), perhaps because this lay variation of the coronation rite fit much better with the civil idiosyncrasy of the kingdom.[45]

As was usual in the kingdom, Charles took his oath. He used the following formula:

---

[41] Mugueta and Tamburri, 'Coronación juramentada', 177–8.
[42] The two records, dated 5 March 1329, are edited in Lacarra, *El juramento de los reyes de Navarra*, 64–8 and 101–6. See also Mugueta and Tamburri, 'Coronación juramentada', 182–3.
[43] *Acta del juramento de Juana II y Felipe de Evreux en la catedral de Pamplona, de acuerdo con el capítulo I del Fuero General* (Comptos, Caja 6, número 60, edited by Lacarra, *El juramento de los reyes de Navarra*, 101–3, here 102).
[44] On a possible coronation of the counts of Evreux see Mugueta and Tamburri, 'Coronación juramentada', 182–8.
[45] An introduction to Charles III's life appears in Eloísa Ramírez Vaquero, *Carlos III de Navarra. Príncipe de sangre Valois (1387–1425)* (Gijón: Trea, 2007) and José Ramón Castro, *Carlos III el Noble, rey de Navarra* (Pamplona: Príncipe de Viana, 1967). See also María Narbona Cárceles, *La corte de Carlos III el Noble, rey de Navarra* (Pamplona: Eunsa, 2006).

Figure 31 Ivory seal of Charles III of Navarra, annexed to the document of the act of investiture of Charles III. Archivo Real y General de Navarra, Camara de Comptos, Documentos, Registro 225, Caja 59, número 10, f. 1, dated 13 February 1390. © Archivo Real y General de Navarra.

We, Charles, by the grace of God, king of Navarra, count of Evreux, swear to our people of Navarra on this cross and these holy gospels touched by our hand, namely, prelates, great nobles, knights, men of good towns and all the people of Navarra, [we swear] all their *fueros*, uses, customs, franchises, liberties and privileges, to each one of them, ... that we will thus maintain and protect them [the *fueros*] and their successors, for our whole life without any corruption, strengthening and not weakening them in whole or in part.[46]

The barons and knights subsequently swore their oath in turn:

We the aforementioned barons of Navarra, in this place and on our own behalf and that of all the knights and other nobles and *infanzones* of said Kingdom, swear to you our lord the King on this cross and these holy gospels touched by our hands, to protect and defend well and faithfully your person and your land, and to help you to defend and protect and maintain the *fueros* in every way possible to us.[47]

Finally, the representatives of the towns, in the name of the citizens and bourgeoisie, swore their oath:

[46] Castro, *Carlos III*, 205.   [47] Castro, *Carlos III*, 205–6.

We, the representatives of the good towns mentioned, in this place and on our own behalf and that of the neighbours, residents and inhabitants of those [towns], swear on this cross and these holy gospels touched by our hands, to protect well and faithfully the person of our lord the King and to help protect and defend the Kingdom in every way possible to us, in accordance with our *fueros*, uses, customs, privileges, franchises and liberties that each of us has.[48]

After the oath, the king retired to the chapel of San Esteban, where he was wrapped in 'a robe and a houppelande of white velvet', used by the king for his consecration. Accompanied by the bishops of Tarazona and Dax, he returned to the high altar, where the bishop of Pamplona, waiting for him at the seat of honour, consecrated him with holy oil. Once the anointing ceremony had been performed, the king changed his white vestments for royal ones and approached the altar, where the sword, sceptre and golden crown adorned with precious stones were. Following the recital of the usual prayers by the bishop of Pamplona, the king took the sword in his own hands and girded himself as he drew it, raising it high and then returning it to the scabbard. Then he took the crown and put it on his own head, and finally he took the sceptre and, placing himself on his shield, on which the arms of Navarra were painted, he was raised by the barons and representatives of the Borough of San Cernin, of San Nicolás and Navarraría in Pamplona, in the name of the chartered towns. While he was raised aloft, all cried out three times, 'Royal, Royal, Royal' (in a clear reminiscence of the traditional popular 'acclamations' or *Laudes Regiae*), and the king scattered his coins to the people, as was the custom.

The account of Charles III's self-coronation is preserved in three documents in the General Archive of Navarra. One general account appears in a document entitled 'Auto de la jura, uncion y coronación del rey Carlos III en la catedral de Santa María de Pamplona' ('Register of the Oath, Unction, and Coronation of King Charles III in the Cathedral of Santa Maria in Pamplona').[49] Yet the most specific mention of the self-coronation is presented in two parallel documents that give slightly different versions of the ceremony, but they basically give the same account of it.[50] They use the same words to explicitly state that the king took the crown and crowned himself with his own hands, since we can read in the

---

[48] Castro, *Carlos III*, 206.
[49] Archivo General de Navarra, *Camara de Comptos*, Registro 225, Caja 59, número 10, f. 1, dated 13 February 1390. On the place of royal coronations in Navarra, Luis Javier Fortún Pérez de Ciriza, 'Catedral y poder político, 1276–1512', in *La catedral de Pamplona, 1394–1994, Vol. 1* (Pamplona: Gobierno de Navarra, 1994), 81–90.
[50] Archivo General del Navarra, *Camara de Comptos*, Registro 209, fols. 1r–3v and Registro 210, fols. 1r–3r.

document that, after being anointed, the king crowned himself 'with his own hands'.[51]

The change of clothing between the anointing ceremony and the coronation is extraordinarily expressive of the transition from the sacred to the profane, from the spiritual to the temporal, that each of these rites signified. We thus see that the two poles of the ceremony, the civil (legal raising up) and the ecclesiastical (unction-coronation) have blended into one. But the fact is that the oath comes first, and then the unction-coronation, and the raising up on the pavis – and, importantly, to round it off, the acclamation of the people as a means of confirmation of the whole ceremony and of the final acceptance of the sovereignty of the king.

The scant participation of ecclesiastics is also striking. They have to content themselves with leading the king to the throne once all these ceremonies are over, seating him thereon and intoning the customary *Te Deum*. The Mass, celebrated by the bishop of Pamplona, follows, wherein the king took communion and offered his gifts: rich golden drapes.[52]

Charles II and Charles III sought to consolidate their French ancestry, which also had a ritual implication. Many have placed in this new context the damaged but exceptionally high-quality copy of the ritual used in England in the late fourteenth century, now in the General Archive of Navarra, which was probably commissioned by the Navarrese kings.[53] The ceremonial practices in France were much more favourable to the laying of sacred foundations for royal authority than the customs traditionally practised by the Navarrese royalty. The enrichment of the rite of accession to the throne from the time of Charles II, with the incorporation of unction and coronation, is also explained by the wish of the Navarrese sovereigns to enrich and consolidate their image beyond what was envisaged in the *fuero* and by their desire to place themselves on the same level as their neighbouring monarchs. At the same time, this diversification of the ceremonies entailed a symbolic complexity that is perfectly expressed in the duality – civil and ecclesiastical – of the new rites.[54]

---

[51] 'Postea, coronam premissis orationibus debitis per dictum episcopus Pampilonensem prefatum etiam accepit, de qua manibus proprius se coronavit' (Archivo General del Navarra, *Camara de Comptos*, Registro 209, fol. 2v, lin. 16–18, and Id., Registro 210, fol. 2r, lines 29–31). See Cierbide and Ramos, *Documentación medieval*, 284–5, and Osés, *Documentación medieval*, 381.
[52] For the coronation of Charles III in 1390, and that of his wife, Eleanor of Trastámara (who was crowned years later, in 1403), see Castro, *Carlos III*, 203–11.
[53] See Ramírez, *Ceremonial de la coronación, unción y exequias*.
[54] Tamburri, 'Liturgia', 392–3.

The Autonomy of the Kings in Navarra: The Function of the Oath and the Self-Coronation

In Navarra, the dynamic evolution of the rites of accession to the throne from the restoration of the kingdom in 1134 until the self-coronation of Charles III in 1390 expresses in a very graphic way the close connection between the political context of each period (from the establishment of a foreign dynasty to the growth of the native dynasties) and the interests of each one of the agents involved in the struggle for power (the monarchy, the nobles, the citizens and the ecclesiastics). From its origins, the Navarrese monarchy developed from a social pact, the substance of which is explicitly expressed in the body of laws and regulations contained in the *fueros*. Without doubt, the aristocracy, symbolised by the twelve nobles who participated in the ceremonies of access to the throne, represents the kingdom.[55] The presence of the towns is highly significant and materialises in the intense diplomatic activity connected to the swearing in of kings, above all from the beginning of 1231.[56] And finally, the role of the ecclesiastics is extraordinarily laconic when compared with their active (not to say monopolising) participation in the corresponding ceremonies of accession to the throne in other European monarchies.

In this whole story, and in contrast to many other European monarchies, the oath assumes an essential function. The oath sworn by the monarchs in Navarra has the potential to keep awareness alive that the content of what is sworn is not a concession or a revocable privilege, but an essential part of the constitution of the kingdom. In 1134, the election of García Ramírez brought about the establishment of a civil ritual, far from any sacred liturgy and ecclesiastical mediation, with the raising on the pavis.[57] A century later, in 1234, the arrival of a foreign dynasty, with a sovereign 'from a strange place' and 'of a strange language', and with profound feudal convictions, spurred the nobles and bourgeoisie to put into writing what had been generically agreed with the preceding, indigenous monarchs, which led to the establishment of the *fueros*. The new king accepted the new ceremonial of the oath, which he combined with the raising on the pavis in the royal accession ceremony. The acceptance of all this protocol by the first count-king and his successors implied a pact

---

[55] Eloísa Ramírez Vaquero, 'El pacto nobiliario, preludio del diálogo entre el rey el reino', in *Du contrat d'Alliance au contrat politique*, ed. François Foronda and Ana Isabel Carrasco (Toulouse: Le Mirail, 2007), 263–96.

[56] Juan Carrasco Pérez, 'El pacto "constitucional" en la monarquía navarra (1234–1330): El rey y las buenas villas del reino', in *Avant le contrat social*, ed. François Foronda (Paris: Sorbonne, 2011), 507–40.

[57] Pascual Tamburri, 'Liturgia de la realeza bajomedieval', in Martín Duque, *Signos de identidad*, 387–98, here 389.

which some have even labelled 'constitutional', confirmed by the solemn swearing in of the monarchs Joanna II and Philip III of Navarra in 1329.[58]

Finally, the fusion in a single ceremony, on Charles III's accession to power in 1390, of unction and (self-)coronation on one hand, and the raising up and oath on the other, represents the culmination of a long process. With this fusion, two long-term lines of ceremonial development converge and finally combine, in a rather bizarre, if deeply symbolic, manner, full of significance both civil and ecclesiastical, profane and sacred, temporal and spiritual. Charles III's self-coronation is the best metaphor for the singularity of the kingdom of Navarra, while also a confirmation of all the external influences (especially from its counterpart Iberian kingdoms of Castile and Aragon) experienced by a realm materially poor but symbolically rich.

No other European monarchy in the thirteenth century had reached the point where the estates imposed on the crown an oath on the laws and redress of grievances as a prerequisite of royal investiture. In Byzantium, the practice of swearing in of the emperor was introduced very early, but the content of the pledge was essentially religious, related to his promise to preserve the Christian faith, rather than containing anything strictly political. In France, the oath that the monarchs swear in the ceremonies of royal accession serves as an effective weapon for reaffirming their supreme authority, rather than as a counterweight or control on their sovereignty. In Aragon, the king did not swear a solemn oath in the ceremonies of accession to the throne until Alfonso III, in 1286, as a result of the General Privilege of 1283.[59] Castile had inherited the strong pactist tendency of the kingdom of Leon, which had established its Carta Magna, approved by Alfonso IX in 1188. However, Castile opted clearly for the path of monarchical absolutism and those Leonese restrictions on power were not continued by the Castilian kings.[60] In England, by

---

[58] Carrasco, 'El pacto "constitucional"', 539. On the political and constitutional meaning of the oath as a cell of modern constitutions see Percy E. Schramm, *Il simbolismo dello Stato nella storia del medioevo* (Firenze: Olschki, 1966), 265; Marcel David, *La souverainité et les limites juridiques du pouvoir monarchique du IXe au XIe siécle* (Paris: Dalloz, 1954); Eugen Wolhaupter, *La importancia de España en la historia de los derechos fundamentales* (Madrid: Centro de Intercambio Intelectual Germano-Español, 1930).

[59] Tomás Ximenez de Embún, *Ensayo histórico acerca del origen de Aragón y Navarra* (Zaragoza: Imprenta del Hospicio, 1878), 130, argues that the first oath should be that of King Alfonso III. For his part, Palacios Martín, *La práctica del juramento*, 62–3, and Palacios Martín, *La coronación de los reyes de Aragón*, 131–84, describes evidence regarding the asserting rather than the normative condition of the first Aragonese kings' oaths.

[60] Irene A. Arias, 'La Carta Magna leonesa', *Cuadernos de Historia de España* 9 (1948): 147–53; Claudio Sánchez Albornoz, 'Sensibilidad política del pueblo castellano en la Edad Media', *Revista de la Universidad de Buenos Aires* 2 (1948): 86. See also Julio González, *Alfonso IX* (Madrid: Consejo Superior de Investigaciones Científicas, 1944), II: num. 11; Lacarra, *El juramento de los reyes de Navarra*, 27.

contrast, the pactist tradition had been greater. Sectors of the high clergy, the aristocracy and bourgeoisie would make use of the anointment oath and others to mitigate the effects of the monarchical tendency towards absolutism. Henry I (1100–35) introduced the *Coronation Letters*, which are frequently sworn by the monarch and in which, after having been anointed, he pledges in writing to observe certain modes of government. However, the limited efficacy of such measures did not reach the standards of the Navarrese oath in submitting the monarchs to the rule of pacted law.[61]

Resulting from the tradition of the swearing in of kings, *pactism* had deep roots in Navarra, and probably also influenced the kingdom of Aragon in the same direction, above all in its Catalan area.[62] In any case, it is likely that the peculiarity of the Navarrese oath, and the ritual nature of Charles III's gesture of self-coronation, resulted from three factors: first, because of the limited size of the kingdom; second, due to the impossibility for the kingdom to expand territorially, given the enormous energy of the three adjoining monarchies of Castile, Aragon and France; finally, because of the direct influence of very local French counties such as Bayonne and Bearn, which had put these restrictive rules to good effect, in their case with their counts.

These two specific characteristics of Navarra reflected in rituals – lack of ecclesiastical mediation in self-coronation and the tendency towards consensualism through oath – must be borne in mind when it comes to analysing its royal accession ceremonies. The symbolic and legal dimension of the royal oath and the self-coronation in Navarra has deep implications in its political conception, thought and practice, and it influenced the other Iberian kingdoms on their way to the unification by Catholic kings at the end of the fifteenth century. The word and the gesture have a dual effect, legal and ritual. This endows them with enormous force, both in semantic content and in the ritual form that its representations take.[63]

---

[61] Marcel David, 'Le serment du sacre du IXe au XVe siécle', *Revue du Moyen Age Latin* 6 (1950): 5–272, here 269; Palacios Martín, *La práctica del juramento*, 40–1.
[62] For the concept of the 'pactism' of the Iberian monarchies, especially the Catalan-Aragonese, see Jaume Vicens Vives, *Notícia de Catalunya* (Barcelona: Destino, 1960). For Castilian monarchy see Valdeavellano, *Curso de historia de las instituciones españolas*, 422ff.
[63] Martín Duque, 'Imagen originaria de los fueros', *Signos de identidad*, 405–8.

12   Early Modern Dramatisation
The Road to Napoleon

After Charles III of Navarra's and Ferdinand I of Aragon's investitures, the trail of self-coronations in modern Europe becomes hard to follow, or at least it is difficult to trace one single line of evolution.[1] The shifts between re-sacralisation and desacralisation continue from the sixteenth century to the eighteenth. Just as the Christianisation of the pagan world had been essential to the development of self-coronations around the fourth century, the appearance of the modern state shaped the monarchies associated with the new state from the start of the sixteenth century.[2] In any case, the practice of self-coronations and its increasing theatricality is probably explained by the fact that early modern monarchs and their courtesans were aware of the power of ceremonies, as a page at the court of Louis XVI of France acknowledges:

> Ceremonies are the most important support of royal authority. If one takes away the splendour that surrounds him, he will be only an ordinary man in the eyes of the multitude, because the populace respects his sovereignty less for his virtue and rank than for the gold that covers him and the pomp that surrounds him.[3]

Apart from the transgressive coronation of Elizabeth I of England in 1559, the two most characteristic samples of self-coronations in this period are those of Frederick I of Prussia (1701) and Napoleon I of France (1804), coinciding also with two foundational political and

---

[1] I have used some studies on early modern rituals for this chapter: Peter Burke, *Popular Culture in Early Modern Europe* (London: Temple Smith, 1978); Roy Strong, *Splendour at Court: Renaissance Spectacle and Illusion* (London: Weidenfeld and Nicolson, 1973); Edward Muir, *Civic Ritual in Renaissance Venice* (Princeton, NJ: Princeton University Press, 1981); Ralph E. Giesey, The *Royal Funeral Ceremony in Renaissance France* (Geneva: Droz, 1960); Sydney Anglo, *Spectacle, Pageantry and Early Tudor Policy* (Oxford: Clarendon, 2003); David M. Bergeron, *English Civil Pageantry, 1558–1642* (London: Edward Arnold, 1971).

[2] See some useful approaches in Ralph E. Giesey, *Rulership in France, 15th–17th Centuries* (Aldershot: Ashgate, 2004).

[3] By Count Hezecques (Felix de France), *Souvenir d'un page de Louis XVI*, quoted in Sergio Bertelli, *The King's Body* (University Park: Pennsylvania State University Press, 2001), 4.

dynastic periods.⁴ The self-coronation gesture retains its effective power, but takes place within very different political, ideological and liturgical contexts from those of the Middle Ages. For early modern sovereigns, self-coronation became a formal gesture, a simple rhetoric of power, a more dramatised and theatrical one.⁵ Thus, the practice of self-coronation in the early modern period shows once more that the same ritual can take on different meanings as its use changes. Rituals may be repeated without any understanding of their original message, since rites cannot be enclosed in a logical system – the 'total ritual system' anthropologists speak of.⁶ Sergio Bertelli explains the need to take this variation into account through time.

A particular ritual or symbol is never fixed or fossilized; instead, it changes and develops along with the society that expresses but may not entirely comprehend it. Its very obscurity may assure its effectiveness. A single comportment or gesture can assume different meanings depending on the 'culture' using it; but it can also change its message within this culture. We must thus distinguish formal acts, intentions, and stylization from what we could call 'behavioural gesture', and remain attentive to their nature and function.⁷

The traditional anointment performed by medieval kings progressively turned into a secular gesture in early modern Northern Europe. In three decades, Europe witnessed three solemn self-coronations: Christian V of Denmark (1671),⁸ Charles XII of Sweden (1697)⁹ and Frederick I of Prussia (1701).¹⁰ As Christopher Clark argues, Frederick I's coronation

---

[4] On Elizabeth I's coronation and her transgressive gesture during the Mass, see Richard C. McCoy, 'The Wonderful Spectacle: The Civil Progress of Elizabeth I and the Troublesome Coronation', in *Coronations: Medieval and Early Modern Monarchic Ritual*, ed. János M. Bak (Berkeley: University of California Press, 1990), 216–27.

[5] It is important to clarify here that I am not arguing that 'whilst modern rituals are supposedly mere remnants, "empty" pomp and ceremony, medieval ritual is credited with the ability to have created community, consensus, and power', so that we treat medieval actors as superstitious and pre-rational primitives – an essentialist and anachronistic position which Pössel has rightly unmasked (Pössel, 'The Magic of Early Medieval Ritual', 113). Rather, I am referring to the particular evolution of the ritual of self-coronation, which, I contend, is an exception to that rule.

[6] Turner, *Forrest of Symbols*, 43. See also Pierre Bourdieu, *Le sens pratique* (Paris: Minuit, 1980), 27, and Bloch, *Ritual, History*, 41.

[7] Bertelli, *The King's Body*, 2. See also Bertelli and Centanni, *Il gesto nel rito e nel ceremoniale dal mondo antico ad oggi*.

[8] Sebastian Olden-Jorgensen, 'Zeremonielle Innovation: Die erste dänische absolutistische Königsalbung (1671) und die erste Preußische Königskrönung (1701) im Vergleich', in *Die Preußische Rangerhöhung und Königskrönung 1701 in deutscher und europäischer Sicht*, ed. Heide Barmeyer (Frankfurt: M. Lang, 2002), 185–92, here 192.

[9] Hans Liermann, 'Untersuchungen zum Sakralrecht des protestantischen Herrschers', *Zeitschrift der Savigny-Stiftung für Rechtsgeschichte, Kann. Abt.* 30 (1941): 311–83, 359–60.

[10] On Frederick I's self-coronation, see Clark, 'When Culture Meets Power', 15–35; Eduard Heyek, *Friedrich I. und die Begründung des preussischen Königtums* (Bielefed-Leipzig: Velhagen & Klasing, 1901), 40–50; Theodor Schieder, 'Die preussische Königskrönung von 1701 in der politischen Ideengeschichte', *Begegnungen mit der Geschichte* (Göttingen:

was a deliberate amalgam of elements from ancient and medieval Western and Eastern coronations, since 'fragments of diverse "traditions" were assembled, modified and recombined in such a manner as to achieve a highly focused array of effects. ... It was a highly instrumental act, designed and executed by the late seventeenth-century's equivalent of a modern event-management agency.'[11] Thus, the strong liturgical dimension of medieval self-coronations was replaced by 'an artificial thing fabricated by very skilful and cunning artisans'.[12] Frederick I sought both aesthetic impact and a strong political message. Johann Christian Lünig, who witnessed the ceremony and wrote its most authoritative account, explains what a gesture of self-coronation could mean in the context of the late early modern period.

Kings who accept their kingdom and sovereignty from the Estates usually only take up the purple mantle, the crown and sceptre and mount the throne *after* they have been anointed: ... but His Majesty [Frederick I], who has not received His Kingdom through the assistance of the Estates or of any other [party], had no need whatever of such a handing-over, but rather received his crown after the manner of the ancient kings from his own foundation.[13]

What began as a transgressive ritual became a natural ritual because of the increasing sovereignty of early modern European monarchies. Philippe Buc defines Frederick's self-coronation as 'hypocrisy and [a] manipulation' of an invented ritual,[14] while Christopher Clark uses the adjective 'artificial'.[15] Philip Dwyer classifies as 'contradictory' the concepts that supported Napoleon's self-coronation in 1804, marked by ritual and symbolic ambivalence.[16] This process of divorcing the actual ceremonies of early modern self-coronations from their own ritual and symbolic meaning culminated with the self-coronation of William I of Prussia in 1861, in which the king was not even anointed. William took the crown

---

Vandenhoeck und Ruprecht, 1961), 183–209 and 287–94; Susan Richter, 'The Prussian Royal Coronation: A Usurpation of Ceremonial?', in *State, Power, and Violence. III. Usurping Ritual*, ed. Gerald Schwedler and Eleni Tounta (Wiesbaden: Harrassowitz, 2010), 561–73; Heinz Duchhardt, 'Die preussische Königskrönung von 1701. Ein europäisches Modell?', in *Herrscherweihe und Krönigskrönung im frühneuzeitlichen Europa*, ed. Heinz Duchhardt (Wiesbaden: Steiner, 1983), 82–95. For the general context of this self-coronation, see Christopher Clark, *Iron Kingdom* (London: Penguin, 2007), 67–77.

[11] Clark, 'When Culture Meets Power', 20–1.
[12] Ernst Cassirer, *The Myth of State* (New Haven, CT: Yale University Press, 2013), 281–2.
[13] Johann Christian Lünig, quoted in Clark, *Iron Kingdom*, 69. The quote is almost contemporary to the facts: Johann Christian Lünig, *Theatrum ceremoniale historico-politicum oder historisch und politischer Schau-Platz aller Ceremonien*. 2 vols. (Leipzig, 1719–20), 2:96.
[14] Buc, '1701 in Medieval Perspective', 123.
[15] Clark, 'When Culture Meets Power', 20.
[16] Philip Dwyer, 'Citizen Emperor: Political Ritual, Popular Sovereignty and the Coronation of Napoleon I', *History: The Journal of Historical Association* (2015): 40–57, here 40.

with his own hands from the altar and crowned himself, saying that he was receiving the crown from God's hands. These gestures and words carried not only symbolic meanings but also very realistic ones, since they were intended as a warning to Prussian Liberals and Constitutionalists.[17] Frederick's self-coronation in 1701 confirms Buc's intuition when he compares medieval with early modern ceremonies of royal accession.

To simplify, the understanding of ceremonies shifted from a hermeneutic-exegetical approach to a proto-sociological one. One passed also from a thought-world in which the political instrumentalization of ritual, while practiced and often feared, was considered a transgression, to one in which the essence of ritual was considered to be political.[18]

'Political' is exactly the meaning of Napoleon's self-coronation in 1804, which in addition serves as a kind of epilogue to the story of self-coronations I examine in this book.[19] Everything in Napoleon's ceremony carried an air of disenchantment, to use an expression by Max Weber, suggesting that this self-coronation marks a pivotal point in the symbolic meaning of these rituals, analogous to the turn from paganism into Christianity around the fourth century. Napoleon's self-coronation even lost Peter de Ceremonious' romantic improvisation, as everything appears to have been planned ahead of time between Napoleon and Pope Pius VII.[20]

After Napoleon's investiture, the ritual of self-coronation was practised by other sovereigns in the nineteenth and twentieth centuries in Europe, Russia, Africa and Asia.[21] It has been usually performed by absolute sovereigns or dictators who have erased any possible tension between the spiritual and the temporal in favour of the latter, so that these ceremonies have lost part of their symbolic meaning. One typical example of this dysfunctional use

---

[17] Clark, *Iron Kingdom*, 75–6, and David E. Barclay, *Fredrick William IV and the Prussian Monarchy, 1840–1861* (Oxford: Oxford Scholarship, 1995), 73–4 and 287–8.

[18] Buc, '1701 in Medieval Perspective', 105.

[19] For discussions of Napoleon's self-coronation and its political dimension see Frédéric Masson, *Le sacre et le couronnement de Napoléon* (Paris: Société d'éditions littéraires et artistiques, 1908); José Cabanis, *Le sacre de Napoléon* (Paris: Gallimard, 1970); Schnapper and Sérullaz, 'Le Couronnement de l'Empereur'; Jean-Marie Ticchi, *Le voyage de Pie VII a Paris pour le sacre de Napoléon* (Paris: Honoré Champion, 2013); Martin Kirsch, 'Wie der konstitutionelle Monarch zum europäischen Phänomen wurde', in *Die Macht des Königs. Herrschaft in Europa vom Frühmittelatlter bis in die Neuzeit*, ed. Bernhard Jussen (Munich: C. H. Beck, 2005), 350–65.

[20] Brühl, 'Auto-couronnements d'empereurs et de rois', 103, note 9.

[21] The self-coronations performed by three eighteenth- and nineteenth-century tsars deserve a specific analysis. Since Byzantine emperors did not practise the gesture of ritual self-coronation at all, as we have seen in Chapter 3, the gesture performed by tsars Elizabeth Petrovna (1742), Nicholas I (1826) and Alexander III (1883) was probably imported from Persia, where the custom of the kings being self-crowned was practised from antiquity. See Richard S. Wortman, *Scenarios of Power: Myth and Ceremony in Russian Monarchy* (Princeton, NJ: Princeton University Press, 1995).

of the self-coronation was that famously enacted by Jean-Bédel Bokassa (1921–96), known as Bokassa I of Central Africa. He organised a pompous coronation ceremony on 4 December 1977, emulating his hero Napoleon by putting the crown on his own head and posing with all the regalia, taking on the title of 'Emperor of Central Africa by the will of the Central African people'.[22]

Figure 32 Coronation of Jean-Bédel Bokassa as emperor of the Central African Empire. Bangui, 4 December 1977. © Keystone Press / Alamy Stock Photo.

[22] On the actual ceremony of Bokassa's self-coronation see Olivier Thomas, 'Les dessous de sacre de Bokassa Ier', *l'Histoire* 382 (December 2012): 34. See also Brian Titley, *Dark Age: The Political Odyssey of Emperor Bokassa* (Montreal: McGill-Queen's University Press, 1997).

Comparative anthropology has also given us other examples that could heighten interest in the gesture of self-coronation itself beyond European frontiers.[23] Of course, the tradition of self-coronation was preserved in Persia, reaching modern Islamic Iran, including the self-coronation by Shah Reza Pahlavi in 1926 and his son Mohammad Reza Pahlavi in 1967, as mentioned at the end of Chapter 2 (see Figure 8). Yet we find examples in Africa as well. Shivaji (1630–80), the first leader and founder of the Maratha polity, crowned himself in 1674.[24] The Zulu king Eshubity, chief for Ibadan and a leader among the north-east Yoruba, crowned himself, took the kingship title *Átá* of Ayede in the 1840s, and initiated a new dynasty.[25] Kalakaua of Hawaii crowned himself in 1883, since no one was considered sacred enough to crown an *ali'i*.[26] Finally, an estimated 15,000 people, mainly expatriate South Pacific Tongans, attended their king Tupou VI's coronation in 2015. For Tongans, it is taboo to touch a king's head, so only the king may put the crown on his own head.[27] To my knowledge, this is the last self-coronation performed.

---

[23] Sahlins, *Islands of History*, 84–7 (on Fiji); Marshall Sahlins, *Moala* (Ann Arbor: University of Michigan Press, 1962), 386–8 (on Moala); Valerio Valeri, *Kingship and Sacrifice: Ritual and Society in Ancient Hawaii* (Chicago: University of Chicago Press, 1993) (on Hawaii).

[24] Shri V. S. Bendrey, *The Coronation of Shivaji the Great* (Bombay: Bookstall, 1960); Stewart Gordon, *The New Cambridge History of India. II.4. The Marathas, 1600–1818* (Cambridge: Cambridge University Press, 1993), 87–90; Stephen Frederic Dale, *The Muslim Empires of the Ottomans, Safavids, and Mughals* (Cambridge: Cambridge University Press, 2010), 262.

[25] Andrew Apter, *Black Critics and Kings: The Hermeneutics of Power in Yoruba Society* (Chicago: University of Chicago Press, 1992), 50–1; on the symbolic meaning of these ceremonies see Apter, 'The Embodiment of Paradox', 212–29.

[26] 'Hawaii: A King's Coronation', *Hawaiian Gazette*, 21 February 1883, Supplement.

[27] See a survey of the ceremony at www.yahoo.com/news/tongan-king-crowned-traditional-ceremony-023458829.html (accessed 29 September 2017).

Conclusion

> For all rituals, no matter how venerable the ancestry claimed for them, have to be invented at some point, and over the historical span in which they remain in existence they are susceptible to a change in their meaning.
>
> Paul Connerton, *How Societies Remember*[1]

This book has traced the long-term historical development of the ritual of self-coronation, its political and religious implications and its symbolic meanings. It foregrounds the function of a medieval ritual in the Middle Ages, through an analysis that engages with continuity and change in history, viewing this ritual as imagined or performed, as transgressive or conventional. In this final section, I expose conclusive remarks from the political, social and ritual perspectives, and I finish with a brief note with projections onto the present.

From a political point of view, self-coronations are proofs of the activation of individual agency rather than the stability of established structures in the Middle Ages. Scholars have argued that invariance is usually corporate since the routine and repetition of actions subordinate the individual to a sense of the encompassing and enduring.[2] Yet it is my belief that rituals often can redefine custom itself. The practice of self-coronations shows the dynamic power of rituals to change society as it privileges the king's agency. This ritual demystifies certain anthropological tendencies to constrain the rites to the boundaries of their particular context or to fix them in an essentialist symbolic meaning. Such ceremonies cannot be understood if we push them to the contextualist or essentialist poles. They are more than 'an epitome of the wider and spontaneous social process in which they are embodied', as Turner states.[3] Self-coronations are only transgressive when performed for the first time in a kingdom, as they have to overcome rituals' natural tendency

---

[1] Connerton, *How Societies Remember*, 51.
[2] Terrence Deal and Allan Kennedy, *Corporate Cultures: The Rites and Ceremonials of Corporate Life* (Reading: Addison-Wesley, 1982).
[3] Turner, *Drums of Affliction*, 273.

to be invariable, so that they can 'accommodate both the idea of stability and the reality of change'.[4] Yet they are transgressive not because they are an unconventional gesture in themselves, but their transgressivity arises from the amount of change that the establishment of a new ritual (or a variation of a ritual) naturally implies, as the coronation by the priest became a transgressive ritual when it was first enacted. The 'amount' of transgressivity does not depend on the ritual itself, but on the context in which it is performed, and on the ability of the king to impose his agency in a given moment so as to change a ritual or tradition.

The ritual of self-coronation is thus better understood not as a singular and *extraordinary* ritual, but as part of a whole array of possibilities deployed at certain times and in certain places in medieval Europe (mostly the Mediterranean and Scandinavian worlds) out of political need and within specific contexts. For instance, self-crowned kings' ritual behaviour functions complementarily to that of the rulers who voluntarily claimed to reject or renounce power, or who tried to avoid the ceremonies of installation (*rex renitens*).[5] These reluctant kings convey 'a posture of renunciation of power [which] contains within it an implicit claim to its exercise'[6] – what anthropologists have labelled 'the return of ritual after this denial or rejection'.[7] In Weiler's formula, 'reluctant kingship was most common when the choice of a new ruler posed considerable political problems.'[8] This ritual was then used as a mark of truly deserving royal dignity – reinforced with the subsequent and interested narration of their alleged unwillingness.[9] While the self-crowned Iberian kings felt properly legitimised in their office, usually received through inheritance, the reluctant kings and rulers 'came to the throne in fraught or disputed circumstances. None had assumed the crown in a direct dynastic line from their predecessors, and all had to overcome considerable political difficulties in asserting their authority'.[10] The reluctance of kingship – and its correlative unwillingness to accept the trappings of office, the insignia or any ceremonial of kingship – and the practice of self-coronation differ in their strategies, but they ultimately share the same goal: to strength sovereignty. The comparison of these

[4] Koziol, *Begging Pardon and Favor*, 296. Interestingly, this quote comes from another medievalist whose work is based on a large inductive study on rituals enacted in the Middle Ages rather than on general theories associated with an essentialist vision of the rituals.
[5] Weiler, '*Rex Renitens* and the Medieval Idea of Kingship', 1–42.
[6] Maclean, 'Ritual, Misunderstanding, and the Contest for Meaning', 98.
[7] Hüsken and Seamone, 'The Denial of Ritual and Its Return', 3.
[8] Weiler, '*Rex Renitens* and the Medieval Idea of Kingship', 42.
[9] Weiler actually emphasises that these narrations should not be read simply as 'propaganda' but have to be 'described in terms which [leave] no doubt as to their inherent moral quality and necessity' (Weiler, '*Rex Renitens* and the Medieval Idea of Kingship', 12).
[10] Weiler, '*Rex Renitens* and the Medieval Idea of Kingship', 11.

two (wrongly considered) unorthodox ways of accessing the throne helps explain that the practice of self-coronation conveys exactly the opposite of what it appears to be. It is a reaffirmation of the office by kings whose legitimation has already been conventionally established rather than an extraordinary instrument for kings who were impostors or usurpers.

Other comparative examples exist in medieval Europe of these various political strategies, as promoted by self-coronations. Haki Antonsson analyses the royal saints and royal sacrality in Scandinavia, highlighting the fact that fragments of the *Life of Saint Magnus*, composed in the latter half of the twelfth century, is the first work of prose which deals with any aspect of Orcadian history: 'We encounter a secular ruler placing his authority and resources behind a cult of a murdered or killed relative', so that 'by personally associating their authority with a saintly relative these rulers strengthened their own claim to power.'[11] One then wonders if it is possible to find a clearer sign of sacralisation of a 'national' history. The consequence of these cultural practices and religious beliefs is that, by the end of the thirteenth century, Scandinavian kingdoms had a native heavenly patron who was neither a bishop nor an abbot but a sanctified ruler. But these heavenly intercessors promoted close cooperation, rather than opposition, between secular rulers and men of the church. These relationships were, again, seen as complementary rather than exclusionary.[12]

These comparative examples help us to understand that medieval self-coronations, as other medieval kingship rituals, were created not on the margins – what Turner has described as liminality, 'the seedbeds of cultural creativity' – but in the *centre* of a society.[13] The sacred centre authorises a kind of social and political mapping and gives the members of a society their sense of place.[14] It is the heart of things, the place where culture, society and politics come together, occupied by institutions such as the church or the monarchy and by figures such as the bishop or the king.[15] We could argue that it is easy for the sovereign to create a new ritual because of his authority, but we know how hard it is to change a social, legal, political or ritual tradition. This is particularly valid in medieval Europe, where 'every deliberate modification of an existing

---

[11] Antonsson, *St. Magnús of Orkney*, 1–2. See also, for a parallel secular-spiritual transposition in late antiquity, Philippe Buc, 'Martyre et ritualité dans l'Antiquité tardive. Horizons de l'écriture médiévale des rituels', *Annales. Histoire, Sciences Sociales* 48(1) (1997): 63–92.

[12] For royal sanctity in Central Europe, see Klaniczay, *Holy Rulers and Blessed Princesses*, 1–18.

[13] Turner, 'Liminal to Liminoid', 60.   [14] Geertz, 'Centers, Kings, and Charisma'.

[15] Michael Young, 'The Meaning of Coronation', in *Center and Periphery: Essays in Macrosociology*, ed. Edward Shils (Chicago: University of Chicago Press, 1975), 135–52, here 151.

type of activity must be based on a study of individual precedents. Every plan for the future is dependent on a pattern which has been found in the past.'[16] Rituals were thus more structured, more formal, more mandatory than in current societies, so that they were more difficult to transform or manipulate.[17] Medieval kings took advantage of the liminal dimension of the rituals to perform a supposed 'exception', really an adaptation of the rite to a new context. This would explain why self-coronations have full symbolic sense when performed in traditional societies, but they lose it when enacted in modern societies, in which they tend towards over-dramatisation and spectacle, having lost their original symbolic meaning. This would fit with the idea of some anthropologists who have criticised those who fail to differentiate 'between symbolic systems and genres which have developed before and after the Industrial Revolution',[18] and with my belief that early modern self-coronations must be analysed from a very different approach than those enacted until the fifteenth century.

* * *

Seen from a social perspective, medieval self-coronations pushed for collective innovation and dynamism. These rituals were in a perpetual state of flux, confirming anthropologists' belief that ritual symbols are not static, absolute objectifications, but 'social and cultural systems, shedding and gathering meaning over time and altering in form'.[19] Yet the dynamism of medieval self-coronations had a price, since all aspiration to social change has to be based, at one moment or another, on a transgressive act that implies a break with tradition. Frederick II of Germany, Alfonso XI of Castile, Peter IV of Aragon and Charles III of Navarra promoted a variation of rites in order to achieve specific social and political transformations, and changes in attitude among the participants and in their kingdoms: they shifted between an adaptation to their context – necessary

---

[16] See Joseph Strayer, ed., *The Interpretation of History* (Princeton, NJ: Princeton University Press, 1943), 10.
[17] Ronald L. Grimes, *Beginnings in Ritual Studies* (Waterloo: Ritual Studies International, 2013), 150.
[18] Turner, 'Liminal to Liminoid', 62. This is a classic argument, which further develops Johan Huizinga's treatment of religion as 'play' and approaches to religious ritual as 'lay', and it would explain why today arts and sports create myths and rituals. See Huizinga, *Homo Ludens*; Althoff, 'Demonstration und Inszenierung', 27–50; David L. Miller, *Gods and Games: Toward a Theology of Play* (New York: World, 1970); Lonnie D. Kliever, 'Fictive Religion: Rhetoric and Play', *Journal of the American Academy of Religion* 49 (1981): 657–69; Robert E. Neale, *In Praise of Play: Toward a Psychology of Religion* (New York: Harper and Row, 1969).
[19] Turner, 'Liminal to Liminoid', 54. For the idea of the 'flow' of the ritual see Victor Turner, 'Process, System, and Symbol: A New Anthropological System', *Daedalus* 106 (1977): 61–80.

to maintain social impact in the present – and their ability to recreate and innovate to signal towards a different future.

As scholars on medieval rituals have recognised, 'the evolution of ritual was occasionally interrupted by bursts of creativity, such as that associated with the Carolingians, and even in the absence of innovation an old rite could be invested with a new meaning.'[20] In self-coronations, the change enacted is conceived as a *reform* of tradition, rather than a radical transformation:

> Authors of change in religious ritual sometimes claim ... that they are not inventing liturgy but merely reforming it, or they escape contradiction by claiming that they are merely divesting the ritual of the inconsequential, profane or evil accretions of time and error, returning to it the purity that prevailed in more righteous days.[21]

On one hand, self-coronation shares with all rituals its ability to consolidate tradition and to base its efficacy on repetition: 'One of the most common characteristics of ritual-like behaviour is the quality of invariance, usually seen in a disciplined set of actions marked by precise repetition and physical control.'[22] Yet, on the other, this ritual follows a crooked line, highlighting its malleability rather than rigidity or formalism. Thus, the practice of self-coronation implies a moral dilemma. Rituals are generally associated with the concepts of formalism, traditionalism, permanence, stability and invariance. Thus, any attempt to transform them may be seen as a destabilised operation that could damage social cohesion and lead to instability. Scholars have stressed the direct connection between ritual change, personal neurosis and social instability:

> Psychologists have treated private ritual as synonymous with neurosis. Theologians have regarded self-generated rites as lacking in moral character because they minimize social responsibility. And anthropologists have thought of ritual as traditional, collective representation, implying that the notion of individual or invented ritual was a contradiction in terms.[23]

---

[20] Warner, 'Thietmar of Merseburg on Rituals of Kingship', 73–4; Nelson, 'Ritual and Reality in the Early Medieval Ordines'; Nelson, 'Kingship and Empire', especially 213–18, which emphasises the creativity of the Carolingian clergy in matters of ritual.
[21] Rappaport, *Ritual and Religion*, 33.
[22] Bell, *Ritual: Perspectives and Dimensions*, 150.
[23] Ronald L. Grimes, *Ritual Criticism* (Columbia: University of South Carolina Press, 1990), 109. See also Ronald L. Grimes, 'Reinventing Rites', *Soundings* 75 (1992): 21–41. Other specialists on ritual, especially those coming from symbolic anthropology, have reflected on the moral and ethical consequences of the ritual change: Turner, 'Ritual, Tribal and Catholic', 504–26; Mary Douglas, 'The Contempt of Ritual', *New Blackfriars* 49 (1968): 475–82 and 528–35; Douglas, *Natural Symbols*, 59–76; David Martin, *The*

Certainly, ritual is based on tradition since that tradition is reinforced with the practice of the rituals, and vice versa. When it is performed in a sacred context – such as sacred liturgy or royal coronations – there is more reluctance to propose ceremonial variations. Medieval kings noted this tension as they had to deal with the consequences of their decisions to perform self-coronations. This was particularly remarkable in the discussion between Peter the Ceremonious and the bishop of Zaragoza at the threshold of the king's coronation. For this reason, self-coronation may be conceived by its promoters and perceived by the actors and their attendants as a disruptive practice. Nevertheless, this tendency to 'ritual invention', to borrow Bell's phrase, paradoxically provided the kings who performed self-coronations with that symbolic and unquantifiable amount of *auctoritas* known as *charisma*.[24] Thus, the subversion of an established order entails a devaluation of the former legitimising symbols and promotes the creation of new ones.[25]

This leads to the concept of the sacred. This is one of the key elements of this book, but, I admit, an elusive one.[26] My point, after having analysed in detail the ritual of self-coronation, is that we have to avoid essentialist definitions of the sacred. Rather, we need to actualise them in the particular characters and context of the enacted ritual.

Self-coronations emerged in medieval Europe at a moment when many traditions were changing, the frontiers of the sacred and secular among them. Koziol has demonstrated that the process of desacralisation was the result not only of changes in the relationship between church and state, but of the way that certain monarchies perceived their own right to rule. For instance, he draws a sharp distinction between the essentially desacralised, 'knightly' ethos of Plantagenet kingship – founded upon conquest, seeking bureaucratic safeguards against its inherent instability and bolstered by myths that traced the king's ancestry to such chivalric

---

Breaking of the Image (New York: St. Martin's Press, 1979); Catherine Bell, 'Ritual, Change, and Changing Rituals', *Worship* 63 (January 1989): 31–41.

[24] Catherine Bell gives interesting examples of 'ritual inventions' in modern times in Bell, *Ritual: Perspectives and Dimensions*, 223–42. The idea has been developed by anthropologists (Geertz, 'Centers, Kings, and Charisma') and by sociologists, based on the classical works of Max Weber: Max Weber, *Max Weber on Charisma and Institution Building: Selected Papers*, ed. S. N. Einsenstadt (Chicago: University of Chicago Press, 1968), 39–54.

[25] David Cannadine, 'The Context, Performance and Meaning of Ritual: The British Monarchy and the Invention of Tradition, c. 1820–1977', in *The Invention of Tradition*, ed. Eric Hobsbawm and Terence O. Ranger (Cambridge: Cambridge University Press, 2012), 101–64, and Eric Hobsbawm, 'Mass Producing Traditions: Europe, 1870–1914', in *The Invention of Tradition*, 263–307.

[26] On the difficulties of the concept of 'sacrality' and other related notions, see Nelson, 'Royal Saints and Early Medieval Kingship'.

archetypes as King Arthur – and the sacral, mimetic and largely unmilitary ethos of the Capetian kings of France. He concludes that 'something in the Anglo-Norman experience of politics tended to desacralise political authority, rendering it fit for parody and resistance, while in France something made it possible to adapt the old typologies that held political authority sacred.'[27]

What was sacred and secular in the Middle Ages, and its limits and interactions, greatly depended on the particular circumstances and the context in which a specific event happened or a ceremony was enacted. For instance, coronations greatly depended on the continuity or discontinuity of the location of the ceremony of the investiture. Reims and Westminster are places associated with the political and sacred authority necessary to be considered the conventional sites where coronations are performed. Yet, once more, French and English models should not be expanded as a general practice in medieval Europe. Iberian realms provide a good counterargument, since locations for coronations varied widely. The two extremes of the poles were the French and Castilian crowns. While the Cathedral of Reims survived as the official place where the kings were crowned from medieval times to modernity, Castilian kings received their crown in different places.[28] The different degree of flexibility in the place where these ceremonies were enacted also reflects rigid obedience to the rituals in the French tradition and their variety in medieval Castile. This helps explain why in Castile and the other kingdoms of Iberia the ceremonies of self-coronations were considered, in the end, as conventional, while in other kingdoms such as England and France they were always met with disapproval and never became part of formal ceremonials.[29]

Seen from a conceptual rather than a spatial perspective, Anglo-Saxon, Ottonian and Salian iconographies and rituals can be related to the sacred and secular tendencies at the same time. Dale rightly states that the discernment of this concept has been damaged by 'a teleology that sees the development of the secular modern state as inevitable'.[30] Scholarship has only recently challenged the paradigm of 'the universal explanatory power of the demise of sacral kingship as a catch-all reason for change, at

[27] Koziol, 'England, France and the Problem of Sacrality', 144. See also Vincent, 'The Pilgrimages of the Angevin Kings of England', 12–45.
[28] Jacques Le Goff, 'Ville du sacre', in *Les Lieux de Mémoire. II. La Nation*, ed. Pierre Nora (Paris: Gallimard, 1986), 89–184.
[29] On the dynamics of 'change' and 'continuity' in English coronations see David J. Sturdy, 'Continuity versus Change: Historians and English Coronations of the Medieval and Early Modern Periods', in *Coronations: Medieval and Early Modern Monarchic Ritual*, ed. János M. Bak (Berkeley: University of California Press, 1990), 228–45.
[30] Dale, 'Conceptions of Kingship in High-Medieval Germany', 1.

the expense of complex political, social and economic factors'.[31] New scholarship has noted the alternative vision and the *demystification* of the supposed 'process of secularisation', usually medievalists working on a number of great series of ritual rather than on singular examples.[32] An old great narrative tells of the Anglo-Saxon and Ottonian sacred kingship, which at some point is 'secularised' through the submission of Henry IV in front of Pope Gregory VII in Canossa (1077) and the legalising programme of the Staufen, in which the German king is argued to be a layman not easily submitted to ecclesiastics. But these great narratives should be read within a more nuanced and contextualised analysis of the crooked line which may be traced in a more non-teleological vision of sacred and secularised artistic and cultural manifestations of kingship.

In this nuanced perspective, the practice of self-coronations helps explain why there was a 'dialect of complementation' between liturgy and law, between ritual practice and legal codification in the Middle Ages, as Nelson has claimed: 'Liturgy as a form of political communication ... coexisted with law rather than competing with it.'[33] This approach allows historians to understand the proliferation of legalism and the political use of liturgy as complements to sacral kingship, rather than alternatives to it.[34] Sacrality and politics, the sacred and the profane, continually interact. In long-duration research like I propose in this book, modern conceptions of 'sacral kingship', 'desacralisation' or the 'process of secularisation' are challenged since they must be complemented and enriched by other important factors such as ecclesiastical mediation – one of the central issues in the ritual of self-coronation – and the king's agency itself.

---

[31] Dale, 'Conceptions of Kingship in High-Medieval Germany', 1. Dale gives a typical example of this Weberian paradigm in Sefan Weinfurter, *Canossa: Die Entzauberung der Welt* (Munich: C. H. Beck, 2006) and Ernst Kantorowicz's traditional version, in which 'the sacral and "Christ-centered" kingship of the Ottonians, devaluated in the long and bitter struggles of the late eleventh and early twelfth centuries, had been replaced by a more secular, "law-centered", conception imperial rule' (Dale, 'Conceptions of Kingship in High-Medieval Germany', 5).

[32] The names of Franz-Reiner Erkens and Ludger Körntgen should for instance join the others quoted in this book such as Koziol, Buc, Dale or Weiler, among others. Erkens considers sacral kingship to be a worldwide phenomenon evident across many eras which requires an anthropological-interpretive and historical-analytic approach at the same time: see Franz-Reiner Erkens, *Herrschersakralität in Mittelalter. Von den Anfängen bis zum Investiturstreit* (Stuttgart: Kohlhammer, 2006). Körntgen tries to contextualise the iconographic and eventual evidence of sacral kingship and desacralisation, so that complex political, social and economic factors are considered, despite the explanatory power of the great narrative of secularisation: see Körntgen, *Königsherrschaft*.

[33] Janet L. Nelson, 'Liturgy or Law: Misconceived Alternatives?', in *Early Medieval Studies in Memory of Patrick Wormald*, ed. Stephen Baxter, Catherine Karkov, Janet L. Nelson and David Pelteret (Aldershot: Ashgate, 2009), 433–50, here 441.

[34] Dale, 'Conceptions of Kingship in High-Medieval Germany', 6.

These alternatives to the traditional progressive narrative of secularisation and desacralisation are key for my line of argumentation that the ritual of self-coronation is not an un-sacral ritual per se, as it is seen through modern eyes. Even with all its inescapable political and secular meaning emerging from its rejection of ecclesiastical mediation, self-coronation is always performed in a sacred and liturgical context. Its deepest function was spiritual rather than social and political: 'The liturgy, and any para-liturgies, aimed first and foremost at establishing a connection between this world and the heavens, not at integrating society.'[35] Yet what really singularised such rituals is that they promoted a paradoxical tension between the binary models essential to medieval European societies, the spiritual and the temporal, the bishop and the king.

This contextualised approach to the seminal concept of the 'sacred' and the 'secular' requires us to revise a vision of the past altered by the lens of modern nation states and modern rationalism. In the case of self-coronations, it discredits any possible artificial conception of the different rhythms of desacralisation and secularisation of 'national' monarchies. In this great narrative, German kingship would have been desacralised during the twelfth-century struggle for the investitures, as the English did in the sixteenth-century Reformation and the French did in the eighteenth-century Enlightenment. In this teleological and national story, Spain becomes, along with Russia, that 'historical anomaly' in which historical reasons lead them to maintain the medieval practices of sacralisation and clericalism while rejecting modern disenchantment, industrialisation, bureaucratisation and secularisation. Thus, the notion that 'Spain is different' does not correspond to the reality of the historical facts, at least as far as the whole issue of self-coronations is concerned. The parallels between Iberian and other European kingdoms clearly emerge in Navarra, where Theobald's attempts to secure the privilege of unction echo what happened in Norway in 1160, where an underage king accepted coronation in order to assert his claim, and in England, where the Pope tried to prevent the kings of Scotland from being granted the right to receive unction.

* * *

Another key aspect of medieval self-coronations is their ability to resist the formalisation of the ritual. By 'ritual formalism' I understand the state reached when the symbols connected with the rituals become empty of content. They lead to a certain decontextualisation: meanings of rituals

---

[35] Buc, '1701 in Medieval Perspective', 123.

Conclusion 311

which were created in a particular context are still enacted by inertia, but they have lost their originality and coherence. This connects to the idea of the 'failure of the ritual', as some symbolic anthropologists note.[36] These formalised ceremonies become 'empty rituals', so that 'either formalism or a paucity of ritual, when extreme, may leave members of an organisation in a condition which Durkheim has called *anomie*, unrelatedness to others and pointlessness of existence.'[37] In this context, a self-coronation would have had to be interpreted as a malfunction of a ritual system rather than a creative intervention. Yet to me, the 'failure' of self-coronations as a ritual should not be located in the medieval but in the early modern period, when the dramatisation of this ritual developed. Self-coronation, especially after early Christianisation, fits better with those late medieval societies in which the ritual of royal investiture is seen as a natural consequence of German and Iberian kings' clarification of the autonomy of the temporal and the spiritual spheres.

I therefore posit that, in medieval Christian kingdoms, the meaning of the self-coronation ceremony emerges not from the fact that it implies greater autonomy for the king as regards the bishop, but rather as a step forward in the differentiation between the spiritual and temporal spheres. Significantly, this distinction was chosen as the central idea of the introduction to the ceremonial commissioned by King Peter of Aragon. This idea strengthens my belief that Frederick II Hohenstaufen, Alfonso XI of Castile, Peter IV of Aragon, Charles III of Navarra and Frederick I of Prussia did not enact spontaneous gestures but strategic, premeditated and calculated secularised rites in order to gain self-sufficiency in their sovereignty and autonomy from the ecclesiastics. These kings acted according to the ideas spread by medieval ritual scholars such as Althoff, Koziol, Buc, Weiler and Pössel, among others, who argue that they 'took the risk, and accepted the cost of disrupting ritualized acts, but they tended to do this not spontaneously but in a carefully planned way, and not alone but in significant numbers, thus increasing their chances and minimizing the risk and cost'.[38]

This strategy could be referred to not only from the *orectic* point of view – the ability to move to action – but also as a model of 'creating the truth', defined by Michel Foucault as *alethurgie*.[39] Thus, this book challenges previous theories which consider the actual ceremony of the bishop

---

[36] Edward L. Schieffelin, 'Introduction', in *When Rituals Go Wrong. Mistakes, Failures, and the Dynamics of Ritual*, ed. Ute Hüsken (Leiden: Brill, 2007), 1–20.
[37] Orrin E. Klapp, *Ritual and Cult: A Sociological Interpretation* (Washington, DC: Annals of American Sociology, 1956), 32.
[38] Pössel, 'The Magic of Early Medieval Ritual', 123.
[39] Foucault, *On the Government of the Living*, 1–21.

crowning the king as the more 'conventional' form of royal investiture: Can we keep the label imposed on self-coronations as allegedly transgressive rituals? Were medieval self-coronations an anomaly? Were they unconventional? Were they subversive? How were they perceived by the participants in the ritual?

In most European kingdoms where unction and crowning were practised, crowning oneself or adopting the paraphernalia of kingship without undergoing these ceremonies was certainly the hallmark of an illegitimate usurper. This reflected well-established ideas about kingship being a gift granted by God as a recognition of the moral character and natural authority of the king and the consequent convenience for ecclesiastical mediation. This posed particular problems when new kingships were created or new kings arose after a dynastic change. Then, chroniclers took all kinds of steps to ensure that a king was portrayed as singled out by the divine, rather than as usurping a power only God could grant. Chroniclers found different ways to make these ideas explicit: visions and revelations feature prominently in Hungary, Norway, Sicily and Jerusalem, as do gifts of crowns in Armenia and Poland. Yet, while self-crowning outside Iberia was a source of invective and disapproval, Iberian self-coronations were taken for granted not only by the kingdom's subjects, but also by other kingdoms. The Iberian kingdoms thus emerge at the centre rather than on the European periphery of this ritual.

In recent years, the anthropology of ritual has linked the formal and conventional character of ritualised behaviour to informal, spontaneous and pragmatic activity, as Saba Mahmood has shown for modern rituals.[40] In this book I have described royal rituals in which unconventional ceremonies have broken with tradition and prescribed social and political behaviour, so that they become conventional as they are enacted and re-enacted. These kings were aware that their rituals with the crown could damage tradition. Attendees' emotional responses to this rupture took different forms – from scandal among European rulers and ecclesiastics in Frederick's liturgy with the crown in Jerusalem, to great surprise at Peter's self-crowning, to normality among the attendees of the self-coronation ceremonies of Peter's successors. Even the most apparent sensational reactions of the attendees may respond to unwritten rules of political behaviour. As Althoff argues, public displays of emotions recorded by the chroniclers of these ceremonies 'may represent the playing out of performances agreed through advance negotiations, and not, as had often been argued, of the unrestrainedly

---

[40] Saba Mahmood, 'Rehearsed Spontaneity and the Conventionality of Ritual: Disciplines of *Salat*', *American Ethnologist* 28 (2001): 827–53.

emotional nature of medieval men'.[41] Yet the crucial issue is the extent to which these allegedly transgressive ceremonial gestures, full of intent and agency, achieved their political objectives. The fact is that – with the exception of Frederick II's ritual with the crown, where the Carolingian, Anglo-Saxon and Ottonian ceremonial traditions might weigh very heavily – they actually rendered conventional what was previously considered unconventional: self-coronations were considered a real possibility, at least from the mid-fourteenth century in Iberia.

Stanley Tambiah describes the tension between the conventionality and unconventionality of the ritual, which would historically have moved between 'intentional behaviour' and 'conventional behaviour' by seeking out which of the two poles the ritual is nearest.[42] Following these categories, self-coronation ritual practice is clearly located at the 'intentional' pole. Althoff connects this to medieval ritual:

> The actors on medieval political stages did not carry out established rituals in a servile way but rather used the given rituals in a utilitarian-rational way. They varied, mixed, or updated them in keeping with the given situation or event [and] invented new rituals if there was no suitable pre-existing ritual language at their disposal.[43]

My analysis of medieval self-coronations demonstrates the compatibility of Tambiah's conventional versus intentional dichotomy with Althoff's historical conviction that political ceremonies in the Middle Ages did not necessarily carry out established rituals. Medieval self-coronations may appear to be unconventional rites, but the same could actually be said of most medieval rites. Bishops certainly crowned kings in France, England and Germany. But many other forms of royal inauguration rituals (in these and other areas of medieval Europe) also occurred, such as those carried out by participants who decided to avoid such ceremonies ('the denial of ritual'),[44] the large group labelled *rex renitens*[45] and the different forms of installation without ecclesiastical mediation analysed in this book, among others.

We should ask those who regard some rituals as conventional and others as unconventional where we should locate the boundaries between conventionality and unconventionality. It is easy to unmask anachronisms and

---

[41] Simon MacLean and Björn Weiler, 'Introduction', in *Representations of Power in Medieval Germany, 800–1500*, ed. Simon MacLean and Björn Weiler (Turnhout: Brepols, 2006), 5. Maclean and Weiler refer to Althoff, *Spielregeln*.
[42] Stanley Tambiah, *Culture, Thought and Social Action* (Cambridge, MA: Harvard University Press, 1985), 14.
[43] Althoff, 'The Variability of Ritual', 73.
[44] Hüsken and Seamone, 'The Denial of Ritual and Its Return', 1–9.
[45] Weiler, '*Rex Renitens* and the Medieval Idea of Kingship', 1–42.

presentisms in what some historiographical traditions have established as conventional and unconventional in the Middle Ages, such as the artificial attempt to project *classic* French and English feudalism onto all the territories of medieval Europe.[46] In addition, postcolonial and global history, although it might damage the interpretation of the past in its presentist tendency, is paradoxically helping medieval studies to overcome a narrow vision of medieval Europe, freeing scholars from that traditional model of the centre versus periphery or Northern versus Southern Europe. There is no evidence that any medieval European monarchy looked to England as a model, and the normative character of Capetian royal self-representation appears to have been most evident in the first or second generation after Saint Louis, surviving only in some of the Angevin kings. Beyond these artificial projections of some alleged royal *conventional* models, my argument regarding the conventionality of self-coronations relies rather on the need to study them in the particular historical context in which they were enacted. Their interpretation requires historicist analysis, free of generalised models usually deriving from presentist projections, essentialist approaches or teleological interpretations.

* * *

Up to this point, I have centred the conclusions of my interpretation of the ritual of self-coronation on its political, social, sacred/secular and ritual *medieval* perspectives. Yet it is obvious that some of its qualities may be projected onto the present.[47] First, the practice of self-coronation and the king's skill in avoiding ecclesiastical mediation may help to explain the frontiers and limits between the temporal and spiritual, between politics and religion, which is essential for the stability of modern societies.[48] Second, it demonstrates the efficacy of the political use of ritual and symbols: '(medieval) kings use ritual to shore up their authority, but (modern) revolutionaries use ritual to overthrow monarchs.'[49] At this point, the distinction between medieval and modern rituals, highlighted by historians and anthropologists, should be emphasised. We have the

---

[46] Timothy Reuter, 'Debating the "Feudal Revolution"', *Past and Present* 155 (1997): 177–95; Weiler, 'Crown-Giving and King-Making', 85–6.

[47] This is the approach enacted in Kertzer, *Ritual, Politics, and Power*, and 'Conclusion: Ritual in Modern Society: A Comparative Analysis', in Lane, *The Rites of Rulers*, 252–84.

[48] On this important aspect, which goes beyond the scholarly world, a number of interesting works have been published from the perspective of ritual, myths and symbols studies: see Kenneth Burke, *The Rhetoric of Religion: Studies in Logology* (Berkeley: University of California Press, 1970); Robert J. Bocock, 'Ritual: Civic and Religious', *British Journal of Sociology* 21 (1970): 285–97; Bernard I. Donahue, 'The Political Use of Religious Symbols: A Case Study of the 1972 Presidential Campaign', *Review of Politics* 37 (1975): 48–65; Rappaport, *Ritual and Religion*, 3–29.

[49] Kertzer, *Ritual, Politics, and Power*, 2.

danger of projecting twenty-first-century sociological and secularising concepts and theories back onto mentalities of the Middle Ages. This anachronism has led to multiple misunderstandings of medieval rituals, as Philippe Buc explains:

> That Schramm, followed by many, owed to the illiberal atmosphere of the 1920s and 1930s, and to an even longer genealogy, his model of rituals does not *per se* invalidate it. It is, more simply, doubtful that medieval thinkers saw in royal ceremonies the formative agent of the social-political body. ... What medieval authors could say was that a ceremony displayed the kingdom's unity, which is rather different than attributing to it, in Durkheimian fashion, a formative power.[50]

Third, an interesting parallel can be noted between the practice of medieval self-coronations and the modern theory of the 'state of exception' developed by certain twentieth-century jurists and political scientists in connection with the problems that arose around the state in the interwar era. For Carl Schmitt, the 'sovereign is he who decides on the exception', and thus 'this definition of sovereignty must therefore be associated with borderline cases and not with routine.'[51] The state of exception has been imposed when there is a clear need to secure public order and political stability. Yet, interestingly, self-coronations are not usually related to either of these. They emerge, rather, on the initiative of the monarch, in a context of relative stability, driven by rulers who seek to strengthen their own authority and who find a way to activate exceptional measures through self-coronation.

Neither the essentialism of eternal continuity in the ceremonies nor the contextualism of permanent change fits with the practice of this ritual. The decision of certain medieval European kings to be self-crowned carries some unpredictability, making it difficult to determine a general interpretative rule on the circumstances which make them possible. There is certainly something fixed in the ceremonial and the tradition (i.e. the continuity of certain sacred places, the enactment of the ritual within the celebration of the Mass, and the coexistence of self-coronations with anointments), but this coexists with changes that are introduced naturally

---

[50] Buc, '1701 in Medieval Perspective', 123. See his interesting thoughts on this issue in Buc, 'Political Ritual'.

[51] Schmitt, *Political Theology*, 5. On the tendency of modern politics of turning the exception into the rule, and very useful for a comparative approach to medieval self-coronations as 'exceptional' rituals, see Giorgio Agamben, *State of Exception* (Chicago: University of Chicago Press, 2005). See also Bruno Gillì, 'The Sovereign Exception: Notes on Schmitt's Word That Sovereign Is He Who Decides on the Exception', *Glossator* 1 (2009), 23–30; Bruno Gillì, 'The Ontology and Politics of Exception', in *Giorgio Agamben: Sovereignty and Life*, ed. Matthew Calarco and Steven DeCaroli (Stanford, CA: Stanford University Press, 2007).

depending on the political circumstances at the time of the ceremony and the personality of each new king. Such is the space the self-crowning kings used to achieve that variation within the general rite of coronation.

In the end, the analysis and interpretation of self-coronations lead us to debunk the myth or grand narrative of the *process* of secularisation. Gathering signs of agency in medieval self-coronations helps us challenge that extended grand narrative of the 'mystical' Middle Ages against 'secularised' modernity, or the theory of the *progressive* secularisation of Western societies. In this grand narrative, ancient and medieval societies adopted theories and cultural practices in which the theological absorbed the political, and the modern period functions in exactly the reverse way. Many sacred cultural forms in the Middle Ages progressively became secular in modernity, and it would be hard to speak of the hegemony of secular attitudes until the early modern period. Nevertheless, the practice of self-coronation among the medieval kings shows that, although the ceremony of investiture continued to be enacted within a sacred place, sovereigns found forms to emphasise their lay dimension – a kind of 'hint of secularisation' – so that there is no general, evolutionary, teleological or progressive process of secularisation. Here the methodology of political theology, which focuses on the reciprocal transfers and borrowings between the temporal and the spiritual, works better than a *competitive* approach.[52] Interestingly, Kantorowicz himself uses the verb 'to drift' to describe the evolution of political doctrines and practices from the twelfth-century anonymous Norman chronicler to the early modern Tudor jurists.[53]

The circular meaning of the verb 'to drift' serves the non-linear evolution of the practice of self-coronation. My argument in this book has been governed by the idea that the marshalling or abandonment of certain rituals occurs, not at the margins of those ceremonies, but at their centre. Mixed ritual forms of the ceremony of royal accession – self-coronations, coronations, elevations and acclamations – are combined with the complete absence of any such ceremonies, as happened in medieval and early modern Iberian realms. In that sense, self-coronations and other such rituals were often liminal events, something in between what was normal in the north (the whole elaborate array of ceremonies) and what was often normal in the south (no ceremonies at all). Self-coronations thus become important lenses through which to examine the unique political contexts

---

[52] Montserrat Herrero, 'Carl Schmitt's Political Theology: The Magic of a Phrase', in *Political Theology in Medieval and Early Modern Europe: Discourses, Rites, and Representations*, ed. Montserrat Herrero, Jaume Aurell and Angela C. Miceli (Turnhout: Brepols, 2017), 23–41.

[53] Kantorowicz, *King's Two Bodies*, 506.

of each individual event. That is, each event was *sui generis*, building upon past experience and tradition, but also sometimes departing radically from previous practices. This allows us to see some parts of medieval Europe as capable of following or ignoring certain rituals.

In the end, there is no absolute mystification in societies, just as there is no absolute secularisation, among other reasons because, as Geertz puts it, 'a world wholly demystified is a world wholly depoliticised' – and that is a utopia.[54] Peter the Ceremonious' authoritative defence of the necessity of preserving an adequate autonomy of the temporal and spiritual sphere, in the introduction to his ceremonial of coronations, is very expressive in this context. Thus, the *grand-récit* of the progressive secularisation of the modern world versus the medieval vanishes when confronted with the inductive and persistent reality of the practice of self-coronation in the Middle Ages – among many other ritual, discursive and iconographical manifestations which would be added, and I am sure that historians and anthropologists will continue finding in the future. Historical experience proves that it is preferable to speak of tensions, transactions, transfusions, transferences, alternations or transfers between the temporal and the spiritual ('a crooked line'), rather than to trace a single upward line towards secularisation from the Christianisation of the fourth century to present secular modernity. As early as the fourth century, there was oscillation between the Caesaropapism of Constantine and the clericalism of Ambrose of Milan: the century began with Emperor Constantine dominating the bishops in the Council of Nicaea in 325 and ended with Bishop Ambrose humiliating Emperor Theodosius when he ordered the emperor to abase himself in public in 390.[55] Even today, no one can deny the importance of a harmonious balance between the temporal and the spiritual, and the reciprocal respect for their proper autonomy, for improving the world in which we live.[56]

---

[54] Geertz, 'Centers, Kings, and Charisma', 168.
[55] Bowersock, 'From Emperor to Bishop'.
[56] See, for instance, the intellectual debate among Jürgen Habermas, Tony Blair and Régis Debray, 'Secularism's Crisis of Faith', *New Perspectives Quarterly* 25 (2008): 17–29.

Index

Aachen, Germany, 131–2, 160, 164, 182
Aachen Gospels, 161
Abbey of Reichenau, 161
Abraham, 86
accession, 11. *See also specific King or topic*
acclamation
  Alfonso XI and, 230
  in Byzantium, 97, 125
  in Carolingian Dynasty, 128, 139–40
  Charles III and, 292
  overview, 41, 50, 316
  Roger II and, 178–9
Achaemenid Kings (Persia), 70, 72–3, 74
Acre, Lebanon, 199
Acre (Kingdom), 199
Acts (New Testament), 87
Adelaide del Vasto, 175
Adeliza of Louvain, 9
Aelfgifu of Northampton, 156
Aethelwold, Bishop, 151–3, 155
Africa, coronation in, 24–5, 299–300, 301
Agathocles (Sicily), 175
agency and self-coronation, 49, 53, 302–3
agency approach, 29–31
Aggesen, Sven, 284
Ahaziah (Israel), 257
Ahura Mazda (Persian deity), 13–14, 70–1, 72, 74, 78–80, 81–2
Aínsa, Spain, 278–9
Akkadians, 72
Alberich von Troisfontaines (chronicler), 213
Albert of Aachen, 206
alethurgical function of self-coronation, 50–1, 311–12
Alexander I (Byzantium), 115, 116–17
Alexander III (Russia), 299
Alexander (martyr), 203
Alexander of Telese, 175–6, 178–9, 180, 182–3
Alexander "the Great" (Macedon), 74–6
Alexandria, Egypt, 104

Alföldi, Andreas, 90
Alfonso I "the Battler" (Aragon), 273, 275–6, 281
Alfonso II (Asturias), 225
Alfonso II "the Chaste" (Aragon), 273
Alfonso III (Asturias), 225–6
Alfonso III "the Liberal" (Aragon), 246–7, 254, 294
Alfonso IV "the Benign" (Aragon), 12, 27, 242–3, 245, 247, 248–9, 251–2, 254–5, 273
Alfonso V "the Magnanimous" (Aragon), 272–3
Alfonso VI (Leon), 229
Alfonso VII (Leon), 226, 227–8, 230, 231, 237
Alfonso IX (Leon), 284, 294
Alfonso X (Castile), 231–2, 286
Alfonso XI (Castile)
  generally, 12, 242–3, 245
  acclamation and, 230
  Asturias, influence of on coronation, 222, 224–8
  audience at coronation, function of, 48, 50
  diadem and, 235–6
  dramatization of coronation, 45
  dynamism of coronation, 305–6
  iconographic sources, 21
  independence form ecclesiastical hierarchy and, 237
  Leon, influence of on coronation, 222, 224–8
  mediation and, 230, 232, 236
  miniatures, 226–7
  mitre and, 234–6
  narrative of coronation, 233, 234
  new ceremonial of, 232–3
  overview of coronation, 34–5, 222
  political effect of coronation, 144
  political theology approach and, 239
  scholarship on, 13

318

self-fashioning and, 31
self-knighting of, 233–7
sovereignty and, 228, 230
strategic purpose of coronation, 236, 311
transgressive nature of self-coronation, 143, 273
unction of, 237
Visigoths, influence of on coronation, 222, 224–8
Wamba, influence of on coronation, 222
Alfonso de la Cerda, 232
Aljafería Palace (Zaragoza), 271–2
Álmos (Hungary), 282–4
Al-Nasir (Egypt), 202
Althoff, Gerd, 18, 36, 46, 47–8, 242, 311, 312–13
Amalric (Jerusalem), 208
Amarna, Egypt, 61–2
Amaury, Arnaud, 245–6
Ambrose of Milan, 317
Amen (Egyptian deity), 64
Americas, coronation in, 24–5
Ammenees II (Egypt), 65
Ammianus Marcellinus, 101, 281
Ammonites, 61–2
anachronisms, 24, 313–14
Anacletus II (Pope), 175, 176–7, 179–80, 183, 184
Anahita (Persian deity), 70–1
Anastasius I (Byzantium), 101, 102, 105
Anatolius, Patriarch, 100–1
Ancona, Italy, 175–6
Andrew II (Hungary), 283, 284
angels, 33, 96–7, 110, 124, 166, 271–2
Angevin Dynasty, 313–14
Anglo-Saxon coronation
  Christocentrism in, 151–6
  Christus Rex model, 147–8, 155
  conventional nature of
    self-coronation, 313
  crown and, 151–6
  desacralisation in, 307–8, 309
  diadem in, 151–6
  dual nature of Kingship and, 171
  English Second Recension, 148
  Jesus, Kingship of and, 148, 151–6
  mediation in, 164
  miniatures, 148, 155
  normative nature of accession, 169–70
  ordines, 147–8, 149–50, 151
  ordo of Edgar and, 148, 149–51
  other Kingdoms compared, 170, 171
  overview, 5, 7, 8, 10, 33, 44, 147–8
  sacred nature of Kingship and, 170–1
  unction and, 170

Anjou, House of, 193–4
Annales de Theokesberia, 213
Annales de Waverleia, 213
Annales de Wigornia, 213
Annales Marbacenses, 213
Annals of Tabari, 77–8
anointing. *See* unction
Anomie, 311
Anonymous Norman, 162
Anselm, Archbishop of Canterbury, 207
Antigonos Monophthalmos (Persia), 76
anti-hierocratism, 238
Antioch, Lebanon, 94, 104, 199
Antiquity, coronation in, 32–3, 84. *See also specific Kingdom*
Antonsson, Haki, 304
Apocalypse, 162
Apter, Andrew, 25, 55–6
Apulia, Italy, 175–6, 177, 182
Arabs, 34, 195, 229–30
Aragon (Kingdom)
  Alfonso I "the Battler," 273, 275–6, 281
  Alfonso II "the Chaste," 273
  Alfonso III "the Liberal," 246–7, 254, 294
  Alfonso IV "the Benign," 12, 27, 242–3, 245, 247, 248–9, 251–2, 254–5, 273
  Alfonso V "the Magnanimous," 272–3
  Constanza, 246
  coronation in, 44, 142
  Ferdinand I, 12, 27, 35, 272–3, 296
  General Privilege of 1283, 294
  James I "the Conqueror," 184, 246, 254, 259–60
  James II "the Just," 246–7
  John I, 27, 273
  John II, 273
  Kings of, 183
  Martin I, 12, 27, 44–5, 271, 273
  Navarra, coronations in compared, 274
  oaths in, 294
  Papal influence in, 240–1
  Pere Berenguer, 249
  Peter II "the Catholic," 245–6, 254, 284
  Peter III "the Great," 246, 254
  Peter IV "the Ceremonious" (*See* Peter IV "the Ceremonious" (Aragon))
  queens, coronation of, 262, 265–7
  Ramon Berenguer, 249
  Sibilia, 267
  Sicily and, 246–7
  unction in, 245, 256–7, 260, 269
Arcadius (Rome), 91
archangels, 111, 112–14, 115, 123–4

Index

Archbishop of Toledo, 129, 249, 252
Arch of Trajan, 89
Ardashir I (Persia), 71, 78–81, 82
Ares (Greek deity), 75
Armenia, 312
Aronoff, Myron J., 51
Árpád (Hungary), 283
Arsacid Kings (Persia), 77
Arthur (legendary King), 307–8
ascension, 154
Asia, coronation in, 5, 24–5, 299
Assyrians, 66, 67–8, 73
Astronomer (biographer), 132
Asturias (Kingdom)
  Alfonso II, 225
  Alfonso III, 225–6
  Alfonso XI, influence on coronation of, 222, 224–8
  Pelagius, 278–9
Átá of Ayede, 301
Athalia (Israel), 257
Atkinson, K.M.T., 73–4
Attila (Huns), 283
Auch (Viscounty), 280
Auctoritas, 94, 307
audience, function of, 47–50, 312–13
Augustus (Rome), 89, 142
Aurelian (Rome), 94
Aurell, Jaume, 13
aureole, 91
Australia, ritual in, 25
authorship, 30
autography, 269
Autokrator model, 100–1, 102, 109, 117–19
Aztec people, 25

Babylonians, 66, 69, 73
Bahrâm II (Persia), 82
Bahrâm V (Persia), 82
Baigorri, Viscount of, 288
Bak, János, 18
Bakhtin, Mikhail, 56
Bal'ami (chronicler), 77–8, 82
Baldwin I (Jerusalem), 206–8
Baldwin II (Jerusalem), 203, 208
Baldwin III (Jerusalem), 208
Baldwin IV (Jerusalem), 208
Baldwin V (Jerusalem), 207–8
Bali, ritual in, 41–2
Ballesteros, Antonio, 231
Balliol, John, 238
Banaszkiewicz, Jacek, 11
baptism
  of Jesus, 91, 115–16, 158
  of Pharaoh, 64

Barcelona, House of, 183, 273
Barcelona, Spain, 264, 267
Bardas, Caesar, 112–13
Bari, Italy, 192–3
Basil I (Byzantium), 103–4, 111, 112–15, 123
Basil II (Byzantium), 121–4
Basiliscus (Byzantium), 91
Bayonne (Viscounty), 279–80
Bearn (Viscounty), 280
Behistun, Iran, 73
Beihammer, Alexander, 24
Beikrönung, 12
Beirut, Lebanon, 199
Bell, Catherine, 25, 57, 307
Benedict XII (Pope), 236, 270
Benedictional of Aethelwold, 151–3, 154–5
Benevento, Italy, 89
Beohmond, Italy, 175–6
Berengaria (Castile), 286
Bermudo II (Leon), 224
Bernard le Trésorier, 180–1, 212
Bernard of Clairvaux, 176, 182–3
Bertelli, Sergio, 297
Bertha of Italy, 119–20
Beth Alpha Synagogue, 86
Bethlehem, Israel, 206–7
bishops, coronation by, 5
Bisotun, Iran, 71–2, 74
Bisson, Thomas, 284–5
Blanca (Navarra), 287–8
Bloch, Marc, 18, 139
Bohemia
  accession in, 12
  coronation in, 8, 170
  Papal influence in, 240
  unction in, 170
Bohigas, Pere, 268
Bokassa I, Jean-Bédel (Central Africa), 299–300
Boleslaw I (Poland), 182
Boniface (Saint), 129
Bordeaux (Viscounty), 280
Bourdieu, Pierre, 52
Bousalgus *(campiductor)*, 100
Boyce, Mary, 71
Brindisi, Italy, 200
Brisch, Nicole, 23
British Library (London), 151–3
Broekmann, Theo, 191–2
Brühl, Carlrichard, 13
Buc, Philippe, 13, 14–16, 18, 36, 40, 41–2, 43, 50, 181, 271, 298, 299, 311, 315
Burckhardt, Jacob, 196, 197
Burgos, Spain, 143, 233–5, 236

Index

Burke, Peter, 57
Burkert, Walter, 46
Byzantium
  acclamation in, 97, 125
  Alexander I, 115, 116–17
  Alexandria, strength of, 104
  Anastasius I, 101, 102, 105
  Antioch, strength of, 104
  Baldwin, 124
  Basil I, 103–4, 111, 112–15, 123
  Basil II, 121–4
  Basiliscus, 91
  Book of Ceremonies, 100, 101, 125
  Cantacuzenus, John, 98
  consecration in, 108
  Constantine V, 110
  Constantine VII Porphyrogenitus, 92, 100, 101, 105, 114, 117, 118, 119–20, 123, 126, 162, 187, 190
  Constantine X, 121
  Constantine XI, 98
  Constantinople, strength of, 104
  coronation in
    Autokrator model, 100–1, 102, 109, 117–19
    baptism iconography in, 115–16
    Basileus and, 89, 109–10, 111, 169
    Carolingian tradition compared, 138, 139, 140–4
    coins and, 110, 111, 115, 116–17
    diadem and, 90, 100, 107–8, 111, 119
    divine election and, 95
    Egyptian tradition, influence of, 108–9
    elimination of role of Patriarch, 109–10
    Greek tradition, influence of, 108–9
    "Hand of God" iconography in, 33, 91, 93, 110–11
    heavenly coronation, 96, 108–24
    iconographic traditions, 124–6
    iconography of coronation, 13–14, 108–24
    Jesus, Kingship of and, 153–4
    Jesus as source of authority, 112, 119–24, 125
    mediation and, 104
    mediation as diminishing divine authority, 96
    Ottonian tradition, influence on, 108–9, 158–63, 168, 169
    overview, 12–13, 33, 44, 96–7
    Patriarch, role of, 97–104
    Persian tradition, influence of, 107–9
    religious meaning in mediation, 104–8
    ritual traditions, 124–6
    Roger II, influence on, 187–8, 189, 190, 192–4
    Roman tradition, continuity of, 97
    Sicilian tradition, influence on, 108–9
    symbolic coronation, 96
    transition from symbolic to real meaning in mediation, 104–8
    Visigoth tradition compared, 139, 222
  ecclesiastical hierarchy in, 96, 141, 144
  Eudocia, 121
  John I Tzimiskes, 110
  John II Comnenus, 110
  Justin I, 102, 110
  Justinian I, 103, 104, 141
  Justinian II, 111
  legitimacy in, 98, 112, 116–17
  Leo I, 97, 98, 100–2, 104, 107–8
  Leo II, 102
  Leo III, 105, 108, 222
  Leo IV, 110
  Leo VI, 114–15, 117, 119, 123
  Manuel I, 108
  Marcian, 97–9, 104, 106, 107–8
  Michael I, 105
  Michael III, 103–4, 111, 112–13
  Michael VII, 121
  miniatures in, 91, 112, 121–2, 123, 124, 126
  mosaics in, 141
  Nicephorus Bryennius, 98
  oaths in, 282, 294
  opprobrium, self-coronation as in, 98
  Phocas, 105
  Romanus I, 116–17
  Romanus II, 119–21, 123
  symbolism in, 115, 126
  Theophanu, 121, 158–9
  Valentinian III, 91, 99
  Zeno, 91, 102

Caesaropapism, 317
Calabria, Italy, 175–6, 177, 180, 182
Cambridge myth-ritual school, 17–18, 56
Cambyses II (Persia), 73–4
Campiductor, 100, 101, 102
Campus Martius, 100
Canaanites, 61–2
Canossa, Italy, 309
Cantacuzenus, John, 98
Capetian Dynasty, 288, 307–8, 313–14
Capua, Italy, 175–6
Carbonell, Miquel, 271–2
Carloman (Franks), 130

Carolingian coronation
  acclamation and, 128, 139–40
  Autokrator model compared, 102
  Byzantine tradition compared, 138, 139, 140–4
  consecration and, 129, 135–7
  conventional nature of self-coronation, 313
  diadem in, 132
  England, influence on, 136, 139
  France, influence on, 136
  fusion of anointment and coronation, 128–35
  "Hand of God" iconography in, 91–2
  Iberian Kingdoms compared, 142, 143
  inauguration and, 128, 129–30
  innovation in coronation, 306
  Israelite tradition, influence of, 129–30
  Jesus, Kingship of and, 153–4
  laudes, 140
  legitimacy and, 129, 130
  liturgification and, 133–5, 139–46, 171
  mediation in, 135–46
  miniatures and, 136
  ordines, 144–5
  Ottonian tradition, influence on, 136, 164–6, 171
  overview, 5, 7, 8, 10, 12–13, 33, 44, 102, 127–8
  person performing coronation, relevance of, 130–2
  Roger II, influence on, 190
  role of priest in mediation, 135–9
  royal investiture, 139–46
  sacralisation and, 128–35, 141, 142, 143, 171
  sovereignty and, 134, 139
  unction and, 129–30, 142, 143–4
  Visigoth tradition compared, 142, 222
Cassiodorus, 281
Castile (Kingdom)
  Alfonso X, 231–2, 286
  Alfonso XI (*See* Alfonso XI (Castile))
  Berengaria, 286
  coronation in, 44, 142, 143, 230–1
  desacralisation in, 214, 308
  Enrique I, 230
  Enrique II Trastámara, 236
  Ferdinand III, 230
  Ferdinand IV, 232
  John I, 236
  Navarra, coronations in compared, 274
  oaths in, 294
  Papal influence in, 240–1
  political theology approach and, 239
  Sancho II, 229–30
  Sancho IV, 231–2
  unction in, 230–1, 237
Catalonia, 92, 280, 284
Cathars, 245–6
Catholic Mass, 25, 259, 260, 292
Catlos, Brian, 238
Cefalù, Italy, 194–5
celestial coronation, 13–14, 61, 96, 108–24
Central African Republic, 299–300
ceremony (*See* ritual)
Ceremonial de Cardeña, 228
Ceremonial de Consagración y de Coronación de los reyes de Aragón, 20, 267
Ceremonial de El Escorial, 232
Ceremonial de Toledo, 232
Champagne, House of, 288
Chantilly Manuscript, 157
Charanis, Peter, 106
charisma, 94, 138, 224, 307
Charlemagne (Franks), 8, 130–2, 187, 222
Charles II "the Bad" (Navarra), 289, 292
Charles III "the Noble" (Navarra)
  generally, 12, 296
  acclamation and, 292
  audience at coronation, function of, 47, 48, 50
  clothing at coronation, 292
  consecration and, 291
  dramatization of coronation, 45
  dynamism of coronation, 305–6
  French ancestry, emphasis on in coronation, 292
  fusion of rituals in coronation, 292, 294
  juridical implications of coronation, 35
  lack of mediation in coronation, 292
  Mass and coronation, 292
  narrative of coronation, 291–2
  oath of, 289–91, 292, 294
  overview of coronation, 35, 274–5
  political effect of coronation, 144
  "raising up" of, 291, 292, 294
  sceptre and, 291
  self-fashioning and, 31
  sovereignty and, 292
  strategic purpose of coronation, 311
  transgressive nature of self-coronation, 143
  unction and, 291, 292, 294
  unique nature of coronation, 295
Charles "the Bald" (Franks), 127, 130, 133, 135, 136–8, 142, 161–2, 164–6, 169, 288
Charles X (France), 127
Charles XII (Sweden), 238, 297

Index

Charles "the Younger" (Franks), 222
Chiliastic eschatology, 22
Chindasuinth (Visigoths), 226–7
chrism, 129, 145, 158, 247
Chrism, 129
Christ. *See* Jesus
Christian V (Denmark), 238, 297
Christianisation, 22–3, 92, 130, 296, 311, 317
Christianity. *See specific topic*
Christification, 127
Christocentrism
  in Ottonian coronation, 166, 169, 171
  overview, 34, 147–8, 175
  Roger II and, 185–95
Christomimetes, 189, 191, 193
Christus Rex model, 147–8, 155, 157
Chronicle of Alfonso III, 225
Chronicle of Bal'ami, 77–8
Chronicle of Pelagius, 229
Chronicon S. Medardi Suessionensis, 213
Church of St. Demetrious (Thessaloniki), 111
Church of the Holy Sepulchre (Jerusalem), 34, 196, 197–9, 202–6, 208–13, 214, 216
Clark, Christopher, 13, 29, 297–8
Clovis (France), 9
Cluny Museum (Paris), 158
Cnut (England), 5–7, 44, 155–6
Codex Egberti, 155
Codex Manichaicus Coloniensis, 80
Coggeshall, Ralph of (chronicler), 285
Coimbra, Bishop of, 232
coins. *See* numismatics
College of Cardinals, 176
Cologne, Germany, 169
Comes, Cardinal, 179
comparative anthropology, 301
comparison of coronation and self-coronation, 8–10, 12–13
Compromise of Caspe (1412), 273
Connerton, Paul, 43–4, 56, 302
Conrad I (Jerusalem), 201
Conrad II (Jerusalem) and IV (Germany), 11, 201, 202, 203
consecration
  in Byzantium, 108
  in Carolingian Dynasty, 129, 135–7
  Charles III and, 291
  Egypt, consecration without mediation in (*See* Egypt (Ancient))
  Frederick II and, 213–14, 215

Greece, consecration without mediation in (*See* Greece (Ancient), consecration without mediation in)
Israel, consecration without mediation in (*See* Israel (Ancient))
Mesopotamia, consecration without mediation in (*See* Mesopotamia, Ancient)
in Navarra, 288
in Ottonian Dynasty, 161–2, 163–4
overview, 12–13, 16–17
Persia, consecration without mediation in (*See* Persia (Ancient))
in Pre-Christian civilizations, 32–3
self-consecration, 65
consensualism, 35, 295
Constantine I (Rome), 87–91, 110, 111, 142, 317
Constantine II (Rome), 89, 90
Constantine V (Byzantium), 110
Constantine VII Porphyrogenitus (Byzantium), 92, 100, 101, 105, 114, 117, 118, 119–20, 123, 126, 162, 187, 190
Constantine X (Byzantium), 121
Constantine XI (Byzantium), 98
Constantinople, 89, 90, 100–1, 103, 104–5
Constantius II (Rome), 89, 90, 110
Constanza (Aragon), 246
context of self-coronation, 43–4
contextualism, 315–16
Continuatio Eberbacensis, 213
conventional versus non-conventional nature of self-coronation, 313–14
cope, 151
coronation. *See specific King or topic*
Corrigan, Kathleen, 114
Cosandey, Fanny, 265
Cosmocrator (title), 90–1
Council of Chalcedon (451), 104
Council of Nicaea (325), 317
Councils of Toledo, 222
Counter-Reformation, 42
Coutume of Bayonne, 279–80
Covadonga, Battle of, 225
Cross of St. George, 268
Crown of Aragon (*See* Aragon (Kingdom))
crown
  in Anglo-Saxon coronation, 151–6
  Frederick II and, 202–6, 209–13
  Holy Sepulchre, crown-wearing in, 202–6
  in Iberian Kingdoms, 227–8
  imperial crown, 130, 162, 182
  in Persia, 74–6, 77
  Peter IV and, 257, 260, 265

324 Index

crown (cont.)
  radial crown, 81–2, 89
Crucifixion, 154
Crusades, 199–200, 201
cultural studies, 29–30
curing, 25
Cyriacus, Patriarch, 105
Cyrus I (Persia), 70–1, 73
Cyrus II (Persia), 73
Cyzicus, Turkey, 94

Dagron, Gilbert, 100
Daimbert, Patriarch, 206–7
Dale, Johanna, 10, 17, 18, 41, 208–9, 308
Dalmatic, 151, 259, 265
Dante, 1
Darius I (Persia), 71–2, 74
Darius III (Persia), 74–5
Darnton, Robert, 19, 54–5
David, Louis, 3–4, 21
David (Israel), 61–3, 136, 153–4, 184, 207, 223–4, 256
deacons, 157–8, 255, 259
De Administrando Imperio, 123
De ceremoniis aulae Byzantinae, 119
Deit al Bahri, Egypt, 64
Denmark
  Christian V, 238, 297
  coronation in, 8, 11–12, 170
  oaths in, 284
  unction in, 170
Deo coronatus, 189, 191
desacralisation
  in Anglo-Saxon coronation, 307–8, 309
  in Castile, 214, 308
  in England, 310
  in France, 307–8, 310
  Frederick II and, 214
  in Ottonian coronation, 308, 309, 310
Descoll, Bernat, 250
Deshman, Robert, 153, 154–5
diachronicity, 24, 26
diadem
  Alfonso XI and, 235–6
  in Anglo-Saxon coronation, 151–6
  in Byzantium, 90, 100, 107–8, 111, 119
  in Carolingian coronation, 132
  in Mesopotamia, 67–8
  in Ottonian coronation, 149–58
  overview, 11, 89
  in Persia, 71, 75–6, 77, 78, 79, 81–2
  Peter IV and, 245, 260
"dialect of complementation," 309
discontinuity in rituals, 4, 273, 308
divine election, 94–5

Doty, William, 52
Douglas, Mary, 31, 36, 38, 39, 141
dove, Holy Spirit depicted as, 87, 91
dramatization of coronation, 44–7, 271–3
Dura Europos Synagogue, 86–8
Durkheim, Émile, 311
Dvornik, Francis, 66, 69
Dwyer, Philip, 298
dynamism of self-coronation, 305–6

Eanna, Iraq, 67
ecclesiastical hierarchy
  Alfonso XI and, 236, 237
  in Byzantium, 96, 141, 144
  Frederick II and, 202
  overview, 12–13, 52
  Peter IV and, 259
  Roger II and, 191
ecclesiastical mediation. *See* mediation
Edgar (England), 147–8, 149–51, 239–40
Edward III (England), 6
Egbert of Trier, Archbishop, 155
Egica (Visigoths), 226–7
Eginhard (chronicler), 227
Egypt (Ancient)
  Ammenees II, 65
  baptism of Pharaoh, 64
  Blue Crown, 64
  consecration without mediation in, 63–6
    Byzantine tradition, influence on, 108–9
    divine election and, 95
    humanisation of Pharaoh and, 66
    overview, 32–3, 61
  Dual Shrines, 64
  Haremhab, 64
  Hatshepsut, 64
  kingship in, 25
  legitimacy in, 74
  Per-neser, 64
  Per-wer, 64
  Red Crown, 64
  White Crown, 64
Einhard (biographer), 8, 132
Elamites, 72, 73
Eleanor of Toulouse, 245
election, 4, 9, 74–5, 91, 94–5, 97, 182
elevation, 109, 175, 231, 316
Eliade, Mircea, 23
Elijah (Israelite Prophet), 111, 112–14
Elizabeth I (England), 296–7
Elizabeth Petrovna (Russia), 299
Elliott, John, 21
Elliott, John H., 238–9

Ellwood, Robert S., 24–5
Elze, Reinhard, 180
England
  Angevin Dynasty, 313–14
  Anglo-Saxon coronation, (*See* Anglo-Saxon coronation)
  Carolingian tradition, influence of, 136, 139
  Cnut, 5–7, 44, 155–6
  Coronation Letters, 294–5
  desacralisation in, 310
  Edgar, 147–8, 149–51, 239–40
  Edward III, 6
  Elizabeth I, 296–7
  Henry I, 9, 284–5, 294–5
  Henry III, 209
  Iberian Kingdoms compared, 239–40
  John I, 284–5
  Magna Carta, 284–5
  oaths in, 282, 294–5
  other Kingdoms compared, 128
  projection of feudalism onto remainder of Medieval Europe, 313–14
  Richard I, 5–7, 44
  unction in, 310
  Unknown Charter, 284–5
Enlightenment, 310
Enrique I (Castile), 230
Enrique II Trastámara (Castile), 236
episcopal ordination, 135–6
Erech, Iraq, 67
Erkens, Franz-Reiner, 23, 309
Ermoldus (biographer), 132
Ernoul (chronicler), 180–1, 212
Erstkrönung, 12
Eshubity (Zulus), 301
essentialism, 38, 315–16
Estella, Spain, 278
Estella Agreement (1238), 278, 280
Estoire de Eracles, 212
etymology of coronation, 10–11
Eudocia (Rome), 91
Eudoxia (Rome), 91
Eudoxie (Bertha of Italy) or Eudocia (Byzantium), 119–21
Euphemius, Patriarch, 105
Europe, coronation in, 24–5
Eusebius of Caesarea, 90
Euthymius, Patriarch, 101–2
Exarchate mosaics, 91
exceptionality in rituals, 4, 56, 238
Exodus (Old Testament), 89
Ezekiel (Israelite Prophet), 86
Ezekiel (Old Testament), 89

Falco de Benevento, 179, 180, 182–3
falsifications, 16–17
Father (Trinity), 87
Fears, J. Rufus, 94
Ferdinand I (Aragon), 12, 27, 35, 272–3, 296
Ferdinand I (Leon), 224, 226–7, 230
Ferdinand III (Castile), 230
Ferdinand IV (Castile), 232
Ferdowski, 70, 77–8, 82
Ferentino, Italy, 200
Festkrönung, 10–11, 12
Field of Mars (Campus Martius), 100
Fleckenstein, Josef, 130
Fortes, Meyer, 5, 24–5
Foucault, Michel, 50–1, 311–12
France
  Capetian Dynasty, 288, 307–8, 313–14
  Carolingian coronation (*See* Carolingian coronation)
  Charles III, emphasis on French ancestry in coronation of, 292
  Charles X, 127
  Clovis, 9
  desacralisation in, 307–8, 310
  Henry I, 11
  Josephine, 3–4
  Louis VI, 181
  Louis VII, 181
  Louis IX, 280–1, 286, 287–8, 313–14
  Louis X "the Stubborn," 288, 289
  Louis XVI, 296
  Napoleon I (*See* Napoleon I (France))
  oaths in, 279–80, 282, 294
  other Kingdoms compared, 128
  Peers of France, 9–10
  Philip I, 9
  Philip III, 287–8
  Philip IV "the Fair," 288
  Philip V "the Tall," 288
  projection of feudalism onto remainder of Medieval Europe, 313–14
Franco, Francisco, 237–8
Frankfurt, Germany, 182
Franks
  Carloman, 130
  Carolingian coronation (*See* Carolingian coronation)
  Charlemagne, 8, 130–2, 187, 222
  Charles "the Younger," 130, 133, 222
  Charles "the Bald," 127, 130, 133, 135, 136–8, 142, 161–2, 164–6, 169, 288
  Louis "the Pious," 37, 130–3
  Pippin "the Short," 129–30, 222, 226

326 Index

Frederick I Barbarossa (Holy Roman Empire), 182, 284
Frederick I (Prussia), 13, 31, 35, 238, 296–9, 311
Frederick II (Jerusalem)
  generally, 13, 34, 177
  audience at coronation, function of, 48–9, 312–13
  Chancellery, 203, 204
  consecration and, 213–14, 215
  crown ceremony of, 202–6, 209–13
  Crusades and, 199–200, 201
  date of coronation, significance of, 203, 214
  desacralisation, coronation as, 214
  dramatization of coronation, 44–5
  dual challenge facing, 48
  dynamism of coronation, 305–6
  ecclesiastical hierarchy and, 202
  excommunication of, 201
  historiographic sources, 16
  as Holy Roman Emperor, 199–200, 214
  in Holy Sepulchre, 202–6, 209–13, 214, 216
  iconographic sources, 21
  inauguration and, 206–7, 208
  Jesus, parallel imagery with, 205
  juridical implications of coronation, 206, 215
  as King of Sicily, 199, 214, 216
  mystical dimension of, 215–16
  Napoleon compared, 196–7, 213
  oaths and, 284
  opprobrium, self-coronation as, 216–17
  overview of coronation, 34, 196–9
  political symbols and rituals and, 246
  as "pre-modern" prince, 196
  provocation, coronation as, 216–17
  reaction to coronation, 197–9, 213, 215, 216, 312–13
  reception of coronation, 197–9, 211–13
  Roger II compared, 188, 194–5, 216
  scholarship on, 13
  self-fashioning and, 31
  sovereignty and, 199, 216
  strategic purpose of coronation, 311
  symbolic nature of coronation, 57, 196–7, 214, 216
  third Sunday of Lent, coronation on, 203, 214
  transgressive nature of self-coronation, 143, 197–9, 215, 221, 273
Freudian psychoanalysis, 56
Fructuoso (scribe), 226

Fruzabad, Iran, 78
Frye, Northrop, 56
Fueros (in Navarra), 277–9, 281–2, 284–95
Fulcher of Chartres, 206, 207
Fulk of Anjou (Jerusalem), 208
functionalism, 25, 39

Gabriel (Archangel), 111, 112–14, 115, 123–4
Galla Placidia, 91
Gallican rite of unction, 145
Gallienus (Rome), 94
García Ramírez (Navarra), 274, 275, 276–7, 281, 293
Gardiner, Alan, 65
Gaul, 129, 142–3
Geary, Patrick, 18
Geertz, Clifford, 31, 36, 39, 41–2, 44–5, 317
Gelasius (Pope), 164
Gelmírez of Santiago de Compostela, 228
genealogy, 34–5, 181, 222, 315
General Archive of Navarra, 291–2
Genoa (Kingdom), 202
George of Antioch, 185, 189, 192
Gerald of Wales, 238
Germanikeia, Battle of, 103
Germanus, Patriarch, 105
Germany. *See* Holy Roman Empire; Prussia
Gerold of Lausanne, Patriarch of Jerusalem, 200, 202, 203, 209–13, 216
Gervais, Archbishop, 9
Gesta Comitum Barchinonensium, 183
Gesta Francorum, 206, 207
Gesta Hungarorum, 283
Getty Villa (Los Angeles), 1–2
Gibbon, Edward, 101
Gihon, Israel, 136
Gilbert de Mons, 182
Ginnasi, Andrea Torno, 96, 108–9, 115
Gluckman, Max, 41–2
God
  Father, depiction in iconography, 87
  Holy Spirit, depiction in iconography, 87, 91, 115
  Son, depiction in iconography, 87
  Trinity, 87
Godfrey I (Jerusalem), 11, 206, 214
Goethe, Johann Wolfgang von, 30
Goodenough, Erwin R., 87
Gospels, 91, 154, 281–2, 289–91. *See also specific Book*
Grabar, André, 13–14, 96, 108, 109–10
Graeber, David, 5, 38

Index

grand narrative, 316
Greece (Ancient), consecration without mediation in
   Byzantine tradition, influence on, 108–9
   overview, 32–3
   Persian tradition, influence on, 74–7
Greenblatt, Stephen, 31
Gregory I "the Great" (Pope), 224
Gregory VII (Pope), 309
Gregory IX (Pope), 201, 202, 205, 209–13
Gregory X (Pope), 246
Gregory of Nazianzus, 112
Gregory of Tours, 224
Guillaume de Nagis, 213
Guiscard, Robert, 177
Gundlach, Rolf, 23
Guy de Lusignan (Jerusalem), 201, 208

Habsburg Dynasty, 237–8
Hagia Sophia (Constantinople), 100–1, 107, 141
Haimeric, 176
halo imagery, 164, 226–7
Hammurabi (Babylon), 69
"Hand of God" iconography
   in art, 93
   in Byzantine tradition, 33, 91, 93, 110–11
   in Carolingian tradition, 91–2
   Christian God, 89–90
   in Christian tradition, 86–8
   divine election and, 94–5
   Father, depiction of, 87
   inauguration and, 89
   in Jewish tradition, 86, 87–8, 90
   in late antiquity, 92–5
   legitimacy and, 91
   mediation and, 90
   in medieval period, 91
   overview, 33, 85–6
   Persian tradition compared, 92
   personalization of crowning deity, 92–5
   Roger II and, 92, 93
   in Roman tradition, 88–91
   as sign of sovereign weakness, 94
   transition between pagan and Christian worlds, 86–92
Haremhab (Egypt), 64
Hatshepsut (Egypt), 64
Hauck, Karl, 142–3
Hawaii (Kingdom), 301
heavenly coronation, 13–14, 61, 96, 108–24
Hebrews. *See* Israel (Ancient)
Heimskringla, 181–2
Hellenistic Kings (Persia), 74–7
Henry I (England), 9, 284–5, 294–5
Henry I (France), 11
Henry I (Holy Roman Empire), 169
Henry I (Navarra), 287–8
Henry I "the Fowler" (East Francia), 12
Henry II (Holy Roman Empire), 149, 151, 157–8, 166–8, 169
Henry III (England), 209
Henry III (Holy Roman Empire), 191
Henry IV (Holy Roman Empire), 309
Henry de Saint-Simon, 9–10
Henry of Huntingdon, 6–7
Henry of Vasto, 175–6
heredity, 4, 91, 97
Heriger of Mains, Archbishop, 12
Hermann of Salza, 202, 204–6, 209–14
Herodotus, 74
Herzfeld, Michael, 55
Hildesheim, Germany, 157
Hincmar of Reims, 134–5, 161–2
Hippodrome (Constantinople), 102, 103, 141
Historia Compostelana, 228
Historia Silense, 229
Historia Wambae, 223, 225
historical tradition of self-coronation, 4–14
historicism, 38, 84
historiographical sources, 14–16
Hittites, 68–9
Hocart, Arthur M., 5, 23, 24–5
Holt, James C., 284
Holy Oil, 145, 158, 178, 260, 291
Holy Roman Empire
   accession in, 12
   Conrad II (Jerusalem) and IV (Germany), 11, 201, 202, 203
   Frederick I Barbarossa, 182, 284
   Frederick II (*See* Frederick II (Jerusalem))
   Henry I, 169
   Henry II, 149, 151, 157–8, 166–8, 169
   Henry III, 191
   Henry IV, 309
   Joseph II, 30
   Lothar III, 176, 183
   oaths in, 282
   Otto I, 150–1, 169
   Otto II, 121, 157, 158–64, 166, 168, 169, 191
   Otto III, 158, 168, 169
   Ottonian coronation (*See* Ottonian coronation)
Holy Spirit (Trinity), 87, 91, 115
homage, 41, 47–8, 66, 100–1, 192, 236–7, 245, 246, 281–2
Honoria (Rome), 91
Honorius III (Pope), 200

Index

Hormozd III (Persia), 82
Horus (Egyptian deity), 63–4, 65
Huizinga, Johan, 46
human sacrifice, 25
Hungary
   accession in, 12
   Álmos, 282–4
   Andrew II, 283, 284
   Árpád, 283
   Blood Oath, 282–4
   coronation in, 170
   Golden Bull, 283, 284
   Iberian Kingdoms compared, 239–40
   Ladislaus, 11, 239–40
   oaths in, 282–4
   Papal influence in, 240
   revelation and coronation, 312
   unction in, 170

Iberian Kingdoms. *See also specific King or Kingdom*
   Carolingian coronation compared, 142, 143
   coronation in, 7, 8, 44, 170
   crown ceremony in, 227–8
   England compared, 239–40
   exceptionalism of, 238
   Hungary compared, 239–40
   iconographic sources, 19
   Islamic invasion of, 224
   mediation in, 238
   miniatures in, 236
   opprobrium, self-coronation as in, 240
   Papal influence in, 240–1
   sceptre in, 226, 245, 271, 272–3
   self-coronation not seen as transgression in, 221–2, 312
   unction in, 170, 224–6
   unique nature of coronation in, 310
   Visigoths, influence of, 237–8
iconographic sources, 19–21
iconography
   in Byzantium
      baptism iconography, 115–16
      iconography of coronation, 13–14, 108–24
   Father, depiction of, 87
   "Hand of God" iconography (*See* "Hand of God" iconography)
   Holy Spirit, depiction of, 87, 91, 115
   of Jesus, 13–14, 21, 33
   in Ottonian coronation, 157–69
   Son, depiction of, 87

identity, 31–2
ideology, 38–9, 94, 127–8, 129, 134, 142, 144, 151, 161–2, 189
Imago Dei, 189
imperial crown, 130, 162, 182
Imy-khant (Egyptian priest), 64
inauguration
   in Carolingian Dynasty, 128, 129–30
   Frederick II and, 206–7, 208
   "Hand of God" iconography and, 89
   overview, 49–50, 84, 135–6, 142, 313
   in Persia, 76
Íñigo Arista of Aragon, 268, 275
In-mutef (Egyptian priest), 65
Innocent II (Pope), 176, 183
Innocent III (Pope), 245–6, 254–5
Innocent IV (Pope), 286
innovation in coronation, 306
insignia. *See* crown; pommel; sceptre
Inszenierung, 242
investiture. *See specific King or topic*
investment ring, 71–2
Iran. *See also* Persia (Ancient)
   coronation in, 70, 83–4, 301
   Mohammad Reza Pahlavi, 32–3, 83–4, 301
   Napoleon, influence of, 83–4
   Reza Pahlavi, 32–3, 83–4, 301
Ireland
   coronation in, 8, 170
   unction in, 170
Isaac, 86, 87, 116
Isabella I (Jerusalem), 201
Isabella II (Jerusalem), 199–202, 205
Isabella (Navarra), 286
Ishtar (Sumerian deity), 67
Isidore, Patriarch, 98
Isidore of Seville, 222, 223–4
Isis (Egyptian deity), 65
Islam
   coronation and, 44
   Iberian Kingdoms, Islamic invasion of, 224
   Navarra and, 275
   Roger II, influence on coronation of, 188, 195
Israel (Ancient)
   Ahaziah, 257
   Athalia, 257
   consecration without mediation in, 62–3
      Carolingian tradition, influence on, 129–30
      divine election and, 95

Index

other ancient Kingdoms compared, 63
overview, 32–3, 61
unction and, 62–3
David, 61–3, 136, 153–4, 184, 207, 223–4, 256
Jehoash, 257
Peter IV, influence on coronation of, 255–7
Saul, 123–4, 255–6
Solomon, 63, 136, 137, 153–4
unction in, 62–3, 223–4
Ivrea, Italy, 158

Jackson, Richard A., 4–5, 263
James I "the Conqueror" (Aragon), 183, 246, 254, 259–60
James II "the Just" (Aragon), 246–7
James III (Mallorca), 253
James (Saint), 233–5
Japan, kingship in, 25
Jehoash (Israel), 257
Jerusalem, Patriarch of. *See* Gerold of Lausanne, Patriarch of Jerusalem
Jerusalem (Kingdom)
Amalric, 208
Baldwin I, 206–8
Baldwin II, 203, 208
Baldwin III, 208
Baldwin IV, 208
Baldwin V, 207–8
Conrad I, 201
Conrad II, 201, 202, 203
coronation in, 5
Crusades and, 199–200, 201
Frederick II (*See* Frederick II (Jerusalem))
Fulk of Anjou, 208
Godfrey I, 1, 206, 214
Guy de Lusignan, 201, 208
historical background, 199–202
Isabella I, 201
Isabella II, 199–202, 205
Papal influence in, 240
revelation and coronation, 312
Sibylla, 208
Jesus
baptism of, 91, 115–16, 158
Byzantium, as source of authority in coronation in, 112, 119–24, 125
dual nature of, 22
Frederick II, parallel imagery with, 205
"Hand of God" iconography and (*See* "Hand of God" iconography)
iconography of, 13–14, 21, 33

Kingship of in coronation, 148–9, 151–6, 157
relation to Kings, 37
Jews. *See* Israel (Ancient)
Jiménez de Rada, Rodrigo, 229–31
Joanna I (Navarra), 287–8
Joanna II (Navarra), 275, 287, 288–9, 293–4
Johann von Viktring, 213
John, Simon, 18, 41, 208
John I (Aragon), 27, 273
John I (England), 284–5
John I (Castile), 236
John I Tzimiskes (Byzantium), 110
John II, Patriarch, 102, 108, 110
John II (Aragon), 273
John II Comnenus (Byzantium), 110
John VIII (Pope), 144
John XXII (Pope), 236
John (England), 284–5
John Lateran (Church), 121
John (New Testament), 87
John of Brienne, 200–1, 205
John of Ibelin, 201
John of Paris, 238
John of Salisbury, 187
John "the Baptist" (Saint), 115–16, 158
Jordan River, 158
Joseph II (Holy Roman Empire), 30
Josephine (France), 3–4
Juan, Archbishop of Toledo, 249, 252
Judah (Kingdom), 256
Judaism, 87
Julian of Toledo, 222, 223, 225, 229
Julian "the Apostate" (Rome), 101, 108
Jungian psychoanalysis, 56
Jupiter (Roman deity), 89
juridical implications of self-coronation, 35, 203, 206, 215
juridical order, 56
Justin I (Byzantium), 102, 110
Justinian I (Byzantium), 103, 104, 141
Justinian II (Byzantium), 111

Kalakaua (Hawaii), 301
Kantorowicz, Ernst, 18, 22–3, 116, 129–30, 134–5, 138, 162, 178–9, 191, 196–7, 213, 309, 316
Kertzer, David, 38, 39, 45, 46
Khosrow I (Persia), 82
Khwarazmian Turks, 202
Kingship, 25. *See also specific King*
"King's two bodies" theory, 22
Kitzinger, Ernst, 188, 189, 191, 192

Kluckhohn, Clyde, 28, 53–4
knighting
  of Alfonso XI, 233–7
  overview, 41, 47–8
  of Peter IV, 259–60
  self-knighting, 233–7
Knights Hospitaller, 202, 204–5
Knights Templar, 202, 204–5
Körntgen, Ludger, 309
Korymbos, 79–80
Koselleck, Reinhardt, 24, 41
Koziol, Geoffrey, 18, 34, 36, 40–1, 47, 54, 55, 138, 307–8, 311
Kronentragen, 12
Kuhrt, Amélie, 69

La Crónica General, 230–1
La Crónica Latina de los reyes de Castilla, 230–1
Ladislaus (Hungary), 11, 239–40
lamb, Son depicted as, 87
Lane, Christel, 53
Lane, Philip, 11–12
Las Huelgas Monastery (Burgos), 233–5, 236
Lázaro Galdiano Library (Madrid), 21
Leach, Edmund, 38
Lector, Theodore, 101
legalism, 309
legitimacy
  in Byzantium, 98, 112, 116–17
  in Carolingian Dynasty, 129, 130
  in Egypt, 74
  overview, 36–7, 46–7, 303–4
  in Persia, 76
  of Peter IV, 255, 260
  of Roger II, 177–8, 193
Le Goff, Jacques, 18
Leo I (Byzantium), 97, 98, 100–2, 104, 107–8
Leo II (Byzantium), 102
Leo III (Byzantium), 105, 108, 222
Leo III (Pope), 130
Leo IV (Byzantium), 110
Leo VI (Byzantium), 114–15, 117, 119, 123
Leon (Kingdom)
  Alfonso VI, 229
  Alfonso VII, 226, 227–8, 230, 231, 237
  Alfonso IX, 284, 294
  Alfonso XI (Castile), influence on coronation of, 222, 224–8
  Bermudo II, 224
  Ferdinand I, 224, 226–7, 230
  oaths in, 294
  Ordoño II, 224–8, 230
  Ramiro II, 224, 226–7

Sancho I, 226–7
Urraca, 226–7, 228
Letentur in Domino et Exultentus Omnes, 203–4, 209, 210, 215–16
Life of Saint Magnus, 304
Life of Saint Stanislas, 182
liminality, 52–3, 304
Linehan, Peter, 18, 223, 231, 233, 234–5
linguistic turn, 29–30
liturgical sources, 16–18
liturgification, 133–5, 139–46, 148–51, 171
Lleida, Spain, 248
Lolland, Netherlands, 284
London, England, 151–3
long-term approach in history, 24–9
López de Luna, Pedro, 248, 249, 252
Lothar III (Holy Roman Empire), 176, 183
Louis VI (France), 181
Louis VII (France), 181
Louis IX (France), 280–1, 286, 287–8, 313–14
Louis X "the Stubborn" (France), 288, 289
Louis XVI (France), 296
Louis "the Pious" (Franks), 37, 130–3
Louvre (Paris), 3–4, 21
Luke (New Testament), 87, 89
Lünig, Johann Christian, 298
Lyon, Jonathan, 41

Maastricht Cross, 155
MacCormack, Sabine, 90, 92–3
Macedonian Dynasty, 96, 103, 108–9, 111, 114, 119, 121–2, 124
MacIsaac, John D., 91
MacLean, Simon, 18, 41, 133–4
Mâconnais, France, 28
Madrid Skylitzes, 124, 126
Magi, 154–5, 157
Magna Carta, 284–5
Mahmood, Saba, 312
Maiestas Domini, 152
Mainz, Germany, 169
Mainz, Ordo of, 148–50, 151
Malik Al-Kamil (Egypt), 202
Mallorca (Kingdom), 253
Maltilda (Sicily), 178
Manganaro, Stefano, 169
Manuel I (Byzantium), 108
Manus Dei. See "Hand of God" iconography
Maratha Empire, 301
Marcian (Byzantium), 97–9, 104, 106, 107–8
Marduk (Babylonian deity), 68, 73
Mari, palace (Syria), 69

Maria dell'Ammiraglio (Palermo). *See* Martorana Church (Palermo)
Maria of Alania (Byzantium), 121
Maria "the Marquise" (Jerusalem), 201
Marin, Louis, 36
Martin I (Aragon), 12, 27, 44–5, 271, 273
Martorana Church (Palermo), 34, 92, 169, 171, 180, 185–95
Marxism, 25
Mary (Virgin), 114, 168–9
Massip, Francesc, 272
Matthew (New Testament), 89
Matthew of Paris, 203, 210, 211–12, 215
Maya people, 25
Mayer, Hans E., 13, 204, 215
Medianites, 73
mediation
  Alfonso XI and, 230, 232, 236
  in Anglo-Saxon coronation, 164
  in Byzantium, 104
  in Carolingian coronation, 135–46
  Egypt, consecration without mediation in (*See* Egypt (Ancient))
  Greece, consecration without mediation in (*See* Greece (Ancient), consecration without mediation in)
  "Hand of God" iconography and, 90
  in Iberian Kingdoms, 238
  Israel, consecration without mediation in (*See* Israel (Ancient))
  Mesopotamia, consecration without mediation in (*See* Mesopotamia, Ancient)
  in Navarra, 35, 47, 277–8, 282, 293, 295
  in Ottonian coronation, 166
  overview, 4, 43, 47, 53, 125, 148–51, 309–10, 312, 313
  Persia, consecration without mediation in (*See* Persia (Ancient))
  Peter IV and, 257
  in Pre-Christian civilizations, 32–3
  Roger II and, 189
Mediterranean cultures, 238
Melchizedek (Israelite priest), 63
mentalités, 18
Mercer, Samuel, 66
Merson Medallion, 90–1
Merton, Robert K., 53
Mesoamerica, kingship in, 25
Mesopotamia (Ancient)
  Akkadians, 72
  Canaanites, 61–2
  consecration without mediation in, 66–9
    Assyrians, 66, 67–8, 73
    Babylonians, 66, 69, 73

diadem and, 67–8
divine election and, 95
Hittites, 68–9
Mari, 69
overview, 32–3, 61
sceptre and, 61–2, 65, 67–8, 69, 73
Sumerians, 67
Day of Atonement, 68
Elamites, 72, 73
Festival of Enlightenment, 68–9
kingship in, 25
sovereignty in, 69
methodological approaches
  agency approach, 29–31
  long-term approach, 24–9
  political theology approach, 21–4
  self-fashioning approach, 31–2
Metz, France, 161–2
Mexico, ritual in, 25
Michael I (Byzantium), 105
Michael III (Byzantium), 103–4, 111, 112–13
Michael VII (Byzantium), 121
Michael (Archangel), 113–14, 123–4
Milan, Archbishop of, 211
miniatures
  Alfonso XI, 226–7
  Anglo-Saxon, 148, 155
  in Byzantium, 91, 112, 121–2, 123, 124, 126
  in Carolingian Dynasty, 136
  in Iberian Kingdoms, 236
  in Ottonian Dynasty, 148, 157–8, 161, 164–8
  overview, 19, 108–9
  Peter IV, 21, 35, 243, 244, 261, 262, 264, 265
miracles, 22
missals, 16–17
Mithra (Persian deity), 70–1, 81
Mitkrönung, 12
mitre, 151, 234–6
modern perspective on self-coronation, 314–17
modern state, 21–2, 296, 308
Mohammad Reza Pahlavi (Iran), 32–3, 83–4, 301
Mondéjar, Marqués de, 231
monotheism, 22
Monza, Italy, 87
Monzón, Spain, 259–60
Moore, Michael E., 133
moral dilemma of self-coronation, 306

mosaics
    in Byzantium, 141
    Exarchate mosaics, 91
    Roger II, 34, 92, 169, 171, 175, 180, 185–95
Moses, 63, 80, 86, 169
Mount Horeb, 86
Mount Sinai, 80
Muntaner, Ramon, 247–8, 251–2
Muret, Battle of, 245–6
Museo del Prado (Madrid), 262
Myers, Henry A., 132
mythology, 57
myth-ritual school, 17–18, 56

Nabonidus Chronicle, 73
Nabu, Iran, 73
Naples, Italy, 175–6
Napoleon I (France)
    generally, 28, 238, 296–7
    contradictory nature of self-coronation, 298
    Frederick II compared, 196–7, 213
    historical tradition of self-coronation and, 4, 10
    Iranian shahs, influence in, 83–4
    overview of self-coronation, 35
    painting of, 3–4, 21
    Peter IV compared, 299
    political nature of self-coronation, 299
Naqsh-e Rostam, Iran, 71, 78, 81
Narseh (Persia), 82
Nathan (Israelite Prophet), 136
Navarra (Kingdom)
    Amo, 286
    Aragon, coronations in compared, 274
    autonomy in, 293–5
    Blanca, 287–8
    Castile, coronations in compared, 274
    Charles II "the Bad," 289, 292
    Charles III "the Noble" (*See* Charles III "the Noble" (Navarra))
    consecration in, 288
    coronation in, 44, 142, 143, 281–2
    Counts of Evreux, 287–9
    Fueros, 276, 278, 280–2, 284–7, 289–91, 292, 293–4
    García Ramírez, 274, 275, 276–7, 281, 293
    Henry I, 287–8
    infanzones, 277–8, 288
    Isabella, 286
    Islamic invasion and, 275
    Joanna I, 287–8
    Joanna II, 275, 287, 288–9, 293–4
    mediation in, 35, 47, 277–8, 282, 293, 295
    oaths in, 276, 278, 280–2, 284–7, 289–91, 292, 293–4
    Papal influence in, 240–1
    Papal opposition to restoration, 275–7
    Philip III of Evreux, 275, 287, 288–9, 293–4
    "raising up" of monarch in, 281–2, 287, 291, 292, 294
    reaction against oaths, 285–7
    reinvention of history of, 278–9
    restoration of Kingdom, 275–7
    Sancho VI "the Wise," 276–7, 285–6
    Sancho VII "the Strong," 276–7, 285–6
    sovereignty in, 279–80, 286
    Theobald I of Champagne, 275, 277–8, 280–1, 285–6
    Theobald II, 275, 285–7, 310
    unction in, 276, 287, 289, 291, 292, 294
    unique nature of coronation in, 295, 310
Ndembu people, 43
Neit (Egyptian Temple), 73–4
Nelson, Janet L., 18, 135, 139, 141, 142–3, 145, 208–9, 309
Nero (Rome), 179
New Church of Tokali Kilise, 115
New Testament, 63. *See also specific Book*
Nicephorus, Patriarch, 105
Nicephorus Bryennius (Byzantium), 98
Nicholas I (Russia), 299
Nicholas (Papal legate), 284–5
Nicholas (Saint), 191, 192–3
Nieto Soria, José Manuel, 18
Nigellus, Ermoldus, 37
nimbus imagery, 91
Nkula (ritual), 43
Norman Kingdom in Sicily. *See* Roger II (Sicily)
normativity, 4
Norse tradition, 181–2
Norway
    coronation in, 8, 170, 310
    revelation and coronation, 312
    unction in, 170
Notre Dame (Paris), 24, 213
numismatics, 33, 78, 88, 94, 111, 115, 116

Oakley, Francis, 25
oaths
    in Aragon, 294
    in Byzantium, 282, 294
    in Castile, 294
    of Charles III, 289–91, 292, 294
    in Denmark, 284

Index   333

in England, 282, 294–5
in France, 279–80, 282, 294
Frederick II and, 284
in Holy Roman Empire, 282
in Hungary, 282–4
in Navarra, 276, 278, 280–2, 284–7, 289–91, 292, 293–4
Visigoths and, 282
Oceania, coronation in, 24–5
Ohrmazd (Ahura Mazda), 78–80, 81–2
Old Testament. *See specific Book*
Olympia, Greece, 1–2
Olympic Games, 1–2
Olympius *(campiductor)*, 100
Oppenheim, Leo, 73
opprobrium, self-coronation as
  in Byzantium, 98
  Frederick II and, 216–17
  in Iberian Kingdoms, 240
  overview, 5–7, 44, 48, 143
  Roger II and, 183
ordines, 16–17, 144–5, 147–51
Ordines Romani, 144
Ordoño II (Leon), 224–8, 230
orectic function of self-coronation, 50–1, 311–12
Osiris (Egyptian deity), 63–4
Ot de Montcada, 248, 249
Otto I (Holy Roman Empire), 150–1, 169
Otto II (Holy Roman Empire), 121, 157, 158–64, 166, 168, 169, 191
Otto III (Holy Roman Empire), 158, 168, 169
Ottonian coronation
  Byzantine tradition, influence of, 108–9, 158–63, 168, 169
  Carolingian tradition, influence of, 136, 164–6, 171
  Christification in, 162–6
  Christocentrism in, 166, 169, 171
  Christus Rex model, 147–8, 157
  consecration and, 161–2, 163–4
  conventional nature of self-coronation, 313
  desacralisation in, 308, 309, 310
  diadem in, 149–50, 157–8
  dual nature of Kingship and, 171
  iconography of, 157–69
  Jesus, Kingship of and, 148–9, 157
  liturgification and, 148–51
  loros and, 158–61
  mediation in, 166
  miniatures and, 148, 157–8, 161, 164–8
  mitre and, 235–6
  normative nature of accession, 169–70

ordines, 147–8, 149–50, 151
ordo of Mainz and, 147–9
other Kingdoms compared, 128, 170, 171
overview, 5, 7, 10, 33, 44, 147–8
portraits, depictions in, 157–69
Roger II, influence on, 190
sacred nature of Kingship and, 170–1
sovereignty and, 158–61, 166, 168
stola and, 157–8
unction and, 158, 163–4, 170
white band and, 163–4
Overlaet, Bruno, 80
Oxford, England, 284–5

pactism, 295
paganism, 92, 127, 299
Palacios, Bonifacio, 18, 247, 253, 294
Palatine Chapel (Palermo), 187, 188
Palazzo, Eric, 18
Palermo, Italy, 92, 175–6, 177, 180
Palestine, 61–2, 68
Pamplona, Bishop of, 286–7, 291
Pamplona, Spain, 143, 274, 278, 287–8
Pamplona Cathedral, 143, 288–9
Pamplona (Kingdom), 275–6
panegyric literature, 94
Pannonia, 283
Pantocrator, 86–7, 112, 123
Papareschi, Gregory, 176
Papua New Guinea, ritual in, 25
pardon, 47, 54
Paris, Matthew, 6–7
Patriarch of Constantinople, 82
patrons, 19, 111–12, 114, 157
Paulinus of Nola (Saint), 87
Paul (Narbonne), 229
Paul (Saint), 166
Paul (Visigoths), 229, 230
Pedro Berenguer (Aragon), 249
Pedro de Luna y Ximénz de Urrea, Archbishop, 242, 249, 265, 307
Peers of France, 9–10
Pelagius (Asturias), 278–9
Pelagius of Oviedo (bishop), 229
performativity, 37, 51
Persia (Ancient). *See also* Iran
  Antigonos Monophthalmos, 76
  Ardashir I, 71, 78–81, 82
  Bahrâm II, 82
  Bahrâm V, 82
  Cambyses II, 73–4
  consecration without mediation in Achaemenid Kings, 70, 72–3, 74
  Arsacid Kings, 77

334   Index

Persia (Ancient) (cont.)
    barsom, 79
    Byzantine tradition, influence on, 107–9
    crown and, 74–6, 77
    diadem and, 71, 75–6, 77, 78, 79, 81–2
    divine election and, 95
    farnah, 70–2
    farr, 70–1
    "Hand of God" iconography compared, 92
    Hellenistic Kings, 74–7
    herbads, 81
    investment ring and, 71–2
    kvarr, 70–1
    mobad, 81
    other Kingdoms compared, 72–4
    overview, 13–14, 32–3, 44, 61
    Sassanid Kings, 70, 71, 77–83, 108–9
    Surena family, 77, 81
    xuarra, 78
    Cyrus I, 70–1, 73
    Cyrus II, 73
    Darius I, 71–2, 74
    Darius III, 74–5
    Hormozd III, 82
    inauguration in, 76
    Khosrow I, 82
    legitimacy in, 76
    Narseh, 82
    Patriarch of Constantinople and, 82
    Phraates IV, 77
    Phraates V, 77
    Qobâd I, 82
    Qobâd II, 82
    Sahrabarâz, 82
    Shapur I, 80–1
    Shapur II, 81–2
    sovereignty in, 71–2, 76–7, 78
    Yazdegerd I, 82
    Yazdegerd III, 82
Peter II "the Catholic" (Aragon), 245–6, 254, 284
Peter III "the Great" (Aragon), 246, 254
Peter IV "the Ceremonious" (Aragon)
    generally, 12, 236, 248, 307
    audience at coronation, function of, 47, 48, 50, 312–13
    autobiography of, 244, 248–53
    consecration versus coronation, 256
    crown ceremony of, 257, 260, 265
    diadem and, 245, 260
    dramatization of coronation, 44–5, 271–3
    dynamism of coronation, 305–6
    ecclesiastical hierarchy and, 259
    historical context of, 27
    historiographic sources, 14, 16, 244, 248–53
    iconographic representation of coronation, 244, 261–8
    iconographic sources, 21, 244
    importance of coronation, 251–3
    Israelite influence on coronation, 255–7
    knighting of, 259–60
    languages in coronation ceremony, 255
    legitimacy of, 255, 260
    liturgical sources, 17, 244, 253–60
    Llibre del rei en Pere, 244, 248–53
    Mallorca, conquest of, 253
    Manuscrito de san Miguel de los Reyes, 261
    Mass and coronation, 259, 260
    mediation and, 257
    miniatures, 21, 35, 243, 244, 261, 262, 264, 265
    Napoleon compared, 299
    narrative of coronation, 244, 248–53
    new ceremonial of, 244, 253–60
    Ordinacions, 254, 261
    ordo of, 244–5, 269, 270
    origin of nickname, 254
    overview of coronation, 35, 242–4
    political effect of coronation, 144
    pommel and, 259–60
    prayers and coronation, 258–9
    reaction to coronation, 312–13
    rituals of coronation, 258
    ritual strategies of, 268–71
    sceptre and, 250–1, 259–60
    scholarship on, 13
    self-fashioning and, 31
    sovereignty and, 265, 271–2
    spiritual versus temporal aspect of coronation, 257, 269–70, 317
    strategic purpose of coronation, 311
    symbolic nature of coronation and, 57
    transgressive nature of self-coronation, 143
    unction of, 245, 256–7, 260, 269
Peter of Meaux, 286
Peter (Saint), 166
Peter "the Patrician," 100, 101
Philip I (France), 9
Philip III (France), 287–8
Philip III of Evreux (Navarra), 275, 287, 288–9, 293–4
Philip IV "the Fair" (France), 288
Philip V "the Tall" (France), 288
Phocas (Byzantium), 105
Phoenicians, 61–2

Photius, Patriarch, 103
Phraates IV (Persia), 77
Phraates V (Persia), 77
Pierleoni, Peter, 176
Pipino, Francisco, 181
Pippin "the Short" (Franks), 129–30, 222, 226
Pisa (Kingdom), 202
Pius VII (Pope), 3–4, 299
Plantagenet Dynasty, 307–8
Plutarch, 74, 76, 77
Poema de Fernán González, 231–2
Poland
  coronation in, 8, 170
  Papal influence in, 240
  revelation and coronation, 312
  unction in, 170
political perspective on self-coronation, 302–5
political religion, 24
political theology approach, 21–4, 239
pommel, 250–1, 254–5, 259–60, 271
Pontificale Romano-Germanicum, 168
Pontifical of Huesca, 254–5
Pontifical of Tyre, 214
Portugal
  accession in, 171
  Papal influence in, 240
Pössel, Christina, 18, 40, 41, 49, 50, 297, 311
postmodernism, 29–30
poststructuralism, 29–30
Potestas, 170
Poussay Lectionary (Paris), 155
Powell, James M., 210
Pre-Christian civilizations, 32, 61. *See also specific civilization*
presentisms, 17–18, 24, 313–14
priesthood, 65, 144, 148
profane nature of self-coronation, 21–2, 107, 141, 197–9, 213
Professio fidei (profession of faith), 110, 260, 282
Protestant Reformation, 42, 310
Prussia
  Frederick I, 13, 31, 35, 238, 296–9, 311
  William I, 298–9
Psalms (Old Testament), 154
psychoanalysis, 56
Puente la Reina (Spain), 288
Puett, Michael, 23
Puglia, Italy, 180
Pushkin State Museum (Moscow), 92, 187
Pyrenees Mountains, 275

Qobâd I (Persia), 82
Qobâd II (Persia), 82
Quigley, Declan, 23

radial crown, 81–2, 89
"raising up" of monarch
  Charles III, 291, 292, 294
  in Navarra, 281–2, 287, 291, 292, 294
  overview, 170–1
  in Scandinavia, 281–2
Ralph d'Escures, 9
Ramiro II (Leon), 224, 226–7
Ramon Berenguer (Aragon), 249
Ranulf II (Alife), 178
Rappaport, Roy, 25, 56
Ras Shamra, 61–2
Ratold, Ordo of, 148–50, 151
Ravenna, Italy, 91, 141
Raymond VI (Toulouse), 245
Reccadedus (Visigoths), 229
Receswinth (Visigoths), 226–7
Re (Egyptian deity), 64
referentiality, 19, 126
Reformation, 42, 310
Regensburg, Germany, 157
Reichenau, Germany, 157
Reichenau Gospel, 161
Reilly, Bernard F., 229
Reims Cathedral, 208, 288, 308
relevance of person performing coronation, 11
Remigius, Bishop, 188
republicanism, 142
Reuter, Timothy, 18
rex et sacerdos, 189, 191
rex renitens, 11, 14, 47, 303, 313
Reza Pahlavi (Iran), 32–3, 83–4, 301
Richard I (England), 5–7, 44
Ricouer, Paul, 57
rites of passage, 25
ritual
  acclamation (*See* acclamation)
  agency and, 49, 53, 302–3
  as aggregation of symbols, 46
  alethurgical function of self-coronation, 50–1, 311–12
  ambiguity in, 45, 55
  anachronism and, 41–2
  as anomaly, 27
  artificiality of, 26
  attendants at, 28, 37, 47, 49, 50, 307
  audience, function of, 47–50, 312–13
  ceremony versus, 38–9
  as communicative act, 39
  comparative approach to, 23, 25, 26, 29, 41

336   Index

ritual (cont.)
  condensation of meaning, 40, 45
  content of, 45
  context of self-coronation and, 43–4
  continuity of, 4, 308
  criticism of ritual concept, 40–1
  as cultural system, 29, 31
  debate regarding, 37–42
  defining, 38–9
  denial of, 313
  designers, 51
  discontinuity of, 4, 308
  as drama, 44–7
  efficacy of, 48, 57
  elevation, 109, 175, 231, 316
  emotional response to, 45, 55, 312
  enactment of, 44–5
  failure of, 27, 310–11
  fixation and, 57
  function of, 42
  as game, 45–6
  heterodoxy and, 52
  historicity of, 26
  inertia of, 57
  innovation in, 30, 49, 57–8
  instrumental acts, 49, 53, 297–8, 299
  integrative function of, 42, 51–2
  intention, 49
  invariance of, 57, 306
  knighting (*See* knighting)
  language of, 31, 56–7
  lexicon of, 56–7
  liminality and, 52–3, 304
  liturgification and, 133–5, 139–46,
    148–51, 171
  malleability of, 274–5, 306
  manipulative function of, 42
  as mirror of social reality, 52
  mnemonic dimension of, 57–8
  multivocality of, 45
  mythology and, 57
  nonverbal terms, 56–7
  orectic function of self-coronation, 50–1,
    311–12
  overview, 32, 36–7
  pardon, 47, 54
  participants in, 12, 37, 44–5, 47–50, 51,
    53, 55, 57–8, 305–6
  penance, 47, 48, 68
  political aspects of, 39–40, 41–2,
    51–2, 53–4
  political change and, 52
  political use of, 314–15
  raising on a shield, 98, 101, 110, 126,
    170, 281, 287
  rational response to, 55
  reiteration of, 28
  repetition in, 28, 35, 57
  secrecy of, 56
  semantics and, 27, 29–30, 35, 55
  social aspects of, 39–40, 51–2, 53–4
  social change and, 52
  as spectacle, 46
  symbolic acts, 49
  symbolic element of, 39–40
  symbolic nature of self-coronation
    and, 54–8
  as theatre, 45–6
  tradition and, 306
  transformative function of self-
    coronation and, 50–4
  transgressive nature of self-coronation
    and, 53
  variation in, 12, 28, 43
  verbal terms, 56–7
ritual formalism, 306, 310–11
"ritual invention," 307
ritual perspective on self-coronation,
  310–14
ritual studies, 17–18
Robert of Artois, 287–8
Robert of Capua, 179
Roderic (Visigoths), 278–9
Roger I (Sicily), 175
Roger II (Sicily)
  generally, 166, 169, 171
  accession of, 175–7
  acclamation and, 178–9
  artistic depiction of coronation, 185–95
  audience at coronation, function of, 48–9
  Byzantine influence on coronation,
    187–8, 189, 190, 192–4
  Carolingian influence on coronation, 190
  Christmas, choice of for coronation, 187
  Christocentrism in coronation, 185–95
  coins depicting, 178–9, 188
  Deo coronatus and, 189, 191
  dramatization of coronation, 45
  dual challenge facing, 48
  ecclesiastical hierarchy and, 191
  Frederick II compared, 188,
    194–5, 216
  "Hand of God" iconography and, 92,
    93
  iconographic sources, 21, 34
  Islamic influence on coronation, 188, 195
  King of France, role of in coronation,
    180–1
  legitimacy of, 177–8, 193
  loros and, 187

Martorana Church, artistic depiction of coronation in, 185–95
  mediation and, 189
  mosaics, 34, 92, 169, 171, 175, 180, 185–95
  as Norman King, 175, 176–7, 179–80, 182, 191, 193, 216
  opprobrium, self-coronation as, 183
  ordo of, 184–5
  Ottonian influence on coronation, 190
  overview of coronation, 34
  political symbols and rituals and, 246
  ritual coronation of, 177–85
  self-sufficiency and, 190
  Sigurd, role of in coronation, 181–2
  sovereignty and, 187, 194
  symbolic coronation of, 185–95
  transgressive nature of self-coronation, 143, 221
  tunic and, 185–7
  as usurper, 183
  weakness of mediation in coronation, 190
Roger of Howden, 7
Roger of Wendover, 203, 211–12
Roman Curia, 176
Romanesque art, 91–2
Romanus I (Byzantium), 116–17
Romanus II (Byzantium), 119–21, 123
Rome (Ancient)
  Arcadius, 91
  Augustus, 89, 142
  Aurelian, 94
  Constantine I, 87–91, 110, 111, 142, 317
  Constantine II, 89, 90
  Constantius II, 89, 90, 110
  coronation in
    Byzantium, continuity of tradition in, 97
    divine election and, 95
    "Hand of God" iconography in, 88–91
    overview, 44
  Eudocia, 91
  Gallienus, 94
  Honoria, 91
  Julian "the Apostate," 101, 108
  Nero, 179
  Senate, 98–9, 100, 103
  Theodosius, 317
  Trajan, 89
  Valerian, 94
Romuald of Salerno, 179–80
Rostas, Susanna, 51
royal inauguration. *See* inauguration
royal insignia. *See* crown; pommel; sceptre
Royal Palace (Barcelona), 270

Royal Palace (Palermo), 188
Royal Pantheon (Poblet), 270
Ruffus, Johannes, 212–13
Ruiz, Teófilo F., 13, 18, 233
Runciman, Steve, 106
Russia
  Alexander III, 299
  coronation in, 299, 310
  Elizabeth Petrovna, 299
  Nicholas I, 299

Sabazios cult, 85, 86–7
Sächsische Weltchronik, 213
sacralisation, 128–35, 141, 142, 143, 171
sacral kingship, 308–9
Sacramentary of Ivrea, 158, 168
Sacramentum. See Oaths
sacred context, 12, 53, 307
sacred space, 101, 104
Sahlins, Marshall, 5, 26–7, 38, 54
Sahrabarâz (Persia), 82
Saint-Denis, France, 130
Saint Emmeram of Regensburg Abbey, 166–7
Saint James automated statue, 233–5
Saints, 33, 96–7, 110, 124. *See also specific Saint*
Saladin, 203–4
Salerno, Italy, 175, 176, 177, 179
Samuel (Israelite priest), 63, 123–4, 184, 207, 223–4, 255–6
Sánchez Albornoz, Claudio, 223, 225, 227
Sancho I (Leon), 226–7
Sancho II (Castile), 229–30
Sancho IV (Castile), 231–2
Sancho VI "the Wise" (Navarra), 276–7, 285–6
Sancho VII "the Strong" (Navarra), 276–7, 285–6
Sancho de Rojas, Archbishop, 261–2
San Salvador Cathedral (Zaragoza), 242
Santa Justa, Spain, 248
Santa Maria la Nuova in Monreale (Palermo), 189
Santes Creus, Spain, 246
Santiago de Compostela, Spain, 228
Saracens, 180, 181, 196
Sassanid Kings (Persia), 70, 71, 77–83, 108–9
Saul (Israel), 123–4, 255–6
Scandinavia. *See also specific King or Kingdom*
  coronation in, 11–12, 170, 304
  "raising up" of monarch in, 281–2
  unction in, 170

sceptre
  Charles III and, 291
  Frederick I and, 298
  in Iberian Kingdoms, 226, 245, 271, 272–3
  in Mesopotamia, 61–2, 65, 67–8, 69, 73
  Peter IV and, 250–1, 259–60
Schieffer, Rudolf, 170
Schmitt, Carl, 21–2, 315
Schmitt, Jean-Claude, 18, 193
scholarship on self-coronation, 13
Schramm, Percy E., 14–15, 18, 55, 163, 188, 282
Scotland
  accession in, 171
  coronation in, 8
  unction in, 310
secularisation, 307–10, 316, 317
self-consecration, 65
self-coronation. *See specific King or topic*
self-fashioning approach, 31–2
self-knighting, 233–7
self-representation, 49, 188, 314
self-sufficiency, 190
Sem (Egyptian priest), 65
semiotic codes, 29–30
Serrano-Coll, Marta, 13
Severus, 87
Shapur I (Persia), 80–1
Shapur II (Persia), 81–2
Shivaji (Maratha), 301
Sibilia (Aragon), 267
Sibylla (Jerusalem), 208
Sicily (Kingdom)
  Agathocles, 175
  Aragon and, 246–7
  coronation in
    Byzantine tradition, influence on, 108–9
    overview, 5, 44
  Frederick II as King of, 199, 214, 216
  Maltilda, 178
  Norman Kingdom in (*See* Roger II (Sicily))
  Papal influence in, 240
  revelation and coronation, 312
  Roger I, 175
  Roger II (*See* Roger II (Sicily))
  Simon, 175
  William II, 189
Sickel, Wilhelm, 106
Sigurd (Norway), 181–2
Șimleu Silvanei, Romania, 89
Simon de Montfort, 245–6
Simon (Sicily), 175

Smith, Jonathan Z., 52–3
Smith, Roland, 76
Sobrarbe, Spain, 278–9
social perspective on self-coronation, 305–10
social stability, 24, 31
social structures, 30, 52
social transformations, 4, 31, 51–2
sociology, 22, 29–30, 42
Soissons, France, 129
Solomon (Israel), 63, 136, 137, 153–4
Sommerlechner, Andrea, 204
Son (Trinity), 87
Soubirous, Bernadette, 80
sources
  historiographical sources, 14–16
  iconographic sources, 19–21
  liturgical sources, 16–18
sovereignty
  Alfonso XI and, 228, 230
  in Carolingian Dynasty, 134, 139
  Charles III and, 292
  Frederick I and, 298
  Frederick II and, 199, 216
  in Mesopotamia, 69
  in Navarra, 279–80, 286
  in Ottonian Dynasty, 158–61, 166, 168
  overview, 22, 56, 128, 311, 315
  in Persia, 71–2, 76–7, 78
  Peter IV and, 265, 271–2
  Roger II and, 187, 194
Spain. *See also* Iberian Kingdoms; *specific King or Kingdom*
  Habsburg Dynasty, 237–8
  Spanish exceptionalism, 238
  unique nature of coronation in, 295, 310
Spiegel, Gabrielle, 29–31
Spielregeln (rules of play), 46, 47, 48
spiritual versus temporal aspect of coronation, 257, 269–70, 307–10, 311, 314, 317
Stanislas (Saint), 182
"state of exception," 315
Stegmüller, Wolfgang, 25–6
Stephen, Archbishop and Papal legate, 212, 284–5
Stephen II (Pope), 130, 151
Stewart, Pamela J., 51
stola, 157–8
Strathern, Andrew, 51
Strootman, Rudolf, 38–9, 76
structuralism, 25
Sturluson, Snorri, 181–2
subversive nature of self-coronation, 76–7, 98, 311–12
Sumerians, 67

Index

Sun Dance, 25
Swabia, 182
Sweden
  Charles XII, 238, 297
  coronation in, 170
  unction in, 170
symbolic anthropology, 30, 36, 40
symbolism
  in Byzantium, 115, 126
  Frederick II, 57, 196–7, 214, 216
  "Hand of God" and, 85, 95 (*See also* "Hand of God" iconography)
  Holy Sepulchre and, 208
  overview, 39, 43, 56, 71–2
  Peter IV, 57
  symbolic coronation, 13–14, 96
  symbolic element of ritual, 39–40
  symbolic nature of self-coronation, 54–8
Symeonis Logothetae, 103
synchronicity, 26
Syria, 68, 87
Szilágysomlyó, Romania, 89

Tabari (chronicler), 77–8, 82
Tacitus, 89
Tambiah, Stanley, 313
Taq-e Bostan, Iran, 81–2
Tarazona, Spain, 248
Tarshish, Turkey, 154
Te Deum Laudamus, 184–5, 260, 292
Tell Halaf, Israel, 61–2
temporal versus spiritual aspect of coronation, 257, 269–70, 307–10, 311, 314, 317
Tephrike, Battle of, 103
Teutonic Knights, 202, 204–5
theater. *See* dramatization of coronation
Thegar (biographer), 131, 133
Theobald I of Champagne (Navarra), 275, 277–8, 280–1, 285–6
Theobald II (Navarra), 275, 285–7, 310
theocentrism, 33, 127, 166, 185, 190
Theodosius (Rome), 317
Theophanes, 101
Theophanu (Byzantium), 121, 158–9
Thessaloniki (Greece), 111
Thoth (Egyptian deity), 65
Tokali Kilise, Turkey, 115
Tonga (Kingdom), 301
Toulouse (Kingdom), 245–6
Trajan (Rome), 89
transformative function of self-coronation, 50–4
transgressive nature of self-coronation
  Alfonso XI and, 143, 273

Charles III and, 143
Frederick II and, 143, 197–9, 215, 221, 273
Iberian Kingdoms, self-coronation not seen as transgression in, 221–2, 312
overview, 1–4, 5–7, 10, 27–8
Peter IV and, 143
ritual and, 53
Roger II and, 143, 221
transformation into convention, 273, 296–9
Trastámara, House of, 273
Treaty of Constance, 284
Trier, Germany, 157
Trinity, 87
Tripoli, Lebanon, 199
Tronzo, William, 190
Tudela, Spain, 278
tunic, 115, 151, 178, 185–7
Tupou (Tonga), 301
Turin, Italy, 64
Turner, Victor, 27, 36, 38, 40, 41–2, 43, 44, 50–1, 56–7, 302, 304
Tyre, Archbishop of, 200
Tyre, Lebanon, 199

Ullmann, Walter, 151
unction
  Alfonso XI and, 237
  Anglo-Saxon coronation and, 170
  in Aragon, 245, 256–7, 260, 269
  in Bohemia, 170
  Carolingian coronation and, 129–30, 142, 143–4
  in Castile, 230–1, 237
  Charles III and, 291, 292, 294
  chrism and, 129, 145, 158, 247
  coronation, relation to, 224–8
  in Denmark, 170
  in England, 310
  Gallican rite of, 145
  Holy Oil, 145, 158, 178, 260, 291
  in Hungary, 170
  in Iberian Kingdoms, 170, 224–6
  in Ireland, 170
  in Israel, 62–3, 223–4
  in Navarra, 276, 287, 289, 291, 292, 294
  in Norway, 170
  Ottonian coronation and, 158, 163–4, 170
  overview, 5, 8, 158, 163–4
  Peter IV and, 245, 256–7, 260, 269
  in Poland, 170
  in Scandinavia, 170
  in Scotland, 310

unction (cont.)
  in Sweden, 170
  Visigoths and, 222–4
  in Wales, 170
Unter-Krone-gehen, 12
Urraca (Leon), 226–7, 228
Ursberg, Burchard von, 212–13
usurpation, 4, 97, 229–30, 312
Uta Lectionary, 157–8
utopia, 22, 317
Utrecht Psalter, 154

Vagnoni, Mirko, 189
Valencia, Spain, 264, 267
Valentinian III (Byzantium), 91, 99
Valerian (Rome), 94
Venice, Italy, 121–2
Victoria (Roman deity), 89, 90, 92–3
"The Victorious Youth," 1–2
Vincent, Nicholas, 18, 40, 41, 128
Virgin Mary, 114, 168–9
Virtus (Roman deity), 89, 90
Visigoths
  Alfonso XI, influence on coronation of, 222, 224–8
  Chindasuinth, 226–7
  coronation and
    Byzantine tradition compared, 139, 222
    Carolingian tradition compared, 142, 222
    overview, 102, 129, 162
  Egica, 226–7
  Iberian Kingdoms, influence on, 237–8
  oaths and, 282
  Paul, 229, 230
  Reccadedus, 229
  Recceswinth, 226–7
  Roderic, 278–9
  unction and, 222–4
  Wamba, 129, 222, 223, 225, 229, 231–2, 237
Vita of Saint Ladislaus of Hungary, 239–40
Viterbo, Gottfried von, 213

Wales
  coronation in, 8, 170
  unction in, 170
Wallingford, England, 284–5
Wamba (Visigoths), 129, 222, 223, 225, 229, 231–2, 237
Warmundus of Ivrea, Bishop, 158, 168
Warner, David A., 16
War of the Lombards, 201
Weber, Hermann, 23
Weber, Max, 138, 299
Weeden, Lisa, 29
Weiler, Björn, 11, 14, 18, 28, 41, 47–8, 49, 303, 311
Westminster Abbey (London), 208, 308
Widukind of Corvey, 150–1
William I (Prussia), 298–9
William II (Sicily), 189
William of Malmesbury, 9, 239–40
William of Tyre, 206, 207–8
Winchester, England, 151–3

Yannopoulos, Panayotis, 107
Yazdegerd I (Persia), 82
Yazdegerd III (Persia), 82
Yolande (Jerusalem). *See* Isabella II (Jerusalem)
Yoruba people, 55–6, 301

Zadok (Israelite priest), 63, 136
Zaragoza, Archbishop of. *See* Pedro de Luna y Ximénz de Urrea, Archbishop
Zaragoza, Spain, 242, 246–7, 264, 267
Zaragoza Cathedral, 254–5, 273
Zeno (Byzantium), 91, 102
Zeonis (Byzantium), 91
Zimmerman, Michael, 223
Zimrilin (Mari), 69
Zoroastrianism, 70–1
Zulus, 301
Zupka, Dusan, 12
Zurita, Hieronymus or Gerónimo, 272–3

For EU product safety concerns, contact us at Calle de José Abascal, 56–1°,
28003 Madrid, Spain or eugpsr@cambridge.org.

www.ingramcontent.com/pod-product-compliance
Lightning Source LLC
LaVergne TN
LVHW011758060526
838200LV00053B/3627